BLACK AND BLUE

Also by John D. Brewer

AS AUTHOR

Mosley's Men (Aldershot, 1984)
After Soweto (Oxford, 1987)
The Royal Irish Constabulary (Belfast, 1990)
Inside the RUC (Oxford, 1991; with Kathleen Magee)

AS CO-AUTHOR

Police, Public Order and the State (London, 1988)

AS EDITOR

Can South Africa Survive? (London, 1989)
Restructuring South Africa (London, 1994)

BLACK AND BLUE

Policing in South Africa

JOHN D. BREWER

CLARENDON PRESS · OXFORD

1994

Oxford University Press, Walton Street, Oxford OX2 6DP
Oxford New York Toronto
Delhi Bombay Calcutta Madras Karachi
Kuala Lumpur Singapore Hong Kong Tokyo
Nairobi Dar es Salaam Cape Town
Melbourne Auckland Madrid
and associated companies in
Berlin Ibadan

Oxford is a trade mark of Oxford University Press

Published in the United States
by Oxford University Press Inc., New York

© John Brewer 1994

British Library Cataloguing in Publication Data
Data available

Library of Congress Cataloging in Publication Data
Brewer, John D.
Black and blue: policing in South Africa / John D. Brewer.
Includes bibliographical references and index.
1. Police—South Africa—History. I. Title.
HV8272.A2B74 1994 363.2'0968—dc20 93-40020

ISBN 0-19-827382-7

1 3 5 7 9 10 8 6 4 2

Typeset by J&L Composition Ltd, Filey, North Yorkshire
Printed in Great Britain
on acid-free paper by
Bookcraft (Bath) Ltd
Midsomer Norton, Avon

PREFACE AND ACKNOWLEDGEMENTS

Blaise Pascal wrote perceptively in *Pensées* that the last thing one discovers in writing a book is what to put first. Let me begin with an apology for writing, in the words of William Henry, Duke of Gloucester, another damned thick, square book. I had hoped that it might be thinner, but so little is known of policing in South Africa that it perforce needs to be comprehensive and could be made slimmer only at the cost of deleting important material.

Another good place to begin is with an explanation of the title. Although it is a familiar media contrast, *Black and Blue* has been chosen deliberately to encapsulate two important features of policing in South Africa: that the men and women in blue function to control race relations, specifically, to police the country's Black population; and that their methods for doing so are relatively crude and unprofessional, relying, more often than not, on brute force, leaving Black South Africans literally black and blue, if they survive at all. These qualities reflect the fact that policing in South Africa has never transcended its origins.

This important fact conditions the nature of this volume, which is not solely about the police in the contemporary period. Because policing in modern South Africa is a product of its past, contemporary policing needs to be put in a historical context; hence the volume adopts a historical approach. Even the future reform of the police is constrained by the failure of the South African Police to transcend its origins. The South African Police began, when formed in 1913, as a colonial police force, and along with all the other compatible agencies to emerge since, it has retained features of this model long after similar forces were modernized (most notably police forces in Ireland, Australia, New Zealand, and Canada). Police professionalization has been restricted by the police role in controlling and regulating race relations. The irony is that while colonial policing was deemed by the state to be necessary when the police were established at the beginning of the century, and for a very long time thereafter, it is an impediment when, at the end, the state now seeks, at long last, to abandon internal colonialism and abolish racial discrimination. The inability of the police to reform these long-established traditions and methods seriously threatens the state's wider reform process. A force that was once vital to the state's power is now a positive hindrance.

The title therefore symbolizes a third characteristic of policing in South Africa: that any transition to a non-racial democracy in the country is partly dependent on an accommodation between the police and Black South Africans. The reform of the police in South Africa, to remove the vestiges of colonial policing, which was a real possibility on more than one occasion in the past but always blocked by the state, is now in the state's best interest. This suggests that during the eight decades covered by the book, the relationship between the police and the state in South Africa has changed considerably. Policing in South Africa is thus a good case-study in which to address the broad question of police–state relations, and in the Conclusion the historical material on policing in South Africa is used to this end.

Another point on which to begin a book is acknowledgement of the debts incurred in writing it. The greatest thanks are owed to the co-directors of the Southern African Research Programme at Yale University, and especially Leonard Thompson, who invited me to be a Visiting Fellow at Yale for 1989, during which time I collected much of the material for the book. Access to the vast resources of the Yale library was also facilitated by the helpfulness of the Curator of the Africa Collection, Moore Crossey, a friendly expatriate Irishman. I am also grateful to the President and Fellows of St John's College, Oxford, for awarding me a Visiting Scholarship for the summer of 1992 in order to complete the writing-up of the manuscript and undertake last-minute dips into various archives held at the Rhodes House Library.

The Nuffield Foundation and the Leverhulme Trust kindly awarded me research grants to visit South Africa to consult the archives of the South African Police in Pretoria; I also wish to acknowledge the efforts of Fatima Meer, Jack Spence, Isobella Sholtz, and Hermann Giliomee in trying to reverse the government's initial decision to refuse me a visa; fortunately, their efforts met with success. Simon Baynham was very helpful in organizing some of the itinerary of the original visit to South Africa. The following archivists in South Africa facilitated my eventual visit in the summer of 1991: Colonel Labuscagne and Lieutenant Appel of the South African Police Museum and Archive; the Chief Archivist at the Central Archives Depot in Pretoria; and the Chief Librarian at the Library of Parliament in Cape Town. I am particularly indebted to Gerrit Wagener, from the State Archives in

Pretoria, who helped me greatly to find my way round this impressive collection of archival material. The following people made the visit enjoyable on a personal level: Fatima Meer, Johan Olivier, and David Ginsburg. I am also grateful to the Centres for Criminal Justice at Harvard University and the University of Natal in Pietermaritzburg, for inviting me to participate in a project on the reform of the SAP, which enabled me to talk to senior policemen in 1991 and 1992.

I would also like to thank the Revd Ken Newell, and all my friends at Fitzroy Church, for the kindness, support, and friendship that has seen me through some difficult times. Finally, I would like to record my appreciation to two friends and colleagues who supported me throughout my career and who died in 1990. John Blacking and Roy Wallis were valiant and courageous fighters—against injustice and ineptitude—who sadly lost their final battle.

J. D. B.
Belfast, 1993.

CONTENTS

List of Tables   x

Abbreviations   xii

Introduction   1

1. The Colonial Agenda: 1910–1913   14

2. Policemen Versus Pukkah Soldiers: 1914–1926   56

3. Internal and External War: 1927–1945   105

4. The Transition to Apartheid: 1946–1959   168

5. The Second Phase of Apartheid: 1960–1975   223

6. Policing Reform and Reforming the Police: 1976–1992   268

Conclusion   332

Bibliography   353
Index   373

TABLES

1.1	Police manpower levels, 1911–1913	42
1.2	Police expenditure, 1911–1913	43
2.1	SAP expenditure, 1914/15–1919/20	60
2.2	Police and defence expenditure, 1915/16–1925/6	60
2.3	SAP manpower trends, 1914–1919	61
2.4	SAP budget, 1919/20–1926/7	67
2.5	SAP manpower levels, 1919–1926	68
2.6	The percentage of wastage due to dismissals	83
2.7	Specific offences as a proportion of total dismissals	84
3.1	Trends in manpower, 1927–1945	117
3.2	Manpower trends in the Black police, 1927–1945	120
3.3	Per capita expenditure on policemen by race 1934/5–1945/6	123
3.4	Salary differentials in 1936	124
3.5	Trends in police expenditure, 1926/7–1945/6	126
3.6	Trends in selected crimes, 1926 and 1946	129
3.7	Selected administrative offences by Blacks for selected years	135
3.8	Complaints by Blacks of assault in police custody, 1934–1936	137
3.9	Distribution of complaints and SAP manpower	138
4.1	Wastage and dismissals, 1939–1945	171
4.2	Pay differentials by race in 1948	183
4.3	Police expenditure, 1945/6–1952/3	187
4.4	Trends in manpower, 1945–1952	189
4.5	Trends in Black manpower, 1945–1952	191
4.6	Per capita expenditure on policemen by race, 1945/6–1950/1	194
4.7	Dismissals from the SAP, 1946–1952	195
4.8	Percentage shift in cases sent to trial, 1947–1952	198
4.9	Trends in police manpower, 1954–1957	208
4.10	Trends in Black manpower, 1954–1957	208
4.11	Police expenditure, 1952/3–1958/9	210
4.12	Dismissals from the police, 1954–1957	218
5.1	Dismissals from the SAP, 1960–1975	230

5.2 Police in the Transkei, 1964/5–1971/2 233
5.3 The Transkei Police, 1972/3–1975/6 233
5.4 Trends in Black membership, 1960–1975 236
5.5 Trends in SAP manpower, 1960–1975 239
5.6 SAP expenditure, 1960–1975 244
5.7 Cases of serious crimes reported in 1974 in selected areas 264
6.1 Manpower trends, 1976–1991 276
6.2 Trends in SAP expenditure, 1975/6–1990/1 277
6.3 The Transkei Police 283
6.4 The Lebowa Police 283
6.5 Command structure of the SAP by race, 1983 287
6.6 Percentage of wastage due to dismissals, 1976–1988 301
6.7 Number in thousands of Cases Reported of Selected Crimes 1981/2–1988 325

ABBREVIATIONS

AKPOL   Afrikaanse Kultuurvereniging van die Suid-Afrikaanse Polisie
ANC   African National Congress
AWB   Afrikaner Weerstandsbeweging
BOSS   Bureau of State Security
CIB   Central Identification Bureau
CID   Criminal Investigation Department
DBAD   Department of Bantu Administration and Development
JMC   Joint Management Committee
MK   Umkhonto we Sizwe
MLEO   Municipal Law Enforcement Officer
NAC   Native Affairs Commission
NNC   Native National Congress
NRC   Native Representative Council
OB   Ossewabrandwag
OFS   Orange Free State
PAC   Pan-African Congress
SACB   South African Criminal Bureau
SADF   South African Defence Forces
SAIRR   South African Institute of Race Relations
SAMR   South African Mounted Riflemen
SAP   South African Police
SAPC   South African Communist Party
SARHP   South African Railways and Harbour Police
SB   Special Branch
SSC   State Security Council
UDF   United Democratic Front

Introduction

In President de Klerk's address at the opening of parliament on 1 February 1991, in which he effectively announced the dismantling of all the legal pillars which supported apartheid, the issue of policing warranted special mention at the end of the speech. He noted the enormous pressures already placed on the police but emphasized that in 'the new South Africa', the police will have to be 'manned and managed properly': 'A professional and well-trained police force, which [is] not subject to political expediency, [is] the best guarantee for the maintenance of a safe environment in which everybody is able to live and work.'

For the new South Africa he thus invokes the liberal model of policing, which supposedly operated for so long in Britain. This is a model in which police recruitment reflects fairly the social composition of the wider society, where the police are neutral arbiters in social conflict, are above political manipulation and control, operating on the basis of consensus rather than force, relying on modern management techniques, and well-trained professional officers. The new, non-racial, democratic South Africa envisaged by de Klerk is seen as having no better guarantee for its stability than a police force designed on such lines.

This is an irony of immense proportions. It is being applied to South Africa at a time when the liberal model of policing is recognized in the academic literature as a chimera, no longer able to operate in a modern world, if it ever did. It is also being applied in a country where governments long resisted reform of the police, actually refusing to take the opportunities offered in the past to introduce the liberal model of policing, and which deliberately involved the police in politics and in partisan control of key sections of the population. And it is being applied to a police force which has become so used to time-honoured methods which deviate from the liberal model as to make reform along these lines a task of Sisyphean labour.

However, this volume is not solely about the future of the police in the new South Africa, for it approaches the topic of policing through an analysis of its history and development because these origins determine the nature of policing in modern South Africa and affect possibilities of future police reform. Thus, the study begins with policing in the nineteenth century and discusses developments throughout the twentieth that have brought the SAP to the present juncture, where the radical reform of the police is recognized as a necessity. The vexed question of police reform is discussed in the Conclusion.

LITERATURE ON POLICING IN SOUTH AFRICA

The police have never been of much concern to analysts of South Africa, the major focus being on the military, to which the police are considered an adjunct (a fact noted by Gann and Duignan 1981: 143, and illustrated by such works as Baynham 1990; S. Davies 1987; Grundy 1983*a*, 1983*b*, 1988; Frankel 1984; Seegars 1986, 1991). The dearth of published work on policing might seem a paradox given that the country is often described as a police state, but apartheid made the police invisible. Social control was embedded in every institution and structure of apartheid, so that the South African state could function effectively without a large police force (Gellately 1990 makes a similar point in relation to the Gestapo in pre-war Germany). The portrayal of South Africa as a police state was thus never a literal truth (as emphasized by writers from divergent traditions, such as Adam and Giliomee 1979: 25–32; Wolpe 1988: 44), although some references to the South African Police (SAP) utilize the idea (Adebisi 1976; Cohen 1977; Duncan 1964; Erikson 1973; Philips 1989; Sachs 1975). The ratio of police per thousand head of population hardly grew for sixty years, and was lower than in most liberal democracies in the West; the ratio in 1976, the year of the Soweto uprising, was the same as 1913, when the SAP was formed.

The reform of apartheid since the 1970s, speeded up apace in the 1980s, moderated this social control and forced the state to rely more on its police. The legacy of apartheid, however, made the police incapable of responding, leaving them understaffed, under-resourced, technologically unsophisticated, and unprofessionally managed. The SAP was subject to rapid change once this became obvious, with enormous increases in manpower, forced reliance on the army and relatively untrained reserve forces, and the deployment of new technologies and management structures. The public profile of the police has increased in tandem with its role in social control. This inevitably makes policing a political issue, in White as well as Black politics (Brewer 1988: 274–9; Weitzer 1991). At precisely the time when the public image of the police is important to the reform process, the SAP is called on to reconsider time-honoured structures, methods, and policies, throwing them further into the political arena. Policing has thus become an important litmus test of the state's commitment to reform. As South Africa's *Financial Mail* perceptively wrote on 22 September 1989: 'the crisis in the police force presents President de Klerk with a key challenge—for how he deals with it could make all the difference between the success and failure of his reforms.'

It is in this background of political controversy that academics have discovered the SAP. This is with the exception of the SAP's own commemorative volume on its seventy-fifth anniversary (Dippenaar 1988), which is the only book-length study of the police but very obsequious and uncritical (for an extensive review of the book see van der Spuy 1990). This context inevitably fashions the focus, for most studies address the SAP's role in current politics (for example see: Brewer 1988; Brewer *et al.* 1988; Seegars 1989; van der Spuy 1988, 1989, 1990), mostly in suppressing Black opposition (D. Fine 1989; Frankel 1980; Hare 1985; Haysom 1990; Institute of Criminology 1990; Prior 1989; Steytler 1990), but also in ideological disputes in White politics (Weitzer 1991).

However, there are some studies which look at uncontentious, apolitical issues, such as job satisfaction among policemen (Orpen 1980), or are supportive of the South African police (T. van Heerden 1986). There is little work of a historical kind. Brogden (1989) looks at the origins of the SAP in 1913 as a colonial police force, T. van Heerden (1986: 28–45) emphasizes the Afrikaner tradition of policing developed from the seventeenth century, and van der Spuy (1989) provides a wide-ranging review of the development of policing in the twentieth century in her short commentary on published writings on the SAP. For a historical dimension one can also rely on personal recollections by ex-policemen (such as Attwell 1926; Godley 1935; Hattersley 1960; van Onselen 1960) or the SAP's own versions of its history, whether recent (Dippenaar 1988; SAP 1986) or from the past (F. Cooper 1972–3). However, there are a few studies of policing prior to the formation of the SAP (Elks 1986; Grundlingh 1991; Koch 1978; Nasson 1991), and there is again anecdotal evidence from former policemen (Holt 1913; Lorch 1922; Searle 1928; E. Wilson 1884).

While a great deal of the literature on policing in South Africa is ahistorical, there are many references to features of SAP history. But much of it is inaccurate because of its narrow perspective: 1948 and the rise to power of the National Party is treated as the critical juncture in determining aspects of contemporary policing, whereas many features have a longer historical precedent. I have been as guilty as others of this in my early writings on the SAP (for example see Brewer 1988: 277). The tendency is widespread. For example, it is often claimed that the SAP has done little to shed its military image (S. Davies 1987: 180; Haysom 1989a: 142; Philips 1989: 17; Seegars 1986, 1989: 6; van der Spuy 1990: 87), but this was a source of considerable debate before 1948 and the force made several attempts to demilitarize in this earlier period. The Afrikanerization of police manpower is also seen as something which happened after the National Party victory in 1948 (Brewer 1988: 277; Moorcraft 1990: 409; Nasson 1991: 249; Prior 1989: 192), but was in fact occurring in the 1920s. A similar claim is made in respect of the SAP's manpower shortage (Prior 1989: 194), but this existed from the beginning. Other claims are that the Special Branch had its origins in the 1960s (Prior 1989: 200) rather than during the Second World War, that excessive powers were given the police only after 1948 (Frankel 1980: 484), and that special effort to recruit among Black South Africans occurred only with post-1948 Afrikaner governments (Frankel 1980: 482). One of the most absurd of these suggestions is that the SAP's role in 'race control' only began with the National Party in 1948 (Nasson 1991: 249).

Another unfortunate tendency in the literature is to associate policing in South Africa with the SAP and thus to ignore other functionally compatible forces, such as the old South African Mounted Riflemen (SAMR), railway police, mines police, the location police employed by the Native Affairs Commission, and, latterly, Black forces in the homelands and townships. Although this is understandable because the SAP is the largest single policing body, and eventually incorporated many of these separate forces, restricting the focus to the SAP results in two weaknesses. It encourages a purely institutional and organizational account of the SAP, thus divorcing policing from its structural context (most evident in Dippenaar 1988; T. van Heerden 1986), and underemphasizes the often quite separate dynamics behind the development and practice of other police forces, especially various Black police forces.

In the study that follows, policing is put in its historical context in an attempt to establish the historical record, and correct some inaccuracies that have arisen, so that policing in modern South Africa and its possible reform can be properly located in the failure of the SAP to transcend its origins as a colonial force. Policing is also understood broadly, both in the sense of locating it in its social and political context and by the variety of police forces which are discussed in the volume. The time period covers eight decades, bounded by the formation of the Union of South Africa in 1910 and the momentous reforms delivered by de Klerk's government in the 1990s. This allows consideration to be given to the situation as it existed just prior to the formation of the SAP and SAMR in 1913 and to which these forces were a response, and for the volume to chart the path that has brought the police to the juncture where their radical reform is recognized by the state as a political necessity. Finally, it is necessary to explain that since the chapters address certain key themes and issues in each period of police development, there is some repetition of key ideas and themes.

THE COLONIAL MODEL OF POLICING

The government of the new Union of South Africa established the country's police forces in 1913 on the basis of the colonial police model, with which Afrikaner traditions of policing were largely consistent. It took the Royal Irish Constabulary as the exemplar (Brogden 1989: 7; Enloe 1980: 110), as did many forces in the British Empire (on Palestine see Bowden 1975), although Anderson and Killingray (1991*b*: 4) and Hawkins (1991: 18, 23) challenge the extent to which the 'Irish model' permeated the Empire. What historical work has been done on the police in South Africa points to its colonial origins. It is necessary, therefore, to outline the model before the historical record is recounted.

Colonial policing has provoked considerable academic interest (for a slightly outdated review see Cain 1979: 159–60; for case-studies see

Anderson and Killingray 1991*a*, 1992), and is discussed in a variety of ways. Some studies are detailed analyses of policing in former colonial societies, such as Australia, New Zealand, Rhodesia, Nigeria, Kenya, and Canada (for example: Anderson 1991; Finnane 1991; Foran 1962; Hickman 1960; Hill 1986, 1991; D. Johnson 1991; H. Johnson 1991; Killingray 1991; Morrison 1985; Robb 1991; Skinner 1975; Sturgis 1991; Tamuno 1970), or the Palestine police under the British mandate (Bowden 1975; Courtney 1939). Others analyse the old British Colonial Police Service (Atz 1988; Jeffries 1952), which was used by the British to police its colonial territories, sometimes in conjunction with local forces (Dep 1979). Other studies contrast colonial policing with the liberal tradition of policing found in the metropolitan core of Britain itself (Brogden 1987*a*, 1987*b*; Enloe 1980; Tobias 1972), although Brogden argues that policing in Britain also had strong roots in the colonial tradition (see especially 1987*a*) rather than latterly reimporting it, which is the more usual claim.

The features of colonial policing have thus been long recognized, although recently Anderson and Killingray point to the effects of different local contexts in creating derivations of the model in specific colonies (1991*b*: 12). In the colonial model policing was centralized into one national force in order to facilitate the control of policing by the state. The police were agents of the government rather than the law, lacking political autonomy and independence. This often showed itself in the merging of policing duties with civil, judicial, military, or political administration, so that the police performed, as agents of the government, a wide range of functions outside normal police duties. The emphasis was upon control of the populace in order to maintain the authority of the government rather than ordinary crime-fighting or a service role in the community. Policing was not therefore carried out by means of consent, and force was resorted to readily, making colonial police forces notorious for their brutal methods. Armaments were an important item of police equipment therefore, to such an extent that colonial forces were paramilitary organizations.

Colonial police were thus divorced from the local population, often imposing an alien rule. Police membership reflected this. Recruitment was not from among locals—policing by strangers is how this is normally referred to in the literature (Brogden 1987*a*: 196; also see Anderson and Killingray 1991*b*: 7). Recruitment from among the indigenous population did take place when the force became long established, as in Ireland with the Royal Irish Constabulary (Brewer

1989, 1990), but the bulk of the officer corps remained within the metropolitan or settler group. Promotion from the ranks on the basis of meritocratic criteria was not the norm in colonial police forces, or was restricted by means of a quota system. In colonial forces, therefore, the social composition of police membership or the officer class did not reflect that of society at large.

This tendency to skew recruitment towards members of the settler or metropolitan group resulted in the employment of many adventurers, escapists, and marginal men, attracted to the police because it was less demanding than the military but one which none the less offered an exciting and rewarding colonial life-style (Anderson and Killingray 1991*b*: 7; Bowden 1975: 117). They were not experienced and professional policemen, although there was the occasional recruit from a colonial force elsewhere in the Empire; Hickman (1960: 63) estimated that one-fifth of recruits to the British South African Police in Rhodesia had served as policemen elsewhere. It was the life-style that drew men to the police not service to the community or the more mundane crime duties. The Handbook of the Columbo Police in Ceylon emphasized the attractions of policing thus: 'it is common in Columbo to play in one week, golf on Sunday, soccer on Monday, rugger on Tuesday, hockey on Wednesday, tennis on Thursday, polo on Friday and cricket on Saturday' (quoted in Jeffries 1952: 37).

Colonial police forces could not have functioned effectively if they were totally insulated from local contacts, and many had 'native sections' to act as a link with the indigenous population, although the two sections of the force were often segregated (on the Sudan see D. Johnson 1991; on Queensland see Finnane 1991). These local recruits were often marginal themselves. Brogden emphasizes how 'native sections' were sometimes ethnically different from the local population (1987*a*: 196; on the Caribbean see H. Johnson 1991: 84–7), while Bowden shows them to be from among the poorer, uneducated sections of the indigenous population (1975: 126, 1978). They had a reputation for considerable brutality, which reinforced the low image of policing among the local populace. There was also an emphasis upon very strict discipline among local recruits (itself often brutal), partly because of the social-control functions they were required to perform in the colony but also because they could never be considered completely reliable and trustworthy. Native police, therefore, also suffered from a low image among the main body of the police themselves.

In Africa, 'native sections' were often tribal retainers, based on traditional patterns of communal control (Jeffries 1952: 91–2; Killingray 1991; D. Johnson 1991; Anderson 1991), and did not suffer problems arising from insularity or low image. But this meant that the rural areas were mostly policed by locals and the towns by policemen from the metropolitan or settler group, although tours by mounted police into the rural areas were a necessity in many parts of Africa. This bifurcation often gave policing in rural areas different dynamics than in urban areas, from which came different patterns of development, with policing in rural areas conforming more strictly to the traditions of colonial policing (on this point see Anderson and Killingray 1991*b*: 5, 10; for examples in Queensland see Finnane 1991: 47; for the Gold Coast see Killingray 1991: 106; for Sudan see D. Johnson 1991: 151).

The ranks within colonial forces were thus very heterogeneous in membership, and it was the officer class which acted as the unifying element. Officers were also the most professional in their attitude to the job, mostly being trained in Phoenix Park in Dublin, the strict training depot of the Royal Irish Constabulary (for accounts of training in Phoenix Park by recruits to the Royal Irish Constabulary see Brewer 1990: 44–55). In 1907 the British government insisted that all officers in colonial forces be trained in Dublin (Steedman 1984: 48 shows that many chief constables in English forces were also trained in Dublin). Officers with experience in one force were often employed as commanders in newer forces, disseminating a policing tradition as they went, and making a contribution to the colony when they eventually retired from the police as businessmen, farmers, or in civil or legal administration.

The process of colonialization was thus effected in great part by this model of policing and by the people attracted to enlist. The police were used to impose the state's political authority on those who might be expected to resist it. They were the coercive power of the state, subjugating the population: literally making them subjects of the Empire. The police upheld a system of law that was alien to the population but which was vital to the colonial system of administration, as well as favourable for the supply of cheap labour and the goods and services necessary for an imperial-capitalist economy. In addition to this legal mandate, the police fostered colonial administration through their work for other government departments, whereby they imposed and regulated standards and practices in such things as weights and measures, tax, agriculture, medicine and health, and customs. The police were thus central to the colonial state.

Colonial-style policing therefore contrasts with the liberal model in terms of its organization, methods and duties, and in the way that it mediates relations between the citizenry and the state. However, in writing what remains the classic book on colonial policing shortly after the Second World War, Jeffries saw it developing along liberal lines (1952: 32–3). Colonial forces would eventually shed their paramilitary character and be organized, constituted, and operated like civil police forces. No explanation was given as to why this should occur. Presumably, evolution of this unilinear sort would take place once colonialism had been so complete as to make this style of policing redundant, as occurred in many of the older colonies like Australia, New Zealand, and Canada, or so unsuccessful that decolonization and independence from colonial rule would result in the introduction of different police styles, as occurred in India and many former colonies in Africa.

However, this trajectory never occurred for several reasons. First, independence did not everywhere create the social, legal, and political circumstances which sustain the liberal model of policing, and the hopes for the introduction of civil policing in many former colonies diminished along with those for political democracy (on policing in post-independence India see: Cox 1977; Griffiths 1971; Gupta 1979; on policing in post-independence Nigeria see Odenkunle 1979; Tamuno 1970; on the police generally in British-ruled Africa see Atz 1988). Secondly, many contemporary civil police forces have adopted features of the colonial police model. This is in great part the reason why interest in colonial policing has been reawakened, especially among radical critics of the modern police. The colonialization of civil policing is evident in the militarization of many civil police forces, in the deterioration in their relations with the local population, especially in the inner cities, the move away from consensus policing, the expanding powers given to the police, and their greater role in monitoring and regulating public order and political protest (for a summary of these trends see: Fielding 1991; Hillyard and Percy-Smith 1988: 236–88; Reiner 1985; Scraton 1985).

Thirdly, the historical record does not bear out Jeffries's idea of unilinear progress from the colonial model because colonial societies often operated both models simultaneously (on this point see Anderson and Killingray 1991*b*: 4). For example, case-studies show that in India (Brogden 1987*a*: 194–5; Robb 1991), Rhodesia (Hickman 1960: 14; Jeffries 1952: 108), and West and East Africa (Anderson 1991; Jeffries 1952: 91–3; Killingray 1991) police forces in the rural areas were mounted, paramilitary bodies, without a sustained presence, relying on occasional displays of authority to regulate and control the colonized population. In the towns, with larger metropolitan or settler populations and more stable patterns of industrial and commercial development, civil police functions were adopted, along with crime-fighting and service roles, which normalized relations with the public (on urban areas in Kenya see Willis 1991). In the urban areas police patrolled on foot and were sometimes unarmed. Occasionally the differences in style were reinforced by being the responsibility of different forces, extenuated in some cases by the use of military dress and titles to define the ranks in forces which policed rural areas, while normal police nomenclature and dress were adopted by civil police in the towns. Therefore, both styles of policing coexisted in some colonial societies, reflecting the different socio-political dynamics in certain regions and locations.

A variant of this argument is that the colonial police style can be employed in cases of internal colonialism (Brogden 1987*a*: 193). In this instance, particular ethnic or national minority groups within a society (whether or not restricted to peripheral regions of the territory) are subjected to policies equivalent to colonial exploitation and subjugation, with policing style being one process. Thus, members of minority groups experience policing in a way different from dominant group members: it is often experienced as harassment, intimidation, oppression, political control, and brute force. Such a situation occurred for a long time in the Deep South in the United States (Bayley and Mendelsohn 1969; Black and Reiss 1967; Hawkins and Thomas 1991; Ruchelman 1974; Wintersmith 1974), and is alleged by some to happen in the Catholic ghettos of Northern Ireland (Walsh 1988), and in Britain's inner cities (Cashmore and McLaughlin 1991*a*; for a review of the literature on police relations with Black Britons see Brogden, Jefferson, and Walklate 1988: 124–41; Cashmore and McLaughlin 1991*b*).

POLICING IN SOUTH AFRICA

Police bodies in South Africa began as colonial forces and, it will be argued, retained most of the features of this model as the century progressed. This is why contemporary policing needs to be understood in the context of the history and development of policing in South Africa. It is not difficult to understand why. The country's modernization, and impressive urban and industrial development, has occurred because of the existence of a reservoir of ultra-exploitable social groups, whose underdevelopment is vital if economic benefits for others are to be afforded. That is, the South African state's project has remained one of internal colonialism. It has systematically accorded fewer civil and political rights, economic privileges, and social opportunities to its Black communities in order to maintain and reinforce their status as exploited and subjugated people. Thus, the monitoring, control, and regulation of race relations, specifically Black South Africans, remained a necessity in order for political power and economic wealth to continue as the preserve of Whites. The colonial policing style was central to this project and remained so until de Klerk recast the state's interests in 1989–90.

However, in presenting their public image, the police themselves draw on the liberal tradition of policing, although the Department of Information's Official Yearbook on South Africa for 1989–90 candidly described the SAP as a paramilitary organization (Department of Information 1990: 259). Thus the police creed in South Africa states:

I must possess complete integrity for temptation will bestride my path. I must be tidy in my thoughts and person, for pride [and] ambition will demand this. Patience and courage are my twin companions; patience paves the way for lucid thinking, while courage should be boundless. My rank instills in me a sense of power which I must discipline so that no man need fear me—except for good reason. And by these concepts I will be strong—a true servant and guardian of the law. (SAP 1986: 43)

This idea of independently serving the law rather than partisanly supporting the government is also enshrined in the police motto *servamus et servimus*: we protect and we serve. This is also now the title of the SAP's magazine, which engages in public-relations exercises, such as advertisements for the SAP's campaign 'Die Helpende Hand', which show police officers in public service roles providing a 'helping hand' to children and the elderly. At the SAP's formation the police magazine was called *Nongqai*, a Zulu word meaning watchman, protector, or peacemaker, which was borrowed from the old Natal Police (where it was equally incongruous, given the real nature of policing).

But as if to symbolize the true nature of policing in modern South Africa, the name *nongqai* was recently given to a new bullet-proof police vehicle, resistant to petrol bombs and hand-grenades, and with a large hydraulic scrapper at the front to sweep away large obstructions, such as barricades. The vehicle was originally deployed by the army in bush warfare but redesigned for use by the police in Black townships. The SAP described it as 'a friend to all law-abiding citizens' (Dippenaar 1988: 839), but it is a formidable coercive weapon to defend the state against those who are protesting at their systematic exploitation and exclusion. The vehicle symbolizes the paramilitary character of policing and the central role of the police in defending the racial and class interests involved in the state's internal colonialism, and thus illustrates that within the liberal policing rhetoric of 'protection' and 'peacemaking', evoked by the word *nongqai*, an essentially colonial policing task is still performed.

POLICE–STATE RELATIONS

For these reasons, policing in South Africa is closely tied to the nature and project of the state. The subject of police–state relations has become of central importance in police studies (for a selection see: Bayley 1982; Brewer *et al.* 1988; Brodeur 1983; Enloe 1980; Hillyard and Percy-Smith 1988; Mosse 1975; Reiner 1985, 1989; Turk 1982), reflecting disillusionment with the liberal idea of apolitical policing, as a result of changes in the nature of both contemporary policing and the modern state. Thus, it is now widely realized that the police are an institution within the influence of the state, operating to consolidate and maintain state authority, taking a share of the state's fiscal pie, and having an impact upon people's views of the state. The very word 'police' reflects this relationship, being derived from the Greek *politeia* or Latin *politia*, meaning 'state authority'. *Politeia* is in turn derived from *polites*, which means inhabitants of a state.

In colonial policing there was a close relationship between the police and state because colonial forces were under central political control, performed extra-police duties for the state, were more interested in the suppression of civil unrest against the government than crime-fighting, and were an armed and paramilitary force. The SAP never transcended its origins and remained a colonial force, thus, the SAP have never been autonomous; police–state relations made the police a tool of the state, and the colonial nature of the SAP throughout the twentieth century made police–state relations the critical feature of policing. Therefore, the following study seeks to place policing in the context of the evolving interests of the South African state.

As a colonial force, the SAP was under the direct political control of the cabinet minister responsible for policing, and this was, no doubt, the main mechanism by which the state was able so easily to communicate its interests, decisions, and priorities to the Commissioner. However, the focus of this volume is not on the precise mechanisms by which the state influenced policing, since the formal processes are so obvious in a colonial setting, but the resulting effects of the state's policies of internal colonialism for police policy, organization, and practice.

But while policing in South Africa bears this imprint, the material will also be used to sound a note of caution against reductionism in our understanding of police–state relations. Borrowing a term from Althusser, it is more accurate to describe the SAP as possessing relative autonomy. Policing is not solely derivative of the state, as much modern literature on policing claims, for the police possess a limited capacity for independent action, although this is constrained. The South African case-study is used in the Conclusion to exemplify this relative autonomy. Indeed, current resistance in the SAP to political change can only be understood in the context of a set of police–state relations in which the police possess relative autonomy. And it is in the context of this relative autonomy that one must also locate the difficulties the South African state will face in reforming the police along liberal lines.

I

The Colonial Agenda
1910–1913

INTRODUCTION

The fledgling government of the new Union of South Africa quickly set about planning the Union's police force. All newly established states consider it a sign of national prestige to have their own security forces, and although union of the four territories in 1910 was not strictly an act of independence, the development of a unified and centralized police service was an important national symbol. When they were formed on 1 April 1913, the SAP and SAMR were structured and organized so as to build on the strengths of pre-Union police forces and to avoid the weaknesses. They were not entirely successful in resolving these problems, and in many respects the SAP is still struggling with some of them. Thus, to understand policing in late twentieth-century South Africa, it is necessary to begin with the dynamics of policing in the nineteenth.

PRE-UNION POLICE FORCES

The police forces that existed in 1910, and which were blended into two forces in 1913, represented two policing traditions: the colonial model that operated in the Natal and Cape colonies, which were formerly controlled by the British, and the Afrikaner tradition in the two former Boer Republics of Transvaal and Orange Free State (also known at this time as the Orange River Colony, but the more familiar usage will be adopted throughout). The ease of the merger lay in great part in the compatibility of these two traditions, for Boer police forces shared many features with the British colonial police tradition.

This also explains why the British retained many Afrikaner policing practices when they usurped the Cape from the original Dutch settlers.

The Afrikaner tradition goes further back than the colonial model. Within six months of van Riebeeck's arrival in the Cape in 1652, he appointed a *geweldiger* as an official to deal with growing crime in the Dutch settlement, especially stock theft and contraband with Blacks (T. van Heerden 1986: 28; also see van Onselen 1960). Thus, from the beginning, the Afrikaner tradition made the control of race relations a feature of police work alongside ordinary crime. The class interests of the propertied were also important. By 1689 the first fiscal was appointed and given policing powers. Responsible to the Council of Seventeen in Holland, the fiscal was charged with the duty of protecting the resources, establishments, goods, and interests of the Dutch East Indies Company.

Given that the early settlement of Afrikaners was urban, bringing with it the usual crimes associated with town life, city burghers later employed patrols and night watches to monitor ordinary crime. In this regard, the town watches in London were similar; and the British retained the night watches once they occupied the Cape in 1806. In Britain, these town watches eventually transformed into civil police forces (see Brogden 1987*a*; Critchley 1978; Rock 1983), with a focus upon ordinary crime and service to the local community. This happened over time among the urban Afrikaner communities in South Africa as well. By 1873, for example, there were thirteen town police forces in the Orange Free State, and the Transvaal Republic Police was founded in 1881 and given legal status in 1895. The impetus behind the development of policing in urban areas was thus the growth of crime or the fear of crime, as in urbanized areas in Britain or the United States (for example, on Chicago see Douthit 1975; on Mombasa, see Willis 1991). Policing in rural areas had different dynamics, however, and as many Afrikaners eventually trekked into the hinterland to avoid the British or in search of land, another feature was added to the Afrikaner tradition.

Crime was low within voortrekker communities on isolated Afrikaner farms, so that the need for a police service arose in the rural areas not from any disorder or fear of crime, but to defend settler territory and regulate interaction with the overwhelming number of Blacks with whom they shared territory. The spur to the development of policing in the rural areas was thus race not crime. The Afrikaner police lineage is therefore also one of paramilitary policing by *ad hoc* commando-type units made up of armed local citizens controlling the Black population by displays of superior force and brutality. The citizen-policeman model was used effectively in the rural areas both to defend territory and steal more of it, and protect the different cultural and social habits of Afrikaners against invasion and absorption by Blacks. The boundaries they regulated were thus both geographical and moral.

However, the town police in the Boer Republics had a similar role. In addition to controlling ordinary crime, perpetrated often by the poor Whites and adventurers attracted to the towns, especially mining towns, the borough police also regulated the social and cultural boundaries between Black and White, calmed White fears about Black crime, and harassed the indigenous Black population that was entering or encroaching on the towns. For example, the growth of alluvial diggings in the Transvaal led to city burghers being legally instructed in 1876 to 'take action against vagabonds and vagrants by apprehending any such coloureds' (quoted in T. van Heerden 1986: 30). Clearly issues of crime and race were linked in Afrikaner thinking, and both encouraged the development and growth of the police service in the Boer Republics. It was this merging of the two social processes which led in later years to the linking of Afrikaner nationalist criminology with the racial ideas of apartheid (van Zyl Smit 1990), a link which became ingrained in the mind-set of the SAP because this version of criminology became a compulsory part of police training.

The Afrikaner policing tradition, then, was split between the paramilitary style of the rural areas, where there was very little emphasis on the control of ordinary crime, and the civil police model of the towns (see Grundlingh 1991; Nasson 1991). But even in the latter, features of the colonial tradition remained, as the police took on duties over and above those considered as normal civil police work; specifically, the monitoring and control of race relations. This made policing in the Boer Republics very similar to that in the British-controlled colonies of the Cape and Natal.

In the rural areas of the British colonies, forces such as the Cape Mounted Police, Cape Mounted Riflemen, Natal Mounted Police, and the Zululand Mounted Police took as their model the early Royal Irish Constabulary (Brogden 1989: 7; Enloe 1980: 110), as did most colonial forces in the British Empire. They were militarized in discipline, command structure, and dress, armed, divorced from the local population, and officered by the British. Long forays were taken up-country to impose British rules and standards on the local population, protect territory, put down an unruly populace, or simply to show a colonial presence. Some ordinary crime was monitored, such as stock theft, but often the police acted as general servants of the colonial power, being responsible for criminal and civil justice, enforcing health regulations, and tax collection, among other things (see Holt 1913: 233 for a personal reminiscence of the duties of members of the Natal Mounted Police). In the rapidly expanding urban areas, however, the model was the London Metropolitan Police (Brogden 1989: 7; Hattersley 1960; on Cape Town see Nasson 1991: 236).

The Cape Mounted Riflemen, for example, possess a history which can be traced back to the first British occupation of the Cape, when the name was borne by a regiment of Hottentot auxiliaries. Over time it became a European force, with a small contingent of Coloured soldiers. The Frontier and Armed Mounted Police was absorbed into a reorganized corps of Cape Mounted Riflemen in 1878, making this body the permanent force for both internal police duties in the rural areas and external defence. Thus, the corps served in numerous wars against the indigenous Black population, against Afrikaners in both Boer Wars, as well as dealing with stock theft, the collection of dog taxes, the pursuit of those without appropriate gun licences, and other duties that passed for police work in the rural heartland of the Cape.

Police forces in rural Natal had a similar role and history. The Natal Mounted Police was established in 1874 as the first regular corps of the colony, under the famous Major Dartnell (later Major-General Sir John Dartnell). The force was involved in the numerous wars with the Zulu, participating in the stand at Isandhlwana and the defence of Rorke's Drift (on which see Holt 1913: 40–54), saw service against Boer and Basuto, while simultaneously chasing miscreants for non-payment of licences, or monitoring the health of cattle, and diseases affecting the local Black population.

These rural-based forces were therefore paramilitary bodies, easily transformed into military units in times of internal or external conflict or threat, of which colonial expansion ensured there were many. But even their policing duties were militarized, as they imposed an alien regime on a colonized people, sometimes by force, but often by simply rigidly enforcing imported British rules, standards, and practices in civil, legal, political, medical, and financial matters. Hence their responsibility for duties over and above those now considered 'normal' for police forces. The policeman-soldier tradition therefore featured as much in the British colonial policing tradition as the Afrikaner lineage, although the town police were not liable for military service, with the exception of those on the Rand and Pretoria (once Britain annexed the Transvaal). This was because town police were under the control of the municipal authority not the colonial power, and paid for partly from local finances, which were frugally protected.

One of the attractions of these rural-based forces was that they were paramilitary units, offering adventure, excitement, and a military life-style at less cost than with the British army. This is why applications increased after police involvement in major conflicts and war (Holt 1913: 42), although recruitment tended to fall once the emergency had been contained. Moreover, the whole point of colonialism was that profit should flow one way: to the mother country. Thus, expensive military engagements in the colonies often led to cut-backs in the size of the units as an economy measure once they had been successfully fought, much to the displeasure of senior officers, who had to maintain a semblance of rational planning. In the early days of the Natal Mounted Police, for example, they earned the nickname of 'snuffs' because the British government would only sanction the use of cheap, foul-smelling cloth for uniforms (Holt 1913: 16).

Being a member of a rural-based police force in British colonies was therefore not without some insecurity, but the life-style provided many compensations, as letters home or men's diaries recount (see MSS Afr. r. 102; MSS Afr. s. 1638; MSS Afr. s. 2015). Leaving aside the officer class, the ranks attracted two types: the wealthy 'remittance men' (a term employed by F. Cooper 1972–3: 21), in receipt of a private income from home to supplement their police salary, who were seeking new experiences in the colonies or avoiding the consequences of past ones at home; and the 'social climbers', who used police membership in the colonies to afford a life-style, travel, and adventure unavailable to them at home. On the whole, then, recruits for regular forces were from abroad. Dartnell once complained about recruiting internally, describing men already in the colony as men of respectable family from England who had run out of money and who saw the police as a temporary living, colonial-born men who had led unsettled lives, or ex-soldiers, ex-sailors, and 'loafers of diverse sorts' all 'addicted to drink' (quoted in Holt 1913: 17). Advertisements for the police in South Africa often appeared in the *London Standard*, calling for 'smart, active young men' (E. Wilson 1884: 17), and the minor English public schools proved productive recruiting agencies. Many Cheltenham boys went to the Natal Mounted Police (Holt 1913: 222).

The foreign recruits, however, were often not much better than colonial-born applicants were assumed to be. Writing in the Preface of Holt's personal reminiscence of the force, Dartnell realized in retrospect that the Natal Mounted Police, for example, was attracting 'social failures from home' (Holt 1913: p. vii), and eventually persuaded the government to consent to make all promotions through the ranks to improve the class of recruits. A former policeman from Natal describes his colleagues as 'black sheep of the family who came out to join the force rather than turn over a new leaf' (Searle 1928: 36). Complaints were sometimes made in the Natal Legislative Assembly about the conduct of the police, and in 1876 the Acting Colonial Secretary referred to the 'perpetual blackening of the characters of the men', although he described it as unjust (quoted in Holt 1913: 290). In the Cape, Hattersley described the police in the nineteenth century as not yet having learned 'habits of sobriety and self-control', and monetary rewards were given to men for good conduct (1960: 50). Members of the Cape Mounted Riflemen actually mutinied on one occasion. There were constant desertions as better opportunities presented themselves to fortune-hunters. The 1889 Annual Report of the Commandant of the Natal Mounted Police complained about the desertions of men attracted to the gold-fields. Dismissals for misconduct were common. Personal reminiscences by former policemen recount tales of debt, drunkenness, and debauchery (see Searle 1928: 36–52); Holt described knowledge of the law among Natal policemen as slight, including knowledge of police powers and regulations (1913: 36). The problem of drunkenness led to many quarrels and fights between the men (Searle 1928: 77).

The life-style of a policeman in the outlying rural areas of the colonies was typically colonial. One former policeman described it thus: 'romantic, what with camping out in the open on a dry starry night, songs on the road and around the camp fires, smoking and yarning' (Searle 1928: 77). Searle recounts memories of flirting with farmers' daughters (more than likely Afrikaner farmers), bathing in rivers, looking for relics from tribal graves, shooting the rapids, and hunting game (1928: 98). On the one hand it was exciting, on the other it was a replica of an English country life-style for those without an estate in the mother country to hunt over: E. Wilson described policing in South Africa as 'no better place for someone who likes horse, dog and gun' (1884: 145).

The peculiar inducements of colonial life therefore attracted to the ranks people of higher social status than the working-class recruits who dominated police forces in nineteenth-century Britain (Brogden 1987*a*; Tobias 1972). However, sensitivity to social status differentials within the ranks brought problems for the colonial police. There were obvious class differences within the ranks as the 'social climbers' worked alongside the 'remittance men'. One policeman looked down on some of his colleagues as 'dragged up by the scruff of their necks as half-starved London clerks of middle class parentage' (Searle 1928: 71). Another referred to his colleagues as 'more adapted to take charge of a few pigs than hold [a] position in a police force' (E. Wilson 1884: 124). Non-commissioned officers were often in a situation where they called rankers 'sir'; the ranks contained princes and pot boys (Searle 1928: 31), so that some ordinary constables were the sons of generals, baronets, and, in one instance, a member of the Bourbon Royal Family (who was killed in a skirmish in Natal, his family coming out with a retinue to visit the place of his death). The 'remittance men' often cleaned out their horse's stable with gloves on, and even though they were in the ranks they employed batmen, who were Black (*Nongqai*, Mar. 1922: 144). Duels were fought when work was slack, and they organized gymkhanas, concerts, and contests of all sorts (*Nongqai*, Mar. 1922: 141). Discipline amongst the 'remittance men' was therefore often difficult to enforce, and not just because of their life-style. Many already had a background of indiscipline and misconduct which brought them to the colonial police in the first place, having been expelled from or denied entry to military academies, or sent out by families for being prodigal (Searle 1928: 35). And not surprisingly, their preference was for military engagements rather than the tedium of routine police work, to which they did not take kindly, undertaking it with dissimulation rather than enthusiasm (*Nongqai*, Mar. 1922: 144).

Ordinary crime was almost non-existent; it was a case of either militarily putting down rebellions or performing a variety of mundane tasks for the colonial power that extended beyond normal police work. The key tasks were thus to defend territory and inculcate colonial standards and rules on an alien and hostile population, whether Black or Boer. Policing race relations was thus as much a feature of the British as the Afrikaner tradition, save that it also involved monitoring relations between Britons and Boers as well as those with the indigenous Black population. Police opinions of both were equally poor; both posed cultural and military threats, felt closely monitored by the police, and came into frequent situations of conflict with them. The Natal Police, for example, considered some Afrikaners as loyal (Searle 1928: 121–2), and the occasional Boer was a member of the Natal Mounted Police (F. Cooper 1972–3: 51; on Boer 'collaborators' with the British police see Grundlingh 1991: 171), but this was a minority in both cases. Yet the major towns in Natal and the Cape were different. The population was predominantly British or European, ordinary crime flourished, and paramilitary-style policing was redundant, although elements of colonial policing remained.

The police in Cape Town were modelled on the London Metropolitan Police. Ex-Inspector John King of the Metropolitan Police was appointed as Inspector of the Cape Town Police in 1844, and introduced the practices and procedures of the London force, with an emphasis on the prevention of ordinary crime and modern training methods, such as they were then (Hattersley 1960; Nasson 1991). This model was also applied in many of the smaller towns in the Cape (see Cape of Good Hope 1882). The nomenclature was from the civil police tradition; military titles were avoided. The Cape Town police even adopted the traditional British blue colour for its uniform, although the borough police in Natal preferred military-style uniforms. It was not until 1880 that police in Pietermaritzburg adopted the uniform and helmet of the London Metropolitan Police.

Most of these forces were very small, each with their chief constable, but only a handful of constables in the command, many of whom were Black. Colloquially, these were known as government town police. The local council also employed their own police to detect contravention of the by-laws, again with many such constables being Black, although the government paid up to half the costs. These were known as municipal police. Black policemen were common in both types of urban force because the pay was insufficient to attract most Whites, and urban policing did not have the attractive and exciting life-style connected with paramilitary policing in the rural areas; a commission established in 1882 by the Cape government under Bernard Shaw, the Cape's first Commissioner of Police, recommended increasing the pay of most urban police forces for this reason. Low salary was not the only hindrance to White recruitment. Police work had very low status, in large part due to the employment of a class of White ne'er-do-wells and members from the conquered Black population, the latter consideration being important in a colonial and racially stratified society (Brogden 1989: 7).

Black policemen were used from the earliest time of British colonization. To begin with British administrators drew on tribal forms of law and order, using paid headmen as a police force, although this was primarily an attempt to diminish the power of chiefs who had maintained law and order in the past (Wilson and Thompson 1969: 265). As the colonial project developed, and the need for effective social control increased, various regiments of paramilitary police were formed in the rural areas exclusively from among Blacks, such as the Zululand Mounted Police and the original Cape Mounted Riflemen, although these were always officered by the British. Both forces were eventually incorporated or reorganized into European-dominated forces. Members of the Zululand Mounted Police saw service against their kinsmen in the 1905–6 Zulu rebellion, and earned praise from White officers for their loyalty.

But Blacks formed part of most rural and urban police forces; the smaller urban forces were sometimes exclusively Black, save for a White chief constable. Indians were absorbed into the Natal Mounted Police soon after their arrival in Natal: the first in 1861. There were thirty Indian policemen by 1896 (Poodhun 1983: 170–3). There are good reasons for this that lie in the nature of colonialism. It increases the acceptability of the police among the subject population, as well as enhances the social-control functions of the police among the colonized: hence the eventual employment of Catholics in the ranks of the Royal Irish Constabulary (Brewer 1990: 5). In a racially stratified colonial society it is also cheaper to employ members of the subjugated population. Details of salary contained in Shaw's report on policing in the Cape show that 'native police' were invariably paid less than Europeans, which was thought to be necessary and desirable (Cape of Good Hope 1882: 21), even though there was not always a difference in duty. Black policemen in towns often did foot patrol, especially where there were no White constables in the employ of the municipality to do it instead. However, their primary duty was to police Blacks in the locations and shanties on the edge of town. Other forms of discrimination existed for Blacks within the police. In 1910, for example, only the Transvaal Police had Black non-commissioned officers.

White colonists had an ambiguous attitude towards the use of Black police. On the one hand, it was a necessity for the success of colonialism, but it brought problems. To be truly effective, Black policemen needed to be housed in the town in case of emergencies at night, but mostly they lived in the Black locations; considerations of race and social status prevented the building of quarters for them in the town. Again for the sake of effectiveness, Black police needed to be armed, as they originally were. But this provoked all sorts of fears among White colonists and restrictions were placed on the arms Black police were able to carry (Holt 1913: p. xi). Similar sorts of considerations limited their powers of arrest over Whites in urban areas (Cape of Good Hope 1882: 16). And there were the usual complaints from ratepayers about the lack of education and language abilities of Black police (Cape of Good Hope 1882: 19).

Fewer problems were therefore created when Black police were restricted to keeping the peace in the locations on the edge of the town where Blacks lived. But regulating contact between the races was also part of the jurisdiction of European police. Responsibility for checking passes and for monitoring trade between the races fell to the municipal police. The chief constable of the government-funded police had no authority over these men.

Urban police generally had problems, however, for there were the same civil liberty concerns about the role and conduct of the police that existed in London. There was resistance to certain police powers. For example, in Cape Town the police were not allowed to handcuff people in the street without special authority from the magistrate, and similar disquiet was expressed in Cape Town in the 1860s about the use of plain-clothes police as there had been in London three decades earlier. These were concerns expressed by Whites only, but fear of crime and of the encroaching urban Black population tended to pull in the opposite direction, and later there were complaints from Whites about being under-policed. The Black population was subject to as much control as the urban masses had been in London a century earlier, where Rock notes that the early police in Britain were required to regulate the activities of the community, and enforce order in such ways as monitoring the crossing of parish boundaries, and checking nightly on lodgers and strangers. Watchmen were required to apprehend 'nightwalkers or any other persons whatsoever that are uncivil or cannot give a good account of themselves' (cited in Rock 1983: 196); the Black pass system was similar in South Africa a century later.

Therefore, although Shaw's report described the duties of the town police as 'entirely those of an ordinary and not of a military or semi-military character' (Cape of Good Hope 1882: 3), the town police in the British-run colonies in South Africa were not devoid of colonial-style duties. Ordinary crime flourished, as it did in all colonial towns throughout the Empire (for example in Ontario see Sturgis 1991; on Mombasa see Willis 1991; for other 'settled areas' in Kenya see Anderson 1991: 194). The 1882 Report found that each constable in Cape Town made twenty-one arrests on average compared to eight in London, leading Shaw to infer that either the Cape force was more effective or crime was more rampant (1882: 44). The latter is more likely the case. But in addition to dealing with ordinary crime, the colonial situation gave the police special duties. Social and economic interaction between the races was regulated through various by-laws which restricted the movement and employment of the colonized population (for similar examples throughout the British Empire see Anderson 1991; H. Johnson 1991; Willis 1991).

Despite this, there was still a sharp contrast between the paramilitary police style of the rural areas and the more civilian tradition of the towns. This sometimes led to conflicts of interest between forces in the two areas. An article in the SAP's journal *Nongqai*, which reminisced about policing in the nineteenth century, stated the following: 'in those days the borough police of Pietermaritzburg were at enmity with the Colony's Police, who did not take seriously to police work until a much later date. Many tricks were played on the former' (*Nongqai* 1922: 142). On another occasion in Pietermaritzburg the borough police raided a public house for illegal drinking whilst it was full of members of the Natal Mounted Police, whereupon a fight broke out between the two. And it was often a complaint by members of the town police that ex-military men from the army or the paramilitary police forces were appointed to senior positions in the town police, despite inexperience in civil policing, rather than having promotions from the ranks (Cape of Good Hope 1882: 45).

The greatest conflict, however, was with the interests of the civilians and administrators in the burgeoning colonial towns, who demanded protection from ordinary crime, and greater policing resources and manpower directed towards the urban areas. The clash between the two policing traditions was even more apparent in the larger towns, and after the period of rapid urbanization in the last quarter of the nineteenth century. In Cape Town, for example, the largest of the British-colonial towns, the convention was to appoint the senior officer from the London Metropolitan Police. But after a corruption scandal in 1867, which led to the resignation of the incumbent inspector, a salary of £200 per annum proved unable to attract someone from England, and the Colonial Secretary sent Francis Fishborne, an army officer with experience in Ireland, who was an instructor in musketry. Although described as a gentleman, Fishborne had no experience of civil police work, and the Governor of the Cape took the unusual step of placing him in the Frontier Police, where his military background was more suited. The Governor stated that the demand was for: 'a superior class of constable, thoroughly conversant with the daily routine of police duties and not unfitted by birth or education to be thrown into the company of constables' (quoted in Hattersley 1960: 116). An appointment was eventually made from within the ranks, which is always an index of a commitment to professionalize police work, and was an important development in the modernization of the Royal Irish Constabulary (for similar complaints in Kenya see Willis 1991: 222).

Town police thus witnessed the greatest modernization. Another manifestation of this is the emergence of criminal investigation departments in the town police in the late nineteenth century. In the Natal Police a CID branch was first formed in the boroughs of Pietermaritzburg and Durban in 1894, in association with the reorganization of the force along civil police lines (see Hattersley 1960: 162–3; Holt 1913: 244). It was developed by Sub-Inspector Clark and modelled on the CID at Great Scotland Yard. By 1910 the CID establishment in the Transvaal was 196 personnel, the Cape 75, Natal 74, and the Orange Free State 42, with a total expenditure, including allowances, of £82,117 (Conf/6/8/10). The fingerprint system of identification formed part of the CID. By 1903 there were 3,500 fingerprints on file, and Black recruits to the Natal Police were routinely checked before being accepted into the force, although this was not its primary usage. A similar system was developed in the Transvaal in 1902 by Sir Edward Henry, who was Inspector-General of Police in Bengal on secondment to the Transvaal Town Police precisely for this purpose (Hattersley 1960; T. van Heerden 1986; on the effect of the 'Indian model' of policing throughout the British Empire see Hawkins 1991: 21). This offers a good example of how British policing methods were diffused throughout the Empire, as well as how fear of crime stimulated police modernization.

In the urban areas, and especially the smaller towns, fear of crime and the rapidly expanding urban Black population also led to persistent complaints that the town police were under-resourced, and that the urban areas were under-policed. For townspeople, the relative modernization of the urban areas had changed the policing priorities. Thus, Shaw's report on policing in over a dozen towns in the Cape pointed everywhere to the escalation in crime and the need to increase the resources and staffing of the town police (especially by increasing the employment of White constables). Crime was going undetected and the inhabitants unprotected. Barkly, for example, had one policeman for every 3,700 inhabitants; Cape Town one in 500 (Cape of Good Hope 1882: 6, 44). Comparative figures for Ireland show Belfast with one policeman for every 306 citizens and Dublin one in 365, not surprisingly revealing Ireland to be much heavier policed (Brewer 1990: 7).

The expenditure on rural forces was thus seen by many urban residents in the Cape and Natal as misspent, and their military manner inappropriate. The Governor of Natal once said to Dartnell that his men in the Natal Mounted Police 'swagger too much; we don't want swashbucklers' (quoted in Holt 1913: p. xi), and he was reluctant to release members of the police for military duties in 1899, urging troops be sent from the United Kingdom (HMSO 1900). Many municipal police forces, paid for partly from the rates, were specifically excluded from the obligation to provide military service. The Natal Legislative Assembly often heard complaints that the smaller towns in the colony, which did not have their own municipal police, were being left under-policed as a result of the military duties of the forces, and that the emphasis in training was too much directed towards drill and not civil policing. The Attorney-General of Natal, in moving the second reading of the Police Bill in the Assembly in 1893, said that the colony needed to be governed by police not soldiers.

This was in part a critical commentary on the prevalence of ordinary crime in the towns, fear about the encroachment of Blacks into urban areas, and the nature of the colonial policeman-soldier tradition, but was also an expression of a wish to see colonial life normalized, at least in the towns; to be made, as far as possible, a mirror of that in the mother country. Members of the Natal Legislature from large urban areas encouraged the development of 'normal' policing, while farmers, isolated in rural areas and surrounded by an alien population that was perceived as hostile, favoured the retention of a paramilitary police, as did the MPs who served such areas, other racists, and the police themselves. The 1891/2 Annual Report of the Commandant of the Natal Mounted Police advocated the retention of military duties.

The government's response to this in Natal was completely to reorganize the police into one centralized force in 1894, called the Natal Police, although four borough forces remained independent in the largest Natal towns. The force was demilitarized in dress and training, although the police tried to resist this and still routinely used military terms to distinguish the ranks. Dartnell was appointed Chief Commissioner, nomenclature which reflected the shift in approach. However, in his 1893/4 Annual Report he recorded his regret at the change in title and the deletion of the term 'mounted' from the name of the force. This shift towards civil policing, no matter how reluctant, was enshrined in the separation of policing and judicial functions, and the removal of police from control by magistrates (who controlled many of the localized and smaller forces). Out-stations were built in many of the isolated areas so that there was a continual police presence in even the most rural of areas: there were twenty-six such stations before the reorganization and sixty afterwards. The out-station at Ubombo, for example, was 150 miles from the nearest railway; at Ingwavuma there were only a few Zulu kraals and two White families (Holt 1913: 229). The personal papers of a Lt.-Col. Bamford from the Natal Police record the isolation of the out-stations; native runners were used to keep in contact with the towns, and for mail. At his station in Northern Natal, where he was posted first as a junior officer, mail from Durban took a week to arrive, and there was constant danger from malaria due to lack of medical care (MSS Brit. Emp. s. 308). But the out-stations proved effective. In the first year, the number of arrests increased by 546 per cent, and the number of stock stolen decreased from 100,000 to 2,170 (Holt 1913: 129); there was no overall increase in the size of the force as an alternative explanation of this decrease in crime.

But the agenda of the colonial government often subverted the shift away from colonial policing in Natal. The British government was intent on accumulating land, profit, and gold, so that the Natal Police were involved in the 1898–1902 Boer War (against the wishes of the governor), and the 1905–6 Zulu rebellion. Thus, while the Natal Police invoked the imagery of service to the community in the name of their police magazine (*Nongqai*, meaning 'watchman' or 'protector'), their force song, penned in 1911, drew on the paramilitary ethos.

> For peace or war—whate'er the call,
> The *Nongqai* boys are ready;
> One loyal love embraces all,

One purpose holds us steady:
For King and Country firm we stand
in cause of law and order,
but should a foe raise threatening hand
we'll fight beyond the border.
Oh, long may such service live,
which makes for Empire-building.
Pure, strong and brave—tis this we crave,
shall be the *Nongqai*'s token.

After the annexation of the Transvaal, the British also became responsible for policing in the old Boer Republics, whereupon they delegated to Major-General Baden-Powell the task of establishing a police force in the conquered Afrikaner territories. In doing so they drew on the model in the Cape rather than Natal. That is, of having separate forces, with different policing styles and approaches, for rural and urban areas rather than a single, centralized force. In 1900 the South African Constabulary was formed as a paramilitary body, intended for service in the rural areas, belying the use of civil police imagery in its name (on this force see Grundlingh 1991). Arthur Weatherhead, who served in the force as a junior officer between 1904 and 1907, has left a rather uneventful diary of his experiences (MSS Afr. s. 1638), which reports a round of sporting and social engagements, but policemen performed many administrative functions for the colonial power beyond civil police work. The Transvaal Town Police was formed in 1901 to deal with policing in the urban areas, with a similar body in the Orange Free State. The Transvaal Police and the Orange Free State Police took over from the South African Constabulary when it was disbanded in 1908, and dealt also with policing in the rural areas.

Many of these forces in the former Boer Republics employed ex-members of the Afrikaner police, ensuring that a sizeable number of Afrikaners were serving policemen when members were being recruited for the SAP and SAMR a few years later. It also gave British residents in the former Boer Republics, who rushed there before and after the second Boer War, the experience of being policed by strangers. It was now their turn to complain about a police force which seemed culturally different and out of kilter with their values and expectations. A petition against the police in the Transvaal, organized by the South African League, read:

The police of this state is exclusively recruited from the burgher element, many of them being youths fresh from the rural districts, without experience or tact, and in many cases without general education or a knowledge of the English language. The force as a whole is entirely out of sympathy with the British section of the community.   (taken from Bulpin 1955: 292)

THE STATE OF THE POLICE IN 1910

At the time of Union, the size of the police forces in the various territories was 10,186 men, 38.8 per cent of which were Black. Only Natal's police had more Black members than White, and forces in the Transvaal and the Cape were by far the largest. Nearly three-quarters of the manpower was based in the Transvaal and Cape. In Transvaal's case this led to the highest number of policemen per head of population, at one for every 465 citizens, but the geographical expanse of the Cape ensured that it still had the lowest, at one for every 983. This represented an average for the four territories of one policeman for every 693 citizens, or a ratio of 1.44 policemen per thousand of population, which was not excessive and equivalent to democratic countries in Europe and America. Total expenditure on policing in 1910 was £1.1 million, with Transvaal and the Cape again taking three-quarters of this sum (based on figures provided in SAP/2/14/21). Overall, in 1910 there was one policeman for every fifty-two square miles of South African territory, varying from one for every seventeen square miles in Natal to one for every 105 square miles in the Cape (p. 3).

In terms of resources, the pre-Union police were in a strong position, but in other senses South Africa's police were in a parlous position at the time of Union. In the former British-controlled colonies there were four types of force: those whose appointment was made solely by the government and paid for out of the general revenue; forces under the appointment of the governor; those employed by several municipalities for additional town duties, paid for half from the rates; and those under the appointment of regional or district councils, paid for one-third from the rates. In addition there were both urban and rural forces in the old Boer Republics.

Policing was therefore localized and decentralized. Some police forces were under the control of magistrates, some of local and regional politicians, others of the colonial government administration. Thus, in Natal there was the Natal Police, various borough police, local board police, magisterial police and magisterial native police, various messengers and convict guards, and the water police (T. van Heerden 1986: 33). This confusion had to be multiplied by four because each of the provinces had forces of similar types.

Decentralization brought many problems. There was often a clash of interest between the policing priorities of the various forces and the people who managed and controlled them, and the British government's constant emphasis upon economy disrupted rational planning. Decentralization also inhibited co-ordination between the forces. Co-operation was difficult to effect because of the absence of any channel of communication between them, and there was often rivalry and jealousy between the forces. For example, the Acting Commissioner of the SAP, Colonel Truter, wrote in 1910 to the Acting Secretary of Justice in Pretoria complaining about the poor relations between the CID and the regular uniformed police in the Transvaal, and made recommendations as to how this might be overcome with the eventual formation of the SAP (Conf/6/8/10, pp. 1–2). Such rivalry and jealousy prejudiced the effectiveness and efficiency of the police, which caused consternation among politicians and public alike in view of fears about the high level of crime in urban areas and relations between the races.

Lack of uniformity was also a consequence of decentralization. Police standards varied in dress, duties, procedures, discipline, and training. In the Orange Free State recruits were instructed in first aid and ambulance work. In the Cape the police insisted that recruits be fluent in at least one other language besides English, either Afrikaans or a native language, and by 1910 was able to recruit solely from among South African-born people. Recruitment of White police, however, was still ethnically structured, with Natal and Cape forces employing British men. The situation was different in the Transvaal. In order to favour Afrikaners, the Transvaal authorities insisted on a two-year residence qualification in the Transvaal before being eligible to apply to the police. While keeping out adventurers and British colonists, this also prevented the employment of experienced policemen from other forces, which the Commissioner of Police, Burn-Beggs, complained about to the Transvaal Attorney-General (SAP/2/14/21, pp. 349–50). Some localized forces were extremely lax in discipline, as Bernard Shaw remarked in his report on policing in the Cape (Cape of Good Hope 1882: 22, 57). It was so lax in some that chief constables could be found living with Black women (F. Cooper 1972–3: 29), obviously a heinous indiscipline in a colonial and racially stratified society where moral and cultural boundaries between the races needed to be enforced by the police rather than eroded. Lack of standardization also manifested itself in variable levels of police resources and manpower, with some areas being under-policed compared to others.

It is possible to summarize the legacies of pre-Union policing. First, it was decentralized and possessed several weaknesses as a result of localization. Secondly, policing was routinely a political activity associated with the interests of the colonial state, so that constables were responsible for dealing with ordinary crime and performing a whole range of extra duties for the state. One of the most important of these special duties was monitoring and regulating race relations, the mandate for which resulted in different styles of policing for Black South Africans compared to Whites, reserving for Blacks methods of extreme crudity and brutality. A third legacy, therefore, was a constant tension between the civil police tradition and the colonial model, as the police in South Africa responded to contrasting demands by applying different policing styles and approaches. Another legacy, therefore, has been to give Black South Africans a common experience of policing from their childhood: that of police impoliteness, brutish-ness, and intimidation (Ndibongo 1991: 22). Other important legacies were the incorporation of Blacks into policing roles so that they co-operated in their own oppression, and the marginal status of Black policemen by being subject to unequal and discriminatory treatment within the police force.

PLANNING THE NEW POLICE

The problems which presented themselves when the state set about planning the new police force in 1910 were therefore obvious; so transparent perhaps that in a letter to the Commissioner of the Transvaal Police, dated 15 April 1910, the Attorney-General initially tried to prevent the chiefs of police from holding a conference to discuss policing matters (Conf/8/431). However, a conference of chiefs of police in the four provinces was held in Pretoria in August

1910 by order of the Union's new Minister of Justice, and the police themselves identified two key issues, with a number of subsidiary problems (see SAP/2/14/21). The two major concerns reflected the conflicting directions the police were being pulled in under the tension between the liberal and colonial police models.

The first key concern was that there be a single national force, with control centralized under one head (SAP/2/14/21, p. 4). Hence senior police officers were opposed to the idea, expressed at the time, of a separate railways police, as existed in Natal. The Natal Commissioner pointed to what he described as the evils of decentralization by referring to the British example, claiming that there was much jealousy between the various constabulary forces in Great Britain. He quoted with approbation an article written by an English policeman that police control should be centralized, 'because the local police system of Great Britain is the most glaring among many glaring examples of inefficiency and extravagance' (p. 5). Commissioners were in favour of this as a strict principle in terms of both their relationship with the government, and in internal police organization. Thus, in a letter dated 26 April 1910, the Acting Secretary for the Transvaal Police wrote the following to one of his district commanders: 'the terms of [your] letter display an anxiety to put yourself right with your local people at the expense of your headquarters, which is not quite what is expected' (Conf/8/438).

The government readily took on board the demand for centralization. In October 1910, in pursuance of the policy, they appointed Mr T. G. Truter, then Transvaal Provincial Secretary and a former magistrate from Standerton, as Commissioner of the Transvaal Police and simultaneously Acting Chief Commissioner for the Union. It was significant that Truter was not at that point one of the chiefs of police in the provinces. The Chief Commissioner of the Transvaal, Commissioner Burn-Beggs, retired in October, and the government took the opportunity to appoint someone without experience of pre-Union policing, who could bring a fresh perspective. The corollary, however, was that Truter was not a professional policeman and had no managerial experience of running a police force. He needed, therefore, to establish legitimacy for himself among policemen and to assert his authority, both of which he did by instituting firm leadership in the planning, and eventual management, of the force.

Yet the parallels which the chiefs of police made at their planning conference with police in other countries were deliberately selective.

The civil policing tradition, so epitomized by local constabularies in Great Britain, was taken as the model in another sense, for the commissioners complained about the tendency for the police in South Africa to be used in the past in spheres which fell outside police duties as conceived in the liberal tradition (SAP/2/14/21, p. 6). Under the Child Life Protection Act in the Cape the police had to judge whether a child was being properly tended and nursed; they even searched for absent fathers who were not paying maintenance to families in Britain; the Transvaal Police did likewise. Seeing this duty as somewhat sensitive, the Secretary to the Transvaal Police instructed the Johannesburg CID to pursue one case in October 1910 as follows: 'it is desired that [name of the father] should not be interviewed by a man in uniform and that care should be taken to interview him out of hearing of other persons in order that he may have no cause to resent or complain of the interference of the police' (Conf/8/513; also see Conf/8/566).

Extraneous duties were performed by all provincial police forces. The Commissioner of the Transvaal Police, for example, wrote to the Attorney-General on 6 January 1910 complaining about the use of his men by government departments without even asking his permission to do so (Conf/8/385), which was an extraordinary managerial malpractice indicative of governmental views of police–state relations. A later letter on 2 May 1910, by the Commissioner to the Secretary of the Law Department, complained of the government's proposal to use the police as a permanent force for military service (Conf/8/431), a duty which also lay outside that which the Commissioner deemed appropriate. At their conference the commissioners resolved that while such duties might have to be discharged on occasion, 'the more patently extraordinary duties' needed to be curtailed (SAP/2/14/21, p. 7). Similar complaints were being made at this time by the police in Kenya (see Willis 1991: 222).

In this regard, the commissioners were oblivious to the contradictions in their demands, for the move towards centralization worked against the demand for professional autonomy, since it gave effective political control of the police to the government and defined the main formal mechanism by which the state could communicate its interests to the Commissioner. In this instance it enabled the state to define police functions. Thus, while the Minister of Justice later agreed to curtail some of the extraneous duties, such as the commitment given in November 1910 that they would be relieved of their duties as post office officials and telegraphic duties as soon as circumstances allowed (Conf/8/504), the demands of the government's policy of internal colonialism led to continual conflict between the police and government as to what constituted proper police duties. And this was not just a feature of policing in rural areas. Within months of the reassurances given by the Minister of Justice, foot patrolmen in the Transvaal Town Police were still, for example, inspecting the registers and books of butchers, pawnbrokers, auctioneers, poundmasters, and cigarette factories; displaying a penetration into civil society that went beyond strict crime-fighting and prevention. Indeed, the issue of appropriate police functions became one of the main areas where the tension between the civil and colonial traditions was manifested within the police, as well as a major source of conflict between the state and sections of the police. The government continued to use the police in a wide variety of ways for most of the century. In the very moment of their birth, therefore, the modern police in South Africa were leaving various contradictions unresolved, from which arose difficulties that have beset them ever since.

Two further problems were of concern to the provincial chiefs of police in 1910, the inferior quality of recruits and the poor public image of the police. The government was similarly troubled by these issues, and they offer a glimpse of police–state relations at the time. The Attorney-General's Office wrote to the Commissioner of the Transvaal Police on 25 January 1910, complaining about the poor quality of recruits taken on by the Transvaal Police. In reply, the Commissioner asserted his professional autonomy by pointing out that he alone was responsible for recruitment and was the only person to know what is required to be a policeman (Conf/8/397). Indeed, there had long been tension in the Transvaal between the police and the government over recruitment. The Commissioner often expressed the desire to appoint ex-policemen from other South African forces, but the Transvaal government imposed a two-year qualification period of residence in the Transvaal. The Natal Commissioner's suggestion at the planning conference was to form a Reserve Police of ex-colonial policemen, both to draw on their policing experience in an emergency and to maintain 'sympathy between colonists and the police' (SAP/2/14/21, p. 349); the suggestion was not taken up until 1960, although *ad hoc* reservists were deployed during several major periods of internal unrest. But the forthcoming unification of the four provinces solved the difficulty of mobility between the separate forces, as the commissioners noted at their conference (pp. 349–50), although simultaneously locating political control of the police in the hands of the Minister of Justice eventually gave the latter enormous influence over all police matters, including recruitment; and not all commissioners asserted their professional autonomy as fiercely as Burn-Beggs. However, the move to a centralized, national force left the problem of how best to integrate policemen from the Afrikaner and British communities, which the commissioners did not address at this stage.

A further difficulty the commissioners identified was the poor public image of the police. There were many features to this. In the Transvaal the employment of uneducated, rural-based Afrikaners in preference to experienced ex-policemen from the Cape or Natal led to problematic relations between the police and the British community living in the Transvaal. In some instances it was their ethnic origin which was the problem; in others their lack of education. So poorly educated were some policemen in Transvaal that the Transvaal Commissioner of Police sent a circular to all officers, dated 26 February 1910, complaining about the paperwork of constables, accusing some of stupidity and gross carelessness. This was a particular problem when discharging judicial powers, often resulting in cases being thrown out because of incorrect paperwork (Conf/8/415). The Commissioner saw this as indicative of a general lack of discipline in the Transvaal Police, which had a consequential effect in 'lowering the tone of the force' (p. 2).

Many Whites were also dissatisfied with the police in dealing with the encroachment of Blacks into the towns and in protecting them from the increase in reported crime among Blacks. Commissioners were particularly sensitive to fears among Whites about rape attacks on women and children by Blacks (pp. 351–2), and noted that convictions of Blacks for offences against the person had increased 23.4 per cent between 1908 and 1910, and those against property by 13.4 per cent (p. 351). Concern about Whites living in isolated rural areas was high, for if the increase in reported Black crime continued, they argued, 'for some years to come the White people, especially those living outside the towns, will not be safe' (p. 351). Black South Africans also had a poor relationship with the police, although the commissioners only expressed concern about their image among Whites. The relation between the police and Black South Africans was prejudiced by police harassment, and the excessive remedies taken against the Black population, such as restricting and regulating their use of liquor, controlling the movements of known criminals, and banning known criminals from certain areas or employments. This was all made much worse by the deployment of the police in suppressing incidents of Black resistance to colonial rule.

These problems set the agenda for the senior police officers who were planning the new police force. They demanded a single national and centralized police force; the police should be free to determine their own organizational priorities and functions; the public image of the force needed to be constantly monitored and improved; the police needed to become more modern and professional; a strict disciplinary ethos was necessary within the police, to avoid both unprofessional conduct and disunity between Black and White, and Afrikaner and British policemen; and Black South Africans needed to be minutely regulated and controlled so as both to assuage White fears about Black crime and to maintain White colonial rule. However, the state did not accede to the wishes of the police in all these matters.

THE NEW POLICE

Upon being appointed as Acting Chief Commissioner of Police, Theodorus Gustaff Truter was given the honorary rank of colonel but very little control. The police forces in the four regions owed their allegiance to their respective chiefs of police, and Truter exerted influence more through his position as Chief Accounting Officer to the existing forces (Dippenaar 1988: 7). His authority could not be institutionalized until an act of parliament formally established the police force; and Truter's main task was to mould the separate forces into such a unit in advance of legislation, making his formal position very ambiguous.

The experience of this early period convinced Truter even further of the folly of a decentralized force. He wrote to the Minister of Justice to express his dissatisfaction with the situation he encountered: 'a more complex system can hardly be imagined . . . organization appears to be absent. There is no uniform policy regarding the organization and control of the police' (quoted in Dippenaar 1988: 7). Rivalries and jealousies within the separate forces required Truter to appoint his own personnel to assist in planning the administrative aspects of the merger, jealousies which had led to the appointment of an outsider like Truter in the first place.

The main objective of this group, established in Pretoria as the first national police headquarters, was to impose a centralized management structure and organization. Thus a uniform salary structure and conditions of service were quickly developed. Only the Transvaal Police had terms of service better than those planned for the new police. Personnel selected for entry into the new force had three months to decide whether or not to accept the new terms; if not, they served out the time of their existing contract and left. In fact, only ninety-five people offered service in the new force declined the terms of service (Dippenaar 1988: 9). Policemen who were formerly part of a mounted force took particular exception to being transferred to foot duty (F. Cooper 1972–3: 19); but the humiliation was anticipated and softened by foot patrolmen being paid sixpence more per day than those on mounted duty.

More problematic were those serving policemen who were refused entry into the new police. Police files are full of correspondence from disgruntled policemen who complained about being refused a service contract; and only a few successfully challenged the decision (see: Conf/6/657/18/13). An additional problem causing equally voluminous correspondence in police files was that of promotion; the prospects of career advancement for many personnel were adversely affected by the regrading involved in merger and the new conditions of service (see: Conf/8/414; Conf/8/533/A).

By 1911 a draft Police Bill was able to be placed before parliament, based substantially on the 1908 Transvaal Police Act, together with police regulations, which were also based on those pertaining in Transvaal, themselves copied from the police service in India (Conf/6/8/10/A), confirming the importance of the Indian example to policing in other colonies (R. Hawkins 1991: 21). However, the legislation was delayed until 1912 because the Defence Act of that year needed to be promulgated first. When the 1912 Police Act became law, it fixed the date for the establishment of the new police for 1 April 1913, an ironically inauspicious date.

The delay between the draft police legislation and its formal enactment reflected the government's intention to determine police duties, which was but one measure of how it saw police–state relations. Union was in part an act of decolonization for Whites, but it left a tremendous task of internal colonialism in monitoring, regulating, and controlling the Black population. The state's need, therefore, was for a centralized police force on the colonial model, which could act as its agent in regulating race relations rather than as a neutral arbiter of the law. But there was also a need for a modern, professional police force which could police Whites, and the urban areas where Whites lived, according to the requirements of the civil police tradition, which called for conventional crime-fighting and prevention, and the development of a service role in the community. The question of appropriate police duties was thus a contentious issue, and the state met the demands of Truter and the former chief constables half-way.

The government maintained a feature of pre-Union policing in establishing two separate police forces, with different functions, styles, and areas of jurisdiction. The SAP was formed to police the urban areas, and the SAMR the rural areas. This allocation of responsibility has been described as representing the disjuncture of the civil and colonial policing models, itself a description of ethnic differences in the populations being policed (Seegars 1989: 6), but it was only a near approximation to these divisions. The SAMR was a typical colonial force, mounted and paramilitary in style, intended exclusively to police Blacks, and specifically given military duties in both internal and external defence. It was promulgated under the 1912 Defence Act rather than the Police Act of the same year. Moreover, Section 76 of the 1912 Defence Act explicitly granted the defence forces a policing role inside South Africa (a fact often alluded to in the 1980s when the South African Defence Forces swamped Black townships).

The SAP, on the other hand, took on features of the civil tradition, focusing on law and order and crime-fighting in the urban areas. Section 7 of the 1912 Police Act defined police duties as the preservation of internal security, the maintenance of law and order, and the prevention of crime. But the entry of Blacks into urban areas prevented the abandonment of colonial-style duties, and the SAP increasingly became responsible for policing race relations in the towns. Moreover, Section 8 of the Act required the SAP to perform military duties 'within or outside' the Union in cases of war or other emergencies, and to be subject when doing so to the regulations pertaining in the defence force.

This was a skilful manœuvre by the government. Although senior managers in the police had not got a single national force, their other demands had been met. The two forces were centralized in their control, and at least one of them was nominally free of the burden of performing duties for the state which fell outside those considered normal for a modern police force, save in states of emergency. The state had also ensured that the large Black population in the rural areas would be policed by different standards compared to Whites, thus maintaining strict police control in the country as a whole but without deleterious consequences in White areas or for the way Whites were policed. And it was able to use the army and sections of the police as equivalents even outside state emergencies.

This division of responsibility between the police forces may well have been permanent but for three factors: the movement of Blacks into urban areas; the preference of senior policemen for a single national force; and the SAP's demand that it be the sole force, which was reinforced by its experience of policing the entire nation during the First World War, when the SAMR was absorbed temporarily into the army. As it was, the SAP became the effective national force within a year of its formation. It never focused exclusively on civil policing, and was routinely used by the government as an agent of the state. This is perhaps summed up in microcosm by the fact that the arms, equipment, and clothing of the police were initially supplied by the Defence Department. In his annual report of 1916, Truter complained that they were often defective (Annual Report of the Commissioner of the SAP 1916: 2). It was not until 1918 that the SAP had their own stores and quartermaster.

The SAMR was composed of five regiments. The first was based on the old Cape Mounted Riflemen, and had its headquarters in King William's Town, serving the Transkei and Eastern Cape; the second comprised elements of the Natal and Orange Free State forces, and was based in Pietermaritzburg, serving parts of Natal and the Orange Free State; the third had its headquarters in Dundee, Natal, and was drawn from the Natal Police, serving parts of Natal and Eastern Transvaal; the fourth regiment was based in Pretoria and comprised former members of the Transvaal Police, serving most of the Transvaal; and the fifth was based on the Cape Mounted Police and had its headquarters in Kimberley, serving the Western Cape. These were isolated rural areas, with some White farmers, but densely populated by Blacks. The major towns in these regions, inhabited mostly by Whites, were policed by the SAP. The Inspector-General of the SAMR was the former commander of the Cape Mounted Riflemen.

In times of war, it was intended that the SAMR be used for military service, but in times of peace they were used exclusively for police duties. Thus, it was intended to use the SAP for military service in very rare cases, while the paramilitary SAMR was expected to do policing duties most of the time. In peacetime, Section 12(4) of the 1912 Defence Act granted them the same powers, duties, and indemnities as those of constables under the 1912 Police Act, although their deployment meant that they worked exclusively in Black areas. Dippenaar, the SAP's official historian, defined the function of the SAMR as follows: 'the point of departure was that a military unit equipped with arms would be able to enforce law and order more effectively in [larger Black] areas and be in a better position to prevent or effectively put a stop to pointless, irrational tribal fights' (1988: 8). However, the SAMR did not only deal with quarrels among Blacks themselves, but also with Black resistance to White domination.

The SAP was divided into two main branches, each with a deputy commissioner: the uniform branch and the detective service. The ranks were civilian in nomenclature (they were militarized in 1919), and further links with the British liberal policing tradition were emphasized by the blue uniform and the use of a Tudor crown as part of the SAP badge. Headquarters was in Pretoria, and there were five divisions, each headed by a deputy commissioner, covering the Western Cape, Eastern Cape, Orange Free State, Transvaal, and Kimberley. These divisional areas represented broad geographical boundaries, and did not at this time reflect patterns of urbanization and associated crime. Johannesburg and the Witwatersrand area, for example, did not yet have their own division, an anomaly corrected only later.

The under-policing of the heavily urbanized and industrialized Rand area was identified as a problem before the inception of the SAP. Two responses were made at that time: reorganization of the urban police, and the transfer of police from rural areas. The Sub-Inspector in Benoni, for example, wrote to the Deputy Commissioner of the Transvaal Police on 19 January 1911 indicating that he had but thirteen men on patrol for twenty-five miles of streets. The case for an increase was made on the basis that the developing mining industry brought both more residents and crime. Truter replied as Acting Chief Commissioner, agreeing to the increase but indicating that it would have to be at the expense of withdrawing men from the East Rand (Conf/8/553). The *Transvaal Leader*, serving this rural area, subsequently complained that the East Rand was now under-policed, editorials from which were kept on police files (see Conf/8/848). At the same time, the Acting Chief Commissioner was requesting a report on how best to improve policing in Johannesburg, which recommended the reorganization of the police in the city (see Conf/ 8/551). The reorganization amounted to the centralization of manpower into three districts, and within that the centralization of men into various beat units: those done on foot, foot and bicycle, and on horseback. The rationale behind this centralization was expressed in the report: 'centralize your men so that a large body may be turned out at any time to meet an emergency in or out of town, to cope with mines or town riots, etc. Married men are difficult to get in cases of emergency. Centralize them into married quarters' (Conf/8/553, p. 2). Centralization became the key principle for the whole of the SAP, but it was not always possible to implement it.

Natal was excluded as a district within the SAP's organizational structure because the rural areas came under the jurisdiction of the SAMR, and the major urban areas of Durban and Pietermaritzburg, with strong connections with Britain, insisted on retaining their own municipal police. They did so against the wishes of the Minister of Justice and the Commissioner of the SAP, who disliked the further elements of decentralization this caused, which was already a problem with the split between the SAP and the SAMR. While Section 3 of the 1912 Police Act enabled municipal police to be incorporated into the SAP, this was only in exceptional circumstances. In Durban and Pietermaritzburg the SAP performed detective work only; in addition Durban had its own water police. Thus, there was triple authority in Natal, which ran against the whole thrust of Truter's new policing strategy. The political leaders in Natal, the most British of the pre-Union colonies, wished to retain the decentralization which characterized the British police system, and the new Union government felt too uncertain of its authority to challenge them on this issue.

Other tendencies to decentralization were created by the existence of separate Black police in new government departments. Except in times of emergency, police in the Department of Native Affairs were at the disposal of the department, although they received their pay and equipment through the police budget and were under police discipline. In 1910 there were sixteen corporals and 206 constables provided for in the estimates of the Department of Native Affairs, spread over thirty-five centres (Conf/8/233/A). There was also Native Labour Bureau Police, under the direction of the Native Labour Bureau but in receipt of pay and equipment from the police budget, and also under police discipline. In 1910 there were six non-commissioned Black officers in the Native Labour Bureau Police and 118 constables, spread across fourteen centres. Black policemen were transferred to these departments from the old Transvaal Police and the former South African Constabulary, and were distinct from those Black policemen transferred to the SAP and SAMR. Police files show that Black policemen in these government departments were sometimes employed merely as servants to senior departmental staff (Conf/8/571). There was also compound or mines police, who were Blacks selected by mining companies from amongst their workers to police fellow employees.

Since some former members of pre-Union police forces were transferred to the SAMR and the permanent defence force, the number of policemen responsible for civil policing actually declined with the establishment of the new police. In 1913 the authorized complement of the SAP was only 5,884 men; actual staff was slightly above this at 5,938, 29.6 per cent of which were Black. The proportion of Blacks in the force thus fell considerably from pre-Union strength, and many Black policemen in the former pre-Union forces seem not to have been taken on in the new police. In fact, the Union government reduced the total number of policemen in both forces following Union, although Black policemen more than their White colleagues; the number of Whites in the police fell by 20.3 per cent between 1912 and 1913, but Black police by 47.8 per cent. In 1910 the combined manpower of the separate forces was 10,186, but from 1911 the size of the police fell markedly, as Table 1.1 shows.

Thus, the ratio of police per thousand of population fell from 1.42 policemen in 1912 to 0.93 in 1913. Expenditure also fell by 18.4 per cent between the same period, as shown in Table 1.2, although this

TABLE 1.1 *Police manpower levels, 1911–1913*

Year	Manpower: authorized	Manpower: actual		%Black*
	All races	White	Black	
1911	—	5,507	2,871	34.2
1912	8,705	5,617	2,807	33.3
1913†	5,884	4,473	1,465	29.6

* Based on actual manpower.
† Includes SAP only.

Source: *Department of Information 1917*, ii. 342.

TABLE 1.2 *Police expenditure, 1911–1913*

Year	Expenditure £m.	% on detective work*	% on equipment
1911	1.27	1.5	0.7
1912	1.34	1.6	0.4
1913†	1.1	1.5	1.3

* Excludes salaries.
† Includes SAP only.

Source: *Department of Information 1917*, i. 620.

is explained entirely by the proportion of expenditure diverted to the SAMR in 1913. The SAP was able to maintain its rate of expenditure on conventional crime-fighting, as reflected in the budgets for equipment, which actually increased, and detective work.

On establishment, personnel from the separate pre-Union forces which went to make up the SAP and SAMR were not allowed to transfer between the two new forces unless they found someone of equal rank who was willing to swop, although there were few requests to do so because of the different policing traditions and styles they each represented. Members of pre-Union forces taken into service in the new police were given twelve months in which to wear out their old uniform before having to purchase the appropriate new uniform. This resulted in a colourful array of uniforms being worn in the first year, with many rankers in the new police wearing uniforms of grander style and adornment than their officers. This link with the past was reinforced by the tendency of some transferred personnel to wear luxuriant Victorian-style side-whiskers, and hair below the collar; the standing orders of the new police were only finalized some time after the SAP's formation, so many practices continued which were permissible in the standing orders of pre-Union forces.

However, Truter quickly set about standardizing police discipline, dress, and training. Initial standing orders were defined within the year, although the final set satisfactory to Truter did not appear until 1918, and the SAP's new central training depot was established in Pretoria West by 1914. Training was for White recruits only, and Truter used personally to test every one at the end of the three-month training period (Dippenaar 1988: 14). Training was eventually extended to five months for foot patrolmen and six months for mounted police. Four foot patrol troops were trained at any one time (thirty-six men), and three mounted troops. Training for each differed, and there was little contact between the two sections. Van Onselen reports that there was often conflict between the two sets of recruits; the military-style riding breeches of the mounted men made them figures of fun to ordinary constables (1960: 35).

However, the transfer to the new police of experienced men from pre-Union forces ensured that they did not have to begin recruitment anew. This continuity of personnel made the SAP very experienced, especially at the managerial level. In 1916, for example, the average length of service for officers was 19 years, head constables 16.4 years, and sergeants 13.7 years (Annual Report of the Commissioner of the SAP 1916: 3). Constables, however, had an average length of service of only 4.9 years in 1916; only 8.5 per cent of constables had 12 years service or more, compared with 95.3 per cent of head constables. Thus, the new force failed to retain many of the former policemen taken on as ordinary constables; only 37.5 per cent of constables in 1916 had been in service since 1913. With this turnover in the lower ranks, manpower shortage was a problem from the beginning, particularly in the Transvaal. In part this was due to the fact that the terms of service in the SAP were inferior to those operating in the old Transvaal Police, but there was also a reticence among all but the poorest Afrikaners to enlist in what was initially seen as a British-dominated police force. The attraction of other forms of employment on the Rand was also great. In 1913, for example, ex-soldiers from the defence force in Transvaal were being recruited as policemen, and senior officers in the Transvaal undertook a campaign to encourage magistrates and clergymen to persuade young men known to them to join the police (Dippenaar 1988: 16).

Thus, experienced constables were being replaced by low-status and poorly-educated Whites, most of whom were therefore Afrikaners from the farms. The recruitment examination at this time involved testing linguistic skills in English and Afrikaans, and mathematics, and was equivalent to Standard 6 in education. However, a former policeman described the examination as merely a test of bilingualism (van Onselen 1960: 32). The Afrikanerization of the lower ranks was thus initiated from the outset, but by dint of circumstance rather than design. In a letter to the Attorney-General, dated 26 March 1913, only days before the official establishment of the SAP, Truter wrote the following description of Afrikaner policemen: 'the great majority are badly educated and can hardly write out an intelligible statement in their own language. This is certainly their misfortune and not their fault. The educated class of Dutch South African, with few exceptions, does not join the police force' (Conf/8/796). He was led to make such a remark because the Attorney-General had earlier complained about the over-use of English by policemen, and had asked that policemen who were prosecutors in the Transvaal (all of whom were apparently English-speakers) reply to him in Afrikaans when he addressed them in that language. In 1910 General Hertzog had complained to Truter that the list of police instructors he had submitted to the Attorney-General's Office for use in the new police contained people with an insufficient proficiency in Afrikaans, and directed Truter to substitute 'at least one with a fully-educated Dutch-speaking and writing' policeman (Conf/8/540). The political control over the police that accompanied centralization enabled the Attorney-General to issue this command, reflecting police–state relations.

The SAP therefore inherited the conflicts that still simmered between Afrikaners and British following the Boer wars, and Truter had difficulty in integrating policemen from the two communities. Leading Afrikaners in the Union government, some of whom had been senior Boer generals in the last war against the British, were sensitive to criticisms that the police, as a powerful arm of the new state, was British dominated. The officer class was overwhelmingly made up of English-speakers, even in the Transvaal. Not only did the Union government insist that the new police employ ex-policemen from the former Boer police forces, young Afrikaners were encouraged to join the new force, and they did what they could to assert bilingualism as a practice within the SAP. This presented senior officers with a series of problems. Those Afrikaners attracted as recruits were poorly educated and in other circumstances would have been deemed unsuitable for the police. Most of the ex-policemen from the former British colonies in the Cape and Natal were poor Afrikaans-speakers, if at all, and since the officer class was English-speaking, business was mostly conducted in that language. Thus from the beginning, Afrikaners felt marginalized. Suspicions, rumours, and ill feeling festered in such an atmosphere, and the Union government took allegations of unfair treatment of Afrikaner policemen very seriously, forcing Truter to do the same.

In a situation where the officer class was English-speaking, disgruntled Afrikaner policemen tended to voice resentment through confidential letters to Afrikaner newspapers rather than through official channels, hoping to mobilize the Afrikaans-speaking community and the government on their behalf. This occurred frequently in the early days of the SAP, and when the new force was being planned. Some Afrikaner policemen in pre-Union forces feared the English might dominate the new police. The editor of *Volkstem*, F. V. Engleburg, wrote to Truter on 26 December 1912, indicating that he had received several such letters from Afrikaners in the Johannesburg Division of the Transvaal Police. The anonymous writer complained that his senior officers, who were all English-speakers, had refused him his request for an interview with Truter; that staff jobs in the SAP were being reserved for English-speakers; and that examination papers for entry into the new force were written in English and were thus unfair to Afrikaans-speakers. A similar complaint was made against examinations for promotion.

Truter got one of his own men, earmarked for a senior position in the new police, to investigate. The Acting Commissioner of the Johannesburg District wrote to Truter on 31 December 1912, the day after he was contacted about these complaints, describing them as 'devoid of truth and most unfair'. 'It is true that all the officers and non-commissioned officers in Johannesburg are English speaking, but they treat all the men serving under them alike and make no distinction ... there is certainly no unfairness' (Conf/8/796). This may have reassured Truter, but not the Afrikaners in the ranks, and it was a problem which resurfaced several times. In 1912 Truter received an anonymous letter from an Afrikaner policeman alleging irregularities in the allowances being claimed by an English-speaking colleague (Conf/8/772). It served as an omen for what the SAP would experience in later decades.

Truter, on the other hand, was well liked. An Afrikaner policeman, disgruntled at his treatment, wrote an anonymous letter to an Afrikaner newspaper stating that the Acting Commissioner, as he was then, 'is a straightforward and just man' (Conf/8/796). However, those who breached police discipline or who damaged the SAP's image in any other way were sorely treated. It was necessary that Truter improve the public image of the police in order to attract recruits and assuage public fears and criticism. Files were kept in police headquarters of newspaper cuttings alleging misconduct by the police, and of the correspondence sent to local newspapers by irate members of the public or disgruntled policemen; senior officers at headquarters invariably demanded reports on the allegations. Senior officers were sensitive to alleged offences against the law, police regulations, and social mores. Thus, the files cover allegations of wild use of firearms against natives which endangered other townspeople; drunkenness (Conf/8/771); adultery with married women (Conf/8/520); corruption in the SAP's diamond and gold sections (Conf/8/423); illegitimate children born to policemen (Conf/8/556); and other aspects of their social life which provoked comment in gossip columns (see Conf/8/580; Conf/8/581). A Board of Inquiry was set up on one occasion in 1912 to pursue an allegation, brought by a constable, that a senior officer who had overlooked him in promotion was continuing to farm and keep pigs while employed in the police (Conf/8/533/A); the constable was an Afrikaner, the senior officer British.

In a racially stratified colonial society like South Africa, the police were required to regulate social boundaries between the groups, so allegations that the police breached these boundaries were taken very seriously. The Acting Secretary of Justice for the Union contacted Truter about a report in *Volkstem*, subsequently carried by the English-language *Transvaal Leader* on 3 March 1911, under the headline 'Police, Settlers, and Native Women'. It ran:

In a certain dorp in the Transvaal the police have been playing tennis with the coloured girls. The girls stroll through the town almost careless of what they say or what they do, for the police take no notice whatsoever . . . Apart from the indignation felt, we can expect to have no good service from policemen who consort with coloured women, for the reason that in the first place they have to keep coloured folk in due restraint, and that whoever lives on a friendly footing with a family tends involuntarily to show towards them soft indulgence. Since kaffir families have wide ramifications, such friendship can injuriously affect law and order. (Conf/8/591)

As Acting Commissioner, Truter made exhaustive efforts to discover the station concerned but to no avail. When guilty policemen were discovered, however, they were either discharged or transferred, although some district commanders complained to headquarters about having to receive errant policemen (Conf/8/446). The disciplinary ethos was strict. In a letter dated 12 June 1913, the Deputy Commissioner wrote to all senior officers on behalf of Truter. Referring to recent cases of misconduct by policemen, 'which have not only brought disgrace on themselves but also discredit to the force generally', senior officers were instructed to tighten up on discipline and take more interest in their men, getting to know them personally.

What is desired is that police officers should get in close touch with the men and their work. Classes of instruction should be held, particularly in the interests of recruits. At these classes, instances should be brought up where men had taken action which was incorrect, the mistakes should be pointed out and instructed what to do in the future . . . Our watchword should be 'constant supervision and encouragement'.   (Conf/8/8838)

Truter was clearly concerned to modernize and professionalize the new police via strict but sensitive leadership.

However, wider colonial divisions made this a more difficult task than it might otherwise have been. Black South Africans had not yet developed sufficient leverage in South African society to make them significant forces. The primary conflict at this time was between Afrikaners and the British. This affected the police in two ways. British officers often had difficulty in getting close to the rural, uneducated Afrikaners who dominated the ranks; and Afrikaner citizens tried systematically to undermine the image of the police, some based on allegations by Afrikaner policemen. The fears, concerns, and racial sensibilities of the Afrikaans-speaking community were thus important pressures on Truter. These were mediated particularly by the government, especially General Smuts and General Hertzog, to whom were sent some of the anonymous letters written by Afrikaner policemen, and whose concerns were communicated to Truter. The main problematic relationship for the SAP at this time was thus with Afrikaners, outside and inside the force. One letter by 'Disgusted' warned Hertzog that the men in Germiston would soon mutiny at the way the station was run (Conf/8/771).

POLICING THE UNION

Three essential tasks fell to the new police after Union: responsibility for ordinary or routine police work, the maintenance of public order, and the regulation and control of race relations. South Africa's rapid urbanization and industrialization, and the government's policy of internal colonialism ensured that from the beginning the SAP and SAMR had a busy time in dealing with all three.

These tasks, however, were not hermetically distinct. Notions of race and crime were often linked in the consciousness of people, although in different ways by the various 'races' and by the police themselves. Ordinary crime was sometimes responded to by the police in a way that escalated it into a major public-order incident, mostly as a result of the police responding to the fears of one 'race' about the real or imagined criminal activity of another. A complicating factor at this time was that race was not understood within South African society to be a simple differentiation between Black and White, as it later became, but also to describe the ethnic differences between the British and Afrikaners. Therefore, the groups whose activities were policed, and between whom the boundaries were monitored by the police, were broader at the beginning of the century than they were at the end. At this time, ordinary crime committed by Whites was given as much attention as that by Blacks, Afrikaners were seen as more of a threat to public order than Blacks, and ordinary policing had not yet been made entirely secondary to the police's internal security role.

The level of ordinary crime committed by Whites was high. Many of the adventurers and immigrants attracted to South Africa's mining areas from Europe had a tendency to drunkenness and rowdiness that was characteristic of any frontier town. Thus, the meeting of provincial chiefs of police, held in 1910 to plan for unification of the police, discussed the problem of crime and noted, for example, the high number of bicycle thefts (the equivalent to today's car thefts). Machines to the value of £8,812 had been lost on the Rand in 1909–10, for which a family of Russian Jews had been successfully prosecuted (SAP/2/14/21, p. 3); 6,202 people had been charged with drunkenness in Johannesburg in 1910, at a conviction rate of 72.6 per cent. Of the convictions, 73 per cent were Blacks; Afrikaners only 2.3 per cent. Drunkenness among Whites was thus mostly a problem for people from the colonies (p. 352), as it also appeared to be in Ontario (see Sturgis 1991). Prostitution by White women was also a problem in the mining towns. Reviewing the crime figures, the chiefs of police concluded that most of the murders were committed in January, rapes in February, drunkenness by Whites in June, native drunkenness in July, house-breaking in January, stock thefts in July, pass offences in February, thefts in March, robbery in April, and fraud in January (p. 352). While they suggested that there was thus a seasonal trend to crime (rather than this being an artefact of statistics), the trends show the range of crimes committed. The overall rate of offending among the population, however, was not as high as it was to become in later decades. The prosecution rate per thousand of population was 46 in 1912, and 45 in 1913.

The police ran a sophisticated system of informers and 'trap boys'. The latter were young Black children used by the police to trap Whites into crime, for which the children received a small payment. Most of these crimes concerned special prohibitions placed on the activities of Black South Africans which some Whites sought to contravene, such as selling them illicit liquor. Some Whites saw 'trap boys' as a form of harassment, and one prominent member of Het Volk, an Afrikaner cultural and political organization, complained that the SAP was deliberately hounding him because of his political activities (Conf/8/447). Mostly, however, the dealers were colonists, making an enormous profit from illicit sales to Blacks, who were prohibited from making their own when living in urban areas, in an attempt to reduce the level of drunkenness and associated crime among 'natives' (for a Kenyan parallel see Willis 1991). One detective on the East Rand ran so many informers and trap boys as to amass expenditure of just over £40 in a year, out of a total budget for the whole district for this purpose of £50 (Conf/8/534). The Deputy Commissioner of the Transvaal reported, however, that illicit liquor-dealing existed on such a scale on the East Rand that he considered it 'imperative to employ these trap boys even if the sanctioned expenditure for secret service is exceeded' (Conf/8/534). Illegal gambling and whippet-racing among Whites was also problematic on the Rand (Conf/8/579). One of the activities engaged in by many Whites which received considerable police attention was attendance at local bioscopes, now known as cinemas. The crowds attracted to them were sizeable, thus proving a lure for criminals, and they were thought to over-excite people in the audience, encouraging some of them to crime.

One dimension to this concern with White crime was the fear that sophisticated criminals from within the White community would pass on their skills to Black accomplices, thus provoking further Black crime, the reverse of later years when young suggestible liberal Whites were seen as under the spell of Black agitators. The Head of the SAP's CID, Mr Mavrogordato, once stated his belief that 'natives' came to the urban areas innocent and learned crime there, often under tutelage to White criminals and others who could lead them astray so easily (SAP/2/14/21, p. 352). Thus, Whites who were known to have a criminal record or to be prostitutes were prohibited from employing Blacks, and Blacks with a criminal record were subjected to considerable restriction in employment and movement. Indeed, bioscopes were seen by the police as posing a particular problem for Black crime, stimulating the sexual fantasies which Blacks were thought to have about White women and thus encouraging sexual attacks on them, and generally over-exciting them so that they became out of control. The cultural image of Black South Africans which infused police work, therefore, was that they were both simpletons and potentially violent.

The policing of ordinary crime and the regulation of race relations thus merged on occasions into one activity. If it was the case that policing in Britain's large cities at the turn of the century amounted to keeping the poor off the streets, as Brogden has claimed in Liverpool (1991), South Africa's police were required to keep Blacks in their designated places, in both the status hierarchy and areas of residence (for examples from the Caribbean see H. Johnson 1991; and for Kenya see Anderson 1991: 198, and Willis 1991: 222–3). Fears among Whites about Black crime were often instrumental in the deployment of police personnel in order that interaction between the two sections of the population could be regulated. Thus, mine compounds received considerable police attention, in addition to that already given by independent mines police, and the police attached to the Department of Native Affairs; in this way fear of Black crime stimulated the employment of Black policemen.

Given the collective memory of past battles over land, Afrikaners particularly feared attacks on isolated rural farms by Blacks, and complained when the police seemed to treat these fears too lightly. Upon receiving word that Blacks, or 'whitemen dressed as such', were to attack a laager on Dingaan's Day in 1912, a Mr Landman wrote a letter of complaint to the Attorney-General when the police took no evasive action. Smuts took the complaint seriously given his Afrikaner heritage, and he had the Acting Commissioner of the SAP institute an inquiry. The senior officer for the area replied that 'Landman is one of that class of idiots who have a perpetual grievance, who thinks that the government is not properly governed and could show them how to do it . . . Landman is just the sort of person to believe nonsense' (Conf/8/787). The British-dominated hierarchy in the SAP ignored such fears because they were treated as part of the wider conflict between Afrikaners and the British, but when other sections of the White population expressed fear about Black crime, the SAP listened very hard.

Whites in the urban areas, overwhelmingly colonists from Britain and Europe at this time, feared attacks by Blacks on White-owned property and White women. On 14 February 1911 the *Rand Daily Mail* ran a story about a White civilian who had fired at a Black person fleeing on the assumption that he must have been a criminal; property thefts were high, and the rapidly growing urban population of Blacks was readily used as the scapegoat. Cases of rape and sexual attack on White women and children were low, but very sensitive as an issue. In 1910 there were 206 rapes reported, with 213 persons arrested, although the conviction rate was only 27.2 per cent, which suggests that the police were arresting Black people without firm evidence to bring or carry a conviction (SAP/14/21, p. 351). Sentences ranged from hanging to fines.

Public demands for an increase in police protection for Whites and surveillance of Blacks routinely followed notorious outrages. The Minister of Justice sent the following telegram to the Commissioner in February 1911:

On Monday Minister wishes to reply to a question whether his attention has been drawn to the large number of cases of brutal outrage on white women by kaffirs and whether he will take immediate steps to increase police force in districts where whites are living in vicinity of compound locations or any other aggregation of kaffirs. Please wire number of such cases within last three months and whether force up to strength in Rand areas and if increase in force is necessary. Urgent and confidential.

The Acting Deputy Commissioner reported only six rapes or attempted rapes, and thirteen indecent assaults. None the less, the Mayor of Johannesburg added to the chorus of complaint, and forwarded a petition to Truter, signed by enrolled voters of the municipality, pointing out that: the honour of womenfolk is sacred and must be protected; that the penalty for attempted rape should be death; that increased police protection is imperative; and that the gradual elimination of the employment of male domestic servants be started (see Conf/8/566). Copies went to the Governor-General, the Union government, and all members of parliament, and provincial and municipal councils.

The police were able to use such public fear as a powerful lever to demand increased resources and manpower. Public fear also affected the focus of police attention. Greater manpower was devoted to areas where Blacks lived in sizeable proportions, and close attention was given to behaviour which might feed the fantasies Blacks were supposed to have about White women. Thus, access by urban Blacks to alcohol was strictly limited, bioscopes were heavily policed, and on one occasion the police even banned the sale of a tobacco product which contained picture cards of White women in alluring poses (Conf/8/572).

The methods the police used in pursuing ordinary Black crime often escalated incidents into major threats to public order. Raids on compounds for illicit liquor were common, and some deteriorated into mass riots. The Report of the Native Grievances Inquiry 1913–14 (Union of South Africa 1914a), on the disturbances that had followed several police raids for liquor in 1913, recommended the continued use of police raids but that the SAP in future be accompanied by the compound manager, as a 'familiar authority'. Even in 1913, therefore, it was recognized that ill feeling between the SAP and Black South Africans was caused by the brutality of the police, but White concerns over law and order allowed no curtailment of police powers or methods.

The Report was instructive on how compounds were policed at this time. In every compound the manager was assisted by a number of workers who were called 'compound police', although they were not technically police, having no legal powers as police but possessing authority over mine employees in terms of mine regulations. Even then, these 'powers' were vague and depended on company regulations, and the discretion of the manager. Since these 'powers' were so *ad hoc*, there was potential for great oppression, and complaints were often made against the behaviour of compound police (Union of South Africa 1914: para. 144). Pay was also not fixed. The head of the compound police, known as the *induna*, was a person whose appointment was based on the possession of great status and authority among workers, normally as a result of some tribal position. Often, however, the work-force was inter-tribal but the police were selected solely from the largest tribal grouping, such that ethnic and tribal conflicts exacerbated the oppression wrought by compound police. Indeed, the Report found that managers often selected *indunas* for the number of potential recruits they could bring with them to the mine rather than an ability in policing or mediating skills (para. 149). The compound police, in other words, were seen by the Committee as little different from the people they were policing. Thus, the Report objected to arming compound police because of the problem of putting 'an offensive weapon into the hands of a native' (para. 146).

Liaison between the compound police and the SAP was also unregulated and *ad hoc*. The Report was opposed to making the SAP responsible for policing the mine compounds, pointing out that where this had been experimented with in the past, disputes arose between the SAP and mine management, and it caused an inevitable reduction in the authority of the mine manager. The SAP therefore only entered the compound when called to do so by the management of the mine, or when undertaking a raid for illicit liquor with the permission of the management. Great disorder accompanied both interventions. In the former situation, the incident had already deteriorated beyond the management's control; and illicit liquor raids were perceived by Blacks themselves as an unreasonable intrusion into aspects of their everyday life and culture. A riot followed one raid by the SAP in July 1913, which the appearance of mounted police could not quell. Police were stoned and troops were necessary to restore order; the Report saw the use of stones to attack the police as indicative of the general lack of respect which White authority now commanded among Blacks (para. 429). A similar point was made following racial unrest in Natal during 1913.

If this were true, it was not only Black South Africans who lacked respect, for major disturbances accompanied industrial strikes on the mines in 1913. The SAP's responsibilities for the preservation of internal security ensured problematic relations with the growing urban proletariat as well as the colonized Black population. A senior officer in the SAP saw the SAP's mobilization for strike duty as an opportunity for the standardization of practice, discipline, and dress (F. Cooper 1972–3: 20). Advantage was taken of the mobilization to practise drill; many of the officers had not before been in charge of such a large body of policemen. Other opportunities for organizational refinement were therefore provided by the railways strike in 1913, and the march in 1913 by Indian sugar workers from Natal to Johannesburg, protesting about working conditions and pay.

The SAP had barely existed officially for two months when a strike by White miners broke out on the Rand. The SAP did not have a uniformly trained personnel capable of dealing with a strike involving over 19,000 workers, and yet the state considered the strike as a major threat to public order, which required the largest concentration of police yet assembled. As it was, the number of police drafted to deal with the strike represented a third of the total strength of the SAP, but was only 1,974 personnel (Dippenaar 1988: 17), so that the police were massively outnumbered. The SAMR was also made available, but the strikers were still more preponderant, so special constables were empowered from among civilians (see SAP/1/185/13/8; police files on the strike are extensive, see SAP/1/185/13/1–52). Considerable unrest occurred, in which buildings were set alight, shops looted, policemen fired upon, and firemen attacked; street-fighting lasted for forty-eight hours. It is against this that one can locate the injuries sustained during the strike. Seven members of the SAP were detained in hospital, and one member of the SAMR. This was out of a total of 161 injuries, eighty-eight of which were gunshot wounds fired by the police; there were twenty-two deaths, all from among the strikers, including two Blacks and nine Afrikaners.

Since Afrikaners were moving increasingly to the towns to work in the mines, many of the strikers were Afrikaans-speakers, such that two notable Afrikaners, Generals Botha and Smuts, were called on to speak to the strikers on behalf of the Union government. None the less, there appears to have been no disquiet among Afrikaners in the police ranks about using force against their compatriots, although the police were under strict instructions from senior officers to use minimum force. A telegraph from the Secretary of the SAP, S. J. Lendrum, to the Deputy Commissioner of the SAP in Bloemfontein, where strike leaders were meeting to negotiate an end to the dispute, read: 'in circumstances you must not use force. You must use tact and have no recourse to violence unnecessarily' (see SAP/1/185/13/8). The Report of the Commission of Inquiry into the Witwatersrand Riots, published in 1913, congratulated the police for their patience and good temper (quoted in Dippenaar 1988: 19). Given the difference in the level of unrest to which the police responded, the contrast with how the liquor raids were carried out in Johannesburg in the same year could not have been greater: the SAP showed from the beginning that criminal activity would be policed differently depending upon the racial composition of the perpetrators (on the contrast in the policing of liquor laws among Whites and Blacks elsewhere in the British Empire see Anderson and Killingray 1991*b*: 11; compare also Sturgis 1991, and Willis 1991).

But if the SAP thought its first months were a baptism of fire, problems continued to flare up between 1914 and 1926, when the force grew and matured.

Policemen Versus Pukkah Soldiers
1914–1926

INTRODUCTION

The period covered in this chapter is marked by the SAP's first full year and the government's first major review of policing in the 1926 Te Water Commission. During this time, the modernization of the police proceeded apace and centralization was finally achieved, with the SAP becoming the single national police force, ensuring that the state had strict control over the police. But the police continued to suffer from the peculiarities of South African society and politics. Police professionalism was hampered by the tension within the police between the civil and colonial policing models, and the negative effects of the state's policies on race were ongoing. These effects were two-fold. The police continued to perform extraneous duties for the state in regulating and monitoring race relations, but they also bore the consequences of wider social conflicts between the British and Afrikaners, and between Black and White South Africans.

Therefore, on the one hand, the police were proactive in the way they intervened in race relations directly on the side of the state, but they also had to respond to the negative effects of state policies on police organization, resources, and manpower deployment, among other things. This led to an uneasy relationship between Truter and his political masters, and to numerous organizational problems for the SAP, which the Te Water Commission attempted to resolve.

WORLD WAR AND ITS AFTERMATH

Even in terms of other momentous times in South African history, 1914 was an unusually difficult year for the police, then only eight months in existence. It began with an industrial strike on the railways, which saw martial law imposed for the first time. It witnessed the outbreak of war, an Afrikaner rebellion, and the march into Namibia, where the SAP acted as the personal bodyguard of the Commander-in-Chief, General Botha, who undertook the strange task as Prime Minister of personally leading his troops into battle.

The intermixing of the racial and class interests of the various parties involved made labour relations particularly problematic in South Africa's rapid move towards industrialization at the beginning of the twentieth century. White workers were militant in their conflicts both with management and the Black working class, and the government feared any compromise with the White working class lest their militancy spread dangerously radical ideas to the Black population. Although the police reacted brutally to the strikers, the 1913 strike on the mines saw the Union government concede the recognition of the miners' union, and acceptance of conciliation mechanisms on the mines. Due to the types of industries involved in the 1914 strike, particularly in the case of the railways, industrial action was not limited to a specific geographical area. The government feared that riots would break out throughout the country. Thus, the call for a general strike at the beginning of 1914 found the government more militarily prepared (for greater detail see Lacey 1989: 31), and martial law was passed. Press censorship was enforced, private telegrams held up, telephones cut off, and travel restricted. General de la Rey surrounded the Trades Hall in Johannesburg with machine-guns and eventually forced the surrender of the strike leaders after a three-day siege, in which some shots were fired at policemen. Some strike leaders were eventually deported to Britain.

Later defending the imposition of martial law, Botha referred in parliament to the strikers as communist-inspired agitators, who, when linked with the 'Black peril', would swamp White civilization (quoted in Lacey 1989: 32). In fact, many were fellow Afrikaners, led by H. J. Poutsema, and the strikers actually advocated the repatriation of the Black work-force in order to protect White jobs. But the state feared the spread of revolutionary ideas to Blacks, and Botha warned in parliament of 'natives being driven to a state of panic' by the strike. However, the use of martial law prevented effectively the disorder which marked the 1913 strike, but the state had done so only by employing the police in a military role and in co-operation with the defence force, and by abandoning civil liberties. While this had long been a feature of the pre-Union colonial forces, the state had set a precedent for the SAP that was affirmed repeatedly thereafter.

With most of the police being from the British community, policemen were automatically assumed to be loyal to the Empire and thus in support of South African involvement in the First World War. The situation would be quite different at the outbreak of war in 1939, when the Prime Minister gave policemen the opportunity to choose the side to which they wished to be loyal, with disastrous consequences for the internal cohesion of the police. In 1914 loyalty to the Crown was expected and realized, even among Afrikaner policemen; Afrikaner nationalism had minority support in 1914 compared to 1939, as the Afrikaner rebellion of 1914 was dramatically to illustrate within weeks.

Although the SAP did not participate in the war as a unit, some policemen were called upon for military service. In terms of the 1912 Defence Act, the SAP was required to provide seventy-nine artillerists, as well as a number of men on intelligence work: 326 men were allocated to the Department of Defence, while another 138 purchased their discharge in order to fight in the war or volunteered for active service (Department of Information 1917: 342). Some men who were refused permission to enlist deserted from the police in order to fight. Police files show that many of those who deserted in order to enlist were Afrikaners (SAP/1/93/27); four of the six men who deserted from the Johannesburg police in 1917 were Afrikaners. In 1920 the government deleted this blemish from their police records, although the men concerned could not reclaim the fine imposed on them for desertion. However, in terms of pension rights their service in the war was taken as continuous with their police service. In fact, a later commissioner of the SAP, Major General Palmer, deserted from the police in the Orange Free State at this time, was fined £5 and allowed to join the new airborne squadron that later became the RAF. In addition to the men lost in this way, a squadron of policemen, known as Hartigan's Horse, was detailed for service in Namibia, and over a hundred men from the SAP were assigned as the personal bodyguard of the Prime Minister. Throughout the period of the war, the SAP lost 2,518 men who purchased their discharge or who retired, although recruitment was always ahead of losses, with 3,417 new members joining the SAP (Department of Information 1917: 342).

The main police contribution to the war effort, however, was provided by the SAMR, who were immediately mobilized. As a consequence, the SAP undertook policing in all the areas formerly under the jurisdiction of the SAMR. Existing police divisions lost 82 officers and 493 constables to areas formerly policed by the SAMR, representing nearly one member in ten. This stretched the manpower resources of the SAP considerably, with many smaller stations in urban areas having to close; but it still left the rural areas under-policed. Half of the territory of South Africa, including the whole of Natal and vast regions in the Cape, was to be policed by barely more than five hundred men. Moreover, men transferred to the rural areas were not always fluent in local languages. Thus, a citizen force of volunteers, the forerunner of the current Police Reserve, was formed at the outset of the war, primarily from among the special constables employed in the 1913 Rand strike (SAP/1/185/13/8). Members of the SAP were spread thinly throughout the citizen force to provide leadership and knowledge. This citizen force would eventually be called upon to render assistance in other internal emergencies, such as the 1922 Rand strike. The colonial citizen-soldier tradition in South Africa always ensured enthusiastic public support for citizen forces among the British and Afrikaans-speaking communities.

In his 1914 Annual Report, Truter urged the government to increase the budget so that more policemen could be employed, warning of the increase in crime and the failure of the police to meet the public's demands for better protection of lives and property. In the 1916 Annual Report, the Commissioner pointedly explained that South Africa was more under-policed than other colonial societies, such as New Zealand, Canada, and Australia, at one policeman for every 706 citizens. For the first time in 1916, the SAP employed policewomen to take over the burden of some men in dealing with cases involving women and young girls, although the declaration of peace brought this experiment temporarily to an end.

However, the wartime economy measures introduced by the government permitted a modest increase in the police budget through-out the war, as Table 2.1 shows, although the proportion spent on civil police work such as detective services decreased. Moreover, minus the expenditure on the war itself, the police budget was bigger than that of defence, as shown in Table 2.2; it remained so until the outbreak of the Second World War. And while both budgets fell after the war, the defence budget did so at a faster rate. Thus, the ratio of police to defence expenditure was always in favour of the police even in the middle of the war. With 100 representing the base figure for police

TABLE 2.1 *SAP expenditure, 1914/15–1919/20*

Year	Expenditure £m.	% increase	% on detective work*	% on equipment
1914/15	1.1	–	1.5	1
1915/16	1.3	8.9	1.5	0.7
1916/17	1.36	4.7	–	–
1917/18	1.5	9.6	–	–
1918/19	1.7	17.3	1	0.6
1919/20	2	16	1	0.6

* Excludes salary.

Source: Annual Reports of the Commissioner of the SAP.

TABLE 2.2 *Police and defence expenditure, 1915/16–1925/6*

Year	Defence expenditure £m.	Police expenditure £m.	Ratio of police to defence expenditure*
1915/16	1	1.3	76
1916/17	1.3	1.36	95
1917/18	1.3	1.5	86
1918/19	1.3	1.7	73
1919/20	1.5	2	74
1920/1	1.25	3.4	36
1921/2	1.3	3	45
1922/3	0.94	2.6	36
1923/4	0.93	2.5	36
1924/5	0.96	2.5	37
1925/6	0.89	2.5	35

* 100 = base figure for police expenditure.

Source: Annual Reports of the Commissioner of the SAP and Annual Reports of the Auditor General.

expenditure, defence expenditure fell to 35 in 1925/6, having fallen from its highest point of 95 in 1916/17. Further, police manpower increased at a faster rate than police expenditure, at least at the beginning of the war, as Table 2.3 illustrates.

Thus, despite Truter's complaints, the ratio of police per thousand of population increased during the war. Although the increase in manpower levels slowed down as the war came to an end, the cumulative effect of earlier recruitment made the SAP less understaffed at the end of the war than at the beginning, as measured

TABLE 2.3 *SAP manpower trends, 1914–1919*

Year	Authorized	Actual	% increase	% under-staffed	% Black*	Ratio of police per 1,000 population
1914	6,267	5,805	–	7.4	22.8	0.99
1915	7,912	6,571	13.1	16.9	23.9	1.23
1916	8,043	7,572	15.2	5.8	29.6	1.22
1917	8,239	7,907	4.4	4.0	29.8	1.23
1918	7,769	7,582	−4.1	2.4	30.3	1.14
1919	8,215	7,655	0.96	6.8	31.5	1.22

* Actual manpower only.

Source: Annual Reports of the Commissioner of the SAP.

by the difference between authorized and actual manpower. However, the increase in actual manpower was disproportionately of Black policemen. A common strategy in times of labour shortage among Whites in South Africa is to increase recruitment of Blacks. Thus, between 1916 and 1920, actual manpower in the SAP grew by 19.2 per cent for White policemen compared with 63.9 per cent for Black policemen.

This policy was recommended by the 1917 Report of the Committee on Retrenchment in Public Expenditure, which established the rationale behind it. The unit cost of a White policeman in 1917 was £173.50, while that of a Black policeman only £70, such was the measure of apartheid within the force. However, the Commissioner stated in evidence before the committee that there were limits to this as a cost-cutting mechanism 'because due consideration must be given to the views of residents most likely to be affected by it'. The racial sensitivities of White South Africans ought, he argued, to limit the number of Black policemen roughly to the proportion that pertained at that time, 29.8 per cent. Dint of circumstances eventually saw it rise to well above that level, however. But the same sensibilities eventually restricted the formal powers of Black policemen, such that in his 1920 Annual Report, the Commissioner noted that members from the various Black communities would from then on only deal with offenders from their own group, a practice which did not pertain rigidly in pre-Union days. And where White and Black police patrolled together, the latter were required to walk discreetly some paces behind their White colleagues (Brogden 1989: 271; van Onselen 1960: 54), presumably both to offer protection to White constables while also maintaining, within the organization and practice of the force, the social distance and moral boundaries between the races.

Two views were thus emerging within the main body of the police about Black policemen, although they shared a common starting-point. One view of Black policemen saw their alleged gormlessness as leading to the unfailing loyalty so characteristic of poor people towards their betters. Thus, when describing 'the kaffir as spy and detective' in 1911, Blackburn and Caddell referred to their 'ludicrous failure at fraud, duplicity and low smartness', for doing what they are told by 'white bosses', and their eagerness to act as informers (quoted in Brogden 1989: 271). This view is perhaps expressed best by Attwell, who refers to a Black policeman as follows.

He is the best tempered, easiest managed man in the world, understands discipline by instinct; is docile, plucky, proud of himself and his corps, kindly disposed toward his officers, full of mettle and capable of enduring the extremes of marching and hunger. He is clean in his habits. In all his fighting service, not a single case of treachery or breach of faith has ever occurred, truly a remarkable feat when one is fighting one's own kith and kin. (1926: 207)

The Commissioner, however, shared the other view, which put Black policemen in the same stereotype as Black South Africans generally, their gormlessness giving them a tendency to crime, indiscipline, and untrustworthiness. Thus, in his 1926 Annual Report, Truter wrote:

Strict discipline has to be maintained. Even stricter methods have to be adopted with the non-European police, who, invested with a certain amount of authority over their fellows, must of necessity possess unblemished characters. Any serious or repeated lapses are usually attended by dismissal for unsuitability, hence the rather large number under this heading. (p. 5)

However, Truter also employed a system where Black policemen, greatly underpaid compared to White colleagues, could receive monetary rewards as incentives for the sorts of behaviour that were expected as the norm from White policemen, such as commendable service and successful convictions. Ten Black policemen received these awards in 1926 (p. 12). Given this working assumption of the basic untrustworthiness of Black police, Black policemen could not be placed in positions of leadership, and Truter failed to increase the number of Black non-commissioned officers to keep pace with the increase in Black constables. The percentage of Black policemen who were non-commissioned officers thus fell from 6.9 per cent in 1916 to 5.9 per cent in 1919; by 1926 it was 4.7 per cent. Apartheid was as strong inside the police as outside.

All through the war, the police were involved in dealing with ordinary crime and Black unrest, but the SAP's war, as it were, was over within twelve months. Within two weeks of Britain's declaration of war, General Botha announced in the South African parliament that his country would attack Namibia, then known as German South West Africa, entirely by its own forces, in accordance with an undertaking that was given to the British Prime Minister as far back as 1911 (Dippenaar 1988: 21), although it was on Britain's instruction and the cabinet were not unanimous in support of the decision (Garson 1962: 133). However, the invasion did not take place until February 1915 because the state had first to deal with the Afrikaner rebellion which was provoked by the announcement of the intention to support Britain in its conflict with Germany.

The rebellion was directed against an Afrikaner government, led by Botha and Smuts, both Transvaalers who were military leaders in the last Anglo-Boer War. Together they dominated the South African Party, which initially embraced all Afrikaners but had some English-speaking support. They accepted as irrevocable the verdicts of the 1902 Vereeniging Peace Treaty and the 1910 Act of Union, which made South Africa a member of the British Empire, the very same connection which they had fought so strenuously to avoid being thrust upon them by their former foe. The view of Sir Herbert Stanley in 1910, then Private Secretary to the Governor-General, was that the Crown was the most popular of British institutions in South Africa, and he supported Smuts's belief that there would be a 'general growth' of sentimental bonds of attachment with Britain (MSS Afr. s. 1250). Not all Afrikaners supported Smuts's position (on the rebellion see T. Davenport 1963; Garson 1962; Webb 1916). Most notable of the dissenters was another famous Boer general, General Hertzog, who had left the Botha cabinet in 1912 and formed the National Party in 1914, primarily from amongst former members of the South African Party in the Orange Free State. The National Party attacked conciliation and the fusion of Afrikaners and Britons into one nation, and advocated segregation of the two 'nations', leaving them to evolve separately. Hertzog's party was thus an early expression of Afrikaner nationalism, although surprisingly it attracted some English-speaking support. The general secretary was H. S. Webb, an English-speaker, whose account of the rebellion (Webb 1916) is partisan but none the less instructive.

Some Afrikaners opposed the war. This was not out of support for Germany (which was the case in 1939) but because of a reluctance to provide aid to a former enemy, against whom there was considerable resentment following the last Anglo-Boer War. Compulsory military service was thus unthinkable to some Afrikaners. Webb claims that such was the festering hostility towards Britain, that some Afrikaners volunteered for the police and defence as an opportunity to arm themselves for eventual liberation (1916: 7). The war therefore provided them with the opportunity to rebel. Lacey (1989: 35–9) recently added another motive to that of ethnic hostility, in claiming that Afrikaner farmers were resisting Botha's attempt to introduce capitalist methods of production in the farming industry. Hence, in addition to notable Afrikaner nationalists, there were among the rebels many poor White labourers who had been thrown off the land; the very people who were active in industrial disputes and class conflict on the Rand.

Racial considerations were also important, however. These poor Whites were in competition with Blacks for work on the farms and the mines, and the Botha government had a more liberal policy on race relations than many of them favoured. For example, General de Wet, another former Boer general who was prominent in the rebellion, complained that the government's race policies were not designed to 'maintain the prestige of the white man in the mind of the native' (Webb 1916: 79) specifically citing a case where he had himself been fined five shillings for whipping a herd boy for disobedience and negligence, whilst the boy was dismissed by the court without reproof, leaving him with the impression that de Wet was in the wrong.

Plans for the rebellion were laid by General de la Rey, who had earlier defended the state against strikers on the Rand, five days after Botha's parliamentary speech committing South Africa to attack German-occupied Namibia (Webb 1916: 9). General de la Rey was a former Boer general and a serving senator in parliament, although the commandos were led in the field by Generals de Wit and Beyers, and Major Kemp, all heroes from the last war with the British. A provisional government was planned with Beyers as president and de la Rey as commandant general of the commandos. German prisoners of war were to be released. This was the only positive act in support of Germany, although one rebel, Lt.-Col. Maritz, fled to German-occupied Namibia to work in the war effort against Britain, taking some rebel Afrikaners with him.

The rebellion tested the loyalty of the police and defence force as never before, given that many of the rank-and-file members were Afrikaners. President Steyn of South Africa refused to condemn the rebels (see the correspondence in Webb 1916: 58–9, 75–7). General Beyers, the Commander-General of the Citizen Force (not to be confused with the citizen force of special constables), resigned to lead the rebels, and some members did not respond to their call-up notice. Some members of the permanent defence force went over to the rebels. In all, 11,500 rebels took the field, mostly from the Orange Free State and Transvaal; about a thousand were members of the defence and citizen forces (Garson 1962: 136). Only in the case of Maritz's unit did a whole section of the defence force rebel. Six rebels were policemen (Annual Report of the Commissioner of the SAP 1914: 2); Afrikaner nationalist hopes of an uprising in the police were dashed.

Perhaps because of the loyalty of the police, police stations were among the most frequently attacked symbols of state power by the Afrikaner rebels, although this was also an attempt to steal horses, arms, and ammunition. The SAP's official historian describes the views of some rebels towards the police: the SAP was seen 'as part of the enemy forces' (Dippenaar 1988: 29), despite the number of Afrikaners in the ranks. The police were also heavily involved in suppressing the rebellion, with a squadron of the SAMR and 400 police recruits being used to defend Pretoria against an attempt by the rebels to capture the capital city. Martial law was declared, giving the police sweeping powers. It was a police unit, commanded by an Afrikaner, N. J. Pretorious, and an Englishman, Harry Trew, which eventually defeated the last rebel resistance, based around the former defence force officer, Jopie Fourie. The SAP formed part of his firing squad.

When the police accidentally killed de la Rey, when he refused to stop his car at all three of the road-blocks set up in pursuit of the Foster gang, notorious criminals and police killers (they also shot another citizen, a member of the Grace cricketing family, at a second road-block), the rebels were given their martyr. His funeral saw widespread unrest; Afrikaners, like Blacks decades later, politicized the funeral. A government commission on the shootings (Union of

South Africa 1914*b*) absolved the police of blame, although suspicion was rife that it had been deliberate (on the de la Rey killing see also Dippenaar 1988: 24–6; Meintjers 1966); certainly the police fired recklessly, although no criticism was directed at the police for this. However, it did eventually transpire that once the Grace killing was made known to them, senior policemen in Johannesburg gave instructions to men at road-blocks to act with great caution and not to fire indiscriminately, but these did not arrive in time to save de la Rey because the telephone lines were down and the man carrying the message on foot was too late (Conf/6/268/14).

However, when Beyers was also accidentally killed, drowned while escaping from government forces, the heart of the rebellion died with them both. Ill-equipped and heavily outnumbered, the rebels retreated to the veld, some joined with the Germans in South West Africa, but most surrendered. The rebellion had cost 332 lives, 190 on the rebel side, and 600 were wounded (Garson 1962: 136). Government forces in the field against the rebels numbered nearly thirty thousand, most of them Afrikaners who had fought with Botha and Smuts in the previous war. Botha deliberately avoided use of British members of the police and army to quell the rebellion in order not to deepen the bitterness between the two ethnic groups. Subsequent hostility and bitterness among Afrikaner nationalists were directed at Botha and Smuts rather than the British, especially that aroused by the court martial and execution of Jopie Fourie, who became a folk hero to later generations of Afrikaner nationalists. The rebellion and its aftermath thus served to signal the deep divisions within the Afrikaner community, in which the police would again become involved at the outbreak of world war. The events also left a legacy of suspicion of the police among Afrikaner nationalists, which affected government relations with the SAP once the National Party came to power in 1948.

With the rebellion quashed, the invasion of German-occupied Namibia took place, with Botha and a sizeable force of policemen landing in Walvis Bay on 9 February 1915, half of whom were Afrikaners. The campaign was over within three months. As a comment on the degree of police involvement in the invasion, Commissioner Truter was accorded the honour of hoisting the Union Jack in Windhoek's main square, in the presence of Prime Minister Botha, the colonial-style soldier-policeman model in epitomy. To further reinforce this, the 1919 Public Services Commission also accorded the SAP the right to use military titles for its senior ranks, with Truter thus becoming a colonel.

TABLE 2.4 *SAP budget, 1919/20–1926/7*

Year	Budget £	% change	% on detective work*	% on equipment
1919/20	2,042,242	–	1	0.6
1920/21	3,496,327	+71.2	0.5	0.6
1921/22	2,933,538	−16	0.6	1
1922/23	2,604,140	−11.2	0.6	0.7
1923/24	2,533,043	−2.7	0.8	0.7
1924/25	2,555,104	+0.8	1	0.6
1925/26	2,539,433	−0.6	1	0.9
1926/27	2,584,912	+1.7	0.9	0.9

* Excludes salaries.

Source: Annual Reports of the Commissioner of the SAP.

With the annexation of South West Africa, the SAP's war was over, except for a group of eighty men who fought in central Africa, although many policemen fought as individuals. Over a thousand policemen were mobilized to fight in Europe; seventy-three were killed in battle. The effects of the war were keenly felt for a long time after. The world economic recession which followed the conflict affected police organization, manpower, recruitment, and pay. The SAP's budget fell markedly after the war, save for the 1920/1 financial year, when most of the SAMR was absorbed into the SAP, as Table 2.4 shows. The SAP's budget fell by 26 per cent between the financial years 1920/1 and 1926/7. Defence expenditure fell by 29.2 per cent in the same period. The proportion of the police budget spent on detective services, a measure of expenditure on civil police work, had fallen by a third in the 1926/7 financial year compared to the 1914/15 financial year, while overall the police budget had doubled, although the expenditure on equipment was roughly the same in 1926/7 as in 1914/15.

This forced the management to reduce administrative costs, among other things, by cutting the number of administrative districts, and to delay its planned massive building programme. Some police buildings had been in use since before the unification of the police in 1913. In his 1920 Annual Report, Truter called for more accommodation for married policemen, describing some married quarters as 'disgraceful and dangerous to health' (Annual Report of the Commissioner of the SAP 1920: 7). The absence of accommodation or its poor quality restricted his autonomy in transferring men. The same complaint was made at a meeting of deputy commissioners in Pretoria six years later. Nor were there sufficient number of police stations and buildings. In 1916 a two-roomed house and iron shack that had been in use as a police station since before the Anglo-Boer War was dismantled and re-erected elsewhere as a temporary measure; it was still in operation as a police station in 1964 when visited by a former policeman (F. Cooper 1972–3: 31). In the Orange Free State they were still using wooden buildings in 1926 built just after the Anglo-Boer War. Being unable to build stations quick enough, even though the police budget gave funds to employ native labourers, many police stations comprised buildings hired by the police from various types of landlord. In 1926 there were more hired than government-owned police stations in the Cape and on the Rand. Some of the government-owned buildings were described by Truter in his 1926 Annual Report as uninhabitable.

However, the greatest effect of the budgetary restrictions was evidenced in manpower. As Table 2.5 illustrates, there was a marked increase in the SAP's manpower once it absorbed the SAMR, but only modest increases thereafter, if at all, which senior police managers found inadequate for the demands of police work in South Africa. Accordingly, the ratio of police per thousand of population actually fell throughout the period as the country's population rose faster than the authorized complement of police. However, from 1924 onwards the actual manpower levels began to exceed those authorized in the police budget, something which had never occurred before. But

TABLE 2.5 *SAP manpower levels, 1919–1926*

Year	Authorized manpower	Actual manpower	% change*	% Black*	Ratio of police per 1,000 population
1919	8,215	7,655	–	31.5	1.22
1920	10,503	10,030	+31	36.6	1.53
1921	10,608	10,129	+0.9	37.4	1.52
1922	10,214	9,944	–1.8	–	1.44
1923	10,210	10,065	+1.2	–	1.42
1924	10,261	10,294	+2.2	–	1.40
1925	10,194	10,219	+0.7	37.8	1.36
1926	10,195	10,441	+2.1	37.9	1.35

* Actual membership only.

Source: Annual Reports of the Commissioner of the SAP.

despite in this sense being slightly overstaffed (by 2.4 per cent in 1926), Truter pleaded with the government for more men. Special constables were employed on beat patrol in some of the larger urban centres from 1920 onwards, and Truter demanded that he be allowed to recruit from abroad. The Minister of Justice expressly forbade Truter to do this in a letter dated 20 June 1921, and reprimanded him for the 'semi-official' recruitment from abroad that had been engaged in up to that point (Conf/6/766/20/1). The chief complaint was that South Africa's unemployment rate made it undesirable to offer employment to people from overseas. The political control that accompanied centralization and was embedded in police–state relations allowed the minister to dictate to the chief commissioner in this way. Thus, Truter was forced to decline the request from Durban and Pietermaritzburg that the SAP take over responsibility for policing the boroughs, even though it would have completed Truter's ambition to make his force truly national (Conf/16/760/20). He even weakened the bilingual rule; the special permission of the minister could be sought to employ a unilingual recruit with exceptional qualifications. In reply to the minister regarding the request from Durban and Pietermaritzburg councils, Truter wrote exasperatedly on 11 May 1920:

The South African youth appears to have a rooted antipathy to foot duties, and I therefore consider that there will be no option but to recruit for this branch from abroad. Every possible source in South Africa has been tried through the medium of posters, personal letters to magistrates, ministers of religion, heads of schools, etc., so it cannot be said that opportunity has not been offered to the South African eligible. It is in this branch that the taking over of the Durban Borough Police will affect us ... My present difficulty in meeting the demands of other large towns would merely be accentuated. (Conf/6/760/20)

The borough of Durban had itself been having difficulty in recruiting sufficient White policemen, and Lt.-Col. Hartigan, who had been active in the Namibian campaign during the war, took it upon himself to recruit from England under the auspices of the British Empire Service League. The Minister of Justice stopped this, pointing out that it added to the number of 'roaming unemployed' in the country, and inflamed the grievances of Afrikaner nationalists against the government (Conf/6/766/20/1).

Manpower shortage in the SAP was made worse by three factors. There was a reluctance to recruit Blacks to compensate for the shortfall in White recruitment, and the apartheid operating within the force prevented Black policemen from patrolling White suburban areas, leading to the use of White special constables instead. Thus, for example, the Public Services Commission of 1926 and the Minister of Justice both opposed any increase in the complement of Black police as a solution to manpower shortage (Annual Report of the Commissioner of the SAP 1926: 3). Even so, the proportion of Blacks in the SAP continued to increase during this period as recruitment among Whites proved harder than among Blacks. A second factor was the influenza epidemic just after the war. The SAP lost 160 men to the epidemic in 1918, 100 in the month of October alone, and the Police Provident Fund went bankrupt, having to be rescued by a massive loan from the government. Above all, however, manpower shortage was made worse by the demands made on police time by other government departments. In his 1920 Annual Report the Commissioner estimated that these extraneous duties were the equivalent of 458 men who were therefore lost to normal police duties (Annual Report of the Commissioner of the SAP 1920: 9). This was another way in which the persistence of features of colonial policing exacerbated the organizational difficulties of the police, leading Truter to complain vociferously about the state's use of the police in this way, which he did in every annual report. In his 1926 report Truter urged an increase in the police budget to the equivalent of the work done for other departments. He estimated that the department of justice alone benefited in this way by £36,000 per annum (Annual Report of the Commissioner of the SAP 1926: 4). He also estimated that the extra work-load imposed on the police as a result of extraneous duties made the average working day twelve hours long.

Another effect of the post-war budgetary restrictions was on pay and promotion, and this was almost immediately felt. In a letter to the Minister of Justice, dated 21 June 1918, Truter complained about the deleterious effect which poor pay was having on recruitment and retention of staff, resulting in many areas being under-policed; he pointed out to the minister that police manpower in the Witwatersrand area was lower than in 1904 (Conf/6/611/18). The war curtailed promotion, and many of the extra allowances paid to policemen during the war were stopped at its end, resulting in a reduction in salary for many policemen. This particularly affected the morale of constables, amongst whom there was considerable turnover. Consequently, the quality of recruits had deteriorated; senior officers estimated in 1918 that between 75 and 80 per cent of constables could not make out a report properly (Union of South Africa 1918*a*: 41). Throughout the war Truter had tried, unsuccessfully, to persuade the government to give an extra allowance to men with fourteen years' service or more, in an attempt to keep experienced policemen. Moreover, the pay structure of the SAP contained numerous anomalies. Allowances were larger in the Transvaal, where the cost of living was lowest. Thus, men transferred from the Transvaal experienced a real reduction in salary and a drop in its purchasing power.

The government was deaf to all the special pleading, and a group of 101 constables in Cape Town held a meeting on 17 November 1917 announcing their intention to go on strike on 1 January 1918 unless something was done to improve pay and promotion. A petition was drawn up signed by another ninety-nine constables. The government did not use the intervening period to negotiate a settlement, and the strike duly followed. A strike of policemen was illegal. The government refused the strikers an interview, called in the defence forces to arrest them, and prosecuted the ringleaders the next day. Many were kept in prison awaiting trial because they could not afford the relatively high bail figure set by the magistrate, although a member of the public eventually purchased their release. The strikers were subsequently found guilty, and given a suspended sentence of imprisonment or fine. None was dismissed from the force and no internal disciplinary steps were taken against them; Truter even spoke in the trial as a witness in their defence. In fact, their actions proved useful in his struggle with the government for proper funding for the police. In his 1918 Annual Report, Truter used the strike to bargain with the government for an increase in the pay and working conditions of the police: a contented and efficient police force required proper remuneration by the state, such that the state got the police force its miserliness deserved.

These arguments had force, and the government appointed a select committee to look into the causes of the strike and asked the Public Services Committee, under Mr Justice Graham, to review the pay and working conditions of all government employees. The Select Committee on the strike revealed some interesting features. The immediate grievances were economic. Despite the attempts of police management to create the impression that policing was a career, constables tended to see it as a stage in the search for something better. By 1918 the average length of service was only seven years, four in the Cape (Union of South Africa 1918*a*: p. xxv). The typical recruit was thus a 'poor White', mostly Afrikaans-speaking rural migrants. The police management derogatively referred to them as the 'bywoner class' (p. 147): young, poorly-educated, landless Afrikaners who formerly worked as hired hands on farms. The Deputy Commissioner for Johannesburg complained to the Select Committee that there was a noticeable lack of intelligence in policemen compared to 1913, which he attributed entirely to the unattractiveness of the salary.

Racial considerations were apparent in this concern. The pay was so low that policemen had to find lodging in areas where Blacks lived, some even lodging with Coloured and African people. Racist notions of what was respectable for a White person were manipulated by senior police officers to suggest that low pay in the police was undermining the social status of Whites (pp. 11, 35, 38). However, the ethno-centricism of the English officers was perhaps the most important motivation. Pay was too poor to attract any other recruit than the bywoner Afrikaner; not even educated Afrikaners were attracted to the force. Officers thus had no option but to put bywoner Afrikaners into urban forces, where their insular rural and Afrikaner background made them unsuitable, provoking complaint from the public and magistrates alike because of their poor facility in speaking English and lack of knowledge of 'town conditions' (p. xxv). Truter admitted that some residents in South Africa's largest towns objected to having Afrikaner policemen on the streets, and they faced a 'good deal of prejudice' from the public (p. 77). In evidence before the committee Truter noted, with obvious regret, that some police stations in urban areas were policed entirely by 'young South African Dutch' (p. 55).

The strike revealed, in other words, the depth of hostility between the Afrikaner and British members of the police. All the strikers save one were Afrikaner, and although Truter suggested that this hostility was not a precipitating factor of the strike, and that relations within the force were good (p. 40), the evidence of his men did not bear this out. The policy of bilingualism, in which both languages could be used equally within the force, did not operate in practice. Some of the young Afrikaner constables also complained of aggressiveness and rough treatment from English officers (p. xlii). Officers often returned reports when written in Afrikaans; one constable complained that only four of his officers understood Afrikaans (p. 51). Truter pointed out in evidence that knowledge of Afrikaans among the British community was slight, and insistence on bilingualism thus restricted recruitment from this section of the White population, which was undesirable. And insistence that young bywoner Afrikaners learn English would cut off the force's main constituency. But in order to improve bilingualism among existing members, he said that he was thinking of introducing a 'language allowance', whereby extra money could be earned for proficiency in other languages. He also admitted that officers 'did not always take sufficient interest in constables and were not always sympathetic to them' (p. 80).

The Afrikanerization of the rank and file thus caused two sorts of problem in 1918: poor relations between the police and the public in those settings where citizens were hostile to Afrikaners; and aggravation of the poor relations between officers and the men within the police. Low pay was both cause and effect. Low pay ensured that the police attracted predominantly bywoner Afrikaners, and it damaged further the poor morale of constables who were suffering under a management which was perceived as hostile to them. Not surprisingly, the Select Committee recommended that constables be allowed to use Afrikaans as their working language within the police, and that they be treated with more sympathy by officers. The 1918 Public Services Commission (Union of South Africa 1918*b*) recommended substantial increases in police salaries, but not before the police nearly mutinied again when the government indicated its intention to delay the increases until April 1920. Although technically illegal, irate policemen held mass meetings throughout the country, eventually persuading the government to introduce the increases with effect from 1 October 1919. However the deterioration of the post-war economy in the 1920s forced the government eventually to renege and police salaries were actually cut in 1926 as a cost-saving exercise.

In his study of the 1918 police strike in Liverpool, King (1988) reveals that its dynamics were similar to those in South Africa but its outcome entirely different. Low pay, wartime inflation, low social status, poor relations with management, and persecution of specific individuals motivated the British strike, but its effects led to the modernization and professionalization of the police. The 1919 Police Act began the task of establishing national standards for the police in pay, pension entitlements, discipline, training, recruitment, and education, and to the formation of the Police Federation, the nearest body in the United Kingdom to a police trade union. By contrast the outcome in South Africa was a pay increase that proved temporary.

The underlying problems that motivated the South African strike remained, and had to be addressed again by the 1926 Te Water Commission.

POLICE PROFESSIONALIZATION AND MODERNIZATION

In another sense, however, the police in South Africa were already in a better position than counterparts in Britain, because national standards existed as a result of the centralized structure of the police, and this was shortly to be reinforced by the absorption of the SAMR into the SAP. But in South Africa the standards were generally lower, and other features restricted the modernization of the force. None the less, in the period from 1914 to 1926 the SAP underwent some modernization and professionalization. The measures of police professionalism employed in the literature normally include such items as the adoption of modern technology and management techniques, improvements in the educational standards required of recruits and in training, the development of mechanisms of accountability to the public, improvements in discipline within the force, public relations skills in dealing with citizens, impartiality in relations with contending social groups, and increasing effectiveness in protecting the public from crime and in its detection. Professionalism, in other words, is evidenced in features of police organization, in the way the public are dealt with by members of the police, and by the manner in which police work is accomplished.

Professionalism is not solely equivalent to the civil police tradition; police forces can, in a restricted sense, be professional in the way they perform sectarian or colonial policing. But many of the measures of professionalism are incompatible with styles other than civil policing. In some senses, therefore, the SAP has never become a professional and modernized force, but by other standards it has, and this relative modernization was evident from the beginning. By its own perception, however, the SAP has always been professional, and successive commissioners have employed the rhetoric of modernization and professionalism. This discourse has not just been utilized since de Klerk's reforms, as Rauch claims (1991: 10), for senior managers have always believed that they were professional in the internal management of the organization and in aspects of public-service delivery.

But the partisanship of the police in South Africa, and their brutality both in policing race relations and in discharging colonial-style policing, sits incongruously with this discourse and seriously limits the achievement of modernized and professional police work. Most senior police officers did not see the contradiction between their emphasis upon professionalism and modernization and the deployment of the police in an essentially colonial task to control, partisanly, one section of the population. Some did, of course, resulting in conflict within the organization over the relative priority given to civil and colonial police work. But even those who whole-heartedly supported the colonial style and enthusiastically policed Black South Africans with considerable brutality and partisanship, none the less saw themselves as professional policemen. Yet their use of the discourse of modernization and professionalism belied their retarded progress compared to other forces in former colonial societies. This is apparent in the period from 1914 to 1926, when the SAP, for example, was modernizing some of its organizational and managerial practices, and establishing an effective CID, but also dropping bombs on protesters from aeroplanes and adopting military titles to designate their ranks.

For Commissioner Truter, centralization was the main measure of modernization because it overcame the problems of localism associated with pre-Union policing. Thus Truter did all he could to establish the SAP as the single national, centralized policing body. By the end of the war, the SAP had shown itself able to be a national force. In 1918 it was granted its own quartermaster stores independent of the defence force and began lobbying to win recognition from the state as the single policing body. Truter's ambition, however, was hindered by the existence of borough police in Pietermaritzburg and Durban, a separate railways police, and the SAMR, but the post-war period witnessed considerable movement towards his goal.

The absorption of the SAMR into the SAP was advocated during the war by the 1917 Committee on Retrenchment in Public Expenditure as a cost-saving exercise, estimating a saving of £25,000 per annum from amalgamation (Union of South Africa 1917: 140). This centralization brought with it, however, the problem of political control over the police, and the Commissioner suggested in evidence that the new single force be under the jurisdiction of the ministry of defence rather than justice, so as to avoid a conflict of interest between the policing, judicial, and penal responsibilities of the justice minister. Without there being a minister of police, just where political responsibility for the police lay proved to be problematic for Truter. Neither option was desirable. If it lay with the justice ministry, it symbolized the colonial tendency to merge policing with civil and judicial administration, and thus was an obstacle to the modernization of the SAP. But placing control under the defence ministry tended to merge policing with the military, which was also unacceptably colonialist and pre-modern. However, the government's wish was for control to remain with the department of justice, and this remained so even after it conceded the argument for amalgamation in 1920; police–state relations ensured that the government got its way.

Part of the reason for this lies in the nature of police work in the early part of the twentieth century. As Pinnock argues, South Africa's rapid industrialization at this time saw the emergence of an urban proletariat that required a focus on internal rather than external threat (cited in van der Spuy 1989: 268). This is most evident in the expansion in the police budget relative to defence expenditure during the 1920s, as shown in Table 2.2. But more than that, the focus of the internal threat had shifted from the predominantly Black rural areas to urban locations. The emergence of an urban threat had been made apparent to the police and the government by the industrial unrest in urban areas during 1913 and 1914, and the continuing urbanization of the Black population brought problems of race relations into the towns. The war delayed the separation of policing from the work of external defence, and prevented a reassessment of the viability of retaining a separate, exclusively rural-based police force. With the end of the war, the government distinguished external defence from policing by insisting on control of the police remaining with the justice department, and amalgamated all but one regiment of the SAMR with the SAP (the final regiment was absorbed in 1926). But while the government wished to separate the two sorts of functions, circumstances required the SAP to assume military-style duties in dealing with internal urban unrest, and the incorporation of the SAMR gave the SAP an even more pronounced paramilitary character.

Other reasons for the amalgamation were more pragmatic; it effectively cut the costs of police work, and senior officers in the SAP demanded it. The Assistant Commissioner of Natal repeatedly complained in the Commissioner's annual reports about the tripartite system of policing in Natal, where police work was shared between the borough police, the SAP, and the SAMR. In the 1919 Annual Report the Assistant Commissioner for Natal described this as reducing police efficiency and creating 'numerous difficulties' (Annual Report of the Commissioner of the SAP 1919: 73). In correspondence with the Minister of Justice, Truter was very enthusiastic about the proposed merger and urged it on the minister (Conf/6/657/18/2). Some members of the SAMR were also in favour. Sergeant Lane, from the Natal district of the SAMR stationed in Pietermaritzburg, wrote to a Colonel Godley in the SAP on 22 May 1919, mentioning the inappropriateness of the SAMR for the type of problem encountered in Natal. The need was for policemen not pukkah soldiers:

The class of inhabitant (Indian and native) on the out-skirts of Durban require a good number of plain clothes men. Northern Natal is going ahead in leaps and bounds. Coal and chemical propositions are opening, with the resulting need for more police. Zululand is opening up . . . Industrial troubles are for ever on the horizon. We have just had a dust up with the colliery natives in Dundee . . . Present times are very disturbing and one looks for the time when our future is settled and we shall know whether we are to be pukkah soldiers or policemen. I hope the latter for myself. (Conf/6/657/18/2)

This was Truter's realization as well, and he tried to limit the number of men transferred from the SAMR because of their more military background and limited policing experience. In doing so, he was setting himself against the wishes of the Prime Minister, whose Private Secretary wrote to Truter on 28 February 1920 urging more men from the SAMR to be retained. Truter replied that the civil police tradition of the SAP required fewer men than the military duties of the SAMR, although he pointed out that while many non-commissioned officers had not been accepted into the SAP, most ordinary riflemen had, 'except those with very indifferent characters'; forty volunteers from the ranks were rejected (Conf/6/657/18/2). It was not just a question of their lack of competence in ordinary police work. In rejecting a disproportionate number of officers, Truter was trying to satisfy the concerns of his own constables, who feared that their promotion prospects would be severely affected by the arrival of new officers. The self-interest of members of the SAP was also at stake. In a series of letters to the minister, Truter said that the morale and contentment of men in the SAP should be a major factor in the number and type of men transferred to ordinary police duties from the SAMR, and that the transfer was causing 'grave dissatisfaction' and 'genuine grievances' among his men (for other correspondence in police files on the transfer see Conf/6/657/18/1–13).

The government, however, was reluctant to abandon the skills and expertise of the military men in the SAMR, and the Minister of Justice accepted the appeal of many young officers whose request for transfer had been rejected by Truter (for the case of a Captain Woods see Conf/6/657/18/13). Clearly, senior managers in the SAP were mindful of the possible negative effects of transfer on the SAP's attempts to modernize itself from the colonial-style, pukkah-soldier tradition, while the government saw a continued need for men with this background (it retained a regiment of the SAMR until 1926). However, given police–state relations, Truter could do little but complain, and he was forced to accept 26 officers and 3,505 members of all races (Dippenaar 1988: 46); another 138 men were transferred upon the final disbandment of the SAMR in 1926. The government at this time also refused Truter an increase in expenditure in order to meet the request of the boroughs of Pietermaritzburg and Durban that their police be absorbed into the SAP; so some areas of Natal kept a bipartite police system, against the wishes of the SAP. In a letter to the Minister of Justice, dated 11 May 1920, Truter regretted that costs prevented him from achieving his aim of a single national and centralized police force (Conf/6/760/20). Pietermaritzburg was eventually incorporated in 1927, and Durban in 1936.

The incorporation of the SAMR required the SAP to expand their organization, and two new districts were established in the Transkei, based in Umtata, and Natal, with headquarters in Pietermaritzburg, although there were mobile squads based in each as a throw-back to the mounted paramilitary-style policing of the SAMR. A separate district for the Witwatersrand was established in 1921, with head-quarters in Johannesburg. The SAP realized at last that the dynamics of crime in the urban Witwatersrand area required the district to be policed differently from the rural conditions of the rest of the Transvaal. Thus, by 1926, the SAP had expanded to eight districts.

Centralization was Truter's obsession, despite the control it gave to the Minister of Justice. At the end of the war, the SAP prepared a planning document on the policing of Namibia (Conf/6/726/19), which had been policed during the war by the South West African Military Constabulary. But the government decided that a separate force should be established, called the South West African Police, and that the 1912 Police Act be applied to it by proclamation. Members were taken exclusively from the military constabulary. In a letter to the Secretary for Defence, dated 24 October 1919, Truter suggested that the protectorate be policed by members of the SAP, and his accompanying report indicated that this could be done without a large detail of men, and that members of the military constabulary lacked the necessary experience in ordinary police work to enable this force to suffice. Again, the government overlooked his arguments, and it was not until the outbreak of the Second World War that the SAP took over responsibility for policing Namibia.

The state also ignored the Commissioner's advice on the question of a separate railways police. Consistent with his view that centralization was a measure of modernization, Truter was against the establishment of a separate railways police, and he did what he could to have it absorbed into the SAP. Up to 1916, the railway companies employed their own private police, although the old Natal Police was responsible for transport duties in Natal up to Union in 1910. In 1916 the Railways and Harbours Police was established, with headquarters in Johannesburg, as part of the South African Railways and Harbours Service, although the police were under the authority of a chief inspector. The 1916 Railway Act conferred upon them the same powers as the SAP 'when carrying out the duty of maintaining order upon the railways and harbours'. They also had the same liabilities and indemnities as the SAP. However, the railways police had no association with the SAP, and there was little formal co-ordination between them. Indeed, Truter complained at how the two forces got in each other's way when the SAP was called upon to deal with incidents at docks.

The 1925 estimates of the South African Railways and Harbours Service indicate that there was provision for 338 White and 214 Black policemen, at a cost of £104,551; the 214 'native police' cost £41 per head, compared to £262 per head for White policemen. In a letter to the Minister of Justice, written on 19 August 1925, Truter again demanded that they be absorbed into the SAP: statute gave the SAP the role of maintaining law and order; the SAP could do it more efficiently than any other force; and justice demanded that policing on the railways be discharged by an independent body (Conf/6/7/10). The Commissioner of the Natal Police had made a similar point to the latter one in his annual report in 1911 when responsibility was taken away from his force and given to the private railway companies, although the General Manager of Natal Railways replied in his annual report of the same year that any allegation of a conflict of interest was 'totally unwarranted' (p. 55). However, in 1925 Truter marshalled a letter in support of centralization from the Assistant General Manager of South African Railways and Harbours Service in Durban, in which the person wrote: 'I am not satisfied that the railways police are efficient or even necessary' (Conf/6/7/10). The ministry of justice were themselves convinced of the necessity for centralization. A letter from the Minister to Truter, dated 30 July 1925, indicated that he was informing the Minister of Railways that 'it seems to [me] highly desirable in the interests of justice that we should have one police force in the union. It is incongruous that the railways department should have its own special force' (Conf/6/7/10). The 1926 Te Water Commission also made this recommendation (Union of South Africa 1926: 53). Yet the powerful transport lobby in the government, linked to even more influential industrial lobbies, resisted the loss of control over policing, and it was not until 1986 that the two forces were eventually amalgamated.

The Commissioner could thus only have been half-satisfied at the modernization of policing in South Africa, if centralization was his measure. On other counts, the SAP was also moving forward, albeit erratically when taken in the round. At one level, the SAP was being called on to help with the formation of other police forces in Africa, as happened in 1917 with the East African Police, and it was also attending to features of its internal organization during this period. One was improvement in the standard of recruits and in training. In 1918 a recruit was required to be aged between 18 and 35, five foot six inches tall, and have a thirty-three-and-a-half-inch chest at the age of 18. He had to be able to read and write either English or Afrikaans, and supply two testimonials from well-known people in his locality. No educational standards were specified in 1918, although those without educational qualifications did one hour of schooling per day during training. This standard was poorer than the Royal Irish Constabulary half a century before (Brewer 1989, 1990).

In 1920 the SAP raised the educational standard of entry to Standard 6 for White recruits, but was forced to accept those with Standard 5 because of manpower shortage (Annual Report of the Commissioner of the SAP 1920: 3); no formal entry requirements were specified for Black recruits, and they received no training. Modernization in this sense was restricted to White policemen, a sign, in fact, of the limits of professionalism within the force. The Commissioner also expressed concern about the number of long-serving policemen whose level of formal education was poor, hoping that they might retire to allow the employment of the 'more educated type of man' (p. 3). But throughout this period Truter bemoaned the poor quality of recruits. Van Onselen describes the entry examination at this time as involving tests in English, Afrikaans, and mathematics, and was not a scholarly test but primarily one for bilingualism (1960: 32).

However, even though bilingualism was official policy, they were letting in men whose knowledge of both official languages was as poor as that of men recruited earlier. It was only in 1926 that the *Police Gazette*, which supplied general information about crime as well as photographs of wanted criminals, was published in both official languages. In his 1926 Annual Report, Truter noted that most sergeants who failed the promotion examination did so because they failed to reach the 60 per cent pass mark on one of the official languages (invariably Afrikaans); the pass mark was accordingly reduced in that year to 40 per cent. This reflected the fact that the Afrikaners in the ranks had not yet affected the social composition of the officer class, which was still predominantly English-speaking. In the Public Service List of 1925, for example, there was only one Afrikaner on the divisional inspectors list, and none above that rank, and three sub-inspectors. This could only be temporary, however, given their preponderance in the ranks, and in the 1934 Public Service List there were two Afrikaner chief inspectors, four inspectors, and thirty-six sub-inspectors.

By 1926 the force also had become more experienced, with less turnover of younger men. The average length of service for constables in 1926 was eight years, compared with just under five years in 1916; that of sergeants, first class, 21.6 years compared to 13.7 years in 1916 (Annual Report of the Commissioner of the SAP 1916: 3, and 1926: 6). This indicates that policing was coming to be seen as a career by some of the younger recruits, although they were not necessarily those 'educated types' whom the police wanted to attract. Recruits were also always male, the SAP having abandoned its wartime experiment of using policewomen. Branches of the National Council for Women in Cape Town, Durban, Johannesburg, and Port Elizabeth brought proposals to the 1926 Te Water Commission for patrols by police-women in their areas, to take care of child and female prisoners, and to be at events where women and children were present (Union of South Africa 1926: 115–16), but this was to no avail. Their request was not even mentioned in the final report.

Also in this period, for the first time, a refresher training course was established for officers. Up to this time officers were left to themselves to perfect drill and develop tactics. It was only during emergencies, such as crowd disturbances, that officers had large assemblies of men under their command. F. Cooper quotes one officer at the first training course in 1927 as saying that this was the first time in twenty-three years that he had the opportunity to drill more than four men at a time (1972–3: 33). However, Cooper notes wryly that some of the old lags found the pace too quick, and withdrew as medically unfit after finding it strenuous.

Another measure of modernization is the development of a disciplinary ethos within the force. A set of internal regulations satisfactory to Truter was established in 1918, and these were very strict, but what was important for the disciplinary ethos of the SAP was their enforcement. One index of this is the number of dismissals from the force. In one sense this is a measure of indiscipline, and thus lack of professionalism, such that the more policemen dismissed, the less professional the force is. But looked at another way, the higher the number of dismissals, the greater is the emphasis by management on professional standards and proper conduct within the force. However, a low number of dismissals can reflect either the absence of misconduct, or a failure by management to take acts of unprofessional conduct seriously. But from what we know of the occupational culture of rank-and-file policemen, and of the conduct of the SAP, especially towards Blacks, it probably reflects the latter. Thus, the rate of dismissal from the force, especially in the context of extreme shortage of White policemen, is a rough measure of the enforcement of modern standards of discipline and ethical conduct.

Wastage, as the Commissioner's annual reports described it, was always high. Most of this was caused by younger men purchasing their discharge in order to find better employment elsewhere. However, on only four occasions in the entire period from 1914 to 1926 did the number of men leaving exceed those joining (1918, 1921, 1922, and 1924), although men of equal quality may not have been swapped. The proportion of the wastage that was due to dismissals was often high, as shown in Table 2.6. The overall level of dismissals varies considerably year from year, but declined markedly in 1926, which saw the lowest number of dismissals of White policemen, either as a result of greater tolerance by management or improvements in police behaviour. Black policemen are clearly dismissed at a greater rate

TABLE 2.6 *The percentage of wastage due to dismissals*

Year	White	Black
1916	12.5	41.5
1917	61.6	38.9
1918	28.1	28
1919	37.4	33.2
1920	33.1	35.3
1926	12.2	40.4

Source: Annual Reports of the Commissioner of the SAP.

than White colleagues. This reflects the absence of formal entry requirements and educational standards for Black policemen; the greater willingness of management to address misconduct among Blacks because of the ready supply of willing recruits; and apartheid within the force, resulting in the conduct of Black policemen being given greater attention by management, and their failure to receive the same organizational support as Whites when transgressing. Table 2.7 seems to confirm the operation of discrimination, for it shows that the offences for which Blacks were dismissed from the SAP were less serious on the whole than those for which White colleagues were dismissed. Unfortunately, the annual reports did not always provide this sort of information, which is why statistics for some years in this period are missing, but the 1926 Annual Report did indicate that there were 378 dismissals, fifty-three of which were of White policemen. Thus, Black policemen were dismissed at over six times the rate of White colleagues. This suggests that the drive to professionalism in the conduct of members of the SAP had a distinct racial component, with Black policemen having to meet higher standards of conduct than their White counterparts. The problems affecting recruitment of Whites, which were absent in Black recruitment, seem to have influenced the severity with which unprofessional conduct by White policemen was dealt with. Either that or White policemen were genuinely becoming more disciplined in their conduct. However, White policemen seem not to have been dismissed for their brutal treatment of Black citizens and protesters, for which there is plenty of evidence of undisciplined conduct, as we shall shortly document. Thus, while the Commissioner congratulated the force in his 1926 Annual Report for its professionalism, because of the low number of dismissals (by which he meant of White policemen only),

TABLE 2.7 *Specific offences as a proportion of total dismissals*

Year	Convictions		Drunkenness		Misconduct		Other	
	White	Black	White	Black	White	Black	White	Black
1916	29.6	100	19.7	–	23.4	–	27.2	–
1917	24.4	20.3	7.4	13.4	24	5.5	49.1	61.1
1918	14.7	20.5	3.5	6	21.7	7.6	60.6	65.8
1919	16.4	12.3	3.5	4.4	23.5	11	56.5	72.3

Source: Annual Reports of the Commissioner of the SAP.

professionalism was being construed in narrow terms which excluded police behaviour towards three-quarters of the population.

On other measures, however, the SAP was indeed modernizing. Its technology was advancing. A few police dogs were used by the Natal Police in 1909, and police in the Transvaal imported three Dobermann pinschers from Holland in 1911, but it was not until 1923 that the Police Dog Training Corps was established. Initially the dogs were used solely for investigative purposes rather than as part of routine patrol work or crowd control. The 1926 Annual Report of the Commissioner of the SAP noted 104 cases in which criminals were brought to trial due to the use of police dogs. Motorization was also occurring, although at some of the isolated rural out-stations taken over from the SAMR, the police were required to remain a mounted force. Debeden station, for example, was 190 miles from a railhead, and few such stations had mechanical transport in 1926. In 1920 the Commissioner reported that the SAP had fifty-three cars; those stationed at headquarters in Pretoria had done 38,000 miles on official business that year. Other cars had covered 293,000 miles, and motor cycles 472,000 miles. As an indication of the switch from mounted to foot duties, the Commissioner estimated that nearly nine million miles had been covered by mounted policemen, and nearly thirteen million by foot patrolmen (Annual Report of the Commissioner of the SAP 1920: 9).

This is also a useful index of how police work was becoming increasingly urban-centred. Van Onselen's experiences as a policeman in Cape Town during the 1920s recount working life on the beat (1960: 50–2). Young men on the beat were accompanied by a senior constable. Standing orders stated that the beat should be walked at two and a half miles per hour; twenty miles were expected to be covered in the average eight-hour relief. Each foot patrolman thus covered 280 miles during a fortnight's duty. While on duty, patrolmen were visited four times by the section sergeant, although standing orders prevented him from trying to trap constables into an offence or breach of regulations. Telephone and radio equipment was not used by the police until much later. While on the beat, policemen were not allowed to smoke. At designated points on the beat, patrolmen were required to take notes and record them for later inspection. Thus, standing orders gave ample opportunity for management control and the monitoring of work activity.

Perhaps the greatest development in technology and technique at this time was evident in the professionalization of the CID. In his report of 1922 Truter made a recommendation to the government, in the wake of the 1922 Rand strike, that it set up an intelligence service to monitor the nature and extent of infiltration by radicals and revolutionaries. The government ignored his suggestion, and the special branch was not formed until during the Second World War, and then as a result of conflicts between the state and Afrikaner nationalists. The CID, however, developed apace.

In drawing up plans for a CID in 1912, Truter drew on the Indian Police, as well as the criminal investigation departments in the Natal and Transvaal police. In a letter at this time to the Acting Secretary for Justice, Truter urged that the SAP's new CID be based in Pretoria rather than Johannesburg. In part this was because Truter himself was based in Pretoria, and the Chief Commissioner could thus 'watch the criminal barometer daily and give instructions which his experience teach him are required ... he will be more in touch with crime than he is at the present' (Conf/6/8/10, p. 2). In other words, siting the CID in Pretoria was consistent with the centralization which Truter so admired. But he also had dissatisfaction with the CID in Johannesburg, who had shown themselves unable to 'co-operate [with] officers in charge of police areas along the reef. Detectives at the CID regard [others] with contempt' (p. 1). Centralization of the CID at Pretoria thus allowed some degree of control over their tendency to élitism and separation. The CID in Johannesburg were described in Truter's letter as an *imperium in imperio*; 'a state of things which was far from satisfactory and did not conduce to efficient working' (p. 3).

Truter got his way, and the CID in Johannesburg became one of four district headquarters, others being based in the three remaining provinces, with headquarters in Bloemfontein, Pietermaritzburg, and

Cape Town. Central headquarters was in Pretoria, and the CID's central identification bureau, and its record of statistics and finger-prints, were relocated in Pretoria. In 1920 it was decided to place the CID in the hands of a deputy commissioner, who would supervise its entire operation. This was a considerable upgrading of the CID's place within the SAP's overall organization, although the proportion of SAP expenditure devoted to 'detective services' fell from this year until 1924/5 (see Table 2.4). By 1926 the CID comprised the Diamond Detective Branch, the South African Criminal Bureau (SACB), and eight divisional CID branches throughout the country. Kimberley, the centre of the diamond fields, also had its own diamond detective department as well as a divisional CID. The former Gold and Diamond Branch of the SAP was overhauled in 1922. The Gold Branch was incorporated into the command of the Witwatersrand district, while the Diamond Branch continued as a separate unit. Its work involved high-profile duties such as diamond thefts and illegal possession of uncut diamonds, but also routine monitoring of the monthly records of diggers.

Managerial· improvements, however, did not solve some of the problems Truter identified in 1912; they also created some of their own. Some senior officers in the CID complained of over-centraliza-tion. The central management were being kept informed of incidents, and receiving information which bypassed senior officers in divisional headquarters. The Deputy Commissioner of the Transvaal CID, for example, wrote angrily to Truter about an incident where he felt his department had been ignored. Nor was this unusual: 'since my assumption of duty in this area I have had a considerable amount to contend with, calling for the utmost tact in order to avoid any friction. But I am no longer prepared to tolerate instances such as [this] one' (Conf/6/758/20). Moreover, jealousy, rivalry, and conflicts over status had not been resolved.

The management contributed to this sense of competition by introducing in 1922 a differential of £20 in the salaries of uniformed policemen and detectives; allowances were also given to detectives for purchasing civilian clothing. Extra pay was granted in view of the special training detectives received, the higher level of educational qualifications required for entry to the CID, the need to compensate detectives for the greater unsocial hours worked, the greater danger faced by detectives in the course of their duty, and to avoid corruption because of the greater temptations presented to men in the CID.

Feelings of élitism were reinforced by the management's insistence that before being transferred to CID, uniformed officers needed a probationary period of six months, during which time they were assigned to a senior detective. The 1926 Te Water Commission addressed the complaints which the uniformed branch raised about this. It found no evidence to support differentials, challenged the grounds on which they had been introduced, and recommended their abolition. In challenging the evidence used by the management in 1922 to justify differentials in pay, the Te Water Commission revealed that ordinary police work was the more dangerous. Between 1920 and 1924, 195 detectives were injured in the course of their duty, and five killed. The figures for uniformed men were 2,725 injured and forty-one killed (cited in Dippenaar 1988: 72). This casualty rate also usefully indicates the high level of unrest and disorder in South Africa at this time, as we shall see in the next section.

One of the important sub-departments in the CID was that of the SACB, formerly the Central Identification Bureau (CIB). The developments in this organization illustrate well the CID's use of the latest scientific techniques, and thus its relative modernization and professionalism. However, this process was in part motivated by racist considerations. In 1916 the CIB comprised three departments, finger-prints, by far the largest of the three, as well as photographs, and drawings. In 1916 there was a staff of sixty, all of whom were initially English-speaking, spread over four provinces, and a small central staff in Pretoria. Lectures were often given by staff to policemen on how to improve the quality of the fingerprints sent to the CIB, and on the proper way of compiling criminal records. In 1916 the Inspector of the CIB still felt it necessary to urge on colleagues the need to recognize the importance of fingerprints in criminal investigation (Annual Report of the Commissioner of the SAP 1916: 78). It was a source of complaint that while police in urban areas used the CIB freely, police in more isolated areas seemed not to; the Inspector hoped that the CIB would become like the criminal records office at Scotland Yard was supposed to be: routinely used by all people in the force. By this time, however, the work of the CIB had become easier as a result of the Department of Justice imposing a standardized format for the compilation and presentation of criminal records across the SAP, prisons department, and the SAMR.

The main task of CIB staff, however, was that of identification via fingerprints. In 1916 71,722 prints were sent to them for identification,

92 per cent of which were of Black people; 66 per cent of the photographs recorded were of Black people. The Inspector reported that thirty-six cases were successfully tried solely on the basis of evidence supplied by the CIB. However, the use of such scientific evidence in court was not widely accepted at this time. Evidence by fingerprint experts was admissible by statutory law in the Transvaal and Orange Free State; in Natal fingerprints were accepted as prima-facie evidence provided it was read in court by the expert; but in the Cape it was not accepted on its own, needing other supporting evidence for a conviction. However, the 1917 Criminal Procedures and Evidence Act provided for fingerprints and photographs to be permissible as evidence. In addition, staff from the CIB could be called on to draw plans of crime scenes, sometimes making plasticine models. Plasticine was apparently more readily used in cases involving Blacks. The Inspector explained why in the Commissioner's 1916 Annual Report: 'plasticine plans are more easily taken in by the native mind' (Annual Report of the Commissioner of the SAP 1916: 80).

But identification was not restricted to criminal cases. All Black applicants for employment in the police were required to submit their fingerprints for routine identification to ensure they had no past criminal record. In 1916 13.2 per cent of Black applicants for the police were shown to have had previous convictions, which is indicative both of the poor quality of some of the applicants and the SAP's efforts to improve selection of Black policemen. A similar identification process was undertaken for Black applicants to the prison service. Private mines police checked on the recruits to mining on behalf of mine employers. So heavy was this use by employers of Black labour that the Inspector of the CIB complained, in the 1917 Annual Report of the Commissioner, of the burden placed on his staff. The number of prints sent to the CIB in 1917 had increased by a half over the previous year, leading the officer in charge of the mines police employed by Consolidated Goldfields to support the Inspector's demand that more staff be employed by the CIB. In 1919 the Inspector in charge of the CIB reported an increase of 171 per cent in the work done for the Chamber of Mines. Work for mine companies was estimated to take up a quarter of the time of CIB staff. Thus, although the expansion in the number of fingerprints sent to the CIB is explained in part by the increasing use of the technique in crime detection, and therefore of the increase in crime, it is also explained by its routine use in monitoring the Black population. In 1902, for example, 28,994 prints were sent for identification (at this time the technique was used only by the Natal Police). By 1919 the number had increased to 88,080.

The identification rate also increased over the years. Several factors explain the greater success in positive identification of criminals through their fingerprints. The CIB was becoming more efficient, the fingerprints sent them improved in quality, and the number of records on file had increased, permitting more people to be identified. The busiest district office was Transvaal, because the Rand was a centre both for crime and for employment. It was not the most successful in getting positive identification, the honour of which went to the CIB in Natal. This is partly the result of the larger number of files on record in Natal, which had been using fingerprints for a longer time, and the number of first offenders attracted to the business and employment hub of the Witwatersrand.

The CIB at this time was pioneering the use of fingerprints for identification, and in 1916 had staff seconded to the defence department in Windhoek and to police in Nairobi. During 1917, staff were also loaned to the Native Labour Bureau in German East Africa, now occupied by allied forces, to train local staff in fingerprint identification. From this time also, the CIB became involved in the identification of corpses; twenty-nine cases were referred to them in 1917, fourteen of which were successfully identified.

By 1918 lectures by CIB staff were made part of the training of all new recruits to the SAP, and in this year the department was instrumental in persuading senior management to publish a *Police Gazette*, three times a week, listing details of crimes and criminals. The obvious use of fingerprint identification in intelligence work was realized in 1919, when the Inspector recorded that the CIB was 'employed on confidential work in connection with political propaganda' (Annual Report of the Commissioner of the SAP 1919: 80). In 1922 the CIB was renamed, and became the SACB and absorbed into the centralized structure of the CID. By 1927 there was an expansion of 32 per cent in the number of prints sent to the SACB for identification compared to 1919, and the identification rate was 34.2 per cent. However, it was not until 1929 that the first Black policeman was employed in the SACB, although Afrikaners had been used since 1918.

The modernization of the SACB in this way illustrates the tension between civil and colonial police models within the SAP. At one level, it seems to represent the development of liberal policing, with an emphasis on detection of ordinary crime, the development of scientific evidence, and neutral service to the law. This was epitomized by the SACB deliberately modelling itself on the Metropolitan Police in London. However, these developments had a conscious racist and colonial element, in that they were also used to monitor the Black population in areas of life lying outside civil police work; and the state continued to use the police in this way despite complaints from the police that it was a burden to them. But the police were not simply being held back in their modernization by the state, for the professionalization of crime detection occurred simultaneously with the deployment of colonial-style policing in other areas of police work. The job of work done by the SAP in policing Blacks, and the brutality with which this was accomplished, pointed to an inability and unwillingness to dispense with colonial policing.

CRIME, RACE, AND POLITICS

Some of the SAP's job specification involved civil police work and the pursuit of ordinary crime. This ranged from tracing errant fathers who had failed to pay maintenance to wives and families in England (for cases on police files see: Conf/8/513; Conf/8/564), to searching for the notorious Foster gang.

During the period 1914 to 1926, crime increased in South Africa quite markedly. Dippenaar explains this as due to the high number of foreign criminals who fought on the British side during the Anglo-Boer War and who remained in South Africa (1988: 38). When caught, most of these were deported rather than imprisoned. However, the post-war economic depression also affected the crime rate, which is why the Commissioner's annual report always mentioned the unemployment rate in police districts. Considerable attention was given in the reports to the 'poor White problem', as it was becoming widely known. The expansion in mineral and gold diggings also increased criminal activity wherever deposits were found, requiring police to set up temporary stations in such areas until the deposits were worked out; mobile stations were also employed in times of epidemic and for stock theft. This was a recognition that levels of crime varied with local circumstances, leading the Commissioner in

1926 to note 'the growing importance of locality' (Annual Report of the Commissioner of the SAP 1926: 10).

This reasoning lay behind the formation of the Witwatersrand police district in 1921. But this reorganization did little to stem the increase in crime. Thus, the monthly average of crimes reported to the police in 1921 was 2,599, which rose to 4,323 in 1926 (Annual Report of the Commissioner of the SAP 1926: 4). Since some of these crimes involved attacks upon policemen, in 1926 Truter allowed members of the SAP to be armed with hand-guns when on beat duty, although this caused considerable public outcry among Whites. In his 1927 Annual Report Truter justified the decision on grounds that the guns were intended only for the policemen's self-defence; he failed to qualify this by remarking that this was with the exception of police dealings with Blacks. He also failed to note that those crimes where policemen were assaulted by members of the public in 1926 amounted to a paltry 0.7 per cent of all serious crimes reported that year. And while the Te Water Commission in the same year drew attention to the number of police deaths between 1920 and 1924, this was less than ten a year. Most occurred in incidents of major public disorder, such as the 1922 Rand strike, where over half of police deaths in this period occurred, and for which the police were already armed under emergency regulations. If one takes away the twenty-nine deaths of police officers which occurred in the Rand strike, the annual rate of policemen killed while on duty between 1920 and 1924 falls to four, or one death for every two and a half thousand members. Thus the grounds on which the SAP justified arming themselves while on routine beat duty were quite spurious. As a solution to rising crime, a display of superior force in this way was a typically colonial response, although one which policemen routinely advocate.

The police were mightily concerned by the soaring crime rate. From figures supplied by the Te Water Commission, it is possible to calculate that the number of 'serious crimes' reported to the police in 1924 had risen by 20 per cent from the previous year (Union of South Africa 1926: 87–9). The increase in the number of reported serious crimes between 1921 and 1926 was 66.3 per cent (Dippenaar 1988: 76). Serious crimes included sexual attacks, gold theft, and public violence. The most common crimes, however, were stock theft, burglary, motor and cycle theft, assault with intent, and fraud. Witwatersrand and the Transvaal were the two police districts with the highest crime rate, at 37.6 per cent of all serious crimes reported in 1924, although the crimes there were more urban, such as housebreaking, which was the most common crime on the Rand. The Te Water Commission indicated that while Witwatersrand had 8.3 per cent of South Africa's total population in 1924, it alone had 20.7 per cent of all crime, the highest in all police districts (Union of South Africa 1926: 89). This is indicative of how crime was linked both to urbanization and industrialization.

In addition, in 1924 there were also 417,925 'minor crimes', ranging from cruelty to animals to drunkenness. The increase in this type of crime, however, was much slower, at 6 per cent from the previous year (Union of South Africa 1926: 88). All of the administrative offences committed by Blacks came within the classification of minor crimes, such as labour and pass offences, offences under the Master and Servants Act, and for possession of kaffir beer and other liquor offences. These offences were peculiar to Blacks, in that they were measures to control the urbanization of Blacks and to regulate their behaviour when in towns, and the increase in these offences between 1923 and 1924 was nearly twice that for minor crimes as a whole. In fact, over a quarter of all minor crimes in 1924 were administrative offences by Blacks, and the bulk of these were committed in the Witwatersrand police district, since the Rand was the industrial and urban centre for Black South Africans: 44.5 per cent of all pass offences, 50 per cent of all offences for illegal possession of kaffir beer, 57 per cent of other liquor offences, and 62.7 per cent of all 'native labour offences' were reported in the Witwatersrand police district.

Like all official statistics, crime figures have limitations and are only gross approximations of the real state of crime in any society. Moreover, these figures refer only to reported cases rather than prosecutions, and some of them would remain unsolved or thrown out by the courts. In 1924 there were 420,170 prosecutions compared to 459,585 serious and minor crimes reported. Witwatersrand police district had the largest amount of unsolved crime at 24.4 per cent of all reported cases (Union of South Africa 1926: 89), showing it to be the busiest and least effective police district, although the two are no doubt related. None the less, for South Africa as a whole, the rate of successful prosecutions increased progressively in this period. The number of prosecutions per thousand of population was 42 in 1914, 47 in 1920, and 61 in 1926, representing a 45.2 per cent increase between 1914 and 1926, although the rise was more rapid after 1920 than before. This trend towards a general improvement in successful prosecutions can be a reflection of several factors. Crime was on the increase after the war so there were more offences to pursue successfully, courts may have increased their proportion of guilty verdicts, and the police may have increased their crime-clearance rate. But certainly some of the increase in the prosecution rate was down to improvements in police effectiveness.

Ordinary crime, however, was often the least of the SAP's worries. Public-order policing of industrial agitation, and ethnic and racial unrest, consumed much police effort and time. The dynamics of South Africa's racial and class politics always ensured it would. Thus, police files are replete with reports on various communist and socialist groups, meetings of Black groups and visiting speakers, such as Gandhi and Marcus Garvey, and reports on strikes and protests of several kinds. Policemen were often incognito in the audience and would report back when strikes or other protests were discussed; files even contain details of conversations overheard in bars and hotels (see, for example, Conf/6/610/18/1–2). This illustrates a high degree of police penetration into politics, and the sensitivity the state felt about labour and race relations. Most commentators describe this period of South Africa's history as involving a race and class war amongst its peoples and with the state (e.g. Lacey 1989: 29).

Race and class were closely intertwined. The government's view in the 1914 Rand strike was repeated again in 1922. As Prime Minister, Smuts spoke in parliament on 21 March 1922 about the Rand strike, and said: 'the fear that obsessed me above all things was that owing to the wanton provocation of the revolutionaries, there might be a wild, uncontrollable outbreak among the natives' (cited in Frederikse 1990: 7). This mind-set was absorbed by the police. The District Commandant of the East Rand wrote to his deputy commissioner on 4 March 1920 about 'native unrest' in his district:

As you are aware, the cause of this strike was purely industrial, due to increased cost of living, and not without real grievances by those concerned, which calls for full consideration as early as possible. If some steps are not taken it will be playing into the hands of native agitators and so-called National Congress, who will undoubtedly bring about another strike. (Conf/6/658/18/1)

One police response to this explosive mix of race and class politics was therefore relatively liberal, in that it sought to persuade the state to ensure that Blacks had no legitimate grievances in the labour market. In the above letter, the district commander went on to state that displays of force by the military in controlling Black crowds were politically unfortunate, and recommended that if mining houses were unable to increase wages, they should sell goods in mine shops only at cost price. Another police response, however, was typically colonial in its policing style, in that industrial strikes, and incidents of ethnic and race unrest, were policed with brutal and crude displays of force that were intended to persuade participants of the folly of further protest.

The 1922 Rand strike illustrates how ascendant the colonial style was within the SAP. On 9 January 1922 White mineworkers on the Rand went on strike because of the intention of mining companies to cut wages and abolish the colour bar as a way of saving costs. The strike quickly spread to other White workers on the Rand. Senior police officers had preliminary discussion with strike leaders, and relations between the police and strikers were initially very good (Attwell 1926: 169). As a precautionary measure the SAP moved nearly eight thousand men into the area, but the strike leaders gave senior officers the assurance that they would not interfere with the execution of police duty.

On the night of 18 January strikers took two policemen hostage, whence began an assault on the police in the hope of destroying their morale. Most of the strikers were poor Whites and Afrikaner urban migrants, who organized themselves on the same commando system Afrikaners used in the Anglo-Boer wars, and they hoped that the young Afrikaner policemen, from the same insular, rural background, would disaffect. A similar hope was evident in the 1914 Rand strike, and a similar result ensued: policemen got stuck into strikers without fear or favour. Martial law was declared by the government, and the strike was quickly and brutally crushed. The police used small arms as well as tanks and aircraft, from which bombs were dropped on civilians, leaving 153 dead and 534 injured. Twenty-nine policemen lost their lives, with another eighty-six injured. Among the dead were innocent civilians caught in the cross-fire, including children as young as 10 years of age. Eight people were shot by the police while under the protection of a white flag. Allegations were subsequently made that many strikers were murdered by the police in cold blood. Some of the English police clearly took the opportunity to vent their ethnic hostilities against Afrikaners. One later described the Afrikaner women who fought alongside men on the barricades as 'large Amazons'

(Attwell 1926: 182). However, Afrikaner policemen also never wavered, perhaps because of the violence policemen received at the hands of the strikers; the cache of arms retrieved from the strikers at the end was massive. The strike was used by strikers to act out their ethnic hostilities, as many attacked groups of innocent Blacks, as well as the many Black workers used by the mining companies as strike-breakers.

Afrikaner nationalists were appalled at police treatment of the strikers, although the military were also involved in suppressing the strike. In a speech in parliament after the 1914 attack on Afrikaner workers, General Hertzog, leader of the National Party, attacked what he described as the military autocracy of a supposedly civil government, which had robbed people of their freedom of speech, and their fundamental and constitutional rights; words that should have haunted the National Party in its subsequent breach of the same freedoms for Black South Africans. In 1922 he accused the government of engaging in *platskiet-politiek*, literally the politics of shooting down—a reliance on force and the gun. Although sounding strangely ironic given events after 1948, Hertzog had correctly summarized the way in which the state had used the police to crush opposition to it.

Partly in response to criticism of this kind, Smuts set up a commission of inquiry into police conduct during the strike. The familiar pattern of recommendation emerged. The commission described some of the police actions as deplorable, particularly in using bombs dropped from aeroplanes as a crowd-control technique, and the death of children killed in cross-fire. But it said that the use of force was never wanton or reckless (Union of South Africa 1922: 15), and that their discipline had been praiseworthy (p. 16). No blame could be attached to the police, and many stories of atrocities were 'largely exaggerated' (p. 35). In parliament the government supported the police. The Minister of Justice described the SAP as 'having made history, establishing a reputation and created a tradition which will be something for future members to live up to' (quoted in F. Cooper 1972–3: 20), something which was more true than he thought. He denied that the police were an arm of the state or that they acted partisanly: they were acting in a civil policing fashion to maintain law and order. Smuts also defended the SAP as a civil police force, which had acted impartially to carry out the law, simply doing their duty without political consideration (cited in ibid.). Subsequent members of the force have treated the episode differently. The SAP's version

of events in its review of SAP history used the rhetoric of the
communist threat to refer to the strikers, and made no mention of
civilian deaths, whereas policemen were described as being brutally
murdered (SAP 1986: 33). The SAP's official historian referred to
the deaths of civilians as 'the price paid by inquisitive onlookers who,
in the hope of experiencing something sensational, could not tear
themselves away from the scenes of violence' (Dippenaar 1988: 60).

It is interesting that the state felt the need to portray the SAP as a
civil police force rather than a paramilitary, colonial one. It was also
important to allay public fears and to emphasize that in police relations
with Whites at least, civil police notions such as public service, neutral
application of the law, and impartiality were the SAP's watchwords.
No such need was felt when police misconduct concerned the Black
population.

The political strategies of Afrikaner nationalism were based on a
fusion of their ethnic status as Afrikaners, demanding special treatment because of this heritage, and their subordinate class position as
poor Whites. Hertzog's strategy therefore involved advancement of the
Afrikaner *volk* and a policy of preferential employment for Afrikaners,
although Afrikaners tended to obtain work in poorer-paid and low-
status jobs, such as, ironically, the SAP. Smuts's South African Party,
which constituted the legitimate elected government, emphasized the
importance of forging a new identity among White South Africans as
a whole, which was not sufficiently Afrikaner for Hertzog's National
Party. The SAP was thus in the paradoxical position of being drawn
into conflict with Afrikaner nationalists on the side of the legitimately
elected government, while simultaneously benefiting in recruitment
from the policies of the nationalists. But it was precisely this paradox
which later made it easier for the SAP to adapt easily to the transition
to National Party rule in 1948, since the force had been thoroughly
Afrikanerized by then, even its officer class.

However, at this period the effort and time devoted by the SAP to
surveillance of Afrikaner nationalists was considerable, and the
English domination of police management ensured that the usual clash
of interest between rank-and-file members and their superiors in this
or any type of work would be overlaid with ethnic suspicions and
hostilities. Thus, some Afrikaner policemen on surveillance at political
meetings held by Afrikaner nationalists wrote reports which were not
unsympathetic. In one such meeting in Johannesburg on 20 December
1919, Sergeant Visser wrote of Afrikaners having bottles thrown at

them by a crowd waving sticks and Union Jacks. Mounted burghers were pulled off their horses, and horses stabbed: 'it is a wonder that the burghers remained so calm' (Conf/6/731/19). On the other hand, another Afrikaner policeman acted as an undercover informant in a plot by Afrikaner nationalists in 1918 to kill Botha and Smuts (Conf/6/288/15).

Making use of these divisions, Afrikaner nationalists complained of bias against them by the police, and the under-policing of nationalist political meetings, leaving them without protection from hostile crowds. However, after General Hertzog's meeting in Johannesburg on 20 November 1919, some Afrikaner policemen made sworn declarations that confirmed nationalist allegations. Sergeant van der Hoven reported the hostility vented against the nationalists by a British crowd, left unprotected by the police. Only then were nationalists compelled to defend themselves. 'As an Afrikaner', he wrote, 'this action hurted me to view this all, and to think that Afrikaners in their own country must be treated in this way' (Conf/6/731/19). Sergeants Joubert and van Wyk signed an oath declaring that a senior police officer, when witnessing the mayhem, gave the order for his men to disperse and have dinner (Conf/6/731/19).

Truter demanded an investigation into these damaging allegations, and asked for a report from senior officers in Johannesburg. The police response to these criticisms contained complaints of violent behaviour towards them by nationalists, some of whom were alleged to be drunk, and pointed to police restraint in face of provocation by the crowd. The Deputy Commissioner for the Johannesburg district described his men as possessing tact, courage, and attention to duty (Conf/6/731/19). The allegation that some constables in the SAP who were on duty at the meeting wore nationalist colours, was disputed by senior officers. But whether true or not, some Afrikaner policemen sympathized with the nationalists because of the unfair treatment they received from the police, if not also for other reasons. As a reflection of these wider political divisions within the broad constituency of the police, Hertzog's bodyguard contained several ex-policemen.

Part of the objection nationalists had towards the police was that they were not as hard on Blacks as the nationalists would like, leaving the moral and social boundaries between the races policed ineffectively and without rigour. Thus, reports of nationalist meetings now held in police files carry allegations made by speakers about the inability or unwillingness of the police to maintain the appropriate social and moral distance between the races, such as permitting Asian traders to compete with Whites (Conf/6/641/18). Ethnic hostilities within the police also bore on wider race differences, since some Afrikaner policemen no doubt supported Hertzog's more extreme policies on race. English-speaking policemen, however, sometimes adopted a more enlightened view of the rights and treatment of Black South Africans. Thus, the Inspector at Marshall Square police station in Johannesburg noted in his report of the violence at Hertzog's meeting, that he restrained a nationalist supporter when he hit a Black person, who the nationalist said had no right to stand with White people. The policeman's view was that no one had the 'right to hit a native' (Conf/6/731/19). Thus, in clashes between Afrikaners and Blacks, ethnic hostilities sometimes overruled racial ones, and individual policemen intervened on the side of Blacks, although in clashes between the police and Blacks, no such brake applied.

Black political activity was as closely monitored by the police as that of Afrikaner nationalists, and files are full of reports of meetings of the Native National Congress (NNC), later renamed as the African National Congress, as well as extracts from speeches, various documents and pamphlets, and newspaper clippings on Black politics. Black policemen would be used incognito, although sometimes the secret presence of these policemen would be uncovered after the fact, as a result of the wish of senior officers to bring cases of slander against the speaker for some remark about the police (e.g. Conf/6/658/18/1). When it was uncovered during the meeting, the Black policemen concerned were in threat of their lives. On one such occasion in Klipspruit location in 1919, the speaker from the NNC helped to dress the policeman as a woman in order to effect escape; in Vrededorp and Bulhoek, however, policemen ended up attacking or firing at the crowd (Conf/6/658/18). Quite a number of Black people in audiences were killed in this way. Just as there were some Afrikaner policemen with divided loyalties, so some Black policemen were sympathetic to Black protesters or political groupings. Sergeant Thema and constable Memaregane, from the Pietersburg district, were committed for trial in 1920 for conspiracy to aid and abet Black protesters and incitement to public violence. The charges against Memaregane were withdrawn, but Thema was eventually dismissed from the force (Conf/6/658/18/1). It was alleged that he was a member of the NNC, which he denied.

The period of the 1920s marks the first mass mobilization of the Black population (the books on Black politics in this period are legion;

for an overview of Black politics at this time see Feit 1967; Karis and
Carter 1972–7; Roux 1964; Walshe 1971). Although the NNC was
formed in 1912 as a coalition of several political associations in the
separate provinces to parallel the unification of 1910, it only became
effective in mobilizing amongst Blacks after the First World War.
Before that it directed its attention very much towards Whites, in the
hope of persuading them to give greater consideration to the rights
and freedoms of Black South Africans. Various other political groupings emerged at this time as well, such as the Israelites, and Blacks
were successfully mobilized as workers via several trade unions and
socialist groups, such as the Constitutional Socialist League and the
Industrial and Commercial Workers' Union (the books on the early
trade union movement are also legion; for an overview see R. Davies
1979; M. du Toit 1976; Lewis 1984; Luckhardt and Wall 1980;
Yudelman 1983). As Blacks mobilized politically, and became confident and articulate, a critique of the SAP emerged, which was
expounded at every platform. From the beginning it was realized by
Black activists that their confrontation with the state placed them in
conflict with the police, and that in this battle the SAP acted as the
brutal arm of the government. This critique therefore had two strands.
First, policing was seen as a political activity to keep Blacks subservient, and, secondly, it was a partisan activity, in which Blacks were
treated as second-class citizens, devoid of the rights, protections,
and service which Whites expected from the police. Allegations of
brutality, partisanship, and injustice at the hands of the police, even
of sexual immorality by the police against Black women, were made
at most political meetings.

The state-sponsored body designed to articulate the opinions of
Black people at government level, the Native Affairs Commission,
passed no comment on the poor relations between the police and
Blacks, although they came to in a later period. At this time, they
simply expressed the government's fear of 'the Black peril'. In their
1921 Report, for example, they warned that 'the danger of the half-
educated agitator among a wholly uneducated constituency needs no
multiplication of words to be understood' (Annual Report of the
Native Affairs Commission 1921: 6). Urban Blacks were a greater
peril: 'a redundant Black population in a municipal area is a source of
greatest peril. It is this class from which the professional agitator,
liquor seller, the prostitute, and other undesirables spring' (p. 7).
The pass laws were thus a means of dealing with crime, at least

in government thinking. This is a view which dominated early criminology in South Africa, where crime was linked to the requirement for racial segregation (van Zyl Smit 1990: 5), and also conditioned the enthusiasm with which the police implemented the pass laws.

But the police were sensitive to the allegations of brutality that were made. Policemen reported in detail on the meetings at which allegations were made, kept newspaper clippings which reported them, and even compromised the identity of undercover policemen by bringing cases of slander against speakers who mouthed them. All the allegations were strenuously denied, sometimes after police investigation into the incidents referred to or government commissions of inquiry. The police and the government obviously felt it important to suggest there was a semblance of civil policing in the SAP's relations with Blacks, even where police methods were blatantly colonial in style. Thus, as Truter presented it in his 1920 Annual Report, the problem between the SAP and Blacks was simply that 'natives are antagonistic to the maintenance of law and order' (Annual Report of the Commissioner of the SAP 1920: 10). It was not that the police upheld a law that was unfair or unjust to Blacks, nor that the police defended a social order that placed Blacks in a subordinate position; they just lacked the capacity or intelligence to meet acceptable standards of law and order.

A consequence of this view was that the police never saw the brutality of their tactics in suppressing Black political and labour protests as incompatible with the civil police tradition; it was a matter of maintaining a just system of law and order. Thus, they saw no contradiction between crude force in suppressing Blacks and their rhetoric on police modernization and professionalism. Therefore, Truter could describe the SAP as a civil and professional police force, while simultaneously his men killed thousands in the suppression of Black unrest. Former policemen, recounting their experiences in the force at this time, report without hesitation or compunction of 'natives [meeting] with short shrift and a swift bullet' (Attwell 1926: 151). In disturbances in Port Elizabeth in 1920, twenty-five Black protesters were killed and another sixty-six injured when police opened fire. In 1920 in Bulhoek, where a crowd of Black people calling themselves Israelites gathered, Truter himself led a force of 800 policemen armed with machine-guns and rapid-firing rifles. Two-hundred members of the crowd were shot dead. In action against the Bondelzwarts tribe in Namibia in 1922, the SAP mounted machine-guns on aeroplanes and fired on the crowd without warning or call for them to surrender. A government commission of inquiry into the events reported that the police regularly chained and flogged tribesmen, assaulted the women, and persecuted them indiscriminately (Union of South Africa 1923: para. 14). The majority view of the commission was that given the deterioration in relations between the police and the Bondelzwarts, civil rather than police personnel should have dealt with the problem; no comment was passed on the unreasonableness of the force used by the police. A minority report by General Lemmer disputed all the findings, referred to the Bondelzwarts as insolent, lazy, and thievish, and said that 'adequate force' was necessary to protect Whites (ibid.: para. 68(a)).

CONCLUSION

There was clearly tension within the police between the colonial and civil police traditions, reflecting broader tension in police–state relations at the time. In its own perception, the SAP was modernizing into a civil police force, but the government's requirement that it police race relations ensured that it remained firmly colonial in role and conduct, especially in its treatment of Blacks. This tension within the police showed itself in many levels beyond the contrast in police treatment of Blacks and Whites (with the exception of Afrikaner nationalists). In recruitment, for example, many men were still being attracted to the job because of the excitement provided by its paramilitary trappings. Thus, in his 1920 Annual Report Truter noted the preference of many recruits for mounted duty and his difficulty in attracting sufficient men to entertain foot patrol. But in the very same report, Truter revealed plans to improve the educational standards required of recruits, and his hope to attract the 'more educated type of men' (Annual Report of the Commissioner of the SAP 1920: 3).

Police organization was another area where the tension between two different models of policing gave rise to conflict. At the time of the 1918 police strike, Deputy Commissioner Gray, in charge of Western Cape police district, argued that the London Metropolitan Police should be the model for the SAP. The feature of the British system which he admired so much was decentralization, the anathema to Truter's strategy. In his evidence to the Commission of Inquiry on the strike he said:

My remedy is decentralization. You cannot run an enormous force in a highly centralized way. The force must be decentralized so that the local head can get in touch with the minister . . . I think the heads should always be in a position to deal with ministers in important matters. The Union force is too much centralized. There are different people to handle, and different local conditions in each province . . . You cannot run a police force on fixed lines in a large country like this where local conditions are so different. The more you decentralize the more efficiency you will get. (Union of South Africa 1918*a*: 106–9)

As Gray saw it, Truter's access to the political head of the police seemed as much of a problem with centralization as its effect on obscuring locality. And later in his evidence Gray complained about the degree of personal control Truter had accumulated under the highly centralized structure of the SAP (p. 109).

Training also saw tension between the two models. In his evidence to the Commission of Inquiry on the police strike, for example, Truter bemoaned the loss of the ex-soldiers in the force, with their military traditions and experience gained during the Anglo-Boer War (p. 87). A great deal of training involved physical exercise and military drill. At the same time, Mr M. C. Briers, schoolmaster at the training depot, complained to the same commission of inquiry that the emphasis was not enough on the skills of civil police work.

I told the commandant that we were making 'Tommies' of the men. It should not be the chief point to be able to drill. They should be better educated to assist them in studying the criminal laws . . . The men get too much military training. The reason is the men in charge are men with military experience . . . They get too much drill and too little law. Education would be better than drill. It is not essential to a policeman to be able to drill . . . It is not always necessary to give men military training in order to give them discipline . . . There is a feeling that the men want to be policemen and do not want so much of a military force.   (pp. 164–6)

Within months of this remark the number of hours spent on scholastic subjects in training doubled to four hours a day, and within two years Truter was demanding the replacement of the older, relatively more uneducated policemen, by younger, 'more educated types'. But the emphasis on drill, military training, arms, and musketry never diminished in this period. The first refresher training course for officers in 1927 entirely entailed military drill and physical fitness (F. Cooper 1972–3: 33).

If Truter was moving towards a civil police model, as he himself proclaimed, he was not doing so fast enough for some of his senior officers. Yet Truter was vociferous in his insistence on one feature of the civil policing model, that of his own professional autonomy to determine the organization's priorities and duties. His complaint against the extraneous duties which the state imposed on the SAP were continually expressed in the annual reports and at government commissions of inquiry into the police. In 1920 he estimated in his annual report of that year that 458 men were effectively lost to the force because of their work for other government departments; in 1926 he gave evidence to the Te Water Commission that seventy-eight different types of duty were performed for seventeen different government departments. This meant that 517 men were effectively lost to the police. Such men checked, for example, the branding of cattle, acted as plague guards, checked on bioscope films, and escorted lepers and the insane. This also blurred the distinction between police work and civil and judicial administration, which Truter wanted to enforce as a positive feature of the civil police tradition. As it was, the government used the police as its administrative arm, so policemen collected taxes, issued native passes, acted as prosecutors and bailiffs, dispensed medication, did inoculations, and gathered agricultural statistics and meteorological information, among many other things. They also collected evidence for the Department of Lands on the state of 'poor burghers', suffering on the farms as a result of the post-war agricultural depression. This encompassing role explains why annual reports by the Commissioner contained details on trends in such things as unemployment, health and disease, and the demand for labour.

The Te Water Commission, set up in 1925 to review the organization of the SAP and to suggest ways of cutting police expenditure, recommended that these extraneous duties be abolished. This was in small part because it would achieve a saving of £155,000 alone on the salaries of men otherwise lost to normal police duty. But the Te Water Commission also strongly favoured the civil police model, and the ending of extraneous duties was a powerful push towards the SAP's professional and organizational autonomy from the state. With two English-speaking MPs and a Johannesburg magistrate as its sole members, the commission was inevitably biased towards creating a modern, effective, and professional police service. Its support for the civil police model was reflected in other recommendations, such as the abolition of military titles to designate police ranks, the establishment of training for Black policemen, promotion only from the ranks, the abolition of some layers of administration in order to decentralize the management, and the establishment of an inspectorate, based in headquarters, to act as a watch-body over the police, albeit one not independent of them.

In rejecting all these recommendations, the state was effectively admitting its need for the colonial model of policing. The police were too essential to its project of internal colonialism to be made completely autonomous, and in this way the state missed an opportunity to reform the police along the lines of a liberal and civil police force. As this project developed up to the Second World War, the state's need for a colonial-style police force increased, and another subsequent opportunity for police reform between 1927 and 1945 was also lost. The government's view of police–state relations thus prohibited police reform at this time and dampened any enthusiasm for it within the police themselves.

3

Internal and External War
1927–1945

Considerable developments occurred in the state's policy of internal colonialism during the years covered by this chapter, and while not as critical as the period after 1948 in this respect, regulations on the Black population intensified and their rights were severely curtailed. It was in this period that the primary task of policing in South Africa narrowed to be control of Blacks. However, various changes in the material circumstances of the Black population were beginning to take place at this time, which fostered the militancy of later periods. What is more, changes occurred in White politics in this period which were instrumental to the 1948 election victory of the National Party on a policy of apartheid, which became the fullest expression of the state's policy of internal colonialism. These events provide background to developments in policing between 1927 and 1945, and to the role of the police in regulating race relations during this and later periods, and will be outlined in this introduction.

The actions of the police in the Bulhoek massacre, in putting down the Rand revolt in 1922, and the Bondelzwart rebellion of the same year, discussed in Chapter 2, contributed in no small way to General Smuts's defeat in the 1924 general election, which brought Hertzog to power. The policies of the new government towards race were expressed simply in a speech by Hertzog to his constituents in November 1925.

The time has arrived for a definite native policy, a policy which will remove all doubt from the native mind about the position which he will hold in society . . . He will have to be told in the most unequivocal language that the European is fully determined that South Africa shall be governed by the white man, and the white man will not tolerate any attempt to deprive him of that task. (quoted in Ashforth 1990: 69)

Hertzog saw the differences between the races in terms of 'civilization'; a notion which typically underlay colonial expansion into Africa in the nineteenth century, as well as the policing of the 'lower orders' and 'dangerous classes' in industrial Britain in the 1800s (see Anderson and Killingray 1991*b*: 10). In order to reinforce this alleged barbarity, the word 'native' was used in government discourse to describe Africans rather than the more familiar word 'Bantu' or the derogatory term 'kaffir' (Ashforth 1990: 76; also see Dubow 1987). Now as His Majesty's High Commissioner in South Africa, Sir Herbert Stanley wrote to Lord Selbourne in London about Hertzog's racial views, referring, in a letter dated 15 August 1934, to 'poor natives', left 'bewildered' and 'afraid' by Hertzog's 'outbursts'. He reported the view that natives feared that South Africa would become a republic, stating that they wished to remain linked to the Crown (MSS Afr. s. 1250).

The new government under Hertzog addressed racial issues on two levels: labour policies which protected Whites, and especially Afrikaners, which the government actually called policies of 'civilized labour'; and policies of segregation which restricted the material, social, and political development of Blacks. Mindful of the 1922 industrial agitation by Whites on the Rand, the pact government quickly passed legislation which favoured unskilled, poor Whites, who were none the less considered 'civilized workers'. The Industrial Conciliation Act in 1924 provided for the recognition and registration of trade unions, and gave a key role to White workers in determining wages for Black workers. This was reinforced in the Wages Act of 1925, which declared that Whites should be given pay 'at a level which the European employee can maintain his standard of living'. The Mines and Works Act in 1926 gave further legal enactment to job reservation, or the 'colour bar', which provided for the employment of a minimum ratio of White workers. Job reservation was extended to the private sector of the economy by means of the 1925 Customs Tariff Act, which made state protection of local industries conditional on 'satisfactory labour conditions', which included the employment of a 'reasonable proportion of civilized workers'. Employment in the public sector at this time favoured Afrikaners, who were increasingly absorbed into state employment. In the railways, for example, the proportion of unskilled White workers rose from 9.5 per cent in 1924 to 39.3 per cent in 1933, while that of Africans fell from 75 per cent to 48.9 per cent (Adam and Giliomee 1979: 151). Iscor, the big state-owned iron and steel corporation, was founded in 1928 and became a large employer of 'civilized labour'. All this effectively ended labour unrest amongst White workers.

The other strand of government policy on race was complete segregation for Africans, with a more modified form adopted for Coloureds and Indians. Hertzog considered Coloureds as in many respects 'closer to whites [differing] fundamentally from Africans, and should be included among whites industrially, economically and politically' (cited in Lipton 1985: 17). Thus, for example, they were kept on the common voters roll in the Cape in 1936 when Africans were removed, although this proved to be only a temporary reprieve. Social segregation was secured by such measures as the 1927 Immorality Act, which prohibited sexual relations between Africans and Whites, the 1923 Urban Areas Act, which confined Africans to segregated townships or locations, and the 1936 Land Act, based on the earlier 1913 Land Act, which reserved only 14 per cent of the land area of the country for Africans, outside which they could not own land, or in most cases even rent it. Black businessmen were hindered by restrictions on their right to own or lease business premises, and by a licensing system which limited their opportunities for trade even in the African reserves and segregated townships. The 1922 Stallard Commission laid down that Africans should only be in towns to 'minister to the needs of the white man and should depart therefrom when he ceases to minister', and the pass laws were continually refined in this period in order to regulate the influx of African labour into 'White areas', and allocate labour between sectors and regions. Government policy discouraged African families from moving to the towns, and promoted the mining industry's system of housing migrant workers in all-male compounds while their families remained in the reserves.

These policies proved attractive to the electorate, virtually all of whom were White, and the National Party was returned with an overall majority in the 1929 election. The more liberal race policies of Smuts's South African Party failed to resonate with most Whites, although as Rich points out (1984), the ideology of segregation still dominated all liberal discourse on race at this time. The election was followed by the world economic depression, though its effects in South Africa were to some extent cushioned by the country's gold reserves. However, South Africa's agricultural exports were badly affected by the depression. A coalition government was formed with Hertzog as

Prime Minister and Smuts as deputy. Shortly afterwards their respective parties merged to form the United Party. The pro-British wing of Smuts's party objected and formed the Dominion Party, under the leadership of Colonel Stallard, who had earlier chaired the 1922 commission which advocated the development of segregated townships for Africans. The pro-Afrikaner nationalist wing of Hertzog's kept the original National Party alive, under the leadership of Dr Malan.

However, while Afrikaner nationalists anticipated a dissolution of Hertzog's strident protectionist policies in favour of Whites, and Afrikaners in particular, the legislative programme of the fusion government continued the same thrust. The state attempted to solve the poor White problem by expanding the public sector of the economy on the lines of Keynesian interventionism, what O'Meara calls in a South African context 'volkskapitalisme' (1983; on the link between Afrikaner nationalism and economic development for Afrikaners also see Dunbar Moodie 1975). The South African Broadcasting Corporation and South African Airways were established in this period, and the National Roads Act of 1935 initiated a massive public works programme in road-building. Above all, the state came to the aid of the depressed agricultural sector, which was dominated by small Afrikaner farmers. Between the financial years 1927/8 and 1938/9, for example, expenditure on agriculture and irrigation increased by 400 per cent, the most rapid increase of all the categories of the state budget (Adam and Giliomee 1979: 152). Control boards were established which ensured the orderly marketing of agricultural products and stable prices.

The fusion government also aided farmers by legislation which tightened their control over the African labour force, and one important function of the pass laws was to keep a sufficient supply of African farm-hands on White farms. Thus, the 1937 Native Laws Amendment Act empowered the minister to remove Africans from an urban area if they were deemed to be surplus to the reasonable labour requirements of the area; and while such a surplus existed, the government could impose a total ban on further entry into the area by Africans (Posel 1991: 43).

However, the state could do little to prevent Black urbanization. The Native Economic Commission estimated at the beginning of the 1930s that in the previous decade the rate of African urbanization alone had 'considerably exceeded' that of Europeans (Ashforth 1990:

82). In 1904, while only 10 per cent of all Africans were urban-based, this none the less amounted to 29 per cent of the total urban population because Whites were still themselves predominantly rural-based. By 1936 the level of African urbanization had reached 18.5 per cent of the African population, representing 39 per cent of the total urban population in South Africa (Waters 1979: 8; also see Posel 1991: 24). Throughout the 1920s and 1930s, Hertzog's government tried to stem this flow by increasingly stringent controls on African migration to the towns and on the acquisition of urban residential rights (see R. Davenport 1968 for a review of this legislation; and Posel 1991 for an account of the importance of influx control to Afrikaner governments at this time). But the rapid growth of secondary industry led to an irreversible growth in the demand for labour and thus to Black urbanization, industrialization, and proletarianization, which in themselves provided a material foundation to the growth of the trade union movement and Black militancy in the 1940s and 1950s. Although the extent of unionization and militancy in the 1930s is often exaggerated, the latter half of the 1930s saw the beginnings of a modern, industrial Black working class (R. Fine 1990: 5). Thus, the number of Africans working in the industrial sector rose by 194 per cent from 1934 to 1946.

Expanding avenues for employment in manufacturing proved a spur to urbanization. During the ten-year period from 1936, there was an increase of 57 per cent in the number of Africans living in urban areas, outstripping in growth the White urban population, representing 23 per cent of all African people in 1946. The number of African women moving to the towns increased by 85.7 per cent during this period, thereby establishing a basis for settled family life in the towns. Simkins estimates that between 1936 and 1946, the proportion of Africans in the metropolitan areas living in family circumstances increased to 38 per cent (1983: 22). The other spur was rural impoverishment. Successive government commissions and committees documented appalling conditions in the reserves arising from severe land shortage, such as malnutrition, poverty, overstocking, and denuding of the land. So apart from a small prosperous peasantry, rural families depended on remittances from family members who had moved to the towns, legally or illegally (Posel 1991: 27–8). The size of the African peasantry fell by over a half between 1936 and 1946, to represent 17.5 per cent of the economically active African population in 1946 (worked out from figures supplied in R. Fine 1990: 13–15).

Despite an expanding economy towards the end of the 1930s, the huge gap in wealth between Black and White remained; as did that between English-speakers and Afrikaners. In 1939 there were still 298,000 White persons reported to be living in 'terrible poverty', all with monthly incomes below the amount considered to be the minimum for Whites to maintain health (Adam and Giliomee 1979: 154). Afrikaners in the cities generally occupied the low-status jobs; only 27.5 per cent were in white-collar occupations in 1936. Thus, it was estimated that the average annual per capita income for Afrikaans-speakers in 1936 was £86, compared to £142 for Whites as a whole (Adam and Giliomee 1979: 154). Afrikaner nationalism therefore provided a potent force of opposition to the fusion government, which resurfaced towards the end of the decade, requiring the police to shift attention again to militant Afrikaner nationalists. In the 1938 general election the National Party under Malan increased its number of MPs to twenty-seven, becoming the Official Parliamentary Opposition. The upsurge in Afrikaner nationalism was also reflected outside politics. The Afrikaner Broederbond and the Federation of Afrikaner Cultural Associations organized the first Afrikaner Peoples' Economic Congress in 1939, from which followed the establishment of the *Reddingsdaadbond* fund, designed as a poor relief scheme to rescue impoverished Afrikaners, although the fund was eventually used mostly to facilitate Afrikaner business and investment. The cultural organization known as Ossewabrandwag (OB) was formed by nationalists in 1938 to commemorate the centenary of the voortrekker victory at Blood River.

By the end of the 1930s, therefore, the fusion government was under serious threat from two sides. Many Black South Africans were having their material circumstances transformed and were becoming more militant, and Afrikaner nationalism was becoming more successful politically, and culturally strident. These twin pressures put the United Party government under strain, which was reflected in several crises and incidents of unrest. Some of these concerned the government's relations with Britain. The looming conflict in Europe gave the imperial connection special resonance, and when war broke out in 1939, the question of South Africa's neutrality finally led to the collapse of the fusion government.

Participation in the war was a dividing factor of great moment for Afrikaners. Hertzog and Malan wanted the country to remain neutral, while Smuts wished South Africa to join the war. Hertzog narrowly lost a parliamentary vote on the issue, and Smuts returned as Prime Minister after fifteen years. Malan and Hertzog joined forces to form the Herenigde Nasionale Party (Reunited National Party). Most Afrikaners were united against the war, but divided on the attitude that should be adopted towards Nazi Germany. Malan had an indifferent attitude towards the pro-Nazi brand of Afrikaner nationalism, and was concerned about their anti-constitutionalism. Divisions like this weakened Afrikaner opposition to Smuts, and he easily won the general election in 1943 against a divided opposition, leaving him in power until 1948.

These events formed the backdrop to developments in policing in this period. As we shall see, on the one hand, the police were greatly affected by these events, but, conversely, they took an active part in some of them, and not always on behalf of the legitimately elected government. First, however, it is necessary to document developments in the organization and structure of policing during this period.

ORGANIZATIONAL DEVELOPMENTS

The last regiment of the SAMR was disbanded in 1926, so the SAP moved nearer in 1927 to its goal of being the national police force. Also in 1927 the borough police of Pietermaritzburg were incorporated in the SAP. It took another nine years for the Durban Borough Police to be absorbed into the SAP, and the mines and railways police existed separate from them. So Truter, who retired in 1928, never quite saw his strategy realized.

By 1936 Durban City Council were finding it difficult to afford their own municipal police. The administration of the 1928 Liquor Act fell entirely upon the council, while revenue arising from it went to the government. The government withdrew the Water Police from the docks, with the burden falling to the municipal police. Above all, however, the borough police became responsible for the investigation and prosecution of all non-serious crime, defined as goods stolen to a value less than £20. This was an increased financial burden, so that the municipal police often exaggerated the value of the stolen goods in order for the case to be passed on to the SAP (Dippenaar 1988: 85). The council sent a deputation to the Minister of Justice asking for a return to the pre-1930 situation, where the SAP did the expensive police work. The Minister refused, insisting that the borough police be absorbed into the SAP; the council reluctantly agreed, and complained at being railroaded (see Department of Justice 1936). On 1 April 1936, twenty-three years to the day after the SAP was formed, 120 White and 130 Black police from the Durban force were transferred to the SAP, making it a national force, save for policing mines, and railways and harbours.

Senior management in the SAP had always opposed the idea of a separate railways police, and the new Commissioner, Lt.-Col. de Villiers, persisted with the objection and sought to realize his predecessor's goal for the SAP to be the nation's sole police force. He achieved this from 1933 onwards, but not by having the railways police absorbed into the SAP, but reorganized into being a surrogate of the SAP. In 1933 the Railways and Harbours Service reorganized its police to increase the co-ordination and liaison with the SAP. Colonel Cilliers, Deputy Commissioner of the CID, was transferred from the SAP to be chief of the South African Railways and Harbour Police (SARHP) and to effect the reorganization. The reorganization amounted to the introduction of SAP practices and methods, even down to the use of military titles to designate the ranks. Stricter discipline was imposed, based on the SAP's regulations. The chief of the railways police was later involved in a scandal when found to have put pressure on officers adjudicating in disciplinary cases against members of the SARHP to convict them and to impose stricter punishments. A training school was established, based on the curriculum operating in the SAP's training depots. Thus, the emphasis was upon military skills. Thus, education in law took three-quarters of an hour per day, while drill, musketry, and physical education took seven, despite the fact that the SARHP were not subject to military duty under the 1912 Police Act. Pay was less for the railways police, so there was greater difficulty in attracting staff than in the SAP; and the latter's manpower shortages were always severe. Pay could not be increased without knock-on effects for all those in the employ of the Railways and Harbours Service, although bilingualism did not become official policy in the SARHP until 1935, much later than in the SAP, which ensured that it was a greater attraction to unilingual speakers (mostly Afrikaners).

The reorganization did not work well. The SARHP had become almost a sub-department of the SAP, when only a quarter of the time of policemen in the SARHP was spent on police work, the rest being devoted to the protection of the interests and property of the Railways and Harbours Service. The imposition of SAP discipline was thus thought inappropriate by members of the SARHP. Senior officers also resented the arrival of ex-officers from the SAP, and allegations were made that they acted nepotistically, favouring colleagues who had transferred with them from the SAP. But most objection was raised against the militarization of the SARHP. To a civil organization designed mainly to safeguard commercial concerns, the lessons of the parade-ground seemed of limited use. The 1937 Lansdown Commission of Inquiry into the Police (Union of South Africa 1937a) endorsed this view, and recommended the abolition of military titles. It established an important principle: 'For the preservation of the Union's traditional system of justice, the judicial rather than the militaristic must be the prevailing spirit of its police force' (p. 98). The implications of this principle for the SAP will be addressed shortly; it is worth noting here that the Commission was commenting critically in 1937 on what was by then the SAP's prolonged failure to shed its colonial heritage. If anything, this was intensified under de Villiers's command, who fashioned the SAP in such a way that it functioned as a military model for the SARHP.

Isaac Pierre de Villiers came from a well-known Cape family descended from the French Huguenots, a community that had originally migrated to South Africa just after the Dutch and had become fully integrated with them to form the Afrikaner community. De Villiers had a very distinguished record of service in the First World War, and was a practising attorney in Cape Town when, in January 1928, he was surprisingly made a deputy commissioner at headquarters and immediately given the title of lieutenant-colonel. When Truter retired in November of that year de Villiers assumed the position of chief commissioner, with the rank of colonel. Although the 1926 Te Water Commission had insisted that all appointments be from within the ranks, it had exempted the post of chief commissioner on the grounds that it was a government appointment. And in 1928 the government did indeed decide to make its own appointment; and, again, it was given to someone from outside, lacking in knowledge and experience of policing. Hertzog, in fact, had made a political appointment, placing an Afrikaner in charge, although admittedly one from the wealthy Cape liberal tradition of French Huguenots. De Villiers's purpose was to strengthen central control over the police, impose stricter, military-style discipline, and Afrikanerize the officer class.

The new Commissioner was a ruthless disciplinarian, but it was military discipline that was imposed, which explains his nicknames among the men of Mussolini and the Roman Centurion (F. Cooper 1972: 13). Training was militarized and made more physically arduous. On one occasion there was a mutiny among recruits in the training depot because of its transformation into a military training camp. Dissatisfaction was not restricted to recruits. De Villiers believed that his officer corps needed rejuvenation; physical training was introduced for them in refresher courses, and appointments to senior posts were made from the defence force, much to the annoyance of senior policemen. Long-standing police officers resigned, among them Lt.-Col. Gray, who was head of the CID and in earlier commissions of inquiry on the police had expressed his preference for the liberal model of a decentralized, civil police. He reorganized the CID along the lines of Scotland Yard and introduced a decentralized command structure. De Villiers later said in the SAP's magazine, *Nongqai*, that the CID was disorderly and disorganized; Gray was replaced by an Afrikaner, who eventually went to the SARHP to reorganize it along the military lines of the SAP. On first assuming command de Villiers noted that only three senior officers were Afrikaans-speakers, himself included. He set about changing that by means of appointment of Afrikaners from the army, and by accelerated promotion of Afrikaners from within police ranks. Thus, by 1938 the Public Service List indicated that the chief commissioner was Afrikaans-speaking, as were three deputy commissioners, two chief inspectors, twenty-eight inspectors (out of fifty-two), and thirty-nine sub-inspectors (out of seventy). This coincided in 1938 with an instruction that Afrikaans be used jointly with English as the business language of the force; de Villiers himself spoke Afrikaans to his subordinates (Dippenaar 1988: 88). The use of mother tongue in official communications began with de Villiers not, as Seegars claims, with Commissioner Rademeyer in 1954, when more extreme Afrikaner nationalists were in power (1989: 7). Hertzog also permitted de Villiers to restore, within his first months of office, the pay cut that had been imposed on the police as a post-war economy measure.

Thus, it was now the English-speaking press which began a campaign to highlight problems within the SAP. Within two years of de Villiers's appointment, discontent was widespread, and former members wrote letters, pamphlets, and newspaper articles identifying the problems within the police with 'excessive militarism', and a lack of respect for the largely English-speaking officer class. One correspondent, writing to the *Natal Mercury* on 26 November 1930, complained that non-commissioned officers and rankers were writing directly to head office and the Minister of Justice about their officers, thus creating 'a rule of terror; spying is the order of the day throughout the force'.

On first taking office, de Villiers undertook an extended tour of police forces in Europe, including rural constabularies in England, but it was clearly the continental example of centralized and militarized policing which impressed him most. The modernization of the police under de Villiers therefore occurred within a framework of centralization and militarization, which both limited the extent of the process and determined its character. Thus, de Villiers tightened organizational control within the police by various managerial innovations. For example, in 1930 the Commissioner introduced one of the recommendations made by the Te Water Commission four years earlier, for the introduction of an Inspectorate at Headquarters to serve, as Dippenaar puts it, as de Villiers's 'eyes and ears' (1988: 101). Afrikaners were appointed to run it, and regular station inspections were carried out by the Inspectorate. It was also to act as the Commissioner's way of policing the police, being given the responsibility to investigate any unfavourable report which came to his notice. Another purpose of the Inspectorate was to ensure the co-ordination and standardization of police activities throughout the country, thus subverting the regular meetings of the divisional commanders, which were later abandoned.

The military-style discipline did not lead to an increase in the number of dismissals from the SAP for misconduct, as might have been expected. In 1929 there were 71 dismissals of White policemen, representing 1 per cent of the White manpower, compared with 170 in 1919, which was 3.2 per cent of White manpower. The figures for Black policemen in 1929 were 174 compared with 227 in 1919, representing a drop in the proportion dismissed from 9.3 per cent to 4.4 per cent. Clearly, de Villiers was satisfied with the conduct of the men in the ranks, as he admitted in his 1930 Annual Report; it was primarily the English-speaking officer class that he wished to rejuvenate. Within the ranks, many of the minor infringements that had led to men being dismissed in the past were either no longer committed or were no longer considered serious enough for dismissal. Thus, dismissals were increasingly for the more serious offences, such as conviction by the courts, drunkenness, or misconduct; the proportion of dismissals represented by these offences increased from 43.5 per cent for Whites in 1919 to 78.8 per cent in 1929, and 27.7 per cent for Black policemen in 1919 to 92.5 per cent in 1929. Among the serious offences committed at this time was a notorious case of police corruption and bribery in applying the liquor laws (see Bennett 1959); a similar allegation was made against former men from the SAP who had been transferred to the SARHP.

However, although dismissals were lower than in previous years, the renewed military ethos initiated by de Villiers led to many disciplinary offences of a less serious nature, for which offenders were not dismissed but reprimanded in other ways, such as by transfer. Complaining about the high number of minor disciplinary infringements, the Lansdown Commission blamed this on the 'excessive predominance of the militaristic spirit among zealous younger officers' (Union of South Africa 1937*a*: 81). Professionalization of a sort therefore occurred in the police at this time, but in ways which prevented the modernization of the SAP along the lines of the liberal model of civil policing; de Villiers's aim was to make the SAP more efficient as a paramilitary, colonial-style force (for an example of how professionalization amongst the pre-independence Indian police was dictated by the continued colonial task of the force see Robb 1991: 146).

The strict military discipline in the SAP eventually led to many resignations from the police. In 1929, for example, wastage increased 8.6 per cent from the previous year, and in 1930 was up by 14.7 per cent from 1927. But while the number of new recruits always exceeded the wastage, save for the years 1930 and 1939, the greater problem was in finding suitable applicants. With wastage high, dismissals from the force for misconduct were problematic. Over time, the proportion of wastage that was due to dismissal fell considerably as dismissals decreased in number. In 1927 the proportion was 15.4 per cent among White policemen and 32.1 per cent for Black, falling to 14.1 per cent and 18.3 per cent respectively in 1929, and 3.3 per cent and 4.8 per cent respectively in 1945. Manpower shortage might well have thwarted the thrust of the disciplinary ethos, or at least forced the management to treat many acts of misconduct in a less serious fashion.

Trends in manpower for the period are presented in Table 3.1. Some points are worth highlighting. Overall there was a small but steady increase in actual membership, except for a period in the early

TABLE 3.1 *Trends in manpower, 1927–1945*

Year	Authorized manpower	Actual manpower	% change*	% Black*	Ratio of police per 1,000 population†
1927	10,401	10,522	—	37.9	1.35
1928	10,511	10,643	+1.1	—	1.33
1929	10,602	10,544	−0.9	37.3	1.31
1930	10,593	10,686	+0.3	37	1.31
1931	10,595	9,566	−9.6	—	1.32
1932	9,882	9,911	+3.6	—	1.19
1933	9,932	9,963	+0.5	—	1.19
1934	10,079	10,079	+1.1	—	1.19
1935	10,429	10,303	+2.2	—	1.20
1936	10,749	10,347	+0.4	—	1.12
1937	11,020	10,553	+1.9	—	1.12
1938	11,080	10,667	+1.0	—	1.11
1939	11,131	11,430	+7.1	—	1.10
1940	11,185	11,215	−1.8	—	1.08
1941	11,131	—	—	—	1.06
1942	11,139	—	—	—	1.03
1943	11,126	—	—	—	1.02
1944	11,128	—	—	—	1.01
1945	15,778	10,454	−6.7	37.3	1.14

* Based on actual membership.
† Based on authorized membership.

Source: Annual Reports of the Commissioner of the SAP.

1930s when the effects of the economic depression curtailed public expenditure, and the SAP experienced bad publicity about its militarism. However, the proportion of manpower that was Black remained constant at a level that pertained in 1920, showing a preference for White recruits, reflecting the state's use of the public sector to solve the problem of poor Afrikaners. Despite the steady increase in overall manpower, the number of men actually in the job rarely exceeded the complement authorized by the state in the police budget, leading to a constant understaffing within the SAP. Nor was the increase in manpower sufficient to keep pace with the growth of South Africa's population, so that the ratio of police per thousand head of population actually declined throughout the period, falling to a level that pertained when the force was first established. The ratio was never equal across the four provinces, and was always highest in the Transvaal. In 1929, for example, the ratios were 1.15 in the Cape, 1.14 in Natal, 1.45 in the Orange Free State, and 1.48 in the Transvaal (Annual Report of the Commissioner of the SAP 1929: 14). For the country as a whole, the ratio fell to its lowest during the Second World War. At the end of the war, South Africa had fewer policemen than the main liberal democracies. In England and Wales, for example, the ratio in 1945 was 1.56, and 1.46 in Scotland (Brewer *et al.* 1988: 9). This differential takes into account that membership of the police in Britain also fell in the war period, by 18.3 per cent (worked from figures provided in Brewer *et al.* 1988: 9), which is much larger than in South Africa's case, where actual membership fell by 6.7 per cent. On both counts, therefore, the South African state's policy of internal colonialism was being effected in this period by a surprisingly small police force.

The SAP began the period well. In his 1927 Annual Report, the Commissioner noted that there were 1,320 applicants for the police, 471 of whom passed the entrance examination, 331 of whom were finally enrolled. All were South African born, so that the management did not have to recruit from overseas, and all were bilingual. By 1929 the Commissioner noted that there was no difficulty in filling vacancies, and applicants were 'of a superior type' (Annual Report of the Commissioner of the SAP 1929: 6). However, conscious of public criticism of the militaristic spirit within the SAP, he complained of the undue press attention given to 'the black sheep that were weeded out during the year' (p. 6). This was a portent of the future, and by the mid-1930s, a government commission on the police noted with concern the phenomenal increase in the rate of resignations, which it attributed to poor pay, the unsuitability of the uniform (too hot in summer), and bad relations between officers and men due to the militaristic ethos of the police (Union of South Africa 1937*a*: 12). Between 1933 and 1936, the number of people purchasing their discharge increased by nearly a factor of five (p. ii), and the committee complained about the poor educational standards of recruits, whose entrance examination only matched the level of Standard 6.

Members of the English-speaking community were still not being attracted to apply to the police (pp. 10–13), such that poor educational standards amongst recruits was a consequence of the social composition of applicants, most of whom were Afrikaans-speaking, although, judging from positive assessments made by the Commissioner in earlier annual reports, they were no longer from the bywoner class of

Afrikaner. However, the Lansdown Commission did little to change
the social composition of the SAP, for it was against offering additional
allowances for educational qualifications as an inducement to English-
speakers to join. It also repeated earlier objections to the employment
of policewomen, an issue raised again by the National Council of
Women, although there were by this time policewomen in English
constabularies and in European police forces. The police saw no
reason to have women patrolling the streets, and race relations in
South Africa were thought to make it dangerous for them to do so.
The Lansdown Commission agreed: 'owing to the presence of a large
and heterogeneous non-European population, that chivalry which
protects a woman social worker in dangerous localities or situations is
not likely to be extended to a policewoman' (p. 40). The SAP preferred
in the larger towns to use wardresses from the prisons service in the
custody and searching of female prisoners, and for dealing with female
victims of sex crimes. In smaller towns and rural out-stations the wives
of policemen performed these duties. There were nine wardresses
seconded to the SAP for this purpose in 1936, all of whom were White
and in receipt of a rate of pay which exceeded that of a Black police
sergeant.

This is indicative of how apartheid operated in the organization of
the police, despite other evidence of limited police professionalization.
The subordinate position of Blacks in South Africa's racial society was
mirrored in their status within the police hierarchy. However, because
of the overlap between race and class in South Africa, employment in
the police, like the public sector as a whole, was a form of social
mobility for Blacks, no matter how unequal their status compared to
White policemen. There was never a shortage in recruits; nor, as yet,
any political resistance to joining that would later counteract the
economic necessity that drove some Black South Africans to police
their own subordination. There were also lower standards of entry
which facilitated the ready supply of recruits. African police at
this time were not even required to read and write, and language
proficiency in the two official languages could be perfunctory.

In 1927 the Annual Report of the Commissioner provided the first
breakdown of the ethnic and racial composition of Blacks in the SAP,
crude as it was. Table 3.2 provides an outline for selected years,
showing the overwhelming employment of Africans. A trend that was
beginning to be noticeable by 1945, but which became more apparent
after the 1948 general election, was the shift in preference towards

TABLE 3.2 *Membership trends in Black police, 1927–1945*

Year	Asian		Coloured		African	
	No.	% NCOs*	No.	% NCOs	No.	% NCOs
1927	108	4.5	134	5.8	3,755	5.0
1929	95	5.2	135	7.3	3,711	5.3
1945	89	4.4	144	7.5	3,670	6.1

*Non-commissioned officers.

Source: Annual Reports of the Commissioner of the SAP.

the employment of members from the Coloured community. Thus, the number of Africans in the SAP fell by 2.2 per cent between 1927 and 1945, and that of Asians by 17 per cent, while that of Coloureds rose by 7.4 per cent, although Africans still dominated in gross terms. Another noteworthy trend from Table 3.2 is the low proportion from all three Black communities that were in positions of authority within the police bureaucracy, with Coloureds having the highest proportion. Black policemen were thus disproportionately in the lower ranks. In 1927, for example, 79.2 per cent of White manpower was at the rank of constable compared with 94.8 per cent of Black policemen. By 1945 the gap had widened, to 73.7 and 93.8 per cent respectively. Only seventeen staff at headquarters in 1927 were Black. Black policemen were not allowed to progress beyond the rank of sergeant, but most non-commissioned officers were corporals. This rank was abandoned for White policemen in 1929 but kept for Blacks, presumably in order to prevent an expansion in the number of Black sergeants for reasons of economy or to preserve the status of White non-commissioned officers. It was abolished for Black policemen in 1946. While a White sergeant was able to be in command of a small police station, Black sergeants always had to be under the authority of a more senior White officer, even in Black areas.

A rise through the ranks for Black policemen was hindered by their lack of formal training and the absence of educational entry requirements. Each police district employed and trained their own Black policemen according to their needs. Since their task was solely to maintain social control in Black areas (but in co-ordination with White colleagues), often by sheer brutality, knowledge of the law, or skill in personal relations, were not considered necessary for Black policemen. The 1937 Lansdown Commission rejected the idea of establishing a formal training depot for Black policemen, and considered it unnecessary, even dangerous, to give them training in drill.

The increasing urbanization of the Black population brought a change in their expectation of Black policemen. The Lansdown Commission was made fully aware of this by witnesses representing the urban Black population.

By many witnesses in the rural areas it is asserted that the uneducated native makes the better policeman. It is, on the other hand, urged by most of the urban witnesses that a more educated native is urgently required, and that grave injustice is often suffered by the native section of the community at the hands of the uneducated and uncultured native policeman. (Union of South Africa 1937a: 14)

In the tribal reserves, African policemen, most of whom were nominated by their chiefs or headmen, primarily tracked stock thieves, and the Commission felt that country knowledge and tracking skills were more important than formal education; training in law and other police duties was entirely unnecessary (in Queensland, the 'native police' became increasingly marginalized to the role of trackers, see Finnane 1991: 40). In the urban areas, however, the Commission recognized the need to increase the educational standards of Black policemen and introduce some training. It recommended that Standard 4 be the minimum educational entry requirement for Black police in urban areas, and that before being sent on normal police duty, they spend a month at divisional headquarters being trained. It was not until 1952 that the first training depot for Black policemen was opened. None the less, even at this time, the Commission's recommendation showed an awareness that the newly emerging Black urban areas required policemen to adopt a different role than in the tribal reserves, and that police relations with urban Blacks were problematic and required sensitivity.

Farmers in the White rural areas also complained to the Commission, alleging that there was inadequate control of stock theft because of understaffing (a complaint common to White settler farmers elsewhere in the British Empire; for Kenya see Anderson 1991: 188). With the shift of population to the towns by the mid-1930s, occurring amongst White and Black South Africans, a number of police stations in White farming areas were closed down and staff transferred. The SAP took to leaving a disproportionate number of African police there to deal with stock theft, on the assumption that their country knowledge and tracking skills made them more suitable than White colleagues. But the racial sensibilities of White farming communities led to complaints about the over-reliance on African policemen. The Commission sympathized with this, and thought it unlikely to be effective in dealing with crime, expressing the view that African policemen were at root unreliable and untrustworthy: 'native policemen, animated by excessive zeal, and usually not equipped with any appreciable degree of critical faculty, are apt to be led astray by witnesses who may have a nature for untruthfulness' (pp. 62–3). Formal training for Black policemen might have been the simplest answer but instead the Commission urged greater supervision of Black policemen by White officers. Thus, a basic principle was being expressed: White policemen for White areas; Blacks should be used only in Black areas, and then under the command of White officers (something common to racially stratified colonial societies in the West Indies, Asia, and Africa; see Anderson and Killingray 1991*b*: 7). Although legally entitled to do so under law, Black policemen were not allowed by SAP regulations to deal with Whites. Uproar followed one case in 1934 when an African policeman stopped a White farmer for a traffic offence. The Minister of Justice, General Smuts, made a statement in parliament on 26 April 1934, explaining that it was just a case of excessive zeal: 'It is not considered sound that native constables should ever come into touch with European citizens ... Our instructions are that the native constables should be employed on native cases and that they should leave the European population alone. It was a case of entire stupidity and of too much zeal.' As van der Spuy so redolently put it, the White master–Black servant relationship in the wider society was reproduced within the police (1989: 271).

The SAP practised its own internal colonialism. This is perhaps best represented in Table 3.3, which shows the per capita expenditure on policemen from the various communities for the financial years of 1934/5 to 1945/6. As this table makes clear, although there was a substantial increase in the per capita expenditure on all policemen in 1937/8, the proportion of expenditure on policemen from the different communities remained much the same. Moreover, although the percentage increase in the per capita expenditure in this period is lowest for White policemen, at 50.1 per cent, compared to 58.6 per cent for Asian and Coloured policemen, and 65.9 per cent for

TABLE 3.3 *Per capita expenditure on policemen by race, 1934/5–1945/6*

Year	White £	Asian/Coloured £	% of White	African £	% of White
1934/5	274.75	108.35	39.5	82.25	30
1935/6	272	106	38.9	81	29.7
1936/7	274	104	37.9	81	29.5
1937/8	290.25	112.75	38.8	87.75	30.2
1938/9	291.5	112	38.4	87	29.8
1939/40	291	111.5	38.3	84.5	29
1940/1	291	111.25	38.2	84.5	29
1941/2	301.25	115.25	38.2	91.25	30.2
1942/3	320.25	123	38.4	99	30.9
1943/4	338	136	40.2	109.5	32.3
1944/5	378	155.5	41.1	124.5	32.9
1945/6	411	171.75	41.7	136.5	33.3

Source: based on figures supplied in the Annual Reports of the Auditor General.

Africans, there was an overall decline in the proportion of expenditure spent on Black policemen when comparing 1945/6 with 1918. At the end of the First World War, the per capita expenditure on Black policemen was 40.3 per cent of that of Whites, compared to 37.4 per cent at the end of the Second.

This inequality of expenditure showed itself in many ways. White policemen were entitled to one month's leave per annum, Black policemen to only twelve days, although this was later extended to twenty-one days per annum. If Black policemen who were married wished to live with their families when accommodation was available for them in barracks as single persons, they had to build this accommodation at their own expense, a ruling which did not apply to White married policemen. No free medical attendance was given for the wives and families of Black policemen, although this was granted to White policemen in 1934. Black police in mounted sections of the SAP had to pay for their own horses, whereas the government covered this expense for White mounted policemen, although the state later changed this ruling, and Black police were denied the right to wear the blue uniform of a White constable and had to use the cheaper military khaki instead. Above all, it was reflected in the fine racial gradations of pay. The various Black communities were treated differently, with Asians and Coloureds being paid better than Africans

TABLE 3.4 *Salary differentials in 1936 (£ p.a.)*

	Constable		Corporal*		Sergeant†	
	Start	Top	Start	Top	Start	Top
White	150	282	260	305	300	350
Asian/Coloured	64	94	100	112	118	130
African	48	60	78	90	95	105

* No equivalent rank for Whites: figure for Whites is based on that for
sergeants, 2nd class.
† Based on figures for sergeants, 1st class.
Source: Report of the Lansdown Commission (Union of South Africa 1937*a*:
pp. v, x, xi).

at all ranks. This is one of the reasons why growth in police manpower
in the former two communities exceeded that of Africans; the
reduction in salary introduced in 1923 as a post-war cost-saving
exercise did not apply to Asian and Coloured policemen. All Black
policemen received less than White colleagues, as reflected in Table
3.4. The Lansdown Commission felt that this was too low to keep the
best African police, especially in the urban areas with the allure of
better-paid employment, and in 1938 the government granted a pay
increase for all policemen, with African police getting the largest
percentage increase, although the differentials in real terms remained
massive.

The government linked the issue of poor pay with various manpower
problems, such as the high number of resignations of White constables,
the difficulties in attracting well-qualified Black police in the urban
areas, and the widespread allegations of misconduct. Although the
Lansdown Commission refuted allegations of corruption within the
SAP and SARHP, it urged a rate of pay whereby policemen could live
in conditions of decency, and freedom from temptation (Union of
South Africa 1937*a*: p. ii); the government consented to this pay
increase a year later. These 'conditions of decency' involved ensuring
that White policemen were paid well enough to avoid having to live in
'undesirable localities' near to Black people (p. ii).

Yet throughout the period, the government was very frugal in its
expenditure on the police. In 1929 the SAP's own veterinary branch
was formed in an attempt to reduce reliance on expensive contract
work by civilians; it later established its own stud farm for the same

reason. The building programme was severely affected by the economic depression. In his 1929 Annual Report, the Commissioner complained that members were having to work, eat, and sleep under conditions 'vastly inferior to those afforded long-service convicts' (p. 7); and 441 stations were still being rented from private owners, compared to 600 which were government-owned. By 1945 the situation had not improved much, with 306 stations being hired from private owners. The Commissioner echoed his words of 1929: 'the deplorable conditions and unsuitability of the buildings seriously hampers efficient police administration' (Annual Report of the Commissioner of the SAP 1945: 5). During this time the cost of policing per head of population was the lowest in the SAP's history, except for a short period during the First World War. It reached its lowest in 1936/7, when it was the equivalent of 21 pence, although this would have been much higher had the calculation been based solely on the White population. By 1944/5 it had not yet reached the level that pertained in 1927/8.

Trends in police expenditure are presented in Table 3.5. There was a steady increase in expenditure after the 1933/4 financial year, once the worst of the economic depression was over. However, this rise began from a very low base. It was not until the outbreak of the Second World War that police expenditure reached the level that pertained before the cuts imposed in the economic depression following the First World War. Significantly, police expenditure always exceeded that on defence until the beginning of the war. Defence expenditure fell to its lowest in the 1932/3 financial year, when it was only a quarter of police expenditure. Police expenditure also increased at a faster rate than defence expenditure until the financial year 1934/5, when events in Europe may have led the state slightly to refocus. But this only ensured the narrowing of a previously mighty gap. The fact that the state was less frugal with police expenditure than the military throughout the whole period before the war is indicative of where the state saw its enemy. It was internal and managed by policemen rather than soldiers; it was a task of internal colonialism rather than external defence.

Although the state was less frugal with police expenditure than defence, the restrictions it placed on police expenditure limited the SAP's use of the latest modern technology, forcing a reliance on manpower, which was often crude and brutal. This inhibited the professionalization of the police. One index of this in terms of police expenditure, shown in Table 3.5, is the declining proportion of overall

TABLE 3.5 *Trends in police expenditure, 1926/7–1945/6*

Year	Total £m.	% change	% detective work*	% equipment	Ratio police/ defence expenditure†
1926/7	2.58	–	0.9	0.9	34
1927/8	2.59	+0.4	1	0.9	–
1928/9	2.59	−0.02	1	0.7	–
1929/30	2.55	−1.6	0.9	0.6	–
1930/1	2.49	−2.3	1	0.8	34
1931/2	2.35	−5.6	0.8	0.4	32
1932/3	2.27	−3.5	1	0.7	26
1933/4	2.38	+4.8	0.9	0.5	34
1934/5	2.43	+2	0.9	0.6	42
1935/6	2.51	+3.6	0.9	0.8	45
1936/7	2.57	+2.1	0.8	–	57
1937/8	2.79	+5.6	–	–	71
1938/9	2.82	+3.8	0.8	–	62
1939/40	3.04	+7.9	0.9	–	97
1940/1	3.13	+2.9	0.5	–	653
1941/2	2.93	−6.3	0.3	–	979
1942/3	3.09	+3.4	0.2	–	–
1943/4	3.33	+6.9	0.2	–	–
1944/5	3.59	+8.6	0.4	–	142
1945/6	4.18	+16.2	0.9	–	108

* Excludes salaries.

† 100 = base figure for police expenditure.

Source: Annual Reports of the Commissioner of the SAP and Annual Reports of the Auditor General.

resources devoted to detective work, the epitome of modern police work. During war one might expect the focus to shift more to control than civil policing, but this trend was occurring even before the outbreak of the Second World War. Senior managers in the uniform section of the SAP did not have a high opinion of the CID because of its reputation for indiscipline and corruption, and decentralized structure. De Villiers sought to deal with both by placing the CID under the command of the uniform branch in local police districts, by himself assuming direct command of the CID when the post of Deputy Commissioner in charge of the CID fell vacant in 1933 and was not filled for several years, and by insisting that the CID wear a uniform. In 1932 policemen in the CID were ordered to wear uniform, both for ceremonial purposes and while on duty, as a means to impose discipline and respect for higher ranks, and to extend to them the militarism that de Villiers was introducing elsewhere in the force. The CID believed the wearing of uniform to be prejudicial to their duties, and it was only following a recommendation of the Lansdown Commission in 1936 that the order was rescinded, although uniforms were kept for ceremonial wear. The Commission, however, supported de Villiers's attempts to centralize the organization of the CID under the control of the uniform branch. However, resentment in the uniform branch against the CID lingered because of their specialist technical knowledge and plain-clothes work, as became apparent in a later commission of inquiry on police corruption during the war (Union of South Africa 1950a: 11, 30).

Restrictions on expenditure also delayed the SAP's use of modern equipment, such as telephones, the introduction of motorization in the police, and the use of radio communication. As late as 1936 most police stations had yet to install telephones by which the station could be contacted by the public or policemen in other stations. Police cars had been in use since 1934 in Cape Town and Johannesburg, although the preferred mode of mechanical transport was motor cycle. It was not until 1936 that police vehicles equipped with radio communication were used. An experimental vehicle was deployed in Johannesburg, which had the capacity to receive messages from a central transmission point but not transmit them. By the following year another twenty-three cars were equipped in this way in Johannesburg, and one in Cape Town. But the slowness of the move to mechanized police transport prevented the wide-scale use of this innovation. By 1943, for example, there were only 128 police cars in the entire SAP fleet of vehicles, although there were nearly three times as many pick-up vans (Annual Report of the Commissioner of the SAP 1943: 14), used mostly for rounding up Africans who offended against the pass and liquor laws, which is indicative of how the SAP's role in policing race relations affected its deployment of resources and general modernization. A further index of this is the use of five motorized charge offices in Johannesburg from 1936 onwards. Five trucks were equipped with radio receivers and stationed at various fixed points of the city, from where they could move swiftly to a site of trouble in order to process large numbers of offenders quickly, mostly for pass and liquor offences. Within the first five months of their use, these mobile charge offices had worked nearly twelve thousand hours and made

3,904 arrests (Annual Report of the Commissioner of the SAP 1937: 3).

RACE, CRIME, AND POLICING

It was not just that the state saw its main threat to be an internal one, as Pinnock claimed it did from the early 1920s (cited in van der Spuy 1989: 268), it increasingly narrowed to be located as an urban one. In 1927 the number of police districts was extended when the Transvaal district was divided into eastern and western divisions, reflecting the movement of population to urban areas. The deployment of police manpower throughout the four provinces lagged somewhat behind this population shift. In 1930 34.1 per cent of the SAP was deployed in Transvaal, 35.1 per cent in the Cape, 18 per cent in Natal, and 7.6 per cent in the Orange Free State. By 1946, however, deployment of police manpower had caught up with the urbanization of the population, and 36 per cent of the SAP were deployed in the Transvaal, 29.2 per cent in the Cape, 17.5 per cent in Natal, and 5.8 per cent in the Orange Free State.

The urbanization of South Africa's population was reflected also in its crime trends. Stock theft, and other crimes associated with rural areas, such as sheep-worrying and theft of produce from farms, remained problems which the SAP attended to. In 1929, for example, there were 14,546 cases of stock theft (Annual Report of the Commissioner of the SAP 1929: 9), but in the same annual report, the Commissioner noted the emergence of new, urban-based crimes, such as motor theft and motor accidents. In 1929, for example, there were 7,069 motor accidents reported in the year, and the Commissioner called for stricter testing of drivers and for a provision that drivers lose their licence when they became physically incapable of driving (Annual Report of the Commissioner of the SAP 1929: 8). In 1926 traffic offences were not ranked in the nine most frequently committed crimes, but were fourth in 1946 and second in 1952. The burden of traffic duty, including point duty, was so heavy on the SAP that municipalities and the provinces were allowed to establish their own traffic police from 1932. Fifty-two municipalities had done so by 1946. They had jurisdiction only with respect to traffic offences, and were paid for out of municipal and provincial budgets, and although they

TABLE 3.6 *Trends in selected crimes, 1926 and 1946*

Offence	1926 Rank*	1946 Rank*	% increase in no. committed
Municipal	1	3	82.4
Pass laws	2	6	15.2
Kaffir beer	3	1	181.3
Drunkenness	4	2	212
Native hut tax	5	9	50.8
Petty assault	6	8	77.9
Petty theft	7	5	146.1
Master/Servant Act	8	14	13.4
Native labour	9	12	44.3

* Position in the rank order of the most frequently committed crimes for that year.

Source: Annual Reports of the Commissioner of the SAP.

reintroduced an element of decentralization, the SAP supported their establishment. In several of his annual reports, the Commissioner complained about the absurdity of having highly trained policemen, at a time of escalating crime, standing on street corners directing traffic. The only objection raised against the traffic police was that they were initially paid at a higher rate than even head constables in the SAP, in order to attract sufficient numbers to join, although this was later rectified.

The most frequently committed crimes in 1926 are identified in Table 3.6, which provides comparative figures for 1946, although the limitations of all crime statistics need to be borne in mind when reading this as a measure of the real extent of crime. Several points are worth noting from Table 3.6. Crime was becoming urban, with municipal offences against the by-laws of town councils being one of the most frequently committed crimes in 1926 and 1946. Although the Commissioner never provided a racial breakdown of crime statistics in his Annual Reports, many of the most frequently committed crimes were for offences which affected Africans only, and urban Africans specifically, such as the pass laws, African labour irregularities, offences under the Master and Servants Act (affecting African domestic servants), and the illegal possession of kaffir beer. But this is not to claim that crime was an exclusively Black pastime. Besides these administrative offences which regulated race relations, much of other ordinary crime was committed by Whites, although police attention increasingly focused on controlling the urban African population by means of these administrative regulations. Also noteworthy is the overall increase in the level of crime. In this twenty-year period there was an increase of 91.8 per cent for the nine crimes covered in the table, which is far greater than the increase in total population for the same period. With population growth constant, crime still almost doubled, as reflected in the number of prosecutions per thousand head of population. The average number of prosecutions per thousand head of population for the period 1912–26 was 48.4, but was 74.2 between 1927 and 1946, reaching its highest rate of 82 in 1939. But, interestingly, the increase in crime was not uniform across the nine crimes selected in Table 3.6. Many of the offences peculiar to the regulation of the supply of urban African workers increased at a level well below the overall figure of 91.8 per cent, although control of their social life when in urban areas, such as the possession of kaffir beer, continued unabated. This reflected the urgent need for African labour during the war years, the United Party's uncertain attitude towards influx control, which led to divisions in the state over how to enforce it (Posel 1991: 39–49), and public disquiet throughout this period about the conduct of the police in enforcing administrative regulations against urban Africans (on the role of the police in regulating boundaries between the races by means of similar legislation in the Caribbean see H. Johnson 1991; for Kenya see Anderson 1991: 198, and Willis 1991: 222–3).

The period began, however, with a marked penetration by the police in the daily life of the Black population; the plethora of these administrative regulations indicates the extent of the state's control over the lives of Black South Africans, and urban Africans in particular. Beinart and Bundy (1987) claim that it was from 1927 onwards that the police became more pervasive in their penetration of ordinary life. This was in part due to the enactment of legislation by the Hertzog government, enforced by the police, which reinforced the subordinate colonial status of Blacks, but also growing police effectiveness in information-gathering and the infiltration of opposition movements. What initially prompted this role in information-gathering was labour unrest by White workers in the early 1920s. The monitoring of labour and communist activists easily merged into the regulation and control of Blacks because of the state's fear that industrial unrest would spread to general rebellion against their colonial status.

In his 1927 Annual Report the Commissioner could write confidently that the SAP had created an efficient means of information-gathering and infiltration.

I may state that the movements of all the known agitators, of both races, is very well marked, and no gatherings of any magnitude can be attended by them without the police being present to take action should any treasonable utterance be made . . . The agitators are carefully watched, their movements marked, and the tenor of their speeches noted. (pp. 20–1)

Thus, in his 1929 Annual Report, the Commissioner announced that a special unit had been established at headquarters in Pretoria to monitor the activities of communists, trade unionists, and 'other agitators'. This was the forerunner of the SAP's Special Branch, itself formally set up in the war to monitor the activities of extreme Afrikaner nationalists. One measure of the extent of this monitoring role, if not also of its effectiveness, is the increase in the number of crimes known under the category of 'offences against the state'. Between 1916 and 1920, they fell by 9.2 per cent, to number 513 in 1920. Between 1927 and 1945, they increased by 394.6 per cent, to total 10,827 offences. In the two-year period following 1927, supporting Beinart and Bundy's argument, they increased by 54.8 per cent, which was well above the annual average increase for the period as a whole. Further, police expenditure on 'detainees', itemized by the Auditor General in the SAP's annual budget, increased by 52.2 per cent in the ten-year period following the 1935–6 financial year.

The crime profile of the Black population at this time is worth discussing in order to demonstrate the nature of its contacts with the police (for overviews on Black crime see Bonner 1988; Davies and Slabbert 1985; for a comparison with crime trends among Africans in Kenya see Anderson 1991; Willis 1991). Ordinary crime was prevalent among the Black population. Van Zyl Smit (1990: 4–6) shows that there were two criminological approaches to it. The Afrikaner nationalist tradition of criminology explained it as due to deficiencies in civilization caused by racial inferiority. The Liberalists, as van Zyl Smit calls them, people such as Hellman, Hoernle, and Rheinnallt-Jones, and others associated with the South African Institute of Race Relations (SAIRR), although not criminologists, located Black crime in social processes such as deprivation, poverty, unemployment, and dislocation. Afrikaner nationalist criminologists explained crime by poor Whites in terms of the same social processes, but racist notions prevented any parallel with Black crime, thereby enabling them to link crime with their opposition to racial mixing. In this way, Afrikaner nationalist politicians used fear of Black crime as a means to mobilize White support for segregation, making crime a significant part of the so-called 'Black peril' (*swart gevaar*), without mentioning that segregation was the main cause of most of the crime committed by Black South Africans.

The literature written today about Black crime in the 1930s and 1940s is within the Liberalist tradition of criminology. The migrant labour system, for example, divided families, and with such dislocation came illegitimacy, dysfunctional behaviour, and, in the single-sex hostels, sexual deprivation, which encouraged rape, sexual assault, prostitution, homosexuality, and various other forms of sexual acts which Whites considered unnatural vices, even if not, as Dunbar Moodie (1988) shows, actual sodomy, as well as alcoholism, and drug abuse (see: Beinart 1987; Bonner 1988; Marks and Andersson 1990). Shebeens, or drinking houses, mostly set up in the urban areas by African women who had been deserted by their husbands and who needed to care for large families, catered for the emotional and physical needs of migrants and others and encouraged the illicit liquor trade, and, in police demonology, also prostitution, even if it was not what is normally understood as prostitution (Dunbar Moodie 1988: 245). The poverty and deprivation of settled urban residents were often worse than migrant workers, since their market position was always vulnerable to being undercut by the ready supply of migrants employed on cheaper wages. Unemployment particularly affected the children of urban residents, amongst whom crime was a severe problem, which encouraged liberal whites to establish the Johannesburg Urban Natives Juvenile Delinquency Conference in 1938 to discuss the problem.

The main expression of their dysfunctional behaviour was in youth gangs (for studies of specific gangs or township locations see Bonner 1988; Guy 1987; La Hausse 1990; Pinnock 1985, 1987). Youth gangs emerged in the 1930s in both the African and Coloured urban townships (Nasson 1991: 248), but reached their zenith in the 1950s, only to be resurrected again following the township uprisings in the mid-1980s (Scharf 1990). While some were not criminal, and a few members used them merely as social clubs (Marks and Andersson 1990: 37), most members were *tsotsis* or gangsters. By 1934 gangs had become problematic enough to the police to affect training. The

Acting Commander of the Police Training Depot in Pretoria wrote to the Commissioner on 30 October 1934, recommending training in the 'scientific use of the baton' when confronted by gangs. He referred to 'an element of tough low class coloured and native people who resort to violence against the unprotected citizen and count it some feat to knock out, or mark for life with a knife cut, some isolated policeman' (SAP/20/10/24). The Fifth Annual Report of the SAIRR in 1934 noted the emergence of 'native juvenile vagrants' in urban areas who came into trouble with the police because of their criminal behaviour, which it attributed to unemployment and homelessness (p. 27). Without work and schooling (on the effect of education on crime amongst Black youth see Hellman 1940; Bonner 1988: 403), unemployed Black youth were sucked into the gangs when forced on to the resources of the street. So prevalent and pervasive did the gangs become that the preference of employers for youngsters from the rural areas for economic reasons was reinforced by assumptions that all urban Black youths were *tsotsis*, which became a self-fulfilling prophecy pulling more unemployed youth into the criminal gang culture. The gangs tried to control the bioscopes, and became involved in gambling, prostitution, pickpocketing, bag-snatching, and robbing migrant workers of their pay. Fights between rival gangs over territory and women became commonplace, adding to the culture of violence that pervaded the urban townships. Most of this crime was committed against other Blacks, although in the larger cities there was public outcry at the robberies and attacks on Whites by Black gangs. Residents in Cape Town and Durban requested that the police appoint special constables, but the police declined in order not to give the impression that the problem was getting out of control. In the Coloured townships in the Cape, gangs known as the 'skolly boys' would attack White pedestrians, motorists, and sailors (Rheinnallt-Jones 1938: 14).

Complaints by law-abiding Black residents that they too were being under-policed, led in the early 1940s to the formation of citizen patrols, as well as the tribal vigilante groups known as the *maghotla*, which were the forerunners of the African township police established in a much later period. It was Blacks in the SAP who mainly dealt with this crime, although some of the larger White municipalities employed their own private guards to operate in the Black locations they administered (known as municipal native police boys), and there were a few African police deployed in townships under the auspices of the

Native Affairs Department. Both sorts of police were under the direct control of White officers, and acted in co-operation with the SAP. All of these Black police were subject to vicious attack when policing the locations. In his review of race relations in 1935, Rheinnallt-Jones (1936) noted the severe injuries inflicted on policemen by youths carrying knives. This 'growing disposition to use the knife' (p. 3), eventually led to legislation which limited the length of the blade which African youths (but not Coloureds) were allowed to carry to two and a half inches, although it was not until 1937 that violence by Blacks against the police became a public issue when the first two White constables were killed.

The violence by gangs against the police has to be set against the brutality of the police in enforcing administrative regulations against otherwise law-abiding and peaceful Black citizens. Most Black crime, in fact, amounted to minor infringements of administrative regulations which controlled the economic and social boundaries between the races. It was in this context that most Black people came into all too frequent contact with the police. Even the Lansdown Commission referred to these offences as trivial (Union of South Africa 1937a: 62), but with a population ratio in the urban areas in 1937 of three Blacks to every one White, the boundaries between the races required persistent monitoring by means of an increasing number of regulations which affected the economic and residential rights of Blacks, their moral conduct, and social life. The fact that the SAP pursued these offences so rigorously indicates the nature and extent of its role in policing race relations. The rigour of the SAP is shown in Table 3.7, which provides statistics for the number of prosecutions for selected administrative offences for selected years between 1930 and 1936. The rigour of the SAP is also shown in its conduct when enforcing these regulations, such that encounters often became violent, leading to a deterioration in police relations with otherwise law-abiding Blacks. Some encounters descended into major public order incidents. In a township near Harding, Natal, in 1937, the police were set upon by four hundred residents when trying to arrest tax defaulters. In the same year two White constables were killed when they went on a liquor raid in a township near Vereeniging. The public inquiry established to investigate the circumstances of this incident, while not uncovering evidence which it thought justified the attack, commented on the persistent brutality and insensitivity of the police when implementing these minor administrative regulations (Union of South Africa 1937b:

TABLE 3.7 *Selected administrative offences by Blacks for selected years*

Offence	1930	1934	1936
Taxation laws	49,772	69,591	95,716
Pass laws	42,262	25,450	71,052
Municipal by-laws	25,912	31,396	–
Urban Areas Act	20,877	39,765	–
Master/Servant Act	15,861	10,653	19,712
Labour laws	23,293	21,649	19,459
Liquor laws	35,777	48,840	69,077
Drunkenness	25,520	17,290	38,271

Sources: figures for 1930 and 1934 are taken from the Annual Reports of the SAIRR; figures for 1936 are taken from Dippenaar (1988: 126)

paras. 17, 44). The pass and liquor laws were particularly problematic because they epitomized the penetration of the state into the ordinary everyday lives of urban Africans and regulated access to things which they thought were theirs by right: employment and residential rights, and traditional forms of alcohol consumption (on the application of the liquor laws in urban Kenya see Willis 1991). Liberal critics of the police therefore focused attention on the enforcement of these two sets of regulations (for example: Goffery 1940; Hayman 1941; Lewin n.d.; Rheinnallt-Jones 1936, 1938; Simons 1939).

Raids for passes and liquor were common occurrences in urban townships. The events surrounding the Vereeniging incident act as an example. The municipal location at Vereeniging was established in 1907, and since 1919 its population had nearly quadrupled. The White Council in Vereeniging employed one White municipal police-man and eight native police boys, although there was a large SAP station in Vereeniging itself with whom they co-operated. There was pronounced overcrowding in the township, with an average of twelve people per stand. Consequently, public places in the township became sites where families congregated at the weekends. Visitors and relatives thronged to the township at weekends, and the police took to raiding precisely at this moment, one of greatest inconvenience to residents, but also when the largest number of offenders was likely to be caught. Police raids were never less than two a month; there had been thirty-nine in the eleven months preceding the disturbances. During the two summer months of 1937, the police raided the township thirteen times. The police disrupted weekend leisure, social celebrations, and ordinary family gatherings. People in the location who contravened the regulations were herded into the pick-up vans, roughly handled, eventually prosecuted, and fined well beyond their capacity to pay. Police treatment of people in the pick-up vans was brutal. They had been deployed in Vereeniging location only since June 1937, but by September the vans were already objects of fear and apprehension to residents, portending, as the Commission of Inquiry noted, 'harsh treatment and violence by the police' (Union of South Africa 1937*b*: para. 17). Following a second raid on the weekend of 18–19 September, residents attacked the police, killing two White constables and injuring a further ten.

White public opinion was outraged. Farmers protested to the government (influenced by their wish to keep Africans on their farms as cheap labour); threats were made against the lawyers who defended those prosecuted for involvement in the riot. Moderate Africans, co-opted by the state on to the Native Representative Council (NRC), forerunners of the township councillors introduced in a later period, also criticized the demonstrators. Members expressed sympathy with the policemen and asked for chiefs to impose order in the township; no criticism was made of the police, and the perpetrators were described as evil (Annual Report of the NRC 1937: para. 17(*a*)).

The government's response was to establish a commission of inquiry, which exonerated the police but also made critical comments on their methods of enforcing the law. By the 1930s the SAP had become less crude in its use of force, and circumstances allowed the police to be more discriminating in its use. Afrikaner nationalists were in power, and political unrest by Afrikaners was non-existent, although it flared up again at the end of the decade with the outbreak of war. White workers were being successfully co-opted by the state, effectively ending labour unrest amongst Whites. Enforcing the state's administrative regulations against the African population therefore became the SAP's chief task at this time, so that the use of force was on the whole restricted to them. By this time the force was low grade, taking the form of brutal physical beatings with sjamboks rather than the use of firearms, bombs, and aeroplanes, as occurred in the 1920s. None the less, the discipline that was imposed in the internal organization of the SAP as part of the modernization of the police did not extend to their treatment of Blacks, when on raids, in pick-up vans, or in custody. Brutality, violence, and assaults were commonplace in police treatment of Blacks, especially urban Africans. Table 3.8 shows

TABLE 3.8 *Complaints by Blacks of assault in police custody, 1934–1936*

Area	No.	Referred to Attorney-General	On which Attorney-General took action	Convictions	Dismissal
Orange Free State	23	13	7	2	0
Kimberley	17	9	4	2	1
Western Cape	99	49	21	5	0
Eastern Cape	30	23	8	0	0
Transkei	22	16	7	4	0
Natal	107	104	27	1	3
Witwatersrand	219	124	42	13	2
Transvaal	101	77	23	2	2
Total	618	415	139	29	8

Source: Lansdown Commission (Union of South Africa 1937a: 71).

the number of complaints of assault alleged by Black prisoners while in police custody between 1934 and 1936. It reveals the low number of policemen dismissed from the force for assault compared even to the number of convictions let alone of complaints, which confirms earlier points about the SAP's growing unwillingness to discharge men for misconduct. It is also interesting to note the distribution of the complaints across the provinces, as indicated in Table 3.9, revealing a pronounced tendency for the police in the Transvaal to provoke the greater number of complaints. This is not surprising given the attraction of the Rand to Blacks looking for work, and thus the increased role of the police there in regulating race relations. Nasson (1991: 245) argues that the police in Cape Town at this time were restrained in their application of the influx control legislation, and thus more moderate in their use of force, which is supported by the figures in Table 3.9.

Brutality against people in custody, however, was only part of a general recourse to violence by the police when dealing with Blacks. In a survey of race relations during 1935 for the SAIRR's official journal, Rheinnallt-Jones (1936) documented many instances of violence in routine encounters between the police and Africans. Sections of the state became concerned at this level of violence. As early as 1929, the number of complaints against the police had reached such proportions that the government was persuaded to submit most

TABLE 3.9 *Distribution of complaints and SAP manpower*

Province	Distribution of manpower*	Number of complaints†
Transvaal	34.1	51.9
Cape	35.1	27.1
Natal	18	17.3
Orange Free State	7.6	3.7

* Based on manpower distribution in 1930. Figures do not add to 100 because of the manpower allocated to headquarters, the training depot and so on.
† Number of complaints brought by prisoners while in police custody, 1934–6.
Sources: Manpower figures are taken from the Annual Report of the Commissioner of the SAP 1930: 5. Figures for the number of complaints are taken from the Lansdown Commission (Union of South Africa 1937*a*: 71).

to a ruling by the Attorney-General, since local prosecutors were often policemen themselves, although Table 3.8 puts this in context. With respect to complaints of ill-treatment of prisoners when in police custody, Table 3.8 shows that the Attorney-General rarely considered there to be a case to answer (only 22.4 per cent of complaints between 1934 and 1936 were acted upon), and the action taken against offenders mostly fell short of dismissal. A test case in the early 1930s established state liability for the delicts of the police (see Dandy 1989), making them more accountable in law. Liberal critics of the government's race policies also tried to focus public attention on the conduct of the police. In its Second Annual Report, published in 1931, the SAIRR, for example, listed the variety of complaints made by Africans against the police (pp. 62–3). They included: unnecessary and indiscriminate harassment of 'respectable natives' for pass law offences; acts of physical violence against them in the streets, and against African witnesses and prisoners; congestion of the courts for petty offences, resulting in miscarriages of justice because of hurried treatment of cases; acts of perjury by the police; abuse of the bail system; discrimination in the treatment of Black and White prisoners; and lack of any connection between fines and the offender's capacity to pay. Rheinnallt-Jones (1936: 2) also later mentioned complaints about the use of force to secure confessions from Blacks. The Select Committee on the General Law Amendment Bill in 1935 recommended that confessions made to the police be excluded from evidence in all circumstances, although the Minister of Justice, General Smuts, objected and the recommendation was withdrawn. Around about this time also, the SAIRR published a pamphlet specially designed for African readers and translated into several indigenous languages, giving advice on how to deal with the police should they be picked up (Lewin n.d.).

The simple situation was that Africans lived in fear of the police. As the SAIRR admitted in its 1931 Annual Report, 'the large class of law-abiding, self-respecting, quiet-living natives is resentful because the police fail to discriminate between them and the lawless element' (p. 63). It quoted the anonymous views of an African leader, who said: 'You Europeans look upon the police as your protectors and go to them for safety. We natives have learnt to fear the police and run away from them for safety' (p. 63). The SAP's reputation for partisanship in policing the 'races' was already established, and the SAIRR mobilized powerful support in its campaign to persuade the police to improve its relations with Black South Africans. In doing so it played partly on White fears of Black crime. In its Second Annual Report in 1931, it quoted the views of a former senior policeman that imprisoning Africans for minor infringements brought them into contact with real criminals and only taught them how to do more serious crime (p. 66). The SAIRR also played on the fear of Black rebellion, quoting the same ex-policeman to the effect that disillusionment caused by the application of trivial law would provoke 'desperate measures' to free them from repression generally (p. 67). Ironically, both views reproduced the negative stereotypes of Blacks that pervaded *swart gevaar* and on which the police drew in the first place. It also mobilized sections of the business community, arguing that employers of Black labour needed a contented work-force. Thus, in its Fifth Annual Report in 1934, the SAIRR quoted a resolution passed by the Conference of Rotary Clubs in Cape Town in the same year:

This conference, convinced that healthy relations between the various sections of the community in South Africa depends upon a sound justice, is much concerned to find that there is an ever-increasing number of complaints, not only from natives themselves, but also from employers of labour, regarding the unsatisfactory relations which exist between the native population and the police in urban areas, and also in respect of the excessive number of minor offences with which the natives are charged.   (pp. 25–6)

The police were thus interfering in the development of a settled and stable urban African work-force.

In this way, the SAIRR was expressing the views of that fraction of the state which wished to co-opt the more affluent sections of the urban African population by distinguishing between their treatment compared to rural migrants (a policy discussed by Posel 1991: 40). Posel points out that the other approach to race saw Africans as forever temporary sojourners, and once having administered to the White man's needs should return to the reserves (pp. 39–40), a view that did not finally become dominant until the second phase of apartheid at the beginning of the 1960s (pp. 228–35). By their conduct in harassing and intimidating law-abiding and innocent urban African residents during the 1930s and 1940s, the police, especially in the Transvaal, seemed to subscribe to this second position, which is one of the reasons why police relations with Asian and Coloured people, and Africans in the reserves, were never as bad as with urban Africans. Thus, the conduct of the police at this time led to inevitable criticism from those sections of the state which favoured the co-option of an 'insider' group of privileged Africans. Some government commissions made much the same criticisms of the police as the SAIRR, indicating the tensions 'within the state over race policies into which the issue of policing became embroiled.

The Commission of Inquiry into the incidents at Vereeniging, for example, urged the police to be more sympathetic and tolerant. The Commission stated: 'We think that discretion should be used in the methods of enforcement and that to invade gatherings in a location on a Sunday afternoon is neither necessary nor discreet, but is to give enforcement the aspect of oppression' (Union of South Africa 1937*b*: para. 44). This was a significant claim. The Commission suggested, in fact, that law and order were better served by turning the occasional blind eye to minor administrative infringements in order to allow a semblance of normal life for township residents (a similar claim was being made in Kenya, although liquor offences were apparently excepted; see Willis 1991: 232). It was a theme repeated by the Lansdown Commission of the same year: 'there are many cases where the indignity and interference with liberty involved in an arrest serve no useful purpose and tends to interrupt the harmonious relation between the police and the public they serve' (Union of South Africa 1937*a*: 77). The Lansdown Commission criticized the police for alienating sections of the urban African population by their all too ready resort to violence, by their 'spirit of arrogance toward the native', by untruthfulness in allegations of misconduct, and their inability to use discretion in distinguishing between the treatment of urban and rural Africans. In this last regard the Commission criticized policemen who, 'owing to their outlook towards natives as they find them in the rural areas, are apt to arouse resentment and friction when dealing with the very different urban type of native' (p. 76). This was one of the reasons why the Lansdown Commission advocated a limited form of training for Black policemen working in urban areas.

The SAP's response to these criticisms was to fall back on liberal notions of policing, no matter how inappropriate, by claiming that the police were merely upholding the law (for the views of an ex-policeman see van Onselen 1960: 85). Indeed, the Commissioner frequently claimed that the public were fickle in not providing sufficient support when the police were merely discharging their responsibility to protect law and order (for example, Annual Report of the Commissioner of the SAP 1927: 9). It was not the business of the police to advocate the removal of unpopular laws, merely to enforce them. However, critics of the police claimed that they enforced these laws with a rigour that reflected partisanship rather than impartiality. However, given that these unpopular laws were fundamental to the state's policy of internal colonialism, and thus the maintenance of White economic prosperity and political supremacy, most liberal critics of police also withdrew from advocating their removal. The Lansdown Commission thought this legislation entirely justified given the 'lower stage of civilization reached by the vast bulk of the native population' (p. 72). What was needed was more tact, courtesy, and consideration in the way the police enforced the comprehensive powers afforded them by the legislation rather than any change of the law. It was the methods of the police in enforcing the law which made it oppressive, not the legislation itself. Laws were unpopular because of the partisanship of the police in enforcing them: such was the extent of the failure of liberals to understand the problems of Black South Africans. But no matter how ill-informed, these criticisms provided a possible basis for police reform, although not of a more fundamental change in police–state relations.

POLICE REFORM

By the mid-1930s criticism of the police was coming from many quarters, including liberal Whites and sections of the state. Criticisms addressed several complaints. The SAP was criticized for its narrow focus on control of the urban African population, its reliance on violence and brutality in doing so, and a general incapacity to rid itself of other unprofessional practices, ranging from corruption and bribery to its militarism in training and rank structure. In other words, without putting it quite in these terms, critics recognized that policing in the mid-1930s was politically informed, and they attacked the SAP's paramilitary and colonial style.

This groundswell of complaint found its fullest expression in the Lansdown Commission in 1937. The Commission's membership was drawn from the English-speaking liberal establishment, and reflected its views; Lansdown was a senior judge with a reformist background (van Zyl Smit 1990: 2). The composition and chairmanship of the Commission were decisions made in consultation with the imperial power, in the form of the Governor-General, and Hertzog was unable to pack it with loyal Afrikaners. While others have noted that the Commission provided a structural understanding of the SAP's role in policing race relations, by locating it in the broader context of a system of laws which bore down exclusively on urban Africans (van der Spuy 1989: 270–1, 1990: 97; van Zyl Smit 1990: 3), something which was never to happen again with commissions of inquiry in later decades, this misses the central feature of the Commission's criticisms. The main focus of attack was the negative effects of the policing style of the SAP (a similar criticism was made of the Royal Irish Constabulary in 1866 by the Commission of Inquiry under Sir Richard Mayne, although Catholic unrest the following year prevented the recommendation being acted upon. See R. Hawkins 1991: 29. For a parallel situation in Kenya see Anderson 1991: 184, 192). The Commission did not advocate the removal of oppressive laws, but complained instead about the consequences of the SAP's militarism, brutality, intolerance, and lack of tact, consideration, and sympathy for making the legislation unpopular. In doing so it identified simultaneously both the problem and the solution. The problem was not the system of laws but the paramilitary and colonial style of the SAP. The solution was not reform of the law but the transformation of the SAP into a civilian police force, much as was happening at this time to police forces in other former colonies, like Canada, Australia, and New Zealand (on the contrast at this time between police professionalization in the independent commonwealth countries and the colonial dependencies see the case-studies in Anderson and Killingray 1991*a*). In taking this approach, the Commission was reflecting the thrust of the whole South African liberal position on policing at the time.

The SAP itself was divided on which model of policing should be the priority as the country modernized, resulting in several contradictions between colonial and civil policing practices. Thus, while most constables acted in a politically partisan manner in their conduct against Blacks, SAP regulations prevented discussion of politics by the men and participation in political activity (ideas borrowed from the regulations of the old Royal Irish Constabulary). While use of force towards Blacks was routine, an independent complaints procedure was established by which the SAP was made publicly accountable, although this was not independent of the government, since complaints were handled by the Attorney-General and only subsequently by magistrates if the Attorney-General deemed it fit. Some policemen at this time were also critical of the SAP's use of force. The then Acting Commanding Officer of the Training Depot wrote to de Villiers on 30 October 1934 outlining a proposal for 'the scientific use' of the truncheon, expressing concern at the number of people who were injured by head blows, even though blows to the head by a baton were outlawed by standing order 109(1) (see SAP/210/10/24), a proposal de Villiers did not act upon. Concern was mentioned about the damage which head injuries inflicted on the victim and to the public image of the police. Carrying a truncheon incorrectly was also thought to be provocative, and he recommended the baton drill adopted at this time by the London Metropolitan Police. Various alternatives to head blows were suggested, and he encouraged that policemen develop knowledge of the human body in training in order to learn how to incapacitate an assailant without undue violence.

Moreover, senior managers within the police continued to demand organizational autonomy for the SAP from the government. The new Commissioner was as vociferous in this as Truter had been. This insistence on organizational autonomy was expressed as opposition to performing extraneous duties for the state which fell outside those considered by the police as normal police work. De Villiers set the tone of this complaint in his first Annual Report, continuing Truter's earlier objections: 'If the efficiency of the force is to be improved, and crime prevented or detected, these extraneous duties will have to be very considerably curtailed' (Annual Report of the Commissioner of the SAP 1929: 8). The Commissioner estimated that nearly one million hours were spent on services to the government, ranging from checking for lungsickness disease in cattle to pursuing children playing truant from school. In some cases the SAP had to divert precious funds from its diminishing budget to employ special constables to replace regular policemen. In the Transvaal, for example, thirty-eight special constables were employed in 1927 to deal with stock diseases.

From 1926 the SAP were required to assist local school boards to enforce the law relating to compulsory school attendance for children. Truter tried unsuccessfully to resist this. Under de Villiers's command, policemen took to merely informing the local school board of the names of truant children whom they came across in the course of their patrols. When even this was withdrawn in Calvinia, in the Cape, during February 1934, the Provincial Secretary wrote to the Commissioner demanding that the service be restored (see SAP/1/161/26). The Deputy Commissioner for the Cape replied in March, stating that this resulted in a loss of efficiency 'to our legitimate police duties', but agreed to restore the practice of supplying school boards with the names of children they discovered playing truant. That the SAP reluctantly relented is indicative of police–state relations; the demand for organizational autonomy often went ignored by the government, who depended on the SAP for aspects of civil, political, and judicial administration.

However, prior to 1948, the government made some attempt to ease the burden of extraneous duties. By 1947, for example, the amount of time spent on extraneous duties had been cut by half compared to 1929, to total 491,467 hours for the year, or the equivalent of 100 policemen (Annual Report of the SAP 1947: 7). This compared with a figure of 485 policemen lost to the force in 1920 (Annual Report of the Commissioner of the SAP 1920: 9). In other words, the state was responding in some way to the Commissioner's demand for organizational autonomy, but resisted making the SAP completely autonomous. Its services to government were too important to dispense with entirely, which ensured that policing continued to merge at this time with civil, political, and judicial administration. Thus, for example, policemen in the smaller centres of the Union who performed the duties of prosecutors in magistrates' courts, had to balance their responsibility to the Attorney-General as prosecutors with that to the minister in charge of the police (the Minister of Justice, who himself had an intricate balancing act to perform). But this potential conflict of interest amongst policemen was one the government was prepared to accept rather than relinquish what they saw as their right to use policemen as agents of state administration. It is therefore significant that the Lansdown Commission did not address the vexed question of extraneous police duties.

But simultaneous to his demand for organizational autonomy free from governmental interference in decisions about police work, de Villiers was militarizing and centralizing the force, adding further contradictions between different police styles. The evidence which many police witnesses gave to the Lansdown Commission, complaining of excessive militarism, illustrates the tension within the force over the SAP's colonial style. Accusations of excessive militarism focused primarily on the questions of internal discipline and training, both of which were claimed to be too heavily based on the military. Some witnesses pointed out that the duties and responsibilities of policemen were entirely different from those of soldiers, and that what was needed by the former was 'expert knowledge of his technical duties as a policeman' (see Union of South Africa 1937a: 17). They suggested that training be given in skills in public relations, in the handling of station accounts, criminal investigations, and court duty. The Commission supported this and recommended that the training depot build a model station to enable trainees to engage in role-playing in order to learn court duty, public-service skills, and accountancy (p. 18). It was only in 1934 that a syllabus for the teaching of law was introduced at the depot for recruits (who were Whites only), and not until 1938 that they had to pass an examination in law. It was also recommended by some witnesses that training for the officer class be demilitarized, with the emphasis changing from horsemanship, musketry, and drill, to skills in managing the public, police stations, and criminal investigations (p. 29). The Commission particularly wanted to see criminal investigation become a routine, technical skill possessed by all officers and constables in the uniform branch, since this was thought to epitomize police work in a modern society.

The emphasis on learning public-relations skills, and on acquiring various social skills such as politeness, courtesy, and tact, reflected a more basic thrust amongst witnesses who advocated this. They were expressing the principle at the heart of the civil policing tradition. Namely, that police forces should serve the community, because it is from the public that they get their mandate. Their mandate is not granted by government; so policemen should not be servants of the state. In endorsing this principle, the Lansdown Commission was encouraging the SAP to shed its paramilitary and colonial trappings.

'It cannot be too strongly stressed that the police are the servants of the public, entrusted with wide powers only for use in the public's interest, and this should be impressed upon every recruit at the outset of his police career' (p. 78). No better statement could be made of the ethos of the liberal policing model.

By the mid-1930s, therefore, a critical moment appeared when the SAP could have been reformed. The government made some concessions to the critics of the police and seemed to recognize the need for the SAP to lose features of its paramilitary, colonial character. Forms of legal accountability already existed by this time, improvements in training followed the Lansdown Commission recommendations, and the state reduced the burden of extraneous duties, giving the SAP limited organizational autonomy. But the moment was not seized. The government's response to critics was hesitant, and few innovations in training were introduced. In part this was because circumstances overtook it. The Second World War made police reform seem small beer, and during the course of the war, the government became more concerned with police relations with Afrikaners than Blacks. But, in large part, the opportunity for police reform was lost because the government was not committed to it. The paramilitary and colonial character of the SAP was a product of its structural role in the state's policy of internal colonialism, and thus of police–state relations. While it performed the role of policing race relations, and regulating the economic, political, and social boundaries between the races, the SAP could not be transformed into a civil police force; its paramilitary and colonial character reflected the essentially paramilitary and colonial task which the government required it to perform (something which also inhibited the reform of the Royal Irish Constabulary following Sir Richard Mayne's recommendations in 1866 for demilitarizing the force).

This points to the weakness of the liberal position on policing in South Africa. Without a change in policy on race relations, the SAP's role would perforce remain colonial and paramilitary in style. The liberal critics of the SAP, and the Lansdown Commission particularly, wanted oppressive laws to be implemented by the police humanely rather than the laws abolished, in the belief that the colonial character of the SAP could be divorced from its colonial task. It was only decades later, when apartheid was in full operation, that some liberal critics of the police saw the impossibility of this position. From that point they began to focus criticism on the entire social system rather than just the role and conduct of the police within it. Paradoxically, this shifted the attention of liberal critics away from the police because, at this later juncture, criticism of the police was subsumed under a broader attack. Police reform, for example, was not again on the political agenda of White politics until 1989, when it was placed there, ironically, by a National Party government. However, the SAP's flagrant misconduct periodically brought attention back to police methods and style, and policing remained a central issue in Black politics throughout because policing was amongst the chief mediations of oppression. But the focus was always upon the system which the police upheld rather than the character of the SAP alone.

THE POLICE AT WAR

One of the reasons why police reform was taken off the political agenda so quickly was the outbreak of the Second World War. In South Africa the war also proved to be one with an internal enemy, with militant Afrikaner nationalists and sections of the SAP and SARHP being at war with the legitimately elected government.

The police war effort was twofold. A police battalion was formed from serving members of the SAP, who fought alongside soldiers in the North Africa campaign. That the SAP so easily transformed its policemen into soldiers showed the vitality of the paramilitary and colonial style in the force at the time. This demonstrated also that very little had changed from when the SAP marched as soldiers into Namibia at the outbreak of the First World War. The SAP's second role in the war was to maintain social control inside South Africa in the face of a militant Black labour force and Afrikaners who mounted another wartime rebellion. Indeed, the parallel with 1914 was further reinforced by the fact that members of the SAP were deployed in Namibia in 1939 to quell a *putsch* by supporters of Germany.

A Nazi party had been active in Namibia since 1932, and a special unit was established in Pretoria in 1936 to monitor its activities, which was strange given that it accorded the SAP a role in monitoring political activities in another country. The government expected, however, that pro-German feeling might resonate with militant Afrikaners. When it became known that a coup in Namibia was to be attempted on 20 April 1939, discovered as a result of infiltration by an officer from the SAP into the German community in Namibia, a force of 326 men landed in Windhoek on 17 April. General Smuts, the Minister of Justice, is reported by his son (Smuts 1952: 372) as having taken the decision to send in the SAP without the concurrence of the cabinet, amongst whom opposition to the move was expected as a result of 'pro-Nazi feelings' among some ministers. The General feared that Namibia would be used by Hitler as another Austria pr Czechoslovakia, invaded in order to protect German-speaking peoples, thus exposing the Union itself to later invasion, something which militant Afrikaner nationalists would have detested less than subservience to Britain. Some liberal opinion was more charitable to the Afrikaans-speaking community. Mr Justice Saul Solomon, for example, in writing to Sir Herbert Baker in England in 1939, remarked that 'the Dutch regard Great Britain as a decidedly lesser evil than the Reich' (MSS Afr. s. 8, ff. 71–74). But for Smuts the gamble worked, with 2,800 Nazi supporters interned, and in a private letter to Martin, the newspaper and mining magnate, on 3 August 1939, Smuts explained that 'my sending the police just forestalled a coup' (see van der Poel 1973: 468).

Although only temporarily used as soldiers to quell the *putsch*, the invasion of Namibia had long-term consequences for the SAP. From 1 June 1939 the South West African Police was disbanded, and its 423 men absorbed into the SAP. The protectorate became a district within the SAP's organizational structure, policed by the former members of the South West African Police, with another 104 transferred there from the SAP. The former Commissioner of the force was made Divisional Commander of the SAP's new South West Africa division. The fingerprints lodged in Windhoek were transferred to Pretoria in 1940 (as were those in Maseru, presumably because of the large number of migrant workers from Basotholand). The South West African Administration gave the SAP £114,000 towards the cost of policing the district in 1939–40, although this was a nominal sum and the SAP budget was required to cover the real costs. This was a strain on an already tight budget, and in 1939 the new district had only 4.5 per cent of the SAP's manpower, making it the smallest of the divisions, falling even further in 1946 to 3 per cent.

By marching into Namibia the SAP was mobilized as a military force even before war against Germany was declared. On the day following its outbreak in Europe, policemen were called on to act against crowds attacking the German Club in Johannesburg, and used tear-gas, batons, and small-arms fire to dispel the gathering, escalating the SAP's level of violence against Whites considerably. This was a portent of the divisiveness of the war in White politics (on which see: Hancock 1968; Martin and Orpen 1979; Stultz 1974). After Hertzog resigned over the decision to participate in the war, despite having given a reassurance to the British government in 1935 that a well-disciplined brigade of policemen were at their disposal (Martin and Orpen 1979: 7), Smuts became Prime Minister, being invited to do so by the Governor-General. The Union declared war three days after Chamberlain did so in London; Smuts also made himself Minister of Defence and Commander-in-Chief of the Defence Forces.

His problems began immediately. The 1912 Defence Act only made provision for active service inside South Africa's border, so Smuts was forced to appeal for volunteers if South African forces were to fight elsewhere. Thus, participation in the war effort could not be made obligatory for anyone, even those already in the defence force. This willingness to participate in active service was signalled by volunteers signing an oath, known as the 'Africa oath' because it demonstrated that they were prepared to serve anywhere in Africa. Those members of the defence force who had signed the oath wore a red tab on the shoulder of their uniform (so the oath was also known as the 'red oath', although the colour of the tab was orange). Probably for the first time in modern warfare, soldiers were being given the choice of whether they wanted to go to war or not, and their willingness to sign the oath, and therefore wear the tab, became an important symbol of loyalty to the government. This was not something Smuts wished to do, as some critics imply, in order selfishly to demonstrate his political support (Dippenaar 1988: 178); he had no option given the law of the land. In fact, most members of the defence force volunteered, as did many civilians.

There were restrictions placed by the government on the categories of people which could enlist for active service. People could not enlist from 'essential services', such as the railways and mines, or from other key occupations, such as motor mechanics or, strangely, people employed in the government printing works. This included policemen. Most civilians who enlisted, including those from restricted occupations who wanted to make a contribution, formed the Essential Services Protection Corps, which looked after key installations and sites, or joined the civic guards or Police Reserve, which were bodies acting in ordinary policing roles to help with manpower shortage in the SAP. However, there was no repetition of the 1914 experience, where policemen deserted in order to see active service, because the police were allowed to make a formal contribution to the war. The Chief of the General Staff, General Sir Pierre van Ryneveld, made a request to the Commissioner of the SAP, a few days after war had been declared, that he supply policemen to form a Police Brigade, knowing that de Villiers was keen to do so. As a combatant of the First World War who carried his militarism into the SAP, de Villiers was eager to ensure that his men contributed to the war effort, with himself leading them into combat, in order to avoid massive desertions.

But this required policemen to signal their willingness to volunteer, opening up the force to the divisive clashes of loyalty that the war provoked, and providing policemen with a rare opportunity to express political disagreement as a body with the government. Party politics were thus displayed on the shoulders of policemen, so that the force divided into those who were loyal to Smuts and those loyal to the extreme Afrikaner nationalists who opposed the war. While there were some policemen who were too young to sign the oath, and others who refused to go to war for family or financial reasons, the oath became a test of the political loyalties of policemen (Martin and Orpen 1979; SAP 1986: 33; van der Spuy 1989: 275; G. Visser 1976: 32).

There is dispute about the numbers of men who seized this opportunity. The SAP's official historian cites only 1,252 as signing the oath (Dippenaar 1988: 16), so that the majority opposed the government. G. Visser, a member of the SAP's special unit which pursued OB, mentions 2,000 (1976: 31), while van der Spuy argues that on the basis of figures revealed to parliament in August 1940, 4,331 policemen signed the oath (1989: 274). This would mean that a small majority in the force loyally volunteered. Whatever the case, there were too many signatories for the number of men needed for active service, ensuring that some policemen went about their ordinary police work wearing red tabs. Detectives in plain clothes wore lapel badges with a red flash. On the other hand, initial projections about forming a brigade of policemen had to be scaled down, leaving the SAP to form only two battalions, with a third being composed of army reservists from the volunteer Second Transvaal Scottish Regiment. However, it is likely that the unrest inside South Africa, provoked by the war, prevented the government from dispensing with the services of many volunteers from within the police.

The official historian of the SAP discusses these events at length

(Dippenaar 1988: 143–90), and blames the decision to form a Police Brigade for the subsequent open conflict in the SAP. However, he stresses the choice as one between those who wanted to politicize the police by declaring their support for Smuts, and those who refused to sign in order to keep politics out of the police (1988: 145). This is a considerable exaggeration of the men's commitment to political neutrality, and the participation later of some policemen in terrorist activity against Smuts's government indicates the strength of political support for Afrikaner nationalism. The government appears to have suspected disloyalty, for a serving policeman at this time records that policemen who had failed to sign the oath were not allowed to guard sensitive installations and sites (van Onselen 1960: 122).

However, as a measure of the political divisions within the Afrikaans-speaking community, most of the policemen who volunteered for active service were Afrikaners (van Onselen 1960: 120), which contradicts van der Spuy's claim that ethnic status determined the decision about whether or not to sign the oath (1989: 274). The casualty list printed in the Commissioner's 1942 Annual Report is almost entirely composed of Afrikaners. In contrast, G. Visser claims that some of the volunteers were Afrikaner nationalists, and even supporters of the extreme terrorist group OB hoping for a German victory, who signed the oath out of fear of doing otherwise (1976: 32), although this seems illogical on a large scale given that it was not unusual to abstain. Black police also enlisted, but most served in the Native Military Corps, which was eventually incorporated into the remnants of the Police Brigade in 1944. Black South Africans generally made a large contribution to the war effort, with 45,000 Coloured soldiers and 70,000 Africans fighting in the war (Hellman 1943; Grundy 1983). The NRC in 1939 passed a resolution in support of an amendment to the 1912 Defence Act to enable 'all loyal South Africans, irrespective of race and class, to take part in the hostilities' (Annual Report of the NRC 1939: para. L(ii)); a recommendation from them to which the government for once listened.

Although members of the Police Brigade were predominantly Afrikaner, officers were mostly English-speaking (63 out of 102). One of the battalion commanders was an Afrikaner, but overall command was given to Brigadier Cooper, Quartermaster of the SAP since 1931, who had military background and knowledge, and later wrote a study of the Police Brigade (F. Cooper 1972), as well as a history of the SAP (F. Cooper 1972–3). It was Cooper who was instrumental in getting the first official chaplain appointed to the police in order to minister to policemen on active service; the chaplain was a member of the Dutch Reform Church, which shows the preponderance of Afrikaners among the volunteers. De Villiers was promoted out of the SAP in 1940 to the rank of Major-General in the Defence Force and given command of the infantry division which the police battalions formed part of, such was his paramilitary leaning. Colonel Baston was appointed Acting Commissioner of the SAP.

The battalions were initially sent to guard internment camps inside the Union where pro-German Afrikaners were being incarcerated. Lt.-Col. Palmer was in charge of the battalion policing the camp at Baviaanspoort, and it was he who replaced de Villiers as Commissioner in 1945. His men subsequently went to all the camps when Afrikaner inmates rioted, establishing for himself a negative image amongst Afrikaner nationalists, which later made for difficult relationships with the National Party government elected in 1948. Members of the police battalions were also used to suppress internal unrest on one occasion in Johannesburg. It was not until June 1941 that the men were sent to North Africa. When arriving in Egypt, however, they were initially used as policemen to control the local Arab population and police industrial strikes. Some of the members were also transferred back to the SAP due to manpower shortage in South Africa (F. Cooper 1972: 75); de Villiers was himself recalled for a while. But policemen did eventually fight as soldiers at El Alamein and Tobruk. The Second Transvaal Scottish Regiment was virtually wiped out at Sollum, and most members of the police battalions were captured at Tobruk and sent to prisoner-of-war camps in Germany and Italy, including Cooper. The remnants of the police battalions were consolidated under the leadership of Palmer, who was promoted to the rank of brigadier. In all 74 policemen were killed, 54 medals were awarded, and 55 policemen honourably mentioned in dispatches (Dippenaar 1988: 159). A diary belonging to a serving member in the Brigade survives for part of 1941 (see MSS Afr. s. 1277 (9)).

The Second World War also caused the SAP to be at war with itself, although it only precipitated what was a deeply embedded and long-standing conflict. This battle proved to be as great as those with Rommel. The recollections of a young policeman at the time provide a glimpse of the problem:

When war came, an indefinable change came over the men in their dealings with each other. There was much dissatisfaction and controversy. Certain elements were against the declaration of war, whilst others expressed their full support. Where there had been easy camaraderie there was now tension, even between friends. The declaration of war split the force asunder. (van Onselen 1960: 118)

Policemen in many stations refused to share mess facilities with those who had signed the oath, while some of those who refused were persuaded to resign or given long leaves of absence, including a Lieutenant Rademeyer, who became Commissioner in 1954. Smuts is reported by one of his police bodyguards as saying that he could not understand the feelings of the police towards the war (van Onselen 1960: 121), implying that he expected more loyalty. If this was so, it is surprising for the conflict was easy to anticipate, given the long-standing antipathy between sections of the Afrikaner and English-speaking membership that went as far back as 1913, when the police were first formed.

The Lansdown Commission was in part responsible for the Prime Minister's delusion because it disguised the antipathy by denying there were any 'racial feelings' or 'race distinctions' between members of the two White communities in the SAP or SARHP (Union of South Africa 1937a: 2, 75). But this ran counter to the facts because the language issue, for example, was a perennial problem. Both languages had long been recognized as official languages in the police, but complaint was frequently made about the use of English as the business language of the SAP. This was even raised in parliament by Afrikaner nationalists in 1925, and surfaced frequently in the 1930s. Some Afrikaner policemen were so aggressive in the advancement of their language that they would insist that African policemen, whose knowledge of the language was slight and not a requirement for entry to the force, address them in Afrikaans, something which the Lansdown Commission brought to the attention of the government in 1937. The issue came to a head in 1938 when two Afrikaner policemen in Johannesburg completed their paperwork in Afrikaans, as part of a concerted campaign in which colleagues around the country participated. They were severely reprimanded by their superiors but supported by de Villiers.

This is an indication of another schism, namely, the dominance of English-speakers in the officer class. This fissure was also long standing. Since 1927 90 per cent of the annual intake had been Afrikaans-speaking (Dippenaar 1988: 118), and complaints about their under-representation in the higher ranks were uttered frequently and given credence by the Commissioner. Complaints were made in the 1940s that English-speaking officers brought Freemasonry with them into the SAP (Union of South Africa 1950a: 15). As a young Afrikaner policeman at this time, van Onselen recalls how his English-speaking officers were objects of fun, and considered stupid and gullible (1960: 103). Noting this problem, the Lansdown Commission encouraged the SAP to redouble its efforts to recruit English-speakers by following the steps taken by the London Metropolitan Police (1937a: 10), which became the model because the Commission wanted to improve recruitment from urban areas, where English-speakers overwhelmingly lived. It noted the fear which English-speakers might have when entering the force because of being unable to talk in their own language in the station (p. 13), or being sent to a rural, Afrikaans-speaking area (p. 13). On this last point, it encouraged the government to allow English-speaking recruits to remain in their own area 'for a reasonable time' after joining the SAP, although it was against giving an extra allowance for higher educational qualifications, which would have disturbed greatly the poorly-educated Afrikaans-speaking rank and file.

The Afrikanerization of the lower ranks was thus something of a constraint on broadening the social composition of the police. It caused other problems in relations between the police and the public. Part of the thrust behind the liberal demand for police reform was disquiet about the bad public-relations skills of young, rural-based, poorly-educated, and insular Afrikaners in dealing with 'the very different type of urban native', and White English-speakers. In making this complaint (p. 76), the Lansdown Commission cited the example of a European male who was flung into a pick-up van at 11.00 p.m., in pyjamas and dressing-gown, after it was alleged that he endeavoured to rescue his African servant from what he thought was illegal and rough treatment from young policemen (p. 77).

Problems associated with the Afrikanerization of the ranks were therefore well known to the government, and it could have been anticipated that the revival of Afrikaner cultural nationalism at the end of the 1930s would have its effects within the police. The revival was based around the centenary celebrations of the Great Trek, which involved a symbolic ox-wagon trek from Cape Town to the site of the Voortrekker Monument in the Transvaal. The day that the trek began from Cape Town was the time established by the Afrikaner policemen for their gesture to make Afrikaans a business language in the SAP.

The enthusiasm caused by the celebration led to the formation of OB, literally meaning ox-wagon sentinels, whose aim was to perpetuate the ideals embodied in the Afrikaner trek and to revive the Afrikaans culture and language. OB quickly established itself amongst Afrikaners, in a way that similar organizations had not done prior to the centenary celebrations, and within months OB had over a quarter of a million members. Since the government had used the public sector as a means to solve unemployment among poor Afrikaners, many civil and public servants were members, including policemen. Dippenaar states that the majority of policemen were members (1988: 144).

It was formally a cultural organization, and its founders explicitly stated their disinterest in politics. Accordingly, prominent Afrikaners in governmental, judicial, and administrative positions were members, including advocates, senior civil servants, and generals in the defence force. The first leader of OB was General Laas, from the defence force. Another was Dr van Rensberg, Administrator of the Orange Free State, and formerly Secretary of Justice. However, the division between the cultural and political expressions of nationalism is always blurred, and in South Africa at this time culture was politics. Smuts realized this. Six months to the day after the formation of OB, he wrote a private letter to his friend J. Martin, stating, 'the Ossewabrandwag movement is going on pretty strong. This is probably only a secret military organization masquerading as a "cultural organization". I am keeping a close watch on it, remembering our experiences in 1914' (van der Poel 1973: 172). Clearly, even before war was declared, Smuts anticipated that OB would become the vanguard of another Afrikaner rebellion. Thus, within weeks of its formation, the government (at this time still under Hertzog) banned defence force personnel from being members, which is why Laas resigned his post in OB. When war was declared Smuts also prohibited civil servants from being members of the organization. In a letter to van Rensberg, dated 23 April 1941, Smuts later explained this decision: 'the rule of obedience to the organization may cause a conflict between duty to the state and duty to the organization' (van der Poel 1973: 294). In the same letter he expressed grave concern about OB's intention to form a youth section around Afrikaner schoolchildren, thinking this worse than membership by adult civil servants.

At this time, the ban on membership did not apply to policemen. The colonial character of the force obviated the need for a prohibition, since the loyalty of the police to the state was taken for granted by the government, such was the government's view of police–state relations. The force was conceived by the government as an agent of the state, and had acted in this way loyally, perhaps with the exception of the 1918 police strike, since its inception. Thus, when war was declared and OB stated its opposition to the government's decision, Smuts did not believe that a ban on police membership of OB was necessary. Smuts's presumption of police loyalty to the state explains both his confident decision to offer them the opportunity to express their loyalty, by being signatories to the oath, and his eventual disappointment and surprise when the extent of their political opposition became known. But on the outbreak of war in September 1939, Smuts evidently saw no conflict of interest between membership of the SAP and OB because policemen were assumed to be policemen first and Afrikaners second. This also explains why Smuts thought that opposition within the police could be easily bought off by paying the men arrears in pay owing since 1938, and offering them free hospitalization for themselves and their families.

Opposition to the war, however, acted as a powerful mobilization for Afrikaner nationalism, and had its effects within the police. Hertzog and Malan joined forces and waged a campaign of opposition against the United Party, indicting Smuts for having dragged South Africa into a war that could not be won. Cultural organizations were transformed into political movements, and protesters drew on Afrikaner cultural symbols in stating their political opposition. Beards began to be worn by Afrikaner men as both a symbol of their culture and allegiance to OB (Dippenaar 1988: 151). Processions of Afrikaner women, in voortrekker dress, marched in protest against Smuts. Petitions were started, with the aid of several Afrikaner cultural organizations, allowing Afrikaners to express their opposition to the war (for Smuts's discussions of this in his private letters, see van der Poel 1973: 240, 249). OB was wrapped up in all this and by 1940 was publishing manifestos critical of the government, and demanding an Afrikaner uprising. In 1940 it formed an armed wing, called the *stormjaers* (storm-troops), which had its own oath, containing the words: 'if I advance, follow me; if I retreat, shoot me; if I die, avenge me; so help me God' (quoted in G. Visser 1976: 22; also see Dippenaar 1988: 172; Calvinist notions about the Afrikaner nation being God's calling were always woven into nationalist political demands; see de Klerk 1975; Dunbar Moodie 1975).

Although initially established to provide order at OB meetings, the *stormjaers* rapidly went on the offensive, in much the same way as did Blackshirts in European Fascist movements in the early 1930s (on Britain see Brewer 1984). *Stormjaers* attacked United Party meetings. In 1940 and 1941 Smuts frequently received pleas from his party members for action against OB, whose supporters were attacking their meetings or holding provocative ones of their own in areas where United Party members were a beleaguered minority (see, for example, a letter from J. C. Opperman, in van der Poel 1973: 294). On 10 January 1941, *stormjaers* attacked the Minister of the Interior, Harry Lawrence, as he spoke on a United Party platform, with only two policemen to protect him. Allied soldiers and sailors, camped in South Africa *en route* elsewhere, were also frequently subject to assault by the *stormjaers* and OB supporters generally, as were South Africa's own volunteers. During 1940, seventy-nine incidents of soldiers being attacked were recorded in the Transvaal alone (Annual Report of the Commissioner of the SAP 1940: 14), and they occurred as frequently in large ports such as Durban and Cape Town. Servicemen were attacked so often that they used to form protective groups when walking the streets, and often anticipated violence by getting their retaliation in first. Soldiers responded with equal violence, so many of the clashes became riots. On one occasion soldiers went on the rampage and attacked students at an Afrikaner university and teacher training college. On 31 January 1941 a group of allied servicemen attacked a meeting of the Afrikaans Language and Cultural Society in Johannesburg, where the head of OB had been invited to speak. A riot ensued between soldiers, *stormjaers*, people in the audience, and members of the public. Order was only re-established the following day by the intervention of the first battalion of the Police Brigade under Palmer.

The government established a commission of inquiry under S. H. Elliot, Johannesburg's chief magistrate. In the course of its deliberations, evidence was revealed which, for the first time, indicated the political partisanship of some policemen who were Afrikaner nationalists, pointing to a link between OB and some members of the police. In a short paragraph Dippenaar records that the Commission absolved the SAP as an organization from being a party to the unrest (1988: 152), but only states elsewhere that the Commission identified the activities of some of its members, working in concert with supporters of OB, as responsible for escalating the disorder (1988: 160; for a more balanced account see G. Visser 1976: 42–3; van der Spuy 1989:

275). Untabbed members of the police were shown to have committed violence against allied servicemen (see G. Visser 1976: 42), joining with *stormjaers* in charging the soldiers. One untabbed policeman shot a soldier who later died in hospital. The soldiers apparently cheered when police arrived wearing red tabs. The Commission regarded the fact that members of OB had fought side by side with untabbed policemen against the soldiers as proof of disturbing connections between the two organizations. Fifteen policemen later appeared in the magistrates' court on charges of public violence, although they were acquitted. The Commission also recommended that in future the police remove all tabs from their uniform so that distinctions between members could not be made by the public, that severe disciplinary measures be enforced in the SAP, and that the police increase their co-operation with the Military Police (G. Visser 1976: 42–3).

The Commission was eager to stress that not all untabbed policemen could be regarded as disloyal or members of OB, but by now the government felt that tabs were important in telling it which policemen it could trust, so it refused to implement the recommendation that policemen remove them from their uniforms. The government had none the less been made fully aware of the intentions of OB, with the Commission describing it as factional, undemocratic, and sectional. Anticipating its banning, van Rensberg wrote to Smuts on 17 April 1941, excusing the unrest as arising from the inherent difficulties of maintaining discipline in military movements. He ended with an appeal to Smuts's Afrikaner heritage: 'I trust, General, your far-sightedness will not allow the majority of the Afrikaans-speaking people in their largest national organization to be declared illegal on the *obiter dicta* of a commission of officials and unheard' (van der Poel 1973: 291). Shortly afterwards it was declared a subversive organization under the emergency regulations, and the Commissioner of the SAP decreed that all policemen should resign from it.

The activities of OB had become well known by this time, but it took the highly public battle between allied servicemen and OB supporters before Smuts would act against it. They had become well known to him in part because in 1939 the SAP had established its first special branch precisely in order to monitor OB. This is what Smuts was referring to when he wrote in his letter to Martin on 3 August 1939, that he was keeping a close watch on it (van der Poel 1973: 172). In July 1939, five months after the formation of OB, Lieutenant Diedricks was appointed the Union's first Aliens Registration Officer, and instructed to establish a unit called the Special Staff in order to monitor the activities of 'aliens' and investigate political crimes. This was the SAP's first special branch, and was set up because of the government's fear that German nationals from Namibia would infiltrate Afrikaner organizations such as OB. Many of its early number were loyal Afrikaans-speaking policemen in order to enable members to infiltrate Afrikaner organizations, but the special staff quickly grew to 180 men and included many English-speakers. Headquarters were in Johannesburg rather than Pretoria, although special staff operated throughout the Union. They even infiltrated OB. On discovering that one of its members was a police informant, the organization kidnapped the person concerned and severely assaulted him, and would have killed him but he effected an escape. It later transpired that Advocate Jerling, a senior member of OB, was also working with the police.

The SAP's official historian argues that few policemen followed the Commissioner's advice to resign from OB, since many were already too deeply involved in its activities (Dippenaar 1988: 160). This became apparent from the surveillance work done by the special staff, and various incidents where untabbed policemen furthered the aims of the organization by interfering with criminal investigations against OB supporters. In 1940 the special staff, including George Visser, became aware of what the German government called Operation Weissdorn. They intended to use OB in order to provide a base in South Africa by which allied shipping could be destroyed, and the Union's industry and war effort disrupted (see G. Visser 1976: 54–5; Dippenaar 1988: 161–8). The Nazis used Sidney Leibbrandt as their agent, and part of his role was to assassinate Smuts and organize a coup. He was a former member of the SAP, who had transferred to the SARHP in 1935. As part of this effort, the OB began a campaign encouraging 'young policemen with national spirit' to resign, distributing a pamphlet addressed to 'comrades of the SAP' (G. Visser 1976: 63). Police files record that on 14 January 1942, thirty constables in Fordsburg were contemplating desertion, but only three did so; a fourth failed to return from leave (SAP/1/93/27). All were Afrikaners, although no connection was made in the report to the OB's campaign. Although Leibbrandt later broke away from OB, finding them half-hearted in their commitment to national socialism, and formed his own National Socialist Rebels, he had some sympathizers in the SAP, who assisted him in evading police arrest. Policemen loyal to Afrikaner nationalism even managed to conceal the fact of Leibbrandt's presence in the country from their tabbed colleagues and did not reveal his intention to assassinate Smuts (Dippenaar 1988: 163). This became known in part as a result of Advocate Jerling's work. Once it was public knowledge, Smuts was given a bodyguard of loyal policemen, one of whom was van Onselen, who later wrote a book on his exploits (for his account of his activities as bodyguard see 1960: 121). Leibbrandt was eventually captured by members of the special staff, and found guilty of high treason after a lengthy court case, with his death sentence commuted to life imprisonment, reputedly because his father had been an old comrade of Smuts in the Boer War (G. Visser 1976: 65–6).

Connections between OB and the police went deeper than the Leibbrandt affair. Certain policemen assisted OB prisoners to escape custody (G. Visser 1976: 69). One such was Johannes van der Walt, Chief General of OB, and a legendary figure among Afrikaners on account of being the Empire's wrestling champion. He came under close surveillance by special staff and was arrested on several petty charges. He broke out of Marshall Square police station in Johannesburg on 22 December 1941, after having his cell door unlocked by a policeman. Other policemen helped van der Walt find his way to a waiting car. He was eventually shot while escaping from a farmhouse; several prominent Afrikaners visited him in hospital, including cabinet ministers. He died some months later, and became an Afrikaner folk hero.

In this way some policemen were aiding an organization which was declared subversive and, having to go underground, was by now engaging in wanton acts of sabotage and terrorism. Members of the SARHP took special precautions against sabotage on railway lines; citizens whose loyalty was without doubt formed the Essential Services Corps, protecting key installations and sites. By the end of the war there were 8,468 members of the Corps, including 2,539 Blacks, most of whom were veterans from the First World War (Martin and Orpen 1979). There were other citizen forces, such as the civic guards, who took over an ordinary policing role, to which a sum of £5,815 was allocated in 1940/1 for training, and the National Volunteer Brigade, members of which signed up for enlistment in the war but did a range of sensitive duties inside the Union if they were not used in North Africa. The support work of these bodies enabled the SAP to focus on the sabotage and terrorism perpetrated by the OB. During

1940–1, there were twenty-five bomb explosions on the Rand, aimed at bioscopes, shops, newspaper offices, cafés, and theatres. In January 1942 bomb explosions brought down electricity and telephone wires. Water-pipes were bombed in May. Moreover, the *stormjaers* began a murder campaign against witnesses in trials of OB members. They killed a member of the special staff in Bloemfontein in September 1942, shooting him and then setting his body alight. He was lured to his death by someone who was, or claimed to be, a fellow policeman. Another murder was of a witness in the treason trial involving *stormjaers*.

This trial showed the real extent of police involvement in OB sabotage and terrorism against the government. In October 1941 members of the special staff raided a house owned by OB in Durban, and discovered arms and documents. They were eventually led to the home of Constable Kraukamp, in the Transvaal, where they found documents which contained the names of 810 members of the SAP, SARHP, Johannesburg traffic police, and prisons service, including three from the special staff, who were said to be members or supporters of OB. Most of the names were of members of the SAP (699), and all were from Johannesburg. The men were described as the OB's 'police battalion', a reference to the SAP's Police Brigade. Kraukamp was the battalion's lieutenant-colonel. Their intention was to capture senior police officers who were loyal to the government, occupy Johannesburg's radio station, and assist in the overthrow of the government.

Not all names on the list were apparently members of the *stormjaers* (Dippenaar 1988: 175), since it included those thought by others to be sympathetic to OB, but 562 men were subsequently revealed under interrogation to be in Kraukamp's command; at the home of one of these they found eighty hand-grenades. Most were constables (a rank where Afrikaners dominated), although forty-three were non-commissioned officers. However, since the list only contained the names of men in Johannesburg, it is likely to under-represent the number of policemen who supported OB in opposition to the government. The list contained no names from the Orange Free State, for example, where van Rensberg lived and where OB was strongest. Nor did it contain the names of policemen from Durban, where the English-speaking culture of the city created an aggressive assertion of cultural nationalism in some Afrikaner policemen; the first cache of arms and documents was found in Durban, and the language issue was always problematic once the SAP took over the Durban borough police in 1936.

The people named on the list were arrested while on a parade, where they were surrounded by members of the National Volunteer Brigade, and dispatched to Koffiefontein internment camp. Kraukamp appeared as a state witness in the eventual trial and revealed that there were another fifteen battalions of *stormjaers*, totalling 8,000 men. The 'police battalion' in OB thus represented at least one-tenth of its armed force. Most of the policemen identified as active members of OB were interned, while fifty-five *stormjaers*, including twenty-two policemen, considered the more serious cases, were tried at a preliminary hearing, being represented by Albert Hertzog, General Hertzog's son. The Attorney-General subsequently reduced the charge from one of high treason, and the men were found guilty of lesser charges, with sentences ranging from fifteen months to fifteen years. The eight policemen who led the investigation were later given the King's Police Medal, including four Afrikaners.

A damage limitation exercise began immediately the plot was uncovered. In the process, the government made remarks about how it saw police–state relations properly operating. At a press conference the day after the mass arrests, the Acting Commissioner stressed the impossibility of policemen serving two masters, although by implication they were allowed to serve one. Loyalty to the government by policemen was stressed above their political impartiality: 'disloyal policemen cannot possibly be trusted . . . it is the policy of this Department to disregard the political affiliations of individual members, as long as they do their duty loyally and efficiently. However, available evidence appears to indicate that these men were disloyal' (cited in Dippenaar 1988: 176). Government ministers also stressed the importance of loyalty to the state rather than impartiality. The Minister of Justice, Dr C. Steyn, said: 'it is very much regretted that these drastic steps against the police have become necessary, but it is essential that the loyalty of the police should be beyond question' (cited in G. Visser 1976: 96). Clearly, the crime was not political partisanship but loyalty to the wrong political cause.

The cause ended once the extent of OB's anti-constitutionalism became evident. Malan and Hertzog finally disassociated themselves and their party from OB, and asked all Afrikaner nationalists to resign from the movement, specifically urging policemen to do so. But their prevarication damaged Afrikaner nationalism as a whole, and Smuts romped through the 1943 general election. He was exuberant in a private letter to M. C. Gillett, dated 31 July 1943, quoting lines from Southey's poem 'The Battle of Blenheim', to the effect that "twas a famous victory': 'the Ossewabrandwag people are in hiding. It is indeed a "famous victory". The political front is now secure, with a parliamentary majority which is an embarrassment. And we can get on with the job' (van der Poel 1973: 447). He was slightly over-optimistic, in that there were occasional acts of violence by OB supporters, the most notable being an attack on a United Party MP at his home on 21 July 1944, when he was brutally whipped with a sjambok until made unconscious. Visiting South Africa from Tanganyika in order to investigate the 'African question', Sir Robert Hall noted in his diary for 1 November 1944 that leading liberals still feared a campaign of 'far-right violence' (MSS Afr. r. 92); however Smuts was right to state that the OB menace was effectively over by 1943.

But fighting Afrikaner nationalists was not the only problem for the police in South Africa's racial society, for the colonization of the country's Black population remained an important function. The government feared that Black South Africans would use the opportunity of the war to rebel, such that the war fed feelings of *swart gevaar*. Curfew regulations covering the African population, which had always been in existence but had become relaxed in their application, were rigorously enforced at the beginning of the war. In Vryheid, for example, the police used to impose an 11.00 p.m. curfew even though the law stated it should be 9.00 p.m., but after complaints from White residents at the beginning of the war, the law was strictly applied (Annual Report of the NRC 1941: 233). Councillors on the NRC demanded the removal of the curfew, pointing out its unfairness in singling out Africans, and complained about the inability of the police to use discretion in its enforcement (pp. 233–4). The liquor laws were also applied rigidly. A later Commission of Inquiry (Union of South Africa 1950a) pursued allegations of corruption made against the police in their application of the liquor laws during the war, concluding that there was corruption, although this was blamed on the existence of the Police Brigade, which had caused extreme manpower shortage in the SAP (p. 5), an idea that resonated with the new National Party government. It also transpired that a policeman at this time passed on information to a medical doctor that he was about to be raided by immorality staff on suspicion of performing illegal abortions (p. 2). The doctor concerned was paying the police £300 per month for protection from prosecution (p. 3).

The application of the pass laws, however, was more ambiguous. Some sections of the state favoured a more permissive approach to influx control during the war. The Minister of Native Affairs, for example, called for the abolition of pass laws in 1942, as did the Smit Commission in 1943. This fitted Smuts's claim in 1942, during a speech to the SAIRR, that state policy on race had shifted from segregation to 'trusteeship'. However, the tensions within the state over this issue were reflected in only a marginal change in the number of prosecutions for pass law offences, and on the ground the police applied the laws with as much force as before the war. For example, Councillor Thema, of the NRC, claimed that Africans were being molested by the civic guards, which had replaced the SAP on many ordinary police duties, demanding to see passes when they had no legal right to do so (Annual Report of the NRC 1941: 199). They apparently stood by bus terminals and demanded to see the pass of every African passenger, and were known to accept bribes from victims. Pick-up vans were kept busy throughout the war. In 1941 Councillor Sililo of the NRC complained that the vans raided Africans as they came out of church (p. 234), and Councillors Mshiyeni and Baloyi alleged that the police were charging sober people for drunkenness if they could not be found contravening the pass laws (p. 235). In 1942 Councillor Dube complained about his house being raided by policemen at night, his wife driven out naked, and his furniture broken up (Annual Report of the NRC 1942: 6). Rightly, councillors pointed to the contradiction between pick-up vans and call-up papers. The war effort of Blacks was used as a moral argument against their internal colonization. How could natives be bundled into pick-up vans by the police, asked the NRC in 1941, and then go off to war (Annual Report of the NRC 1941: 197)? This is something which a few liberal White soldiers recognized also, and after the war they tried to encourage the Springbok Legion to adopt some progressive views on race issues (for the account of one member see Frederikse 1990: 43–4).

The operation of the pass laws became critical in the war because it stimulated the urbanization of the African population, as they moved into towns to fill the labour shortage in manufacturing industry caused by the hostilities. And even though some sections of the state advocated a permissive approach to influx control at this time, the living and working conditions Africans encountered in the urban areas became the focus of considerable grass-roots protests. Posel documents some of the reports filed by location managers in the early 1940s which noted the proliferation of 'subversive propaganda'. She quotes one who said there was a 'growing tendency on the part of natives to organize concerted resistance on any question which they consider affects them adversely, and at such gatherings to speak extravagantly and defiantly of authority' (cited in 1991: 34–5). Grass-roots protests centred around increases in food prices, hikes in the price of bus fares, and, particularly, squatters' rights. Squatter movements were extremely active during the war, protesting against the poor living conditions in the locations, the unavailability of proper housing, and the attempts by some authorities to flatten the squatter settlements (for the comments of Sir Robert Hall, visiting the country from Tanganyika, see diary entries for 17, 27, and 30 Oct. 1944 in MSS Afr. r. 92). Some of the battles were won, with authorities allowing squatters to settle on municipal land, but others were lost, sometimes after fierce and brutal police action. In one incident, sixteen protesters were shot and killed, with a further fifty-four wounded. A commission of inquiry absolved the police of blame, but condemned the shootings and recommended compensation for the families.

These wartime protests fed into organized political resistance in three ways. First, the NRC became radicalized, transforming the formerly conservative body into a radical forum for African demands (it disbanded itself in 1946 over protest at the government's actions in quelling the miners' strike). Secondly, it reinvigorated the trade union movement. African trade unions grew in strength and size during the 1940s, so that by 1945, over 100,000 workers were unionized, approximately 40 per cent of the African industrial work-force (Posel 1991: 38). This brought the trade union movement back to the heights it achieved with the Industrial Commercial Union in 1927. Initially there was some support within the state to legalize African trade unions, and in 1941 the Minister of Justice wrote to the Commissioner of the SAP instructing the police not to prosecute or harass Africans on strike until there had been an opportunity to settle the dispute (R. Fine 1990: 21). One consequence of this liberal attitude was the increase in strike activity in the war, which saw 304 strikes, involving 58,000 Black South Africans (Posel 1991: 38; also see R. Fine 1990: 5–12). From an analysis of the 284 strikes between 1942 and 1945 mentioned by R. Fine (1990: 10), Black workers participated in industrial action at a level nearly eight times greater than White workers, and there was a total of 280,400 days lost. This number has to be set in the context of renewed repression of strikers after 1942.

Fine shows that after 1942, the liberal approach to African trade unions was replaced by the iron fist (1990: 23–4), and the state abandoned attempts to recognize African trade unions.

The third manifestation of Black political radicalism during the war was the growth of the Communist Party of South Africa (CPSA) and the formation of the militant ANC Youth League in 1944. CPSA had been in existence since 1921, but grew in parallel with the Black trade-union movement during the war (R. Fine 1990: 9). By the end of the war, the CPSA had gained a foothold in many African townships on the Rand and in the Eastern Cape (Posel 1991: 36), and the ANC Youth League, headed by young radicals like Mandela and Sisulu, demanded a strategy for mass action (for an account of Black politics in 1945 and after see Lodge 1983; on the ANC Youth League see Gerhart 1978: 45–84). The scene was thus set for the political resistance of the 1950s, in the suppression of which the police played the prominent role.

CONCLUSION

On 1 December 1944 Major-General de Villiers resumed command of the SAP, allowing the Acting Commissioner to retire. De Villiers himself retired on 31 July 1945, to be replaced by Brigadier Palmer, who in the First World War had deserted from the SAP in order to enlist, and during the Second, was part of the Police Brigade. Palmer's appointment was a significant break with tradition. As a former constable in the pre-Union Orange Free State Police, he was the first commissioner to rise from the ranks and to possess experience of police work. This was a measure of modernization. However, during the period covered by this chapter, in which Palmer's predecessor was in command, police professionalization was limited. An opportunity for police reform was not grasped because of the nature of police–state relations and the state's need for the SAP to police race relations, for it was in this period that this role was clarified and the SAP intensified its monitoring and control of the Black population. This role continued apace after 1948, when the police enforced a policy of apartheid, as we shall see in following chapters. From that point on the state and the bulk of the police were in agreement on what the right political cause was for the police to support partisanly. An opportunity for reform did not present itself again until the 1990s. However, the political opposition displayed by the police during the Second World War acts as a bad omen for police reform today, when the state has recast its interests and finds itself, once more, in conflict with the political partisanship of the police.

4

The Transition to Apartheid
1946–1959

INTRODUCTION

The period covered by this chapter marks the transition to National Party government and the first phase of apartheid, although technically it was the Herenigde Nasionale Party which won the 1948 general election, only becoming known as the National Party when it joined with the Afrikaner Party in 1949. The extent of continuity between segregationism and apartheid at the structural level is widely debated, showing itself in disputes over the periodization of the state and the significance of 1948 as a marker, and whether or not there was any shift in the underlying relationship between race and class interests under the different governments (for contrasting views on this debate see Lipton 1985: 14–48; Rich 1989; Wolpe 1988: 5 *passim*). This debate is less important here than the issue of how broader political changes affected policing. Smuts's defeat and the rise to power of militant Afrikaner nationalists bore upon the police, but this was less presentient than the literature on the SAP suggests (for examples of work which portray 1948 as a radical juncture for policing see: Brewer 1988: 277; S. Davies 1987: 180; Frankel 1980: 482, 484; Haysom 1989a: 142; Moorcraft 1990: 409; Nasson 1991: 249; Philips 1989: 17; Prior 1989: 192, 200; Seegars 1986, 1989: 6; van der Spuy 1990: 87).

The transition from segregation to apartheid did not represent a radical departure for the SAP. The rank and file was already Afrikanerized in manpower, the SAP's reputation for partisanship in the use of force was established prior to 1948, and the regulation of the social, political, and economic boundaries between the races had been defined as the primary role of the police by the 1930s. The significant change under apartheid was in the number of regulations and powers by which the police monitored the boundaries between the races, giving them more pervasive and systematic control than before over the lives of Black South Africans, and Africans especially, and the degree of force policemen used when doing so. But this was something which occurred slowly as apartheid consolidated during its first phase in the 1950s. The transition period itself brought quite limited change for the police.

THE IMMEDIATE AFTERMATH OF WAR

The war depleted the SAP considerably, in terms of morale, manpower, and resources, and Palmer's first task as Commissioner was to rebuild. After assuming office on 1 August 1945, he formulated a three-year plan. Disunity was addressed by his stress that past divisions should be forgotten in the approach to a new era. This theme was important because nearly one thousand policemen, interned in prisoner-of-war camps after being captured as part of the Police Brigade, needed to be reintegrated into the force without conflict being created when working alongside colleagues who had refused to fight in the war. As a part of the reconciliation, Palmer asked the Minister of Justice to allow all policemen interned for support of OB to rejoin the force. Not surprisingly the government found this unacceptable. But it did permit an increase in pay.

The Third Report of the Public Services Commission of Inquiry, published in 1946, recommended sizeable increases in allowances and basic pay, which the government agreed to immediately. Part of the problem was that sections of the state were bidding against each other for similar services, and the Commission found that the pay and allowances of the SAP were inferior to those of the traffic police and SARHP. Men were often being trained by the SAP, purchasing their discharge for the price of £10 within the first year, and immediately joining the SARHP at an increase in annual salary of just over £42. The Commission recommended an immediate increase in allowances and basic pay, plus other fringe benefits, such as free medical attendance and hospital treatment for White members, introduced as a temporary measure during the war, as well as half the cost of dental treatment (Whites only), a free railway ticket once a year for a member and their family (Whites only), allowances to cover the costs of resettlement upon recruitment (Whites only), and various leave privileges and pension rights (all members).

The Commissioner's programme for rebuilding the SAP also literally meant a demand for the provision of more suitable accommodation for living quarters and police stations. In his 1945 Annual Report, the Commissioner noted that 400 stations were needed to replace those which were now in advanced states of decay (p. 5); in 1946 half of the SAP's 947 stations were thought by Palmer to be in need of replacement, many of 'immediate replacement' (Annual Report of the Commissioner of the SAP 1946: 5). He noted ruefully, however, that some had been awaiting repair for twenty years, clearly recognizing that his complaints echoed those of his predecessors. As an immediate measure the government allowed policemen to be billeted in disused military barracks.

The main substance of Palmer's programme was to correct the manpower shortage and promotion blockage that were an aftermath of the war. Rapid promotion for White members was used as a strategy to address problems of morale and high wastage. Upon taking office Palmer found that there were four White constables for every White officer or non-commissioned officer above him; on his retirement in 1951 there were only two (F. Cooper 1972–3: 24). The Commissioner also introduced an annual examinations system by which White members could apply for promotion, overseen by a new Promotions Council (three of whose four members were Afrikaners), which drew up examination papers and supervised the system. The problem of high wastage, which was being addressed through promotion, was made worse by poor recruitment to the police after the war.

Recruitment to the SAP was suspended during the war because Section 9 of the 1912 Police Act prohibited resignations during war without the express permission of the Chief Commissioner. Only 116 men were allowed to resign during the war, although, as Table 4.1 shows, wastage and dismissals were high. The abandonment of recruitment during the war led to severe manpower shortage after it. In 1945 the SAP was 1,333 men short of its complement of White members, and the Public Services Commission recommended an increase in the establishment of all races. This amounted to 2,963 Black policemen alone between 1945 and 1946, for which the Native Affairs Commission (NAC) was mightily pleased (Annual Report of the NAC 1947: 23). However, the government was concerned about the imbalance in the racial composition of the force and agreed to an

TABLE 4.1 *Wastage and dismissals, 1939–1945**

Year	Drunkenness	Misconduct	Conviction by court	Unsuitable	Medically unfit
1939	–	26	15	11	68
1940	–	39	22	23	58
1941	–	46	18	30	55
1942	1	–	9	83	79
1943	–	–	5	60	71
1944	–	3	2	20	71
1945	–	–	–	36	77

* All races.
Source: Union of South Africa 1946: 15.

increase of 2,829 for White members and only 901 for Blacks. Most of the African recruits were Zulu because special recruitment teams went to Zululand, although they also visited the Northern Transvaal.

The Commissioner's problem was in finding suitable White recruits to replace the shortfall, especially since the Civic Guards were hurriedly disbanded in 1946, in part because of their poor reputation in dealing with urban Africans. Palmer tried initially to recruit among trained soldiers. The Deputy Commissioner went with two other officers to the army corps in Egypt, and although the number of applications was high, most were rejected on grounds of poor education or medical disability. The inferior pay and service conditions of the SAP compared to the SARHP and traffic police also proved problematic, although salary increases announced in 1946 solved this. Coinciding with the improvements in police pay, 2,213 White recruits were enrolled in 1946, which added to the accommodation problems being experienced at the time. A Junior Branch of the SAP was also formed from youngsters between the ages of 17 and 19 who had passed their Junior Certificate, employed in 'sheltered positions' (Annual Report of the Commissioner of the SAP 1946: 4).

To improve recruitment still further, policemen throughout the Union were encouraged to nominate names of suitable candidates to their officers, and the press ran large campaigns urging patriotic men to enrol for the SAP. A large public-relations exercise was undertaken by the police when a recruitment team toured South Africa. Within eight months they travelled 15,500 miles, visited 184 towns, held 383 drill and physical education performances, showed 192 motion pictures on careers in the police, and distributed 170,000 posters (Annual Report of the Commissioner of the SAP 1947: 3). None the less, in the same report, the Commissioner was still complaining about the shortage of White personnel, caused primarily by the high number of trained men purchasing their discharge to find better paid employment elsewhere (p. 5). This particularly affected Whites, and it is from the end of the Second World War that the racial composition of the SAP begins to shift markedly in favour of Blacks, as we shall see later. South Africa's Official Yearbook for 1948 indicated a shortfall in White manpower of 3,003 men (p. 450), while figures from the Commissioner's Annual Report for 1948 indicated it to be 3,158.

POLICING UNDER THE UNITED PARTY

The period under review in this chapter includes the last three years of United Party government, enabling a contrast to be drawn later with policing under apartheid. Were a short description to be given it, policing in the final years of Smuts's segregationist policies was characterized by partial modernization towards a civil police force within the overall constraints of the colonial task the police were required to perform. The SAP's continued role in policing race relations therefore ensured that race remained the vital feature of policing, as reflected in the internal structure and organization of the SAP, its deployment of police manpower and effort, and in police–public relations.

Wars quite often facilitate technical innovation, but in the SAP's case the Second World War accelerated the adoption of modern technology that was first deployed before the hostilities. Cars fitted with one-way radio were first introduced in 1936, and the experiment was assessed in 1945, with the Commissioner reporting his satisfaction with it (Annual Report of the Commissioner of the SAP 1945: 6). In that year 40,163 messages were sent, resulting in 5,192 arrests. In 1948 fifteen cars were fitted with two-way radios for use in Johannesburg, Durban, and Cape Town. The number of messages sent by radio that year had increased by 78 per cent from 1945, and the Commissioner estimated that the arrest rate arising from calls to radio-fitted cars was 7.5 per cent (Annual Report of the Commissioner of the SAP 1948: 7). As a point of comparison, by 1952 there were twenty-two cars fitted with two-way radios, the number of radio messages had increased by 56 per cent from 1948, and the arrest rate was estimated to be 34 per cent (Annual Report of the Commissioner of the SAP 1952: 5). A trend was thus established to modernize the technology of the force, which was reflected also in its use of mechanized transport.

In 1927 the SAP's fleet of vehicles totalled 311, by 1945 it was 1,356, and by 1947 1,821. In the period 1945–7, the most rapid expansion was in the number of motor cars, with an 86 per cent increase over two years. There were still more pick-up vans than cars, but the growth in the number of vans, at 24.3 per cent, was well behind that of cars. The SAP was thus beginning to shift to modern forms of transport, enabling men to cover more ground when on duty. In 1927 the average policeman on foot patrol covered 12.6 miles per day, and his mounted colleague 13.4 miles, whereas the average mileage covered by cars per day in 1945 was 32.9 (Annual Report of the Commissioner of the SAP 1945: 8). The advent of mechanized transport therefore enabled the police to rationalize manpower and close down some of the smaller stations. The use of public call boxes, linked to central police stations, reinforced this trend. Call boxes were first introduced in 1940 in the context of severe staff shortage, and by 1945 Johannesburg had twenty; another sixty-six were built in the city during 1946. Other towns on the Rand were planning to introduce them in 1945; fifteen were being built in Springs.

The sheer size of the country meant that motorization was more effective in South Africa than foot patrol, although foot patrolmen remained in some of the White suburbs of the largest cities because some residents complained about the closure of stations (Annual Report of the Commissioner of the SAP 1948: 7). But South Africa's geography also ensured that horses could never be dispensed with entirely, especially in the rural areas, and after the war the SAP purchased its own stud farm and formed a veterinary sub-branch. In 1947 there were thirty-nine members employed in veterinary services, and the SAP had 9,366 animals, including five donkeys, 157 camels, and two oxen (Annual Report of the Commissioner of the SAP 1947: 9). The stud farm, however, was eventually disposed of by public auction as motorization superseded the use of horses, even in rural areas. In 1947 the SAP formed its Mechanical Training Centre as the first training school for police technicians and mechanics.

These figures may seem rather arid but they are important. It is noticeable after the Second World War that the SAP shifted to motorized patrol more rapidly than was the case in the United Kingdom, where men on foot could more easily cover the smaller distances involved. This technical innovation presaged a significant shift in police–public relations after the war, even with respect to the policing of Whites. In relying on motor vehicles, as well as radio calls and call boxes, men were being withdrawn from the beat, and the SAP began to rely on what is now popularly called 'fire-brigade' or rapid-response policing much earlier than was the case in the United Kingdom, for example, where this style of policing was not introduced until the 1960s and 1970s. Critics of this style of policing in Britain have noted that it divorces the police from the community (Alderson 1979; Brewer *et al.* 1988), and can have a deleterious effect on crime detection (Kinsey *et al.* 1986), since it loses the basic point of contact between public and police, which is the beat.

In South Africa's case, however, the negative effects of the fire-brigade approach to policing merely widened the chasm between the SAP and the majority of the public, which was already gapingly wide as a result of the colonial policing task the SAP performed. In fact, the SAP's use of some types of modern vehicle reflected the deterioration in police–public relations in South Africa rather than provoked it, the best examples being the pick-up vans and mobile charge offices.

In addition to modernizing its technology prior to 1948, the SAP was also modernizing its organization by means of the specialization of function. The SAP formed a Special Branch (SB) in 1947 (as well as a veterinary sub-branch), to add to its existing uniformed and CID branches. Despite being a form of modernization, the thrust behind this innovation also reflected the colonial task of police work in South Africa. Although the SAP today present the origins of the SB as lying in a communist onslaught on the country (Dippenaar 1988: 204, 211; SAP 1986: 34), it grew from the Special Staff set up in 1939 to monitor the activities of Afrikaner nationalists. Moreover, the state's primary worry about communism was that it would provide a basis for Black rebellion, so that class interests and racial fears both underlay the establishment of the SB.

The first head of the SB was an Afrikaner, Major du Plooy, who had been in the Special Staff and was based at headquarters in Pretoria. Although the SB was ranked equal to the SAP's two other branches, it was centrally located, and operated at this time from headquarters rather than from the divisions. Dippenaar reports that some senior officers opposed the formation of a special branch on the grounds that it was an alien idea (1988: 211), and perhaps to assuage such fears du Plooy recruited from the existing establishment of policemen rather than directly to the SB, and within months he went on a tour to the Metropolitan Police in London to seek advice on how to 'combat subversion'. Visiting the Metropolitan Police was more an attempt to pacify the few officers who favoured the use of the civil police tradition as a model for the SAP, because the Metropolitan Police could teach du Plooy very little given that the exclusive responsibility of the SB was internal security, something about which London's uniformed police knew nothing. And Dippenaar reports that du Plooy returned more with ideas about the establishment of CID investigation rooms, the use of two-way radios, and extensions to the SAP's Mechanical Training Centre (1988: 211).

Training was also modernized in the last years of Smuts's government. In November 1947 the training depot changed its name to the Police College, because of the military connotations of the word 'depot' (Annual Report of the Commissioner of the SAP 1948: 4). By 1948 412 staff were employed in training, with another 52 Black personnel (p. 5). One of the senior staff was given the title of the SAP's 'Educational Officer'. The changes in nomenclature, however, reflected a deeper transformation. The emphasis shifted towards law and general education, and away from military training, although drill and musketry remained significant features of the curriculum. Visiting lectures were arranged by the Department of Education, Arts and Science on topics such as psychology, ethnology, personality, and race relations. The latter included an early form of 'race awareness training' for White recruits, involving lectures on African culture and administration. Quoted approvingly by the NAC, the Commissioner explained that 'every effort is being made to awaken the sympathy of all ranks for the native population' (Annual Report of the NAC 1947: 23). The reverse of this, of course, is that recruits could easily be fed distorted views about race, culture, and anthropology, with social science being twisted in order to find spurious justification for racial separation and prejudiced notions about a link between race and crime. This is precisely what happened once Afrikaner nationalist criminology became the hegemonic paradigm (van Zyl Smit 1990).

One of the biggest advances taken in 1947 towards modern training was the decision to train Black police formally. The Third Report of the Public Services Commission of Inquiry in 1946 supported the continued employment of 'illiterate natives' for use in rural areas, but recommended an improvement in the educational entry requirements of African police intended for the urban areas, and the establishment of a training school for them. The government agreed, and a training school was opened at Umtata on 10 March 1947, in buildings which formerly housed the now defunct Mobile Police Unit, a mounted, paramilitary squad that once operated in the Transkei. This location for the new school was perhaps symbolic of the trend towards police modernization.

Training for Black police lasted three months (shorter than for Whites), but covered the same syllabus, including a mix of drill, horsemanship, physical training, first aid, law, and 'police duties', such as the wearing of the uniform, powers of arrest, and police regulations. Nearly a thousand recruits went through the school during 1947, and refresher courses were introduced on 12 December 1947 for serving Black policemen (Annual Report of the Commissioner of the SAP 1947: 3). As the number of Black police increased in the post-war period, so temporary training establishments were created throughout the Union's largest cities. In 1952 temporary training schools for Black policemen existed at Cape Town, Port Elizabeth, Durban, Johannesburg, and Pretoria.

The NAC congratulated the SAP for introducing these innovations, stating that the advantages of trained African police were felt by the individual and the country (Annual Report of the NAC 1947: 23). It sent some of its members to visit the school, and as a result of the training it noted a 'marked improvement in the deportment, bearing, and self-confidence discernible among the recruits who have completed the course' (p. 23). The training was inculcating 'a spirit of helpfulness towards their own people' (p. 23), and was encouraging a better type of recruit to apply. Among the recruits, it noted, were a number of Matriculants, teachers, and agricultural demonstrators who had been formerly employed at the Agricultural School of the Department of Native Affairs (p. 23). This stimulated other employers of African police to offer training. For example, the Native Affairs Department of the Johannesburg City Council started to train its location police in 1952. Training was provided by an ex-member of the SAP and covered 'basic theoretical and practical instruction in the performance of their daily tasks', as well as a 'very comprehensive physical training and drill programme' (Carr 1953: 6). Time was quickly to tell just how little improvement in efficiency and bearing this training ushered, and how briefly the 'spirit of helpfulness towards their own people' lasted.

The commitment to modernize aspects of recruitment and training, and to broaden the social composition of the SAP, did not extend to the employment of women. The Sixth Report of the Public Services Commission of Inquiry, published in 1948, thought that the state's interests would not be served by recruiting women (Union of South Africa 1948: 82). The National Council for Child Welfare made representations to the Commission, which repeated those of the National Council for Women to the Lansdown Commission in 1937. Earlier in 1948, the Commissioner of the SAP held a conference presided over by the Secretary for Social Welfare, and attended by social welfare officers and members of the SAP and SARHP, at which he explained his objections to employing women. The Commission repeated these, stating that the Commissioner was flatly 'not prepared to, and would not accept, the responsibility of employing women on beat duty' (p. 83). The country's racial problems made it too dangerous to employ women. Women, however, could be employed as civilians on a part-time basis, for 'clerical work and abnormal cases' in the larger cities. The resistance to recruiting policewomen lasted until 1972, well beyond the date when they were employed even in other divided societies. The Royal Ulster Constabulary, for example, used policewomen in Northern Ireland from 1944.

In all these ways the police were making some strides towards modernization in the final years of Smuts's government. But this was always in the context of the SAP's colonial policing task. Modernization in some areas was facilitated and accelerated by the requirement to police race relations, but mostly this task constrained and limited the process. Race remained the vital feature, conditioning the nature of police work, and determining the structure and organization of the force. The society's colonial relations were still being reproduced by, and within, the police. Thus, at the same time as modernization was occurring in some features of policing, the SAP functioned to monitor and control the Black population, by means of brutal force if necessary.

The 1946 African miners' strike is a good example (on the strike see O'Meara 1975). The strike was a potent mix of two of the state's worst fears after the war, communist agitation and *swart gevaar*: communism as the framework for Black rebellion. With this mind-set, the police response to the strike was brutal. It was the single largest strike in South Africa's history, lasting five days, and left twelve strikers dead after being shot by the police, and thousands more injured (Dippenaar only mentions injuries to fifty-three people, 1988: 196).

The combination of class interest and racial fears not only affected the policing of industrial relations but was a feature of the SAP's handling of disputes around the issue of squatter camps. The chaotic urbanization stimulated by the war had led to many illegal squatter camps being built on the edge of industrial centres. This was made worse by the fact that house-building ceased for the duration of the war. Johannesburg's squatter problem was severe. In the ten years prior to 1946 the city's African population had grown by 68 per cent, and 16,195 people were on the waiting-list for a house in one of the city's townships (Union of South Africa 1947: para. 11). Squatting thus became the only alternative for many migrants, and was an issue around which the African population became politically mobilized (for an account of squatter movements in Johannesburg during the 1940s see Stadler 1979). The Council tried unsuccessfully to persuade the SAP to take over responsibility for policing all its shanty towns and camps, but the Deputy Commissioner declined because of manpower shortage. The police also considered this a civil issue, and would only intervene if the squatters threatened or used violence, thus making it a criminal issue, or the Council obtained a court order enforcing evictions (Union of South Africa 1947: para. 20).

In 1946 Johannesburg City Council decided to remove squatters and resettle them in Moroka emergency camp, and arrested or deported leaders of the squatters. Moroka was a camp holding 55,000 people, without a police station but with some location police in the employ of the Council. The infrastructure of the camp was poor, and facilities were inadequate for the size of population. Crime was a problem in the camp, and criminal gangs proliferated among the young unemployed. There was also discontent over the inability of the Council to issue residents with licences to trade. On 30 August 1947 the police made an early-morning raid for liquor (the incident was not sparked by a group of residents attacking the camp's trading store as Dippenaar claims, 1988: 207). In typical 'fire-brigade' fashion, reinforcements were driven into the camp from a nearby station in 'White' Kliptown. Force was used as a first resort, with shots being fired at the crowd. After running out of bullets, three policemen from the contingent dispatched to Moroka were cornered by the crowd and killed. All were young Afrikaners, described later by the Minister of

Native Affairs as 'three beautiful young men' (*Nongqai*, Sept. 1947: 1); the government was outraged and established a Commission of Inquiry (for other accounts of the incidents see the Annual Report of the NAC 1947: 43–9; Annual Report of the Commissioner of the SAP 1947). The Commission's report absolved the police from blame, but did point out that they needed to change the way locations and camps were policed: 'the essential thing is that they should routinely patrol the area for the protection of the residents themselves not merely sweeping down on them to seize liquor, to check passes or to effect arrests' (Union of South Africa 1947: para. 104).

This repeated a criticism made by similar commissions in the 1930s, and the SAP was as deaf now as then. Its enforcement of administrative regulations against Black South Africans, one of the critical ways in which it policed the boundaries between the races, provoked unrest in other places during 1947. The application of the liquor laws led to disturbances in Langa township, in Cape Town, in May 1947, and restrictions on the trading and land rights of Indians led to a campaign of passive resistance in the Transvaal and Natal, lasting for over three months. One feature of the last incident acted as a portent of the future, in that the police used powers to prevent the press from reporting the resistance.

But not all policemen refused to listen to criticism of police methods, and the police's recourse to brutality tended to be influenced by local factors. For example, the officer responsible for dealing with Indians engaging in passive resistance decided to wait them out rather than launch in with force, and after three months those involved in the sit-in eventually dispersed of their own accord. In Evaton township, near Vereeniging, local White farmers complained to Commissioner Palmer about the lawlessness of the residents, but he endorsed the view of the Police Commandant that the crime rate was very low considering the size of the population. Both policemen regarded the behaviour of residents as 'unusually good' (Annual Report of the NAC 1947: 38). When the SAP raided a hostel in March 1947, they found over 3,200 trespassers but prosecuted only those that had no bona fide employment. Nine out of ten trespassers were allowed to go free (Union of South Africa 1947: para. 99). The police responsible for Moroka refused to participate in evictions of squatters while they remained peaceful. By way of contrast, however, police twice demolished shacks in Alexandra township during November 1946 (Union of South Africa 1947: paras. 64–5), and in Newclare, in

September 1946, the squatters were rounded up, passes inspected, and their shacks demolished (para. 56). In Orlando township, in April 1947, the police cordoned off the township and combed it looking for potential offenders, making 396 arrests for passes, liquor, and defaults on tax (para. 72).

This illustrates that the tension between colonial and civil policing styles resurfaced within the police in the final years of United Party government. This particularly showed itself in two areas which were critical to the SAP's role in policing race relations: its use of force, and enforcement of the regulations which monitored the boundaries between the races. At a local level, some policemen were tactfully using their discretion in not enforcing some of the administrative regulations against the African population, something urged on them by various commissions in the 1930s. Senior officers also gave instructions to limit the use of force, although the discretion of policemen in other local areas operated in the direction of escalating violence. The SAIRR, for example, which had long protected the rights of Africans subject to police brutality, made several complaints to the Commissioner during 1947, and reported that they received 'sympathetic treatment' (Annual Survey of Race Relations 1947/8: 23). Following the 1946 miners' strike, the Commissioner warned the government about the undesirability of placing policemen in situations of confrontation with Blacks where there was a likelihood of police over-reaction, and he issued an order that policemen would have stern action taken against them if they were found guilty of wilful assault and maltreatment of Blacks. Senior officers met with African representatives several times during 1947 under the auspices of the Department of Justice, 'in order to bring about better understanding between the SAP and natives'. The SAIRR's regular newsletter, *Race Relations*, in its April 1948 issue, quoted the Deputy Commissioner's liberal views on police–public relations: 'the position of a police officer is that of guide, philosopher, and friend of all law-abiding citizens' (p. 48).

Such tension resurfaced in the police at this juncture because it was an expression of a wider conflict within the state at this time over the issue of race, which reproduced itself in tension in police–state relations. Notions of 'trusteeship', which were developed during the war when the Black population was making a significant contribution to the war effort, were used by Smuts in the run-up to the 1948 general election to distinguish the position of the United Party on the so-called 'native question' from Afrikaner nationalists. As Posel notes, there had always been elements within the state which sought to create a privileged group of urban Africans, who wished for influx control against this group to be relaxed or abandoned, and other restrictions eased (1991: 40). Reflecting this view in 1942, the Minister of Native Affairs called for a reform of the pass laws and for African political representation at the municipal level. In a speech to the SAIRR in 1942, Smuts concurred, saying that African urbanization could not be stopped: 'you might as well try to sweep back the ocean with a broom' (cited in Lipton 1985: 21). After the war, the job colour bar, pass laws, and migrant labour were all described as unjust and inefficient. In 1947, for example, the Minister of Native Affairs argued that the country's rapid industrialization in the last decade made certain restrictions on labour movement outmoded. The Deputy Prime Minister, Jan Hofmeyr, urged that the colour bar be scrapped.

The conflict within the state between its liberal and authoritarian approaches to the 'native question' became reflected in the Fagan Commission Report of 1948 (for an account of the Commission see Ashforth 1990: 114–48). Fagan was a former member of the fusion government cabinet, breaking from the United Party in 1939 over the issue of participation in the war. He was a member of the bar and described as a 'conservative democratic', with views on trusteeship which were not far removed from Smuts (Ashforth 1990: 121). His Commission was established in 1946 to investigate the Union's 'native laws' and their bearing upon labour supply in manufacturing industry. The terms of reference specifically called for a review of the pass laws and the migrant labour system. The final report, published in 1948, was made a crucial part of Smuts's electoral programme. But it reproduced all the contradictions of the liberal position on race. On the one hand, reform was restricted to socio-economic policy; there was no offer of parliamentary representation for Blacks or participation in government. The farthest it went on political reform was to recommend that 'some responsibility in connection with certain administrative matters in native villages within the jurisdiction of a European urban authority, be delegated to the natives themselves' (cited in R. Fine 1990: 24). Interestingly, part of this responsibility covered 'the maintenance of law and order'. But even in terms of socio-economic policy, it did not recommend the abolition of discriminatory laws or the removal of the restrictions on the movement of urban Africans. It recognized that African workers were a permanent part of the urban economy, and that the migrant labour system was socially and economically undesirable, but African urbanization was an economic phenomenon which needed to be 'guided and regulated'. As Posel argues, the principle of influx control was endorsed (1991: 49).

Thus, the SAP continued to police race relations. But wider political considerations in the run-up to the election required that the police act with as much an appearance of trusteeship as the colonial policing task allowed. Hence the tension within the police at this time over the use of force and the permissive enforcement of some of the administrative regulations. The contradiction was thus the same in 1948 as in 1937; the SAP was being asked to act as a civil police force in performing an essentially colonial policing task.

One reflection of this ambiguity was an official attempt to prevent the police from using military titles to designate ranks. The Sixth Report of the Public Services Commission of Inquiry, published in 1948, indicated that the 1912 Police Act only allowed for this practice in times of war, and that the 1926 Te Water Commission had recommended the discontinuation of the practice, without success. 'It is a striking anomaly', the 1948 Report indicated, 'that some officers of the SAP should be unwilling to use the titles which signify their true function' (Union of South Africa 1948: 81). It quoted a former commissioner to the effect that he had tried his best to get rid of military titles against the resistance of senior colleagues, but that 'the time has now arrived to civilize the police force even more than it is—to demilitarize it. You must aim in that direction' (p. 81). This was an odd thing for de Villiers to say (Truter having died by now), because he was responsible for enhancing the SAP's military character. But the post-war political situation appeared to suggest a change, and the Commission recommended the cessation of the practice, stating that in 'normal times', 'the maintenance of law and order is a function of a civilian and not a military force' (p. 81). Military titles should not even be used when quelling local disturbances in times of a state of emergency. But such was the ambiguity within the state, that Palmer now had the rank of major-general, being promoted in 1946.

Not only did the SAP continue to help to reproduce colonial relations in society prior to 1948, these relations were also reproduced within the structure and organization of the force. Black and White recruits were trained in separate establishments to avoid any suggestion of social integration. Many of the improvements in allowances and

TABLE 4.2 *Pay differentials by race in 1948*

	Constables		Sergeants*	
	Bottom £	Top £	Bottom £	Top £
White	200	400	450	500
Asian/Coloured	120	150	240	300
African	84	150	150	180

* Sergeants first class.

Source: *South Africa Yearbook 1948* (Department of Information 1948: 450).

benefits introduced in 1946 applied only to White members, although in 1948 the Public Services Commission recommended that Black policemen and families be given the same entitlement to free medical care as White colleagues, so long as the marriage was legal and that they resided in the same locality (which was not the case for many African police). In 1948 salary differentials according to race remained large, as reflected in Table 4.2. Salary differentials need to be considered in the context of the relative promotion prospects of policemen from the various communities. In 1945 there were four times as many White commissioned and non-commissioned officers as Black, and the situation subsequently deteriorated because of Palmer's emphasis on selectively promoting White constables as part of his three-year plan. And with the National Party government, promotion for Whites accelerated even faster, as we shall see below.

In short, policing in the final years of Smuts's segregationist policies was characterized by partial modernization towards a civil police force, but this was severely constrained by the colonial task the police were required to perform. Therefore, race remained the vital feature of policing, distinguishing it very little from policing under the National Party (van der Spuy 1989: 277 notes the continuity).

POLICING IN THE TRANSITION TO APARTHEID

It is commonplace to see apartheid as a fully formulated and worked-out blueprint, with all its later features decided and progressively implemented once the brake of a small parliamentary majority was released with each successful election. Apartheid was a *volkskapitalisme* which promised to solve the economic problems of Afrikaners, as well as to deal with White fears of *swart gevaar*, with its means for achieving these ends being both fully clarified at the beginning and representing new choices for the electorate. More recent scholarship has shown that the National Party did not immediately proceed to implement a monolithic 'grand plan' (Marks and Trapido 1988: 7–12; Lipton 1985; Posel 1991: 5 *passim*), and that there was considerable continuity with previous government policies (Rich 1989; Wolpe 1988). 'Apartheid' meant different and at times contradictory things to the various groups of Afrikaners who were in a nationalist alliance in 1948, and the contingent pressures and priorities of the historical moment were more important than ideology in determining its eventual character. This fits the thesis that Afrikaner ethnic solidarity was more an outcome of policies pursued after the 1948 victory than the cause of electoral success (Adam and Giliomee 1979: 61–82; van Zyl Slabbert 1975), and that it was only by its second stage, the 'separate development' or Bantustanization of the 1960s, that apartheid was fully consolidated (Lipton 1985: 29–37; Posel 1991: 227–55).

There are equivalent debates with respect to policing. It has recently been claimed that the electoral success of the National Party brought a sudden and marked change in policing in the Cape after 1948 (Nasson 1991), showing itself in the Afrikanerization of control in the SAP, the redirection of police attention towards race control, and the move into 'political policing' (Nasson 1991: 249–50), what Brodeur calls 'high policing' (1983), being the close surveillance of political activity by alleged subversives and agitators. This is the conventional wisdom for policing at this time throughout the Union, and it is wrong (as noted also by van der Spuy 1989: 277). There were more continuities than differences in policing style and practice, and the changes were mostly ones of degree, extending trends evident before 1948. Changes were also incremental and evolutionary, in that they emerged over time, and were often influenced as much by circumstance as planning.

The differences, such as they were, cannot be explained by the change in top leadership within the SAP in 1951, when Palmer retired through ill health; he died shortly afterwards. His successor was Commissioner Brink, who continued in much the same mould as his predecessor. Like Palmer, Brink was a long-serving member of the police, and a former member of the pre-Union Orange Free State police; so long-serving in fact that Brink himself retired within three years. Brink was an Afrikaner, but had signed the 'red oath'. Like all commissioners, Brink resisted government control over the police and demanded organizational autonomy for the SAP. In his first Annual Report, Brink estimated that 400 full-time policemen were employed permanently on work for other government departments; this was four times as many men as in 1947. It was important, the Commissioner noted in 1951, that the police did not do duties which fell outside 'the category of police work proper' (Annual Report of the Commissioner of the SAP 1951: 7). He warned that 'it is time to resist the imposition of further extraneous duties and to take a careful review of those presently being carried out. Steps are being taken in this direction' (p. 7). This demand for organizational autonomy from government control is a statement on what police–state relations were like at the time. The inability of the police subsequently to resist extraneous duties after having taken steps to evade them is a testimony to how police–state relations developed as the government consolidated apartheid during the 1950s.

One of the immediate steps taken by the new government in 1948 was to allow all policemen interned during the war for anti-government activity to return to their former posts, something Palmer had tried unsuccessfully to do in 1945. However, the National Party government made this part of a general dispensation to Afrikaner nationalists, and many political prisoners were released as well. These included Liebbrandt, who during the war had urged policemen to defect and to help him assassinate Smuts, and Sidney Holm, who had broadcast Nazi propaganda to South Africa from Germany in the war and was imprisoned for high treason in 1947. Immediately after the war, the SAP began investigation of German documents in order to pursue charges of high treason against South African citizens. The investigation team was composed entirely of Afrikaner policemen (G. Visser 1976: 177). A report was sent to Smuts in 1947, but the general election prevented its recommendations being acted upon. The new nationalist government claimed it could find no trace of the report, and no action was taken. In 1952 the government even restored the pension rights of those policemen, and other public servants, whose service had been interrupted by internment or who had been dismissed or resigned during the war for their political support of Afrikaner nationalism.

Although the reintegration of former internees was desired by Palmer in 1945, it was probably not his intention that this should presage the more open expression of Afrikaner nationalist loyalties, but this is what happened during the 1950s. OB membership and internment became a badge of status, within the police and outside; B. J. Vorster, a former internee at Koffiefontein, was elected a National Party MP in 1953, later becoming Minister of Justice, and thus responsible for the police, and, in 1966, South Africa's sixth Prime Minister. His friend in Koffiefontein, van den Bergh, rose rapidly through the SAP to head its Special Branch and then the country's separate secret police, the infamous Bureau of State Security (on the early careers of both see Winter 1981: 19–53, who reputes to be a former member of the bureau). A similar process occurred at the same time in Israel with the Irgun, one of whose members, Begin, was also later to become Prime Minister. Another reflection of the trend to Afrikanerize the loyalties of men in the SAP during the transition period was the formalization of the Chaplaincy Service in 1951, which had first been introduced during the war. The post went to a minister in the Dutch Reform Church, as it had done so earlier. The incumbent had the rank of major and was entitled to wear a uniform, although this was not done at the beginning.

There was no immediate expansion in the size of the SAP's manpower or budget with the National Party government. The rapid growth in police expenditure that occurred under the last years of Smuts's government even enabled the new government to slow down the rate of increase, as shown in Table 4.3, although it rose again rapidly in the 1952/3 financial year, following a considerable degree of political unrest the year before. Police expenditure quite often reacted like this to wider political contingencies. Expenditure per head of population was increasing before 1948 and the trend continued in the transition period, indicating that although the increase in expenditure was variable, it always kept ahead of the growth in the population. Nor was there any shift in the ratio of police to defence expenditure. From the Second World War defence expenditure was always to remain higher than police expenditure, which reverses the case before the war, but the ratio was smaller in the initial period of National Party government than it had been before. Defence expenditure picked up again towards the end of the period but still did not reach the peak it achieved in the penultimate year of Smuts's government. But one noticeable shift with the nationalists is the reduction in the proportion of police expenditure devoted to detective services, which had risen in the final years of the United Party government to a point that pertained

TABLE 4.3. *Police expenditure, 1945/6–1952/3*

Year	Amount £m.	% increase	% on detective work	Expenditure per head population* £	Ratio to defence expenditure†
1945/6	4.18	—	0.9	0.35	108
1946/7	5.59	33.7	1.4	0.47	132
1947/8	6.55	17.2	1.7	0.53	115
1948/9	7.26	10.7	1.1	0.58	—
1949/50	8.07	11.1	1.5	0.63	—
1950/1	8.44	4.5	0.8	0.66	106
1951/2	8.76	3.7	0.8	0.72	126
1952/3	10.14	15.8	0.9	0.80	121

* All races.
† Police expenditure = 100.
Source: Annual Reports of the Auditor General.

at the very beginning of the force, when it was at its highest. This reflects a shift towards the labour power of the uniform section.

The relative slow-down in police expenditure meant that the new government did not mark its entry by a spending spree on law and order to fit the electoral emphasis that it had placed on the issue. Commissioners at this time still complained about the poor quality of buildings and the unavailability of married quarters. In 1951, for example, Brink described some accommodation as unhygienic and primitive, which was in part to blame for the manpower shortage being experienced at the time (Annual Report of the Commissioner of the SAP 1951: 5), and the force was still using many rented buildings as stations in 1952. There was no rapid expansion in police technology either. By 1952, only twenty-two cars were fitted with two-way radios, although the move to motorized transport, which began before 1948, continued under the nationalists. In 1951 the number of horses in use in the SAP was reduced by nearly two-thirds, and it finally got rid of the camels. Yet Dippenaar notes how even the trend to motorization was affected by lack of funds four years after the new government came to power (1988: 236). Thus, between 1947 and 1951, there was only a 25.4 per cent increase in the SAP's fleet of vehicles, although the rate of increase for cars was nearly double this. The type of vehicle which saw the largest increase in this period was pick-up vans, indicative of how the modernization of transport was being conditioned in part by the demands of colonial policing. The relative shift after 1948 from expanding the number of cars to that of pick-up vans is also symbolic of movement in police attitudes towards crime, which will be addressed shortly.

Above all, however, the slow-down in police expenditure prevented the new government from signalling its support for the police in real terms by a wage increase. It was Smuts's government that gave the police a large pay rise in 1946, and by 1948 the Commissioner was complaining that even this was not enough to stem the high wastage that was occurring. Wastage was particularly high among those with short service. In 1948, for example, 691 policemen purchased their discharge, 81.9 per cent of whom had less than three years' service, 13.8 per cent with less than a year (Annual Report of the Commissioner of the SAP 1948: 2). A problem was that wage rates in other parts of the state bureaucracy were raised immediately by the new government, and the Commissioner noted that many policemen were switching jobs to other government departments. Wastage was thus explained by the Commissioner as due entirely to the new government's under-funding of the police; he did not mention whether English-speaking policemen resigned as a result of the change of government.

The new government therefore faced more severe manpower problems than did the old. Van Onselen explains the post-war deterioration in the SAP's relationship with Blacks, and its reputation for brutality, as due to the expansion in White manpower, with the police recruiting people who normally would have been considered unsuitable (1960: 159). Not only does this underscore the poor reputation that the SAP had before 1948, it misrepresents the manpower situation from that year on. Indeed, the new government presided over a depletion in manpower that was as bad as that during the war. Trends in manpower are presented in Table 4.4, which shows that in the last two years of Smuts's government, manpower grew by over a half, and the increase slowed considerably in the first years of the National Party. The growth under the United Party dissipated under the nationalists due to high wastage among new recruits, and the ratio of police per thousand head of population declined in the immediate years following the 1948 election victory, and only picked up again in 1952. But even then it did not reach the point it attained in Smuts's final year of power. But the depletion was not due solely to high wastage caused by uncompetitive wage rates. In the first decade of the SAP there were more policemen than officially established

TABLE 4.4. *Trends in manpower, 1945–1952**

Year	White	Black	% increase	% Black	% under-staffed*†	Ratio per 1,000 population‡
1945	6,551	3,903	—	37.3	18.2	1.14
1946	8,302	5,906	35.9	41.5	3.6	1.31
1947	9,669	6,756	15.6	41.1	6.7	1.55
1948	9,740	6.868	1.1	41.3	19.3	1.73
1949	—	—	—	—	—	1.58
1950	—	—	—	—	—	1.50
1951	9,999	7,291	4.1	42.1	9.7	1.47
1952	9,933	8,591	7.1	46.3	10.6	1.54

* Actual membership.
† Difference between actual and authorized membership.
‡ Based on authorized membership.
Source: Annual Reports of the Commissioner of the SAP.

posts, and Truter urged the government to fund more posts. Thereafter, governments often increased the authorized establishment of the SAP to show their commitment to strengthening the police, but could never get enough recruits to translate this into an increase in real membership. But in the case of the National Party government, they actually reduced the authorized complement by 7 per cent between 1948 and 1949, and did not increase it until 1952, when it was raised by 8.2 per cent, bringing it more or less back to the level it inherited from the United Party. As a comparison, between 1945 and 1947 the United Party increased the official establishment of the SAP by 37.7 per cent, but between 1948 and 1952 the National Party increased it by 0.75 per cent.

Some other trends in membership are worth highlighting. It is interesting to note that the racial composition of the SAP begins to change after the Second World War, with an increase in the proportion of Black policemen, which had remained fairly stable from 1913 to 1945; it was 37.9 per cent in 1927 and 37.3 per cent in 1945. This trend was accelerated by the nationalists rather than reversed. This can be explained in part by the shortfall in White manpower after the war, and by Afrikaner nationalist ideology, in that the new government was soon to pursue a policy of 'own areas' policing. But in fact, to begin with, the government tried strenuously to avoid changing the social composition of the police. The proportion of Black policemen that was authorized in the official establishment was always lower than the proportion in practice, because the state was less able to impose its racial sensibilities on actual recruitment. But the new government reversed the trend in 1948 by reducing the proportion of Black policemen in the authorized establishment of the SAP compared to 1945–7. In 1951 the proportion of Black policemen in the authorized complement was still lower than it had been in 1946 and 1947. Thus, the SAP was always more understaffed among White policemen than Black, as measured by the difference between authorized and actual membership. In 1948, for example, there was a shortfall of 24.4 per cent among White policemen, while the increase in White recruits was only 0.73 per cent. This represented a shortfall of 3,158 Whites. The government reduced the shortfall in White policemen to 14.1 per cent in 1951, representing 1,653 men, illustrating its efforts to recruit Whites, but it still remained more understaffed among Whites than Blacks.

The special efforts to increase White recruitment after 1948 demonstrate the new government's wish to resist the change in the racial composition of the police. It approved a reduction in the minimum age of White recruits to 16 years and the minimum educational entry requirement to Standard 7. Recruits this young were trained until 18 years of age, then placed in 'sheltered positions' until they reached the normal qualification age. Recruitment teams also toured Transvaal, ensuring that the Whites would be overwhelmingly Afrikaans-speaking. In earlier periods the SAP had been urged to increase its recruitment from English-speaking Whites, something which it always failed to do, but with the nationalists even the effort was gone. The government also later reversed usual practice by allowing married men to apply to join the police; normally, policemen were required to be in service for five years before being allowed to seek permission to marry. The Commissioner was desperate to recruit more Whites, warning the public in his 1950 Annual Report that unless more joined the SAP there would be a 'diminution in the degree of protection in which [they] are entitled' (Annual Report of the Commissioner of the SAP 1950: 3). But the rapid industrial expansion after the war ensured that the SAP always offered uncompetitive wages for Whites, and the nationalist government could not resist the trend towards the recruitment of Blacks. Thus, in 1952, when the 'own areas' policing strategy was adopted, the proportion of Black policemen allowed in the authorized complement expanded significantly, to reach its highest level yet. It expanded even further in terms of actual membership because this is more difficult to control, and by this time 46.3 per cent of actual manpower was Black. This suggests that the 'own area' strategy was itself as much a response to manpower shortage among Whites as ideological preference for racial apartheid in policing matters.

Before discussing the 'own areas' policy, it is worth noting membership trends in the Black police, and how they were affected by the transition to apartheid, since this has some bearing on the strategy. Table 4.5 provides an outline, showing that while Africans dominated in gross numbers, the expansion in membership was greatest for Coloureds. In the period from 1945 to 1952, the number of Coloureds in the police grew at three times the rate for Asians and Africans. From 1927, when figures first became available, to 1952, the number of Asian and African policemen just more than doubled, while the number of Coloured policemen grew by 355.2 per cent. But the expansion in Coloured membership was primarily a policy pursued by United Party governments, perhaps reflecting the racial hierarchy of South African society prior to 1948, which placed Coloureds nearest to Whites. From 1945 to 1947, Coloured membership rose by 237.5 per cent, Asian by 100 per cent, and African by 65.9 per cent. However, between 1948 and 1952 the growth in Coloured membership was reduced to 25.2 per cent, the same as that for African policemen. The growth in Asian policemen was 15.7 per cent. The racial hierarchy had not changed with the transition to apartheid, but

TABLE 4.5. *Trends in Black manpower, 1945–1952*

Year	Asian		Coloured		African	
	Number	% NCOs	Number	% NCOs	Number	% NCOs
1945	89	4.4	144	7.5	3,670	6.1
1946	145	6.8	375	7.7	5,386	8.4
1947	178	5.6	486	5.5	6,092	9.0
1948	191	6.2	487	5.3	6,196	8.7
1949	—	—	—	—	—	—
1950	—	—	—	—	—	—
1951	197	11.1	531	7.7	6,563	9.8
1952	221	12.2	610	10.9	7,760	9.6

Source: Annual Reports of the Commissioner of the SAP.

policing policy had undergone a transformation: the 'own areas' policing strategy required fewer Asian and Coloured policemen than African. Thus, in 1952, when the policy was introduced, the increase in African manpower was the largest of all the three communities.

At a passing-out parade on 24 September 1951, the new Minister of Justice, Advocate Swart, announced that the government's policy in policing was that Blacks would in future be serviced by members of their own community. He declared, for example, that eventually all police stations in African areas would be staffed by Africans. To allow for this, recruitment of Black police was to expand, Africans especially. This transformation in police strategy, however, was less dramatic than it appears, for it had always been policy for Blacks and Whites to police their own areas, although Black policemen were always under the command of White officers. In 1947, for example, the NAC congratulated the Commissioner for 'placing a preponderance of native police in areas where natives predominate' (Annual Report of the NAC 1947: 23). This was also a recommendation of the 1948 Fagan Commission. The nationalist government rode this trend but redirected at the same time. The racial distinctions were more finely made. Coloured, Asian, and African policemen were each given responsibility for their own areas rather than deployed collectively in Black areas, as before. What is more, ethnic differences within the African population were taken into account, so that Zulu policed Zulu, and so on. Moreover, in doing this, Black policemen were given command of police stations in their respective communities. This was a considerable extension of previous policy, and is apparent from Table 4.5, which shows the increase in the proportion of Black policemen who were non-commissioned officers between 1951 and 1952. In 1952 provision was made for the establishment of Black head constables, a rank not before attainable. Two were allocated to Asians, two for Coloureds, and twenty-eight for Africans, although nobody was promoted to fill the posts for some time.

On 1 October 1951 Sergeant Thomas Lion, a Xhosa-speaking member of the SAP, was made the first African station commander, responsible for four Xhosa-speaking constables and a local population of 2,327 Xhosa living in a township near to King William's Town (Annual Report of the Commissioner of the SAP 1951: 5). Commissioner Brink described the policy thus: 'policing native areas by members of the SAP who belong to the tribe predominant in the area' (p. 5). The policy was extended in 1952, to include another eight stations mostly in African townships on the Rand or Eastern Cape: Moroka, Orlando, Eastern Township, Germiston, Benoni, Batho, Sandfontein, and New Brighton. In outlining this, the Commissioner identified the advantages of the policy. It provided Black police with the prospects of promotion and more pay, it gave them responsibility, and improved, the Commissioner hoped, police–community relations in the locality. 'There is a chance', he wrote, 'if locations and townships are policed by people of the same race, that a better feeling may arise, and that the police may come to be regarded, as they should be, as friends and protectors of law-abiding citizens' (Annual Report of the Commissioner of the SAP 1952: 3).

This was laudible in sentiment, but never achieved. The 'own areas' policy was a fiction in practice. Black police were not trusted to be left solely in charge. White 'supervisory staff' were left at all the townships save the smallest, Eastern Township. The 'skeleton staff' of Whites left in the others amounted, for example, to fourteen White officers in Orlando, seven in New Brighton, eight in Benoni, and six in Germiston. In practice, therefore, the policy was not all that different from that which operated before. The government was cautious in implementing the policy in another way, in that it was extended to new stations only very slowly. But the main reason why the Commissioner's hopes for an improvement in police–public relations were unrealistic was the conduct of these Black police, which was as brutal as that meted out by Whites. The 'own areas' strategy therefore made no difference to the nature of the police–public encounters in the localities where it was applied.

One consequence of the 'own areas' policy was the advancement in pay and promotion which it afforded a minority of Black policemen. The number of Black non-commissioned officers, however, remained low, as Table 4.5 shows, indicating how apartheid operated within the police. This is perhaps better represented in Table 4.6 on the per capita expenditure within the police by race. The pattern of earlier periods is repeated, with marked inequalities existing according to race. These differentials are reflected in the inequalities of salary highlighted earlier in Table 4.2. One noticeable trend, however, is the attempt by governments, before and after 1948, to narrow the differential. In the period as a whole, the biggest movement was made with respect to Coloureds and Asians, where per capita expenditure increased by 71.6 per cent, compared with 62.6 per cent for Africans, and 23.3 per cent for Whites. Given the cut-backs in police

TABLE 4.6. *Per capita expenditure on policemen by race, 1945/6–1950/1*

Year	White £	Coloured/Asian £	% White	African £	% White
1945/6	411	171.75	41.7	136.5	33.2
1946/7	447.75	203	45.3	156.5	34.9
1947/8	459.25	220	47.9	165.75	36
1948/9	480.25	263.25	54.8	201.5	41.9
1949/50	498.25	233	46.7	262	52.5
1950/1	507	294	57.9	222	43.7

Source: Annual Reports of the Auditor General.

expenditure after 1948, it is to be expected that the increase in per capita expenditure is less, but the relative emphasis is still towards Coloured and Asian policemen, at 11.6 per cent compared with 10.1 per cent for Africans. Per capita expenditure on Whites rose by less than half this, at 5.5 per cent, but the gross differences remained huge. Thus, the 'own areas' policy did not lead to any relative improvement in the position of Africans in the police, and per capita expenditure on this group fell in the 1950/1 financial year.

One of the other surprising occurrences on the nationalists assuming power was the increase in the number of dismissals of White policemen from the force, counter to the trend amongst Black policemen, as shown in Table 4.7, although this had stopped by 1952. This could perhaps reflect the effects of training for Black policemen, the weeding-out of anti-nationalist White policemen, or an increased disciplinary ethos within the force associated with a new government. Whatever the case, discipline was working in opposite directions. Thus, the proportion of wastage represented by dismissals increased for Whites, but decreased for Blacks. The latter clearly behaved better or the decrease was the result of the need for as many as possible to be kept in the force to facilitate the 'own areas' policy. The latter seems more likely, given that, when they were dismissed, it tended to be for the more serious offences. The larger number of dismissals in gross terms between Black and White policemen suggests that the former were less professional (although becoming more so with training) and more likely to have action taken against them by the police authorities (although decreasingly so during this period). Given what is known about the conduct of White policemen, these figures suggest that White colleagues were treated more leniently than Black policemen,

TABLE 4.7. *Dismissals from the SAP, 1946–1952*

Year	White	% White manpower	Black	% Black manpower	% = serious offences* White	Black	% of wastage = dismissals White	Black
1946	27	0.32	248	4.1	62.9	58.8	3.3	29.5
1947	49	0.5	252	3.7	57.1	97.6	3.8	39.0
1948	72	0.73	229	3.3	70.8	98.6	5.7	37.6
1949	—	—	—	—	—	—	—	—
1950	—	—	—	—	—	—	—	—
1951	91	0.91	153	2.0	64.8	92.1	6.2	29.8
1952	46	0.46	121	1.4	89.1	95.0	6.1	30.9

* Defined as conviction by court, drunkenness, and misconduct.

Source: Annual Reports of the Commissioner of the SAP.

and that acts of misconduct by Whites are under-represented in Table 4.7. Misconduct generally is underscored in the Table. In its 1950–1 survey of race relations, for example, the SAIRR revealed that 347 policemen had been found guilty of assault by the courts and 52 departmentally in the sixteen-month period from 1 January 1949, 54 of which were White and 345 Black, but that only 51 were dismissed from the force (pp. 62–3).

The greatest change with the transition to apartheid occurred in the policing of race relations. From their inception the police had three kinds of encounter with Black South Africans, which continued under apartheid. These correspond to the types of Black crime: the enforcement of administrative offences, which involved policing Blacks in primarily White areas by means of the administrative regulations which controlled the boundaries between the races; 'low policing' of ordinary crime in Black areas; and 'high policing' of public order incidents, such as political and industrial unrest.

These encounters did not begin with apartheid but they changed in nature under the new policy. First, under apartheid there was an increase in the number of administrative regulations by which Black life was controlled, and the enforcement of existing ones was made more rigid, so that the police increased their penetration into the ordinary lives of Blacks. Secondly, unrest intensified during the 1950s, due to successful mobilization by political movements and trade unions, which increased both the legislative control of Black opposition and the police role in suppressing it. Finally, ordinary crime in the Black townships escalated in the 1950s, as criminal gangs proliferated among the unemployed and dispossessed. But in this last case, there was no corresponding increase in police activity because the townships were relatively under-policed. Under apartheid, most of the SAP's efforts went into controlling the boundaries between the races in White areas by means of administrative offences, and surveillance of their political activity by means of public-order policing. Therefore, the police failed to relate to township residents in a civil policing role, servicing their need for protection against ordinary crime, but encountered them solely in oppressive terms; oppression either of Black rights to live and work where they wished, or of their right to protest, politically and economically, against systematic subordination.

But the changes that occurred in the nature of police relations with Black South Africans under apartheid are not explained by ideology alone, for only the increase in administrative offences was a direct consequence of the new policy. In other respects police encounters with Blacks reflected historical circumstance: the escalation of ordinary crime and political activity that was only an indirect consequence of apartheid ideology. Further, while these changes were apparent in the transition period, their full effect became obvious only once apartheid was consolidated after 1952. None the less, policing in the transition period was an omen of the future.

The trend towards the urbanization of South Africa's population and crime continued after 1948, resulting in an increasing concentration by the police on urban areas. The deployment of the police throughout the Union reflected this. By 1952 39.1 per cent of the SAP's manpower was based in the Transvaal, 27.7 per cent in the Cape, 16.8 per cent in Natal, 6.3 per cent in the Orange Free State, and 2.4 per cent in South West Africa. By 1954 42.1 per cent of manpower was based in the Transvaal. Both crime and the prosecution rate per thousand head of population increased markedly after 1948. Between 1947 and 1948 there was an increase in reported crime of 5.2 per cent, which increased to 49.1 per cent in 1948–9 (Dippenaar 1988: 224). Between 1948 and 1952, reported crime increased by 56.9 per cent (Annual Report of the Commissioner of the SAP 1952: 4). The average prosecution rate per thousand head of population between 1912 and 1926 was 48.4, 74.2 between 1927 and 1945, but was 92.8 for the period 1948–52. For 1952 it was 99.

Neither the people nor the police changed suddenly; the police did not become more efficient nor people more inherently criminal. Admittedly there were now more policemen, with an increase in actual police membership of 16.7 per cent between 1947 and 1949, but the increase in reported crime was three times the growth in manpower. The sudden change is explained by the increase in the number of offences against which people could transgress, and the unwillingness of the police to be lenient in the operation of discretion. On 1 January 1949 a revised list of crimes and offences came into effect which reclassified previously minor offences as serious, and identified new offences. These included *Crimen Laesae Majestatis*, promoting racial hostility between Europeans and non-Europeans, resisting and obstructing the police, opium law and regulations on habit-forming drugs, motor vehicle ordinances, blasphemy, impersonation of police, suicide, and malicious damage to property below the value of £50 (see Annual Report of the Commissioner of the SAP 1954: 5; Dippenaar 1988: 224–5).

Surprisingly, this process did not operate selectively against Blacks, for there was no increase in the proportion of Black offenders as a result of the change. In 1947, for example, 86.7 per cent of all convictions involved Black offenders, while in 1952 the proportion was 86.5 per cent. But in gross terms, the massive increase in the number of offences brought more Blacks before the courts than ever before: 1,024,131 in 1952 compared with 773,876 in 1947. This was an increase of nearly a third, which is lower than the increase in cases of reported crime, indicating the amount of unsolved crime (on these statistics see: Annual Report of the Commissioner of the SAP 1947: 8, and 1952: 8). There was, however, some shift in the nature of the offences which brought Black South Africans to court. Five of the top nine offences in 1926 remained in the 1952 list: possession of kaffir beer, pass law offences, drunkenness, petty assault, and petty theft. Kaffir beer offences were at the top of the list in 1952, as in 1946. But native hut tax offences had dropped from the list in 1952, as had offences under native labour regulations and the Master and Servants Act (so too had municipal offences, which was the eleventh most committed offence in 1952). But this is only a crude measure of the relative change in the number of offences committed in the period. Table 4.8 lists the changes occurring between 1947 and 1952 in the number of cases sent to trial for the most frequently committed offences.

The change is variable and goes in both directions, since the

TABLE 4.8. *Percentage shift in cases sent for trial, 1947–1952*

Case	Increase	Decrease
Aggravated assault	32.4	
Common assault	9.9	
Theft	57.1	
Dagga (marijuana)	69.1	
Drunkenness		11.4
Kaffir beer	57.4	
Native reserve regulations	75.7	
Master and Servant Act		7.7
Municipal offences		47.0
Labour regulations	36.4	
Pass laws	39.0	
Native (Urban Areas) Act	52.1	
Curfew regulations	105.1	
Registration/production of documents	69.6	
Dog tax	5.9	
Native tax		0.2
Trespass	57.1	
Traffic ordinances		43.4

Source: Annual Report of the Commissioner of the SAP 1947: 8; Annual Report of the Commissioner of the SAP 1952: 8.

number of cases sent to trial for certain offences actually fell. Some of the latter offences were exclusive to Africans, but if not got by these, Africans were prosecuted for other things, and the growth in the number of cases sent to trial is enormous for some offences which exclusively concern Africans, such as curfew regulations, native reserve regulations, possession of kaffir beer, and the failure to register for or produce documents on demand (which is not the same as pass law offences). This demonstrates the fact that the new government tightened up on the enforcement of the administrative regulations by which the boundaries between the races were policed, and extended the control by defining new ones.

The new government, for example, immediately set about tackling the problem of African migration to the towns, and quickly promulgated Bills which restricted urbanization and attempted to distribute African labour between economic sectors (see Posel 1991: 91–115). The government also planned to extend the pass laws to African women, although it withdrew this in the face of widespread opposition from the Black population and liberal Whites. However, the regulation was reintroduced in a different guise in 1952 when legislation was passed requiring all Union-born Africans, men and women, to carry a 'reference book' (rather than a 'pass'), which authorized them to live and work in specific areas. In 1952 parliament passed the Native Laws Amendment Act, which narrowed the categories of African who had urban residential rights, gave powers to the police to exclude those without rights after they had spent seventy-two hours in an urban area, and allowed the Native Affairs Department to prohibit the further employment of Africans in proclaimed areas. This was complemented by the 1950 Group Areas Act, which restricted Africans living in 'White' areas to segregated residential areas, and legislation in 1951 which prohibited Africans from squatting on land beyond municipal jurisdiction. Many long-established shanty towns were therefore demolished and residents forced to return to the reserves.

Those with urban residential rights, however, were enabled to keep them irrespective of whether they were employed or not, thus establishing permanent urban status for a very small minority of the African population. But even this privileged sector of 'urban insiders' became enmeshed in a bureaucratic system which finely controlled African movement, residence, and employment. All Africans were required to have official permission to determine where they could live, work, and travel. Permits became necessary to look for, obtain, and change employment, and for every journey to and within proclaimed areas. The Minister of Native Affairs admitted in 1952 that 950 clerks were needed just to issue the necessary forms let alone process them (noted in Simons 1956: 53).

The police were vital to the enforcement of this regimen, and, for it to work, needed to detect and eject those Africans who overstayed their seventy-two hours in areas where their documents did not permit them to be. They did so not by massively increasing their manpower— attempts to do this failed—but by saturating White areas with what policemen they had. The 'own areas' strategy facilitated this by withdrawing highly-trained White policemen from the Black urban areas, leaving these areas to be relatively under-policed for the level of ordinary crime that existed there, both in terms of the number of policemen in Black urban areas and their degree of training. Under apartheid, therefore, the attention of the police took a slight shift, with the balance tipping even further than it had before towards a focus on White areas rather than Black, and on administrative offences rather than ordinary crime generally. In the Black urban areas, police–public relations primarily involved the enforcement of administrative regulations rather than ordinary crime detection and prevention. Passes and documents were checked, raids for illicit liquor conducted, and illegal squatters evicted, all while murder, rape, and gangsterism flourished in the townships. The 1950s was the period when township gangs were most active. In its 1950–1 survey of race relations, the SAIRR described the 'reign of terror' in the townships: 'gangs of youths impose a reign of terror, and law-abiding people are afraid to venture out after dark' (p. 63). Similar problems existed in Coloured townships in the Cape, where the 'skolly' rivalled the African '*tsotsi*' for gangsterism (see Wollheim 1950).

In an inquiry into disturbances at several African townships between 1949 and 1950 (Union of South Africa, 1950*b*), the Commission linked unrest to the existence of the *tsotsi* gangs and attributed the blame for the gangs to social progress not social deprivation: too many privileges rather than not enough.

Giving natives a European education has caused the schools to impart knowledge to native youths which they can make little use of to make a living. All native youths who attend school want 'office jobs' . . . It leads them to drift into gangs, to become idle, with a loosening of the social bond, and to anti-social tendencies and crime.   (paras. 190–2)

The bioscopes were also disseminating the wrong role models. Cowboy films shown to native youths engendered violence, and because of their low mental capacity, natives failed to grasp that crime does not pay (paras. 224–5). However, Afrikaner nationalist criminology was never hegemonic, and L. I. Venables, Manager of Johannesburg's Municipal Native Affairs Department, countered with a Liberalist version of crime in Johannesburg (1951*a*, 1951*b*). Ironically, he published his account in the journal of the South African Bureau of Racial Affairs, the nationalists' 'think tank' on race, but his views were anathema to Afrikaner nationalist criminology.

Crime in the townships was attributed to social conditions, which did not prepare urban Africans for settled life. It was thus linked to unemployment; there was 80 per cent unemployment of youths aged between 15 and 20 in Pretoria, and Johannesburg had 20,000 youths unemployed (Venables 1951*b*: 20). Venables also linked it to housing shortage, economic insecurity, the lack of recreational facilities in the townships, and poor education. The migrant labour system also caused crime because it affected negatively the social cohesion of families, and increased drunkenness and social instability (1951a: 9). He therefore recommended the abolition of the migrant labour system with a stable, well-housed, permanent, and economically satisfied urban labour force (p. 10). The control of the consumption of kaffir beer also provoked crime rather than solved it (p. 11). In his account of juvenile delinquency (1951b), Venables also mentioned the effects of the high divorce rate, single-parent families, absenteeism from school, and early school leaving (p. 15). The inadequate number of schools, and the lack of opportunity to obtain lucrative jobs were also mentioned as factors promoting youth gangs (pp. 17–18). He concluded: 'the panacea lies in such matters as improved social conditions, better opportunities industrially and commercially for natives, and possible revision of legislation affecting natives' (1951b: 24). Liberal criminology of this sort clearly survived under apartheid but never influenced police training.

Ordinary crime was rife in the townships, although it needs to be kept in proportion, for the overwhelming majority of residents were law-abiding. Venables provides figures which show that in 1948, only 0.73 per cent of Johannesburg's African population had been convicted of serious crime, compared with 0.16 for Whites, 0.26 for Asians, and 0.92 for Coloureds (1951a: 2), although such figures can only be rough bench-marks because of the difficulties in estimating the official population of each group. Despite living in worse economic conditions therefore, African crime was proportionately lower than among Coloureds, although the relatively small Coloured population in Johannesburg could have distorted the figures. While the mass of law-abiding citizens in the townships needed protection from the gangs, the police left the townships under-policed. Even after the 'own areas' strategy was introduced in Moroka, for example, it had a ratio of 1.07 police per thousand head of official population, which was lower than the country as a whole, and does not take account of the large 'unofficial' population living in the township illegally. Based on official population figures, Orlando had 1.7, Germiston 1.7, Benoni 1.9, Batho 1.3, New Brighton 1.2, Sandfontein 0.07, and Eastern Black Township, where African police were solely in charge, 4.3.

In its survey of race relations in 1950–1, the SAIRR complained that African townships were badly under-protected, with inadequate patrolling of the streets, so that 'flying squads' toured the townships in vehicles. Often, White policemen would sit in the police car while

African police patrolled the streets on foot. It attributed the high rate of crime in the townships to the inadequacy of the 'fire-brigade' style of policing (p. 63). The SAIRR recommended that law-abiding Africans be recruited as civic guards or special constables. In some townships residents established 'self-protection groups' or vigilante groups, some formed on conservative and tribal bases, such as the *maghotla*. Contrary to the popular view (for example Marks and Andersson 1990: 53), the state did not condone the *maghotla*, at least not at the beginning. The *maghotla* quickly developed a reputation for brutality, and there were frequent allegations of floggings, assaults, and kangaroo courts. Venables is quoted with approval by the SAIRR when he described them as 'worthwhile in suppressing crime, apprehending wrongdoers, and confiscating dangerous weapons' (p. 78). He noted, however, that sometimes they 'show a tendency to go beyond the powers normally conferred on "peace officers"' (p. 78).

These views are somewhat paradoxical. At the beginning liberal Whites supported the *maghotla* because they offered the prospect of crime detection and prevention in the absence of state provision. The fact that they operated with tribal notions of justice later led liberals to oppose them, and the state directly to sponsor them, but, at the beginning, the state rejected them. The Commissioner of the SAP refused to countenance the development of self-protection groups, pointing out in the SAIRR's 1951–2 survey of race relations that the emergency regulations which permitted the development of African civic guards in the war were now suspended, and there was no legal machinery to provide for vigilante groups. He promised instead to augment the number of policemen in the townships (p. 78). They never appeared in sufficient numbers, however, and unofficial vigilante groups proliferated, so much so that a government notice in December 1952 prohibited 'the establishment of any organization purporting to function as a civic or civilian guard for the protection of property, lives or persons unless approval is given by notice in the government gazette'. The self-protection groups established on the Rand thus came to an end, save those eventually sponsored directly by the state. The government may have feared that others, associated with various grass-roots political and trade union groups, were lending these movements too much credibility. It may also have been unwilling to see policing functions decentralized.

Whatever the case, the control of ordinary crime in the townships was not a high priority. But it was a priority to control Black opposition, such that the policing of race relations under apartheid also involved the SAP putting emphasis on policing industrial and political unrest. This had always been the case, but opposition strengthened after the war, heightening the SAP's profile in political suppression. What was new was the way opposition politics was criminalized. It was criminalized in two senses. At one level, various forms of political activity were made unlawful. In 1950, for example, the state passed the Suppression of Communism Act which banned the SACP and allowed draconian action to be taken against anyone thought to be furthering the aims of communism, including banning and house arrest without such power being regulated by the courts. Communism was defined so broadly as to include 'the encouragement of feelings of hostility between the European and non-European races', and the 'promotion of disturbance and disorder' and 'political, industrial, social, and economic change' (see SAIRR 1978: 412–14; also Mathews 1971). This also resulted in the criminalization of some forms of industrial action and trade union activity. In 1953 the Criminal Law Amendment Act also prescribed severe penalties for 'passive resistance'.

Politics under apartheid was criminalized in another sense because criminal gangs were thought simultaneously to be political agitators. The Commission of Inquiry into township unrest between 1949 and 1950 claimed that ordinary crime and political agitation were the same phenomenon, breeding in the same fertile ground (Union of South Africa 1950*b*: para. 232). The assumed low intelligence and suggestibility of Africans therefore made them at risk of being drawn into both criminal and political activity. The 'idle' unemployed youths who were *tsotsis* intimidated law-abiding residents into crime and political agitation (p. 3). This was the main reason why ordinary crime in the townships went relatively ignored: it was thought to be addressed by suppression of political activity.

A measure of the SAP's role in political suppression is provided by the escalation in offences against the state. These fell in the last three years of Smuts's government by 10.3 per cent, but between 1948 and 1952 they rose by a factor of nearly nine. As another example, the amount of expenditure granted to the SAP for detainees increased by 28.6 per cent between 1945 and 1946 and 1952 and 1953, nearly half of which came in the last year alone. Some specific incidents are worth citing. A Freedom Day demonstration was organized in Johannesburg for 1 May 1950 to protest against the Suppression of Communism

Act, which left seven Africans dead and nineteen injured when the police opened fire on the marchers. That night there were disturbances in several of Johannesburg's townships, leaving two Africans shot dead in Sophiatown, three in Orlando with another five injured, and five dead in Benoni and seven injured. The SAP's official historian describes the slaughter thus: 'the senseless shooting of people has never been police policy and for the first time policemen were now forced to shoot misguided people in order not to be engulfed by a wave of violence' (Dippenaar 1988: 227). Earlier victims of police shootings would probably turn in their graves at the idea that this was the first time the police had opened up with firearms on protesters. In 1952 an industrial dispute left thirteen African workers dead after being shot by the police. The Commissioner's comments on incidents like this in his annual reports always took the same form, providing justification for the resort to force. The crowd was 'truculent', 'hostile', 'throwing stones', 'angry', and otherwise engaging in acts of protest which made police action that of 'self defence', resulting in them being 'compelled to open fire', having done 'everything possible' to avoid the use of firearms (these comments are taken from the Annual Report of the Commissioner of the SAP 1952: 6, and make reference to police conduct in a strike by African workers). But at least it was felt that justification was needed. In later years, deaths were announced coldly without feeling the compunction to provide reason for them.

Details of specific incidents at this time do not bear out the Commissioner's comments. Indeed, the incidents illustrate that the tension within the police in the years before 1948 over the use of force continued for a period after the National Party came to power. Apartheid did not impose its view of police–Black relations on every officer straight away. For example, the Commission of Inquiry into disturbances in Krugersdorp, Newlands, Randfontein, and Newclare between 1949 and 1950 reveals a conflict of approach at the local level in the crowd-control tactics of the police. In Newlands, for example, disturbances arose in 1949 during a transport boycott after the Johannesburg City Council raised fares on the trams. The Council wanted the SAP to protect the tram cars but the commanding officer indicated that this was not the responsibility of the police, and he suggested to the Council that they hold a public meeting with the protesters to defuse the problem (Union of South Africa 1950*b*: para. 22). When violence erupted, the police baton-charged but did not use firearms. Firearms were used on one occasion only, to protect a policeman who had become separated from the rest and surrounded by the crowd. Shots were not fired into the crowd. In Krugersdorp in 1949 a dispute arose between residents and the township management. The police again took a conciliatory role, at least initially. The local inspector of police addressed a public meeting called by residents, and arranged for another to be held at which residents could put their grievances to the location manager. Police were withdrawn when the crowd became angry. The police were about to leave when the crowd attacked them. Shots were fired directly at the protesters, leaving two Africans dead (see para. 68). Firearms were used as a last resort, although when done so they were used to kill.

By contrast, the incidents in Randfontein and Newclare show that firearms were used as a first resort, and intended to kill. In Randfontein in 1949, for example, the police undertook a liquor raid which resulted in residents becoming angry. The Commission's report noted that the police tended to raid the township at night and in the very early morning, disrupting sleep and causing the greatest inconvenience. Residents were treated harshly during the raids and the location manager had tried unsuccessfully to get the police to stop making them (para. 85). During this raid, the location manager asked the police to withdraw when the crowd became angry, which they did. But the police later came back with reinforcements and refused the manager's request to retire. Unprovoked, they opened up on the crowds with rifles, leaving three Africans killed and three injured (see para. 106). In Newclare in 1950, the police undertook a liquor raid and shot and killed a resident who had escaped arrest. When a crowd assembled, tear-gas and live bullets were fired to disperse them. Twenty-seven residents were shot. The report noted how liquor raids tended to provoke conflict, and urged that the police develop more experience and tact in handling them rather than stop them altogether (para. 212). Once again, therefore, an official commission was asking the police to use the civil policing style to perform a colonial policing role.

To add to this ambiguity over the use of force, the police often performed a benign role in addition to their repressive, paramilitary one. Routine policing of sorts still exists in divided societies (on Northern Ireland see Brewer 1991), giving the police the opportunity to act in a benign capacity. Thus, at the same time as police were shooting protesters in cold blood, Africans flocked to police stations in Durban seeking protection from Indians who were attacking them in the riots of 1949, the police acted bravely in rescuing a young African boy trapped down a well in September 1949, and in rescuing Africans who were trapped in the debris after tornadoes demolished houses during 1952, pulling the dead and injured from buildings that were so dangerous as to threaten their own safety. But all too often in divided societies, the goodwill created by the benign role is dissipated by the deleterious consequences of the repressive one.

POLICING IN THE FIRST PHASE OF APARTHEID

The 1950 Population Registration Act classified the whole population according to race, and in consolidating apartheid, the National Party used the Act to draw progressively sharper distinctions between the racial groups and resorted to even further legal intervention to enforce them. In 1951 the Bantu Authorities Act laid the basis for separate political systems for Africans based on tribal distinctions. The parliamentary representatives created for Africans in 1936, and the NRC, were abolished, Coloureds were removed from the common voters roll in the Cape in 1956. Economically, in 1957 the government stopped all trading by Africans outside the reserves, and in 1956 further powers were given to the Minister of Labour to impose job reservation 'in any industry, trade or occupation'. Legislation passed in 1953 barred Africans from forming registered trade unions, and made strikes by Africans illegal. Also that year, separate amenities were legalized, and the 1957 Natives Amendment Act extended compulsory segregation to churches, places of entertainment, clubs, buses, and sports. Separate amenities needed to be provided in factories and offices.

Further restrictions were also placed on sexual relations and marriage between people of different races. The 1953 Bantu Education Act established separate and unequal educational provision for Africans. The school curriculum and language of instruction was changed in order to promote tribal loyalties, and emphasis was placed on teaching manual skills to enable Africans to minister to the needs of Whites. Introducing the Act, the Minister of Bantu Education said that 'natives will be taught from childhood that equality with Europeans is not for them' (quoted in Duncan 1964: 125). And, finally, the pass laws were tightened and extended to women.

However, the country's need for African labour ensured that influx control could not stem the flow to the urban areas during the 1950s, and between 1951 and 1960, African urbanization increased by 47.9 per cent, to total 31.8 per cent of the total African population in 1960 (Posel 1991: 141). Apartheid underwent a transition in its second phase in order to try to deal with this problem, but in its first phase, the government was permitting more and more Africans to reside in White areas. The SAP's role in policing race relations in urban areas thus became critical to the implementation of apartheid.

As the enforcers of discriminatory measures the police were the key agent of state policy, as well as the most immediate symbol of Black oppression. Three features distinguish policing under the first phase of apartheid: the extension of police powers, increasing brutality, and an accompanying withdrawal of legal and political constraint on police conduct. In terms of police powers, a new Police Act was passed in 1958 which gave the police responsibility for the 'preservation of internal safety in the Union', a power which they had in practice but which was not legally defined in the 1912 Act. The Criminal Procedure and Evidence Amendment Act No. 29 in 1955 gave the police the right to search premises and persons without a warrant, and the Criminal Procedure Act No. 56 of the same year broadened the powers of the Native Affairs Department's municipal police, giving them right to search and arrest within the boundaries of townships without warrant. The SAP was also given extensive new powers under this Act, for it allowed for 180 days' detention without regulation by the court.

However, there was no parallel enlargement of the police force, contrary to conventional wisdom (for example Posel 1991: 119). Trends in manpower are shown in Table 4.9, which indicates that there were only marginal increases in overall manpower for the period, and these failed to keep pace with the growth in South Africa's population so that the ratio of police per thousand head of population actually fell. The force was also still considerably understaffed, although this reduced during the period to be at its lowest in 1957, as a result of incremental growth in actual membership throughout the period. The growth was biggest amongst Whites, which demonstrates the government's wish to reverse the trend towards the employment of Blacks, such that the proportion of Blacks in the SAP fell. Indeed, the SAP could not get enough White recruits. It raised the maximum age limit for White recruits in 1955 to 35 years, but the

TABLE 4.9. *Trends in police manpower, 1954–1957*

Year	Number*		% Black	% increase	Ratio per 1,000 head of population†	% understaffed
	White	Black				
1954	10,110	10,829	51.7	—	1.63	8.3
1955	10,573	10,794	50.5	2.0	1.63	7.1
1956	10,926	10,851	49.8	1.9	1.61	6.2
1957	11,250	10,889	49.1	1.6	1.58	4.6

* Actual membership.
† Based on authorized membership.
Source: Annual Reports of the Commissioner of the SAP.

TABLE 4.10. *Trends in Black manpower, 1954–1957*

Year	Asian		Coloured		African	
	No.	% NCOs	No.	% NCOs	No.	% NCOs
1954	296	12.5	839	12.5	9,710	9.3
1955	293	12.2	843	13.2	9,661	11.0
1956	293	12.2	837	12.9	9,721	10.7
1957	293	12.6	834	13.3	9,762	10.4

Source: Annual Reports of the Commissioner of the SAP.

following year there was still a shortfall of 1,012 White policemen. However, the Commissioner noted in his annual reports that 'at no time has there been difficulty in finding non-European recruits' (Annual Report of the Commissioner of the SAP 1954: 1).

In terms of the Black membership, Table 4.10 shows that the trend continued towards the employment of Africans, in order to facilitate the 'own areas' policy. There was also an associated increase in the proportion of African non-commissioned officers during this period, although the proportion remained lower than among other Black communities. The selective promotion of Whites continued apace as the SAP practised its own apartheid. In 1954, for example, 88.6 per cent of all Black police were at the rank of constable, compared with 63.1 per cent for Whites, and rather than promote Blacks to the rank of head constable, a new rank was invented for them alone called 'senior sergeant'. Ten people were given the rank in 1954 (Annual Report of the Commissioner of the SAP 1954: 2). The 'own areas' policy was implemented very slowly, however. By 1955, only three stations were staffed solely by Blacks out of 962 police stations throughout the country, although many more had a preponderance of Black staff under White authority. In his 1953 Annual Report, for example, the Commissioner explained that 'the training of non-Europeans to replace Europeans at stations in non-European areas takes time and demands patience' (p. 3). By 1956, however, there were twenty-four, but most were in the tribal reserves, as a prelude to the formation of separate homeland police forces in 1960 with the Bantustan phase of apartheid.

There had always been sufficient supply of African police to make it unnecessary for the SAP to have formal recruitment campaigns aimed at them, but to facilitate the move to homeland police, the SAP began a formal advertisement campaign in the late 1950s to increase the size of its African manpower. *Bantu*, for example, the journal of the Department of Native Affairs, carried a report on 15 July 1955, where the Under-Secretary for Bantu Education made 'a call to service' to encourage Africans to join the police. The report emphasized the employment opportunities provided by the police, although it incorrectly described it as deracialized. In February 1959 the journal carried a report on the station at Meadowlands (*Bantu*, 1959), which had recently come under the sole charge of Africans, and it often printed photographs of African policemen leading an adventurous and happy life, as an inducement to others to join. However, this growth was a portent of the move to the second phase of apartheid.

But if there was no great expansion in police manpower during the first phase of apartheid, there was in police expenditure, as shown in Table 4.11. The increases were even sufficient to narrow the gap with defence expenditure that had begun since the war. But it is also noteworthy how the proportion of expenditure on detective work declined during the period, indicating a further shift towards the labour power of the uniform branch, which lent itself more readily to the policing of race relations. In addition to the money spent on the SAP, the SARHP had nearly a million pounds devoted to it in the 1955/6 financial year, exclusive of salaries, and had a total manpower of 3,410, 34.4 per cent of which was Black. The same apartheid operated as in the SAP, for only 1.2 per cent of Black personnel were non-commissioned officers, compared with 27.4 for Whites (see South African Railways and Harbours Service 1956). Some of the duties of the SARHP were handed to the SAP in 1953, when the latter became responsible for airports.

TABLE 4.11. *Police expenditure, 1952/3–1958/9*

Year	Total £m.	% increase	% detective work	Ratio to defence exp.*
1952/3	10.14	—	0.9	121
1953/4	11.54	13.7	0.9	116
1954/5	11.98	3.8	0.8	116
1955/6	12.60	5.1	0.8	—
1956/7	14.03	11.3	0.8	—
1957/8	14.96	6.6	0.9	—
1958/9	15.99	6.8	0.7	—

* Police expenditure = 100.

Source: Annual Reports of the Auditor General.

The massive increases in expenditure reflected the state's commitment to solve some of the problems identified by commissioners in
earlier periods. The first was the poor quality and shortage of police
buildings. In 1955 the SAP was able to form the Building Unit,
composed of qualified artisans and tradespeople who became enrolled
as members of the SAP but were employed exclusively on a rebuilding
programme. In the past, artisans had been drawn from existing staff
and retrained, but the new unit had a staff of 100; it even made its
own bricks. In the first year it built 3 police stations, 17 houses, 37
cells, 21 storerooms, 17 garages, and repaired another 19 stations
(Annual Report of the SAP 1955: 7). It used the portable construction
system to quicken the erection of buildings, and made bricks on site.
By 1957 the Commissioner was noting, at long last, 'considerable
progress in the replacement of inadequate and unsuitable buildings'
(Annual Report of the Commissioner of the SAP 1957: 3). However,
304 stations were still hired from private owners. Increased finance
also accelerated the modernization of the SAP's technology. The use
of two-way radio cars was extended to the Eastern Transvaal in 1956,
and in 1956 the SAP only had 515 horses. Its vehicle fleet, however,
was now 2,598. By this time 170 cars were fitted with two-way radio.
Developments were also made in the SAP's riot-control technology.
Two water-cannon were purchased in 1956, and in 1959 47 Saracen
armoured vehicles went into commission. Up to this point, the SAP
had been using converted army lorries to transport large numbers of
policemen to incidents safely. In 1959 244 lorries were used for this
purpose.

One of the SAP's familiar problems which the state did not ease was the complaint about extraneous duties, despite the Commissioner's earlier statement that steps were being taken to reduce them. Police–state relations in the 1950s increased the burden of these duties. In 1953, for example, shortly after the Commissioner issued his warning, 547,240 hours were given to work for other government departments, which increased by a factor of one and a half by the following year. By 1957 the number of hours spent on work for other government departments had increased by another 53.6 per cent, and the Commissioner complained that 'notwithstanding every effort to resist the undertaking of enquiries, there is a steady increase. Many of these have no connection whatsoever with police work and have a detrimental effect on the functions and responsibilities of the force' (Annual Report of the Commissioner of the SAP 1957: 3).

What is significant about this complaint is that it was uttered by the SAP's first Afrikaner nationalist commissioner, illustrating how strong was the demand within the SAP for organizational autonomy from the state. Commissioner Brink retired in 1954 and was replaced by C. I. Rademeyer, who was the first member from the CID to become Commissioner and the first not to have signed the wartime 'red oath'. He spent the war on compulsory leave of absence. His nationalism showed itself almost immediately. Upon taking office he wrote in his own hand a standing order which confirmed the inalienable right of every policeman to use mother tongue in police business. In 1954 he also abolished the British-style blue uniform and helmet, as well as some of the colonial trappings such as riding breeches and the right of officers to wear dress swords. In 1957 the British crown on the cap badge was abolished and policemen started wearing a castle as an emblem of rank. The fullest expression of the Commissioner's nationalism came in 1955 with the formation of an Afrikaans cultural association in the SAP, known as the Afrikaanse Kultuurvereniging van die Suid-Afrikaanse Polisie (AKPOL), under the leadership of the Chaplain. Its emblem featured oxen, the nearest it could come to an ox-wagon. It contributed greatly to celebrations of significant events or people in Boer history, and especially events surrounding the old South African Republic Police. The objectives of AKPOL were: to promote the use of Afrikaans in and outside the SAP; to promote Afrikaans art and culture in the SAP; to promote the intellectual and cultural edification of policemen; to cultivate and foster a healthy spirit of solidarity amongst policemen; to co-operate with similar organizations outside the police; and to publish and distribute a magazine and other reading matter to policemen to promote the Afrikaans language (*Nongqai*, Jan. 1955: 1). In practice, therefore, it acted as the nearest equivalent to a police community relations branch, although exclusively dealing with the Afrikaans-speaking community. It organized hikes for children along trails connected with the voortrekkers, ran inter-school quizzes on the life and work of renowned Afrikaner poets and writers, and ran 'boeremusiek' competitions in the Transvaal, encouraging the development of Afrikaner folk-music. By these means the occupational culture of the force was thoroughly Afrikanerized, marginalizing the few remaining English-speakers in the force.

This also meant that the mind-set of policemen was heavily influenced by the prejudices and racial stereotypes of Afrikaners, many of whom came from an insular, rural background. The brutality associated with the policing of race relations in the first phase of apartheid owed much to this mind-set, especially in a context where police powers were strengthened, Black political opposition and crime escalated, and the legal and political constraints on police misconduct were lifted.

The *tsotsis* continued their rule of terror in the townships, and extended their field of interest in the mid-1950s, when violent armed robberies became common on the Rand. This led the SAP to form its Murder and Robbery Squad within the CID. Allegations were also made that the *tsotsis* were paying protection money to the police in Alexandra township, and several policemen were relieved of their duties after a departmental inquiry. However, ordinary crime was not a priority, because it was thought to be dealt with by focusing on political unrest and the administrative regulations which defined the boundaries between the races. Thus, one of the leading Afrikaner nationalist criminologists, J. van Heerden, Chief Bantu Affairs Commissioner, said that the causes of crime lie in social mixing in residential areas (J. van Heerden 1959: 52). Enforcing segregation thus solved crime; the police could prevent crime, their primary function, by enforcing apartheid's race laws (noted by Bloom 1957: 9; Frankel 1980: 490–1). Black South Africans were therefore caught between the *tsotsis* and the police. The thugs raised the level of fear of ordinary crime in the townships, while the police became objects of fear in enforcing race laws which did not deal with ordinary crime.

The attention given to administrative offences which regulated the boundaries between the races is revealed in statistics which show that by 1957, pass law offences, for example, had risen 123 per cent since 1946 and 76.6 per cent since 1952. The offence of possession of kaffir beer had increased 83.5 per cent since 1946 and 3.1 per cent from 1952. Native hut tax offences had increased threefold from 1946 and fourfold from 1952. In 1957 there were 177,890 native hut tax offences, 169,236 offences of possession of kaffir beer, 129,060 cases of trespass, 88,448 native reserve offences, 69,735 breaches of curfew regulations, and over a million pass law offences (Annual Report of the Commissioner of the SAP 1957: 5). Not surprisingly, the prosecution rate per thousand head of population increased rapidly during the 1950s. The average annual rate for the period 1954–9 is 115.6, compared with 92.88 for the period 1946–52, and 74.2 for 1927–45. In 1959 the figure had reached 118, resulting in just over one in every ten people being prosecuted, most of whom were African. The prosecution rate had increased by nearly a quarter in this period compared to 1946–52.

By 1957 Johannesburg's Native Affairs Department, which had its own municipal police in townships, had set up mobile patrols 'on constant duty in the townships' to apprehend and remove Africans who had overstayed their seventy-two hours, although Posel reports that policemen were often ignoring the seventy-two-hour rule and simply arresting all those without permits (Posel 1991: 223). At the beginning of the decade, Dr Xuma told a government commission that 'flying squads, pick-up vans, troop carriers, and mounted police are abroad irritating and exasperating Africans by indiscriminately demanding passes' (Union of South Africa 1950*b*: 2). By 1957 W. B. Ngakane, on behalf of Black Sash, wrote: 'Pass! No other word in the country conjures up such variety of associations . . . control of Africans . . . police raids, families estranged from one another, fathers sent to imprisonment, and humiliation in its bitterest form' (1957: 5; also see Black Sash 1959*a*). By 1956 passes and the pick-up vans had entered township folklore and there were several songs and poems featuring these objects of fear (for examples see Simons 1956: 55). Punishments for pass law offences were severe. One could be 'endorsed out' back to the impoverished reserve, given a prison sentence, which meant automatic loss of employment, forced to pay a prohibitively expensive admission of guilt fine, or, since 1954, sent to work on White farms as forced labour. The conditions on these 'prison farms' were appalling, and it was suspected at the time that the police were acting as *de facto* recruiters for White farmers (First 1958: 20–1). So common were prosecutions that punishment by the courts soon lost its social stigma.

The 1950s also witnessed an escalation in Black political activity, being the period of the defiance campaign, the formulation of the Freedom Charter, and mass support for the African National Congress (on Black politics at this time see: Gerhart 1978; Lodge 1983). This was reflected in police activity. Between the 1952/3 and 1958/9 financial years, expenditure on detainees rose by 98.7 per cent, and offences against the state rose by 35.4 per cent between 1952 and 1957. Some of the tactics used by the police are worth noting. Pass law enforcement was sometimes used as a weapon of collective punishment for political activity, and early-morning raids were often stepped up in the wake of protests in the townships. This only fed back into political opposition by fuelling further protest against apartheid's race laws. They took to using conservative vigilante groups as surrogates to impose brutal tribal punishments in the townships. In Evaton, for example, the police co-operated with a group called the 'Russians' to attack bus boycotters. The vigilantes loaded and unloaded their guns in the presence of the police unchecked by them, while the police disarmed the victims (see Mphahlele 1956: 61–2).

Infiltration of political organizations was also perfected as a tactic. In the late 1940s, the SB placed informers in the SACP, and by the 1950s it operated an extensive network of spies. It monitored the activities of journalists, trade union and political activists, and even university students. After a revelation in 1959 that political spies were operating at the University of Witwatersrand, Commissioner Rademeyer said in the press that what else could be expected, and that anyone making an issue of it would get a 'kick up the pants' (see Williams 1959: 6). When his remarks were raised in parliament the Minister of Justice said that in his view it was the patriotic duty of all South Africans to be police informers. It later became enshrined in police regulations that members with information which might possibly be of importance to the SB were required to bring it to their attention immediately, and the code-book lists dozens of items which policemen were required to look out for (Poodhun 1983: 324). Since 1954 it had taken to gate-crashing private meetings forcibly and demanding the names of people, often accompanied by members of the regular SAP who checked passes.

However, the primary tactic for policing political opposition was brute force. Live bullets became the main crowd-control tactic, although on one occasion on 20 December 1956 the *Star* reported how an officer had shouted at his young constables to 'stop that firing'. Not many did. The Commissioner's attitude to this was cold. In his 1956 Annual Report, for example, he refers to the fact that 'the police had at times to use their firearms, but the loss of life was insignificant' (p. 4); deaths no longer required justification. The design of townships took the SAP's crowd-control techniques into account. Hirson quotes a young architect from Durban, who in 1957 was told of the conditions to be observed in the design of African townships. The width of the roadways had to be sufficient to allow large vehicles to execute U-turns quickly, the alignment of the houses and the distance between them had to be such as to permit unimpeded firing, and the distance from the township boundary to the nearest main highway had to be beyond the range of a rifle (Hirson 1979: 184). S. Davies notes how houses were typically built in valleys or low-lying areas to facilitate long-distance surveillance from high reconnaissance points (1987: 182).

But the use of force was not restricted to incidents of public order, for police methods generally became more brutal. The SAP had used gratuitous violence since its inception, especially in dealing with Africans. But systematic inhuman treatment and torture occurred for the first time during the 1950s. The first known incident of the use of electric shock to force confessions occurred in the Orange Free State in 1954, when Head Constable Nieuwenhuis admitted use of it to persuade an alleged stock thief to divulge where the cattle were hidden. He also used gas masks for the same purpose. In 1955 a suspect alleged to have stolen cloth in East London claimed that Sergeant Malthys wrapped electric cable around his fingers and put a gas mask over his face (other cases are cited in Duncan 1964: 39–42). In April 1957 a magistrate in Lichtenburg ordered the police to undertake a departmental inquiry when it was revealed that the police had used electric-shock treatment to force a confession. In February of that year a magistrate had thrown out a case because the confession had been extracted by means of electric shock. Seven policemen were charged with assault in January 1957 after using the treatment on a suspect.

Beatings were common. The London *New Statesman* carried a report on 27 June 1959 that businessmen in Cape Town were complaining that their secretaries could not work near the central police station because of the 'pleadings and screams of people being beaten'. The *Cape Times* of 2 July 1959 noted the case of a detective sergeant who had admitted under oath that it was an 'everyday occurrence for prisoners to be beaten, usually with a garden hose'. Other forms of torture were used. On 19 November 1951 16-year-old Leziwe Gwala was forced by Constable van Zyl to drink such large amounts of water that he drowned. In 1958 Willo Smit, a Coloured suspected of theft from a White farmer, was killed after being stretched between two lorries. He had suffered three days of beatings by the police and the farmer. Deaths while under interrogation began to occur. Two members of the SAP in Zululand buried a prisoner on a beach in 1955 after he died under interrogation. In Durban in 1951 police were responsible for the death of a West Indian sailor arrested for drunkenness. Officer Groenewald is reported in the *Star* on 14 June 1951 as saying, 'I just wanted to hit him'; with one blow he was dead. Two police officers were imprisoned in 1956 for beating a suspect to death. The judge cautioned that 'it was better that the guilty go free than the reputation of the police be tarnished by methods such as these' (quoted in Bloom 1957: 10). The cases of people who were alleged to have committed suicide in police custody were often suspicious enough to suggest that the allegation was a cover-up for police brutality. For example, in one such case in Cradock in January 1959 (see Duncan 1964: 43), affidavits were lodged claiming that the prisoner found hanging in the cell had been systematically tortured, and had died of a cerebral haemorrhage; the Minister of Justice would not permit the body to be exhumed.

Incidents of gratuitous violence were commonplace. Constable Visser from Johannesburg attacked a citizen on the street on 13 January 1956 because he had earlier filed damages against him for mistreatment. The policeman attacked him with such force that the citizen, an Indian member of the congress movement, died. Visser admitted that he 'hacked his forehead with the heel of his boot so that detectives would think he was assaulted by natives' (Duncan 1964: 49). The judge described Visser as a beast. A young Afrikaner policeman, Willem Johannes Spence, 19 years of age, when asked why he had shot an African, is reported in the *Rand Daily Mail* of 16 August 1957 as saying, 'I threatened to shoot him and he said "shoot then," so I shot him. He was cheeky.' Twenty-three-year-old Andries van Rensburg, and his 18-year-old colleague, too young to be named, stated that they drove their police vehicle around Cape Town's townships whipping

Africans with sjamboks as they went past, saying in the *Cape Times* of 8 January 1959 that it was fun. By mistake they hit a White man, but van Rensburg explained that he thought he was a native. In February 1959 Constable Terblanche jumped on the stomach of a drunk, killing him. Gratuitous violence extended to sexual attacks on African women. In 1957, 20-year-old Jacobus Retief, a constable in Durban, raped an African woman arrested under the curfew regulations. A 22-year-old Afrikaner policeman was charged with raping two African girls in 1952, one of whom was only 13 years of age, after arresting them for pass law offences. Sex was frequently demanded from women arrested under pass law offences as an alternative to formal punishment, and goods and money were sometimes stolen from victims whose houses were raided for liquor or passes (Duncan 1964: 51).

These incidents show that the maltreatment, humiliation, and rough-handling of former years escalated into systematic brutality. It might be expected, therefore, that the number of dismissals from the force rose dramatically during this period, but as Table 4.12 shows, the reverse happened. The number of dismissals as a proportion of the total manpower was stable for Whites between 1954 and 1957, and actually fell for Blacks by nearly half, which is likely to be the effect of training for Black policemen or the need to retain them for the 'own areas' policy, and the proportion of wastage that was due to dismissal fell for both groups. It was the case, however, that most dismissals concerned the more serious cases. These figures suggest that misconduct was either not widespread, so that cases like the above were isolated, or not serious enough to merit dismissal. Indeed, in 1957 only 2.77 per cent of White policemen were convicted of crime by the courts, which is lower than might be expected, although it compares unfavourably with the London Metropolitan Police, where the corresponding figure was 0.06 per cent (Bloom 1957: 19). However, the figure had increased tremendously with the National Party government. Between 1946 and 1948, 1.34 per cent of all policemen were charged with crime and 1.04 convicted, but for 1956–8, the figures were 5.7 per cent and 3.8 per cent respectively (worked from statistics provided by Bloom 1957: 19, and based on membership figures in 1948 and 1957 respectively). It is also clear from these figures that White policemen were more likely than Blacks to be convicted of crimes. This becomes more obvious by breaking down the figures for dismissals provided in the Commissioner's Annual

TABLE 4.12. *Dismissals from the police, 1954–1957*

Year	White	% of manpower	Black	% of manpower	% = serious*		% wastage = dismissals	
					White	Black	White	Black
1954	49	0.4	302	2.7	83.6	97.3	6.0	30.9
1955	41	0.3	244	2.3	97.5	97.9	4.6	35.8
1956	47	0.4	212	1.9	100	100	5.7	26.7
1957	52	0.4	176	1.6	98.0	94.8	5.3	27.2

* Defined as convictions by the courts, drunkenness, and misconduct.

Source: Annual Reports of the Commissioner of the SAP.

Reports into types of serious offence. In the period 1946–52, 52 per cent of all dismissals of White policemen involved convictions by the courts, compared to 31.3 per cent for Black policemen. The corresponding figures for 1954–7 are 77.2 per cent and 51.2 per cent respectively. Some of the policemen were so young that they were prosecuted before Special Courts set up under the Children's Act; the state was giving to juveniles enormous power to police race relations, and they often acted childishly.

These figures also demonstrate that policemen were not yet above the law, and the escalation in brutality was matched by a growth in the number of men dismissed as a result of being convicted by the courts. Many of the serious incidents cited above came before the courts. However, there are three arguments which suggest that the police were becoming immune in practice. First, only the serious cases came before the courts. Low-level, day-to-day violence was so routine as to be unnoticeable to the authorities. Quite often the sole point of police action was to give people a thrashing rather than bother to arrest them for some offence and tie up the courts. People who were dealt with summarily got a sound beating as their punishment. After an incident in Claremont in 1960, for example, a witness is quoted by *Contact* on 16 April as saying 'police are beating up everybody, blood is everywhere'. The Deputy Commissioner for the Cape Western Division is also quoted as saying that 'our aim is not to make arrests but to deal with people on the spot'. The routine violence involved in this was completely acceptable to the police and no cause for dismissal, let alone appearance before the courts.

Secondly, the courts often treated policemen lightly. For example, the officers involved in killing Willo Smit by manacling him and stretching him between two lorries were prosecuted for 'aggravated assault'. Thus, in some instances, magistrates showed a lack of independence from the government, especially outside the Natal Bench. The government was able to subvert the judiciary in another way, for, thirdly, men found guilty received sympathetic treatment by the Minister of Justice, and were often reinstated or not dismissed at all. In 1952, for example, forty-two White policemen convicted by the court of assault were admitted back to the force; only twenty were dismissed (Bloom 1957: 15). Early in his cabinet career, Charles Swart, Minister of Justice, announced that he would protect 'his' force against criticism of their use of sten guns. It was under Swart that the identity number was removed from the uniform of White policemen (but not Black), although this was restored in 1961. He described claims of lawlessness amongst the police as an exaggeration deliberately conspired by the English-speaking press, and he refused to condemn 'his' police force. His protection went further. Constable Visser, for example, who had hacked a person's head with his boot and been described by the judge as a beast, was moved by the Minister to Cape Town for 'medical treatment', and lived as a free man. Minister Swart also released two other policemen in 1957 found guilty of killing an African prisoner. Swart gave clemency to a White policeman found guilty of murdering a suspect, after serving only six months of a seven-year sentence, and immediately made him a warder in a prison (Duncan 1964: 48). Swart even refused to condemn a policeman who had assaulted a magistrate, claiming that the magistrate was resisting arrest. The victim was subsequently awarded substantial damages by the Appeal Court.

This was the same Minister who pardoned an Afrikaner hotel owner found guilty of assaulting a Coloured person because the conviction, according to the *Star* on 19 November 1957, would have resulted in the man losing his licence. It was Swart who was often photographed with the cat-o'-nine-tails, and who urged the courts to recommend more corporal punishment. Between 1945 and 1958, the number of people given corporal punishment rose by a factor of six. The number of executions also increased. In 1945 29.3 per cent of those sentenced to death were executed, compared with 63 per cent in 1958 (Duncan 1964: 35). When South Africa became a Republic in 1961, Swart was made President. He was replaced as Minister of Justice by F. C. Erasmus and then B. J. Vorster, formerly of Koffiefontein.

With the Commissioner stating that deaths were 'insignificant'

(Annual Report of the Commissioner of the SAP 1956: 4), and the Minister responsible for the police being eager to defend police deviance, the legal and political constraints on misconduct were lifted during the 1950s. Gone was the disquiet expressed in the 1930s and 1940s by government commissions or more liberal-minded policemen who supported a more civil policing style. If there was internal opposition within the SAP to the unrestrained use of force, it was not expressed. The leadership and rank and file had now become more than Afrikanerized, they had become nationalist, with a mind-set which saw Africans as unequal, subservient, and dispensable. But it was not yet the case that all public accountability was removed. The liberal press was not muzzled in reporting misconduct, as it was to be in the second phase of apartheid (although the press was affected by legislation which did not make it entirely free; see Chimutengwende 1978: 59–61), and radical political organizations were still lawful and could articulate criticism of the police, although they, too, were silenced as apartheid moved into its second phase.

But in its first phase, the policing of apartheid was vociferously criticized. The Minister often claimed in parliament, and to journalists, that figures on police misconduct were unavailable, but the press was free to investigate and report, and political organizations were able to mobilize around police atrocities. Thus, it became popular to claim, for example, that Afrikaner nationalists were South Africa's Nazis, the SAP its Gestapo (Black Sash 1956: 1–2; Bunting 1964; Duncan 1964), and that apartheid threatened 'normal society', with the police creating rather than preventing disorder, crime, and instability (Rankin 1957: 5–6). Criticism was made of the powers given the police under apartheid (Bloom 1957; Nokwe 1959; Portia 1956), and specific attention given to the brutal enforcement of the pass laws (Black Sash 1959*a*: 10–11; Ngakane 1957: 5–6; Simons 1956). English-language newspapers drew attention to police atrocities. The *Rand Daily Mail*, for example, described 'young constables' as 'little Cæsers, operating lynch law . . . gangsters in uniform', and in an editorial entitled 'Police Emergency', on 2 July 1959, the *Cape Times* outlined the crisis in the police, arising from their abuse of power, brutality, and criminal behaviour.

The demand for police reform, however, was not isolated from the wider context within which the police operated. Police misconduct in enforcing the pass laws, for example, was integrally linked to the apartheid system which imposed influx control and granted such wide powers to its policing. A clear and extensive programme of police reform was outlined by Doreen Rankin on behalf of the Black Sash, an anti-apartheid organization of women concerned with how apartheid affected Black women (on the Black Sash see Michelman 1975; Spink 1991). 'Speaking as a woman', she wrote, 'I will tell you what our traditional way of life has always been—pampered by the non-European. We have depended on them, lived in indolence because of them, and thought as little about them as possible' (all quotations taken from Rankin 1957: 5–6). Yet this 'traditional way of life' was now under threat. Serious crime was becoming more common, 'murders are appallingly frequent, more houses are being burglar-proofed, while at the same time robberies have become commonplace. The jails are full to overflowing, and people are no longer safe in the streets at night.' This was Johannesburg, she declared, and the cause was the very laws which were supposed to protect them. The pass laws were responsible for thousands of law-abiding people being thrown into gaol. These law-abiding people were 'hemmed in by laws and regulations which made life a perpetual misery, while at the same time criminals remain free to prey on the community'. Influx control was responsible for idleness, vagrancy, and serious crime.

The solution was simple: abolish influx control; the demand to see passes should stop; combing the locations for Africans without passes should cease and the police should patrol the streets only; the police force should be better paid and young men of quality and character should be encouraged to apply; pay of African police should be raised, and a much larger body of men employed—character should be the basis of eligibility for the African police; a system of night patrols should be operated in Black and White areas 'in the same way that the London police work'; the civic guards should be revived while the police force is reorganized, and law-abiding members of the community be encouraged to police their areas; and Africans without work should be given jobs. Such proposals could never be accepted because they affected the heart of the colonial relations under apartheid policed by the SAP, but Rankin clearly understood that civil policing was impossible when the main task was to police a policy of internal colonialism. Therefore she was not optimistic about the prospects of her programme, and ended with some prophetic words: 'the heart quails at the threat of the future'. Within a few years many hearts did quail as apartheid moved into its second phase, and the quality of its policing deteriorated further.

CONCLUSION

The differences in policing under apartheid emerged only over time, and most were differences of degree rather than of quality. The only qualitative difference was the 'own areas' strategy, but this was proceeded with very slowly, and only developed significantly with the Bantustanization associated with the second phase of apartheid. Under the first phase, police powers were consolidated as the National Party regulated relations between the races in the urban areas to a greater degree than before. The police controlled the boundaries between the races with a level of systematic inhumanity which was not known before, and the legal and political constraints which moderated police conduct in the past were lifted.

This was all done, however, with a very small police force, and the National Party did not expand police manpower in the way they did police expenditure. But apartheid did not demand sizeable numbers. What was important to policing race relations under apartheid was brute force, an organizational culture and managerial ethos which encouraged this, and an armoury of equipment which made the police into a killing machine. The simple containment of residents in townships requires fewer men than the patrolling of streets in pursuit of ordinary crime. Apartheid required fewer policemen in another sense because policing roles were diffused throughout society, since social control was embedded in virtually all its institutions and bureaucracies, from the education system to the labour bureaux. Homeland structures were defined in the second phase of apartheid to extend the social control, and these had an effect on policing. Otherwise, the dye was cast and policing in the second was much the same as in the first.

5

The Second Phase of Apartheid
1960–1975

INTRODUCTION

The year 1960 was significant for South Africa and, with hindsight, for the police. The country voted to become a Republic in 1960, and the peak of Black protest was reached with Sharpeville. From this point Black political opposition declined, went underground, militarized, and mostly abroad, forcing the police to focus on the external rather than internal threat, to develop counter-insurgency skills, and rapidly to expand its manpower and resources. It was not until the Soweto uprising in 1976 that the focus changed again to the internal threat. Apartheid's second phase began in earnest in 1960, taking South Africa in a direction opposite to that suggested in Macmillan's famous 'winds of change' speech of that year. To reinforce the impression that the SAP was entering a new era, Commissioner Rademeyer retired in 1960, cutting links with past conflicts within the police during the war, to be replaced by Lt.-Gen. du Plooy, a former member of the Special Branch, symbolic, perhaps, of the SAP's future.

Apartheid's second phase is marked by the development of the supposedly self-governing homelands or Bantustans, and the consequent industrial decentralization and population removals thus caused. This limited enfranchisement was not a knee-jerk response to the international criticism of apartheid following the Sharpeville massacre in 1960, as Lipton claims (1985: 30), but was an extension of previous apartheid policies, albeit a radical departure (Posel 1991: 227). The homeland policy, for example, was presaged in the 1954 Tomlinson Report (on which see Ashforth 1990: 114–48), which urged 'self-development for the Bantu'. Moves in this direction were made in 1958 when the Native Affairs Department was renamed the

Department of Bantu Administration and Development (DBAD), and responsibility for Black education was given over to the new Department of Bantu Education. University education became racially segregated the following year, and the infamous 'tribal universities' were established for the respective ethnic groups in the African population. The Promotion of Bantu Self-Government Act was passed in 1959 as the central legislative pillar of apartheid's second phase.

The Act recognized eight 'national' units among the African population, and promised them self-determination in their 'homeland'. Territorial boundaries were based on the tribal reserves defined in previous land acts, ensuring the perpetuation of past inequalities. The African reserves thus became 'nations', in which the ethnic groups could control their own political destiny and preserve cultural identity; something claimed in Transkei since 1956.

The main feature of the separate development policy was to confer limited political rights rather than economic opportunities, although much later some industrial decentralization did occur to the border areas. In initial legislation, territorial authorities, or governments, were created for the other 'national' units, to whom a constitution and various administrative powers were devolved: Ciskei (1961); Bophuthatswana (1961); Gazankulu (1969); Lebowa (1969); Venda (1969); Qwaqwa (1969); and KwaZulu (1970). Further administrative powers were granted to the authorities in slow stages, although the South African government kept control over key decisions and resources (on Transkei see Southall 1982; on KwaZulu and Bophuthatswana see Butler, Rotberg, and Adams 1977). Between 1972 and 1974, legislative assemblies were established for each of the territories, through which its citizens were supposed to enjoy voting rights. Representative councils were also set up for Coloureds and Indians. The first of the African homelands to become 'independent' was the Transkei in 1976.

In this way Africans lost their citizenship of South Africa to one of these 'nations', irrespective of whether they lived in 'White' South Africa or the homeland. Many living in urban areas were forcibly removed to their respective homeland as the state sought to limit further the number of urban Africans with permanent residential rights outside the homelands. It finally became hegemonic in government thinking at this time that all urban Africans were sojourners, whose cultural links with their 'tribe' needed to be maintained. None the less, the economy's continued need for African labour ensured a steady migration to 'White' South Africa from the reserves, and the government was never able to remove fully the legal right of some Africans to permanent urban residence, with the result that the separate development policy promoted political rather than economic separation.

The second phase of apartheid affected policing in three ways. The task of policing race relations was extended by the police now having to intervene and enforce the removal of many Africans to the homelands, and Coloureds and Indians from 'White' areas. Because the influx control laws were tightened in the urban townships as part of the push towards Bantustanization, the police enforced the pass laws with renewed vigour, resulting in a further deterioration in their relation with urban Africans. Above all, policing was decentralized to accommodate the gradual emergence of homeland police forces.

BANTUSTANIZATION AND THE POLICE

Population relocation was a key feature of Bantustanization. Some was effected by simple means of boundary changes, as cartographers redrew the borders of homelands in order to include communities, sometimes even entire townships, on the edge of homelands. The police intervened here only when this resulted in protest among residents who had lost their residence rights in 'White' South Africa. Some of these protests, however, were significant and required massive police action. Other forms of removal required the physical uprooting and forcible relocation to the homelands of communities from both farming and urban areas, including some illegal squatter camps. This eviction was done by officials from the DBAD, in conjunction with their own police (formerly the police employed by the NAD), and the SAP. Forced removals also became incidents of violent conflict between the police and residents, such as occurred in Cato Manor near Durban in 1960, when residents were being threatened with a move to nearby KwaMashu township in KwaZulu. The crowd attacked the small police station on 23 January killing nine policemen, most of whom were also Zulu. Ten people were later hanged for their murder and twenty-one sentenced to terms of imprisonment ranging up to fifteen years. Cato Manor was first settled in 1928, but within four years of the attack it had returned to a state of green pasture, as DBAD's journal *Bantu* proudly averred in its November 1964 issue (1964*a*).

Another form of removal was the relocation of 'non-productive' Africans from the urban areas by means of influx control. By 1967 Posel records that those targeted in this way were the aged, unfit, widows, and women with dependent children, as well as many middle-class groups. A government document referred to the latter as 'professional Bantu, such as doctors, attorneys, agents, traders, industrialists, etc. Such persons are not regarded as essential for the European labour market' (cited in Posel 1991: 234). The SAP policed this form of resettlement by means of enforcing the pass laws. The pass laws themselves were tightened up in the second phase of apartheid in order to boost the productive capacity of the home-lands, to shed the urban areas of all unnecessary labour, and thus responsibility for the care and welfare of the unfit, infirm, and aged, and further restrict the migration of Africans to the cities, especially dependants of those already working there.

Crime statistics bear this out. According to figures provided in the Commissioner's Annual Reports, there was an overall increase in cases sent to trial of 75 per cent between 1952 and 1968–9, but this was greater for influx control offences, where there was an increase of 328.6 per cent for failure to register for or produce passes, and 685.5 per cent in offences under the Native Urban Areas Act. These offences saw by far the largest increase. In gross terms, there were 138,990 offences for failure to register or produce passes in 1960, 318,825 in 1968–9, and 203,492 in 1973. It was the second most committed offence in all three years, falling only behind traffic offences. Indeed, four of the top five offences in each year dealt exclusively, in one way or another, with the control of the Black population, especially Africans.

It became a standing order for the SAP to arrest and hence prosecute people without a pass, and although later statutory amend-ments made provision for a period of grace to produce the document, the standing order did not make allowance for this. As Black Sash stated in December 1959, 'numbers of women are daily taken off to prison for failure to produce documents on demand even when, as often happens, they have them in their houses a couple of hundred yards away' (Black Sash 1959*b*: 16). Millions of Africans thus landed up in court for pass offences; special courts were established just to deal with the number of cases, and each offence took only a few minutes to try. On 4 March 1966 the *Rand Daily Mail* estimated that each person before these courts was granted a hearing lasting twenty seconds. Katz estimated it to be one and a half minutes (1967: 15). In the Cape Black Sash set up a Bail Fund to help rescue victims from custody. The government even became concerned at the loss to industry of African labour as a result of the upsurge in pass offences, but rather than relax influx control it extended the Bantu Prisoners' Friend scheme. A court officer known as the Prisoners' Friend would discuss with the offender ways in which the fine could be paid in instalments rather than having to go to prison for non-payment. *Bantu* estimated in November 1964 that by that time nearly 84,000 people in Johannesburg had been kept out of gaol as a result of the scheme, and while its origins went long back, the scheme was broadened beyond Johannesburg once influx control was tightened (1964*b*).

While this had deleterious consequences for police relations with Black South Africans, the official view was that relations were good. In a lead article in an issue of *Bantu*, entitled 'Sound Relations Between Police and Bantu', DBAD officials described relations in 1964 as excellent (1964*c*). The Department of Bantu Education's mouthpiece, the *Bantu Education Journal*, ran recruitment features in its 1963 issue under the general heading 'My Future Career' and 'Occupations in the Disciplinary Services'. In one such piece the police service was described as a 'vocation of which one can be justly proud' (1963: 238), and referred to policemen as 'enjoying honour and status in the community' (p. 240). Other sections of the state could not quite accept this as a fair description of some policemen. The report of a commission of inquiry into disturbances in Paarl, in November 1962, under Justice Synman, blamed the riots on the brutality of the municipal police (South Africa 1963: 16).

The new Commissioner's own assessment was in accord with the view that the SAP's reputation among Blacks was good (for example Annual Report of the Commissioner of the SAP 1961: 5); this is shared also by the SAP's official historian when reviewing events during this period (Dippenaar 1988: 348, 353), and by White police-men in their reminiscences (for example see van Onselen 1960: 7). Surprisingly, Black policemen held the same opinion. In the SAP's magazine, which by this time had changed its name, first to *Justitia* and then *SARP* (and eventually to *Servamus*), a regular column was included called 'Non-White News'. This took on the banal features of the journal as a whole, focusing on sporting achievements, events, and news of promotion and of the children of members. It was mostly written in Afrikaans, but in the February issue of 1966 *Bantu* Senior Sergeant Mkwanazi penned the following to mark his retirement:

I joined the SAP on 1 March 1932 and I am still proud to be a member of the force. I am proud to have served the state with dignity and respect, as well as the general public. Today I enjoy a great deal of confidence and integrity in the community. A policeman is cursed and hated by some members of the public, but the majority, especially, the educated class, show a great deal of consideration and often respect ... God bless you all to carry out the good work of the SAP to maintain law and order. (pp. 52–3)

Even allowing for the sentimentality of the occasion, the remarks are indicative of how well the SAP was able to socialize some Black policemen into the ethos of the organization and to blind them to the real nature of police–public relations under apartheid.

This is not to deny that the SAP often related to Black South Africans in a benign role. Citations for medals awarded to policemen often record acts of tremendous bravery towards Blacks in rescuing them from floods and other natural disasters. In 1972, for example, an Afrikaner policeman, Sergeant Fouche, dived into a swollen river from a helicopter and helped thirty-one Coloured people to safety, winning for himself the SAP Star of Merit (Annual Report of the Commissioner of the SAP 1972: 3). Overall, 104 lives were saved by policemen during the flood. This sort of bravery occurred time and again. A letter from the editor of Durban's *Daily News* to *SARP* on 17 October 1972 records the paper's tribute to two Durban policemen from Smith Street Station who found three lost, hungry, and tired African youths who had been robbed, and gave them money for food, clothing, and rail tickets home. The *Daily News* wrote:

The impression these young, raw Bantu have obtained from their experience is that the police are their friends, to whom they can turn for help in times of trouble. A small gesture like this has probably done more for sound race relations than a thousand words.

SARP regularly published tributes like this. The complimentary views of a London QC, Mr Stout-Kerr, about the SAP were published in the April 1973 issue of *SARP*, where he described them as 'equal to the best' (p. 19).

Of course, the tributes rarely came from Blacks themselves, and whatever favourable opinion was created by the benign role of the SAP was immediately undercut by the negative image caused by its repressive, paramilitary role. But the SAP enthusiastically appropriated them to counteract the effect of more widely uttered criticisms. There was much massaging of the SAP's public image at this time. In the September issue in 1962 *Bantu*, for example, described Black policemen as 'keepers of the peace', stressing their public-service role in the townships (1962: 527). The choice of title for the SAP's magazine was also made with import to this issue. *Justitia* was initially chosen in order to emphasize 'we serve justice—our primary and ultimate aim' (quoted in Dippenaar 1988: 298), although ironically it was changed to the more anodine *SARP* shortly afterwards. The SAP ran recruitment campaigns under the title of 'The Helping Hand', showing pictures of policemen helping injured children and the elderly: the white faces in the advertisements revealed this as a campaign to improve the SAP's image among Whites as much as Blacks. It made much of its participation, for the first time, in the International Police Exhibition in Germany in 1966 (Annual Report of the Commissioner of the SAP 1966/7: 10). In 1968 it formed a Police Choir and Theatre Group to perform in White schools and other public venues in order 'to assist in improving the image of the force' (Annual Report of the Commissioner of the SAP 1967/8: 3), and various other public-relations exercises were employed. Lectures were given frequently in Afrikaans-language schools. In 1969 the SAP employed its first Choirmaster, and the new Commissioner appointed that year, General Gous, explained that the choir was in part an attempt to integrate 'young members in the force from rural areas, who are finding it difficult to adjust themselves to the bustle and the intricate social structure of city life', and to be a 'strong propaganda medium for the force' (Annual Report of the Commissioner of the SAP 1968/9: 2).

But while the SAP presented itself as a civil police force to the public, and acted in this fashion to Whites all of the time, and occasionally to Blacks when discharging a benign role, it mostly acted towards Blacks in a colonial policing capacity. The use of force in dealing with Blacks was but one example of this. The role of violence in suppressing political unrest will be discussed shortly, but gratuitous violence was part of the ordinary dealings between the police and Blacks. The ill-treatment of Black prisoners, for example, led to 566 officers being charged with assault in 1963, 311 convictions, but only eleven dismissals from the force (Duncan 1964: 25). The station commander and four White constables at Bultfontein were found guilty of murdering an African while investigating the theft of money. The victim was given electric shocks, hit with a sjambok, partly choked, and eventually suffocated with a plastic bag tied to his head. One of the convicted excused himself by saying that the methods were in common use in the SAP (SAIRR Annual Survey of Race Relations 1964: 100). The Commissioner sent a directive to all police stations drawing attention to standing orders which prohibited ill-treatment of prisoners. He also investigated the use of electric-shock treatment, and admitted that such apparatus was found at some stations, although the new Minister of Justice, B. J. Vorster, said 'it was in private hands' (p. 101). The catalogue of incidents of gratuitous violence is lengthy; notable ones are often horrific. In 1966, for example, sixty-five policemen entered the Flamingo Club in Johannesburg, where over two hundred Black guests were dancing, and loosed a pack of dogs into the throng. Ten people were crushed and killed in the stampede to escape (SAIRR Annual Survey of Race Relations 1966: 93). Magistrates never failed to condemn outrages like this, yet the number of dismissals from the force is low during this period, and declined

TABLE 5.1 *Dismissals from the SAP, 1960–1975*

Year	White	% White manpower	Black	% Black manpower	% serious offences* White	% serious offences* Black	% wastage due to dismissals White	% wastage due to dismissals Black
1960	108	0.7	288	2.4	100	95.8	10.5	27.4
1961	64	0.4	273	2.2	95.3	96.7	6	23.1
1962	98	0.6	412	3.2	97.9	97.8	9.8	35.7
1967	79	0.4	216	1.4	15.1	99.5	5.8	25.2
1968	106	0.6	320	2.1	32.1	95.9	2	31.5
1969	70	0.4	294	1.8	95.7	99.6	3.4	30.4
1970	44	0.2	144	0.9	95.4	100	2.3	15.4
1972	45	0.2	232	1.5	91.1	70.6	2.1	28.7
1973	129	0.7	273	1.7	48	50.9	3.1	32
1974	33	0.1	232	1.4	100	52.1	1.8	22.3
1975†	18	0.1	191	1.2	100	59.1	0.8	14.8

* Defined as conviction by the courts, misconduct, and drunkenness.

† Figures for dismissal were no longer supplied by the Commissioner after 1975.

Source: Annual Reports of the Commissioner of the SAP.

from the peak of 1960, at the time of the Sharpeville massacre, as illustrated in Table 5.1.

In addition to extending the SAP's role in policing race relations, by means of forced removals and enforcement of stricter influx control, Bantustanization resulted in the decentralization of policing. In a sense separate development led to a reinvention of the old SAP–SAMR split, with the latter's role being taken over by the homeland police. It is ironic that decentralization should be reintroduced after the effort of previous commissioners to establish the SAP as the sole national and centralized force. None the less, it was consistent with the 'own areas' policing strategy of apartheid, and gave recognition to the long-standing reality of policing in South Africa: that Black and White South Africans were to be policed differently. On this occasion the decentralization of policing was made part of the state's decentralization of administration to the homelands. This meant, however, that the devolution of policing responsibilities to the homelands followed the pace of the broader separate development policy, which the state introduced only gingerly; and the SAP kept a considerable degree of control over the homeland forces, as did the central government over the homeland authorities. Between 1960 and 1975, only the Transkei homeland developed its separate police force, although many more homelands did so after 1976, when 'independence' was granted on a wider scale. Initially effort went into the 'own areas' strategy rather than a fuller decentralization.

In 1961, in the wake of the Sharpeville massacre, a large ceremony took place in Orlando Stadium, Soweto, to honour an African sergeant with the Queen's Police Medal, the highest attainable by policemen. The presentation was made by the Minister of Justice in the presence of over one hundred VIPs from DBAD, including the Minister, and the SAP. African schoolchildren from nearby Orlando school filled the seats at the football stadium, and 124 African policemen formed an honour guard. It was a marvellous display to counteract the bad publicity caused by police conduct in Sharpeville, but the Minister of Justice took the opportunity to outline how the new homeland policy would affect policing (the speech was reported in *Bantu* 1961: 177–8).

In the decade since the first all-African police station was created in Zwelitsha in 1951, a further 28 stations had been given over to Black control. In 1968 the number was 37. In his Annual Report of that year, the Commissioner referred to the 'own areas' strategy as 'Bantuization', and said that 'good progress has been made in the

Bantuization of police stations, and a number of non-Whites are being trained as station commanders and public prosecutors' (p. 13). Progress was slow, however, for by 1973 only 45 stations were under the control of Blacks: 37 by Africans, 7 by Coloureds, and one by Asians. The Asian station commander was in Durban's Chatsworth township, which in 1967 had 90 Indian policemen for a population of 150,000 (Poodhun 1983: 186). Part of the reason for the sloth in extending 'Bantuization' was the conventional belief in the innate inferiority of Blacks, but also a reluctance to alter the promotion system to the detriment of lower-ranking Whites. On the one hand, the SAP slowly promoted most White members. In 1966–7, 45 per cent of White personnel were of the rank of constable, compared with 84.9 per cent of Blacks. In 1970 42.7 per cent of Whites were constables. On the other hand, the police only slowly and reluctantly created, and then later filled, senior posts for Blacks. Rather than promote Blacks above the rank of sergeant, the management created the rank of chief sergeant in 1961. The rank of lieutenant was created in 1970, although not occupied by anyone until 1972, when there were twenty, although 136 Black officers were in training as station commanders in 1972 (Annual Report of the Commissioner of the SAP 1972: 3). The rank of captain was created in 1974, although nobody filled the vacancies for a year, when ten were appointed. But at this time there were still only 45 stations under the control of Black officers.

Sloth was also a characteristic of the introduction of separate homeland forces, the natural next stage of the 'own areas' strategy. Transkei had been granted a homeland government well before other Bantustans, and development towards self-government was marked by it being the first to be granted 'independence' in 1976. It was the only homeland to develop its own police force in the period up to 1975. From 1964, some staff from the SAP's Transkei Division were transferred to the Transkei government (but by no means all), paid for out of the latter's own expenditure, save for the four senior staff seconded from the SAP who managed the force, who were paid for by the SAP in order to keep salary up to the national level. In addition the Transkei government appointed its own 'home guard', funded out of its grant from central government. Details of manpower and expenditure for both types of force are contained in Table 5.2.

The Transkei Police as such was not formed until 1972, when the home guard was abolished and all staff absorbed into a single force,

TABLE 5.2 *Police in the Transkei, 1964/5–1971/2*

Year	Staff	Expenditure R	Home guard	Home guard expenditure R
1964/5	112	69,400	323	37,600
1965/6	114	81,200	326	38,000
1966/7	114	85,100	241	29,000
1967/8	150	92,200	150	18,000
1968/9	111	98,000	110	14,000
1969/70	111	97,900	75	9,000
1970/1	111	115,700	35	4,200
1971/2	111	116,200	13	1,500

Source: Annual Estimates of the Expenditure of the Transkei Revenue Fund.

save for three posts which were still seconded from the SAP. The four senior officers continued to be paid by the SAP. Details of expenditure and manpower are presented in Table 5.3, which illustrates that the new force was slightly larger than the two earlier ones combined, as a result of the transferral of more men from the SAP's Transkei Division, and that there was a progressive increase in expenditure and manpower up to Transkeian 'independence' in 1976. From this point the Transkei government appointed its own chief of police and became responsible for all staff and expenditure. Many more staff from the SAP's Transkei Division were also transferred to the new force at this juncture. The emergence of this and other homeland forces after 1976 will be considered in the next chapter, although the government was clearly thinking at this time in terms of broadening the experiment with homeland police, for the Commissioner announced in his 1974 Annual Report that 398 'homeland tribal police' were undergoing training.

TABLE 5.3 *The Transkei Police, 1972/3–1975/6*

Year	Expenditure R	% increase	Manpower	% increase
1972/3	197,900	—	169	—
1973/4	222,700	12.5	170	0.5
1974/5	285,100	28.0	173	1.7
1975/6	595,250	108.7	259	49.7

Source: Annual Estimates of the Expenditure of the Transkei Revenue Fund.

One of the characteristics of apartheid's second phase was that the urban townships were considered ethnic outposts of the 'national unit', and the development of homeland police thus had consequences for townships outside the homelands. By Government Notice R1035 in 1966, the state established Community Guards for African townships outside the homelands. This involved further decentralization, with responsibility for policing being devolved to yet another force, the administration of which lay outside the SAP. Many townships already had municipal police connected with DBAD, which dealt with enforcing municipal regulations and the preservation of law and order on 'minor matters'. The new force was to help to maintain law and order in the locality, and was appointed by the Urban Bantu Councils, which helped the Bantu Administration Boards to run townships, although appointments had to be approved by the Bantu Affairs Commissioner and the local commanding officer from the SAP. Control therefore remained with the SAP in the final instance, although each Urban Bantu Council administered its own guards. By September 1967, 510 people had volunteered.

This was supposedly a form of local policing, with communities policing themselves, although the community guards were never allowed to work alone. Guards wore armlets, received training from the SAP, and offered their services entirely voluntarily. They were not allowed to carry firearms, although they were allowed to carry sticks, not exceeding four feet long, when on duty. (Black police in the SAP were only allowed to carry firearms from 1972 onwards.) In practice, most guards were members of the conservative *maghotla*, imposing tribal notions of justice in a form of vigilantism. Much of this was rough justice, with the *maghotla* inflicting floggings as punishment. Eleven members of the *maghotla* in Soweto were prosecuted in 1974 for administering beatings.

The formation of community guards was not only an urban expression of the 'Bantuization' lying behind the formation of homeland police, it reflected the SAP's awareness that they were losing the fight against crime in the townships, as emphasized further below. Community involvement in local policing was seen as a form of crime prevention and detection, although the new force was set up directly to challenge the volunteer groups that had been operating in a policing capacity in the townships for some time. These vigilante groups were abolished in June 1968, giving the state a monopoly in the control of law and order and official endorsement to the *maghotla*, which were exempt from the prohibition. The state-sponsored local forces and the SAP could do little about crime, and some local communities demanded the right to form protection groups again. In 1971, for example, the Masingafi Party was formed in Soweto, the name meaning 'let us not be killed'. A memorandum was sent to the Soweto police, but their only response was to reorganize policing on the Rand and to form the Soweto Division in 1973.

To add elements of further decentralization in the policing of urban townships, some authorities employed a separate traffic police. In 1962 Johannesburg had forty-one African traffic inspectors, and Pretoria twenty-eight. Their function was to control traffic near to African schools, deliver road-safety lectures in African schools, take traffic counts, and make measurements after accidents, but they were not allowed to issue parking tickets (which was the domain of the White traffic police). Pay was below the level pertaining in the SAP for African policemen; in 1962 a traffic inspector could earn R900 per annum at the top scale, compared with R1,080 for an African chief sergeant.

In this way there was a diffusion of policing roles throughout the African community in an attempt to involve them in policing themselves, whether in the homelands or ethnic outposts in the urban areas. This fitted the ethos of the second phase of apartheid, which emphasized 'self-development'. In effect, the 'own areas' strategy asked Africans to police their own subordination. However, the main role for this was recruitment to the SAP rather than to other compatible forces; it was not until the mid-1980s that the separate township forces expanded rapidly. Table 5.4 provides figures for Black recruitment to the SAP for selected years between 1960 and 1976 (the Commissioner stopped providing this breakdown after 1976). Expansion was greatest for the Asian community, although Africans dominate in gross terms. The Table also illustrates the low proportion from each community that occupied non-commissioned ranks or above, with Africans being the worst of all three, although the proportion of men in senior ranks doubled in the period for both Africans and Asians.

Black recruitment to the SAP was therefore healthy, although the number of African policemen fell in the early 1960s because of a reaction to the Sharpeville massacre and the transferral of men to the Transkei. The quality of the recruits matched the quantity. In 1960 the Commissioner noted in his Annual Report that 'the type of

TABLE 5.4 *Trends in Black membership, 1960–1976*

Year	Asian	% NCOs	Coloured	% NCOs	African	% NCOs
1960	368	11.6	1,028	12.8	12,390	8.3
1961	373	10.9	1,088	12.6	12,316	8.9
1962	420	13.5	1,144	12.0	12,319	9.6
1963	419	13.8	1,095	12.5	12,159	10.4
1967	583	18.8	1,275	19.5	12,952	14.4
1968	639	20.1	1,393	19.8	13,134	15.8
1969	639	20.3	1,438	18.7	13,460	14.8
1970	692	20.8	1,438	18.3	13,401	15.7
1972	730	23.8	1,375	21.5	13,113	16.9
1973	733	22.7	1,361	20.9	13,112	16.3
1974	766	24.9	1,454	20.5	13,493	16.3
1975	812	26.9	1,608	19.8	13,483	16.7
1976	833	26.2	1,615	19.8	13,590	17.0

Source: Annual Reports of the Commissioner of the SAP.

non-European recruit . . . is of a good standard, educationally and physically, and no difficulty whatsoever is experienced in filling vacancies' (p. 2). In the 1968–9 Annual Report, the Commissioner indicated that there was a long waiting-list among Asian and African applicants to join the SAP (p. 4). Educational entry requirements for Black policemen were raised in 1963 to Standard 5. Other requirements included being born in South Africa, fluency in speaking and writing one of the official languages, being of 'good character and behaviour', and various physical capabilities. (By 1970, the SAP had availed itself of the services of the Human Sciences Research Council to devise psychological tests for Black applicants to reassure themselves about character and personality.) Training involved physical exercise, drill, 'due attention to religious matters' (involving Christian devotion and attendance at Sunday service), law, criminal procedure and investigation, and first aid.

Recruitment advertisements emphasized the career prospects offered by the police (for example see *Bantu* 1962: 527–9; *Bantu Education Journal* 1963: 230–43), with the opportunity to be put exclusively in charge of a station. Promotion to the rank of senior sergeant, as a result of the development of the 'own areas' strategy, was dangled before readers (*Bantu Education Journal* 1963: 238). The opportunities for genuine social mobility were stressed, with note made of the pension scheme, fringe benefits, and regular salary advancement. The nature of the work came in for special mention. Public service duties were emphasized, as well as the prospect of excitement and adventure; dealing with fierce animals was mentioned as one reason why the work was not monotonous, although no reference was made to the police role in suppressing political unrest as another.

The little we can glimpse of the attitudes of Black police seems to confirm that membership of the police was seen as a mechanism for social mobility. Letters to the SAP's magazine from serving Black policemen, for example, often made direct reference to the value correspondents placed on education as a means of social advancement and the career prospects opened up by membership of the SAP. 'Education is in many ways', wrote Sergeant Tsolo, from the Transkei, 'of paramount importance, for it does not only render or cause one to get well paying jobs, it opens up new spheres of life which thus far have been closed to you' (*SARP* 1967: 51). They stressed this for their children as well, which is why many Black policemen had kinship networks where membership of the police was common. Being aware of the life chances provided for them as a result of the police often made Black policemen very obsequious. Retirement speeches from Black policemen printed in *SARP* were notorious for their deference and respectfulness. That by Sergeant Goya, from Kimberley District, is typical. The Commissioner of the SAP was thanked for his 'intelligent administration because the high standard of the SAP is squarely based on his inspiration'. He went further: 'to His Excellency the Minister of Police, and also the Commissioner of the Police, we take our hats off and say "thank you". "Thank you", "thank you sir"' (*SARP* 1967: 60). When combined with rigid training and discipline, this obsequiousness explains the willingness of Black policemen to commit atrocities against their fellow countrymen and women. (Although hero-worship of the Minister responsible for the police also seems to be a characteristic of Afrikaner policemen; on the loyalty to B. J. Vorster, for example, see Dippenaar 1988: 315, 348, 352.)

Neither the eulogies of serving Black policemen nor the recruitment literature spoke of the apartheid operating inside the SAP; it was concealed by the latter and probably taken for granted by the former. There were marked differences in salary between Black and White members, in fringe benefits and promotion prospects. In 1970, for example, 83.8 per cent of all Black police in the SAP were at the lowest rank of constable compared with 42.7 per cent of Whites. Training was segregated, and petty apartheid operated in subtle ways. Standing orders, for example, stated that at 'White stations' the national flag was to be hoisted and lowered by a White member. In the mid-1960s, however, the state made some concessions to alleviate petty apartheid distinctions in the police. A wreath would now be supplied at state expense for the funeral of Black policemen who had lost their lives in the course of duty; assistance and support could be provided for Black policemen injured on duty; and the housing needs of Black policemen were now to receive 'the sympathetic attention of divisional commissioners'.

Consequently, correspondents to *SARP*'s 'Non-White News' in May 1967 reproduced the official discourse that racial distinctions were not drawn in the SAP. A policeman, whose nickname was 'No Matches', wrote 'we are all one in the force—there is no white and non-white in the force' (p. 56), although the very terms used to deny this reflect the appropriation of society's racial distinctions into police discourse. However, the above is interesting for also illustrating the existence of an occupational culture amongst Black policemen, with nicknames, banter, and friendly rivalry existing amongst them. This was itself an attraction of the job. The contribution of Sergeant Manotsha, from KwaThema township, in the May issue of *SARP* best reveals this:

'Forward' is the watchword of KwaThema. We do not believe in 'marking time'. The sports club has decided to buy a set of weights and the boys are already puffing up like crocodiles or hippopotami. Bantu Sergeant Mtsweni has gone to Swaziland—the land of the mountains. It is said that he nearly got lost on the mountain top but was able to trace his way back. Bah. (*SARP* 1967: 56)

Other membership trends in the SAP are worth highlighting at this point. Table 5.5 shows the progressive expansion in police manpower between 1960 and 1975, although the rate of increase did not keep up with the size of the general population so that the ratio of police per thousand head of population declined cressively throughout the period, making it lower than in most liberal democracies. The ratio is misleading, however, because of the number of men and women in policing roles in compatible forces, such as the reserves force (established in 1961), the traffic police, SARHP, and various Black police forces. In the SARHP, for example, there were 4,038 policemen in the 1962/3 financial year, and 4,724 in 1975/6, 42 per cent of whom were Black. By 1975/6, expenditure by the SARHP was R17.34

TABLE 5.5 *Trends in SAP Manpower, 1960–1975*

Year	Actual membership		% increase	% Black	% under-staffed*	Ratio per 1,000 population†
	White	Black				
1960	11,938	13,786	—	53.5	8.1	1.70
1961	12,249	13,777	1.1	52.9	7.5	1.67
1962	12,778	13,853	2.3	47.9	5.9	1.59
1963	13,770	13,673	3.0	50.1	5.4	1.66
1964	14,528	13,812	3.2	48.7	7.8	1.56
1965	14,678	14,080	1.4	48.9	7.6	1.60
1966	15,437	14,056	2.4	47.6	8.6	1.61
1967	16,316	14,810	5.5	47.5	6.9	1.66
1968	16,587	15,166	2.0	47.7	5.5	1.65
1969	16,376	15,532	0.4	48.6	7.3	1.61
1970	16,346	15,531	−0.09	48.7	8.3	1.46
1971	16,776	15,333	0.7	47.7	7.0	1.44
1972	17,063	15,218	0.5	47.1	6.4	1.40
1973	16,366	15,222	−2.1	48.1	10.9	1.29
1974	16,862	15,713	3.1	48.2	7.4	1.30
1975	17,179	15,903	1.5	48.0	6.8	1.27

* Difference between actual and authorized membership.
† Based on authorized membership.

Source: Annual Reports of the Commissioner of the SAP.

million, an increase of 236.9 per cent since 1962/3 (see SARHS, Annual Estimates of the Expenditure to be Defrayed from the Revenue Fund). The ratio is misleading in another sense because the state tried continually to increase the size of the regular police, permitting generous increases in the authorized membership of the SAP which it never met in actual manpower. Thus, the SAP was perpetually understaffed, in the sense that actual membership failed to keep up with the desired establishment; in 1973 the SAP was as much as 10.9 per cent understaffed. But it is clear from Table 5.5 that the state tried hardest to recruit Whites. The Black proportion of the SAP declined from its peak in 1960, and in the period as a whole White membership increased by 43.9 per cent, and Black by only 15.3 per cent. And only a very small part of this shift is explained by the transfer of Black personnel from the SAP to the Transkei. In order to boost recruitment amongst Whites, the SAP adjusted its regulations in 1964 to permit immigrants with policing experience in African colonies to join the SAP (forty did so in 1964), and alterations were made in 1966 to permit former policemen to rejoin; 313 did so in 1966–7 (Annual Report of the Commissioner of the SAP 1966/7: 2).

The increase in White staff was almost entirely from among the Afrikaans-speaking community. Van der Spuy reports that between 1968 and 1977 English recruits averaged only 12 per cent of the yearly intake of White members (1988: 11). Senior officers tried to increase this. In 1968, for example, special recruitment drives were undertaken in Natal's English-language schools, resulting in 16.1 per cent of the intake that year being English-speakers (Annual Report of the Commissioner of the SAP 1967/8: 5). But the effect of past Afrikanerization of the ranks ensured that the SAP was unattractive to many English-speakers. The occupational culture of the SAP at this time was thoroughly Afrikaner, as a result of the work of AKPOL and the Chaplaincy Unit, which by 1973 had grown in size to thirteen full-time chaplains who wore uniform and underwent proper police training; it was not until 1984 that the SAP employed its first full-time chaplain from outside the Dutch Reform Church. Moreover, English-speakers faced better opportunities elsewhere in the economy because of their high levels of education. In 1969 the English intake dropped back again to 9.8 per cent. In 1975 the proportion was 7.9 per cent (Annual Report of the Commissioner of the SAP 1975: 5).

With expansion in the economy, the Afrikaner recruits were also increasingly poorer, lower educated, and rural-based. The Commissioner once referred to their difficulties in integrating into city life (Annual Report of the Commissioner of the SAP 1968/9: 2), and articles and features in *SARP* indicate that alcoholism was a problem. J. C. Bain, writing in the June 1967 issue, admitted that 'the cruel and terrible disease known as alcoholism exists in our midst' (p. 13). A treatment centre in Pretoria was established, attendance at which was compulsory for people for whom it was considered necessary by senior officers. It was because the police tended to recruit from this pool of Afrikaners that the force was slow in raising the educational standards of entry. In 1960 the minimum was raised to Standard 8, still below the normal school-leaving qualification of Matriculation. To compensate for this, the SAP started to provide recruits with its own educational qualifications. In 1961 a Diploma in Police Science was begun at the University of South Africa, and the National Senior Certificate was introduced to provide policemen with an alternative academic qualification to Matriculation. By 1969 only 28.1 per cent of recruits had Matriculation, which made it rather irrelevant, at least to most members, that the Diploma in Police Science was upgraded to a BA degree in 1972. Bursaries were provided by the government; many were not taken up. From 1970 various other diplomas were also made available to policemen, although the Commissioner's Annual Report noted that only 27 per cent of recruits had the SAP's National Senior Certificate that year (1969/70: 3). By 1975 just over half of the new recruits had Matriculation, and there were five graduate entrants, so at the time of the Soweto uprising in 1976, many policemen were still relatively uneducated.

Two innovations in membership were introduced in this period. The first was the employment of women. For the first time, in 1960 women were engaged for full-time employment in clerical positions in order to relieve physically fit men for active duty. Up to this point they had been seconded from other parts of the civil service. It was not until 1 January 1972 that two women were recruited for police duties, both of whom were Afrikaners, with the intention of supervising, after training, further enrolment by women. Policewomen performed the same duties as men and underwent the same training, including firearms, although there was less drill. By the end of the year 102 had joined, nine of whom were English-speakers; all were Matriculants, with the effect that educational entry requirements were tougher in practice for women than men. In 1973, for example, all 170 female recruits were Matriculants compared with 24 per cent of men; all were White. By 1975 there were 565 policewomen, with another 181 recruits accepted for training. Brigadier Duveen Botha was head of the female section. A former deputy mistress at an Afrikaans-speaking girls' school in Pretoria, she supervised the growth of the Women Police. By 1985 there were 2,750 policewomen. The section was not open to Black women until 1981. Botha retired in 1985, to be replaced as head by a fellow recruit from the 1972 intake.

The other innovation was the establishment of reserve forces. In 1961, after the warning of Sharpeville, the government announced the formation of the Police Reserve, a voluntary body for White citizens composed of four types of volunteer, giving various amounts of time to police work. In 1961 1,261 members were in training. Members provided their services entirely voluntarily, doing it, as the Commissioner said in 1975, only 'for honour and glory' (Annual Report of the Commissioner of the SAP 1975: 4). The force drew on the civic guard tradition that had existed in South Africa since the

First World War; in fact, many White citizen protection groups, set up out of fear of Black crime, were incorporated into the Reserve Police in 1963, and from that year the size of the Reserve Police grew enormously (SAIRR Annual Survey of Race Relations 1961: 35). By 1963 there were 11,057 members, nearly totalling the White man-power in the regular SAP for that year. The Commissioner described their behaviour as exemplary, with no complaints made about their conduct (Annual Report of the Commissioner of the SAP 1963: 4). Training was provided, and by 1963 the volunteers were being instructed in the use of firearms; some even served on the border. The first Reserve member to be killed died while on border duty in 1968. No uniform was provided, although badges of rank were worn; the first lieutenants in the Reserve Police were appointed in 1970.

Initially, the force was exclusively White, although in 1963 the Commissioner announced that plans were being made to recruit among Indians and Coloureds in the future. This did not occur until 1967, when the Reserve Police was also opened to Africans in Soweto 'as an experiment' (Annual Report of the Commissioner of the SAP 1967/8: 2). By the following year, there were 17,530 Whites in the Reserve Police, larger than the White complement in the regular police, although some were in very inactive voluntary service, as well as 600 Africans, 307 Indians, and 555 Coloureds. To give a measure of how inactive some members were, the Commissioner estimated in 1972 that of the 15,806 Whites then in the Reserve Police, 7,120 were active, or 45 per cent. The equivalent figure for Black members was 72.2 per cent (Annual Report of the Commissioner of the SAP 1972: 3). The 'experiment' with African Reservists proved successful and by 1969 there were 1,530 members, operating in 17 police divisions.

African membership drew on the vigilante tradition in the town-ships, such as the 'protection societies' and 'escort committees' which provided some defence against the *tsotsi* gangs (SAIRR Annual Survey of Race Relations 1963: 36), so that motivations had more to do with fear of crime in the townships than service to the state. However, there was also considerable overlap between the African Reserve Police and the conservative *maghotla*. When introduced in Soweto in 1967, the African Reservists helped the police in dealing with ordinary crime— loitering, drug abuse, possession of dangerous weapons, and stolen property. They patrolled the streets in groups of five; two were killed in Soweto in the first year (SAIRR Annual Survey of Race Relations 1968: 52). In 1969 African Reservists were equipped with two-way radios, batons, and handcuffs, but could do little to stem the growth of ordinary crime in the townships.

Two other reserve forces were also established in this period. In 1973 the South African Wachthuis Radio Reserve was formed. It was a collection of 257 amateur radio operators that acted as a communications link for the police, reporting incidents and later the infiltration of guerrillas. Also that year the Police Reserve was established. This was composed of former policemen who were called upon to perform duty for periods of thirty days per year for five years after leaving the SAP, often in police stations where there was a particular shortage. They could also be called upon in times of emergency. In 1974 there were 6,059 members (Annual Report of the Commissioner of the SAP 1974: 5).

Through forces such as these, the SAP was supplemented by thousands of other people in compatible roles, such that the ratio of police per thousand head of population at this time gives a poor representation of the real size of the state's policing capacity. Taking 1974 as an example, there were 32,575 people in the SAP, and another 30,536 in other formally constituted police forces or reserve groups, excluding the mines police and those employed by DBAD. (In addition, from 1975 a small number of SADF staff were deployed by the SAP in policing roles.) Thus, the ratio that year, of 1.30 policemen and women per thousand head of population, needs to be nearly doubled to get a true picture of the state's policing capacity. This puts South Africa on a par with other countries. Comparative figures for 1974 are: Great Britain 2.35, Northern Ireland 2.95, the Irish Republic 2.56, and Israel 3.2 (taken from Brewer *et al.* 1988: 223). The reverse, however, is that South Africa's ratio did not much exceed that of liberal democratic countries, and was lower than similarly divided societies such as Israel and Northern Ireland. This is perhaps a measure of the amount of social control embedded in the very institutions and processes of apartheid.

However, it is the case that South Africa spent roughly twice as much on its police force as Israel when the police budget is measured as a proportion of total government expenditure (for comparative statistics see Brewer *et al.* 1988: 224). The only figures available for Northern Ireland cover the period of 'the troubles' and thus give a poor representation of police expenditure under normal circumstances, even for a divided society. Figures for police expenditure in South Africa are contained in Table 5.6, which shows that the police

TABLE 5.6 *SAP expenditure, 1960–1975*

Year	Total Rm.	% increase	'Secret services' Rm.	% detective work	% equipment*	SAP to defence exp.†	% of government expenditure
1960/1	36.8	—	—	—	—	108	4.03
1961/2	40.2	9.1	0.02	0.1	2.1	170	3.91
1962/3	41.8	4.1	0.02	0.1	1.4	350	3.76
1963/4	45.8	9.4	—	—	—	470	3.76
1964/5	49.6	8.1	0.22	0.1	1.8	460	3.24
1965/6	56.3	13.5	—	—	—	400	3.42
1966/7	64.7	14.9	0.31	0.2	3.5	390	3.17
1967/8	72.6	12.1	0.41	0.2	6.4	—	3.22
1968/9	—	—	—	—	—	—	—
1969/70	85.7	17.9	1.2	0.2	2.4	316	3.16
1970/1	94.5	10.2	1.0	1.4	2.6	290	2.74
1971/2	107.4	13.6	1.0	1.3	2.6	260	2.78
1972/3	112.1	4.3	1.0	1.2	3.0	310	2.74
1973/4	120.6	7.5	1.0	1.2	2.1	370	2.87
1974/5	156.6	29.9	1.2	1.1	2.9	440	2.81
1975/6	170.1	8.5	1.2	1.0	2.4	550	2.36

* Defined as 'arms, equipment, and ammunition'.
† SAP expenditure = 100.

Sources: Worked from figures provided in the Annual Reports of the Auditor General and the Annual Reports of the Commissioner of the SAP.

budget grew steadily between 1960 and 1975, with an annual percentage increase usually in double figures or very near to it. For the period as a whole, the police budget rose by a factor of over three and a half. None the less, this was always a falling proportion of total government expenditure; the police budget nearly halved as a proportion of total government expenditure, although it still remained well above the Israeli equivalent, which itself dropped from 2.24 per cent in 1960/1 to 1.03 per cent in 1975/6 (see Brewer *et al.* 1988: 224). Nor did police expenditure keep pace with the even larger increases in defence expenditure. Another noteworthy trend from Table 5.6 is the miniscule proportion of the budget spent on 'detective work' in the 1960s, although this picked up again towards the end of the period. It always fell well below the proportion devoted to equipment, which was defined in the General Auditor's Accounts as 'arms, equipment and ammunition'. Clearly, investigative skills and CID work were less important for the SAP's colonial policing task than fire-power. From 1969/70, it spent nearly as much in gross terms on 'secret services' as 'detective work'.

While this reflects some ambivalence on the part of the state towards police expenditure when set against its other financial commitments, the substantial annual rises in the police budget were real increases as far as the Commissioner was concerned, allowing expenditure to rise on all aspects of police work and equipment, although not necessarily equally. This allowed some perennial problems to be dealt with. In his 1960 Annual Report, for example, the Commissioner complained about the backlog of new accommodation that the police needed for stations and staff quarters. Over a third of stations were still being hired from private owners (p. 2). Within two years, he described the monies voted for police buildings as 'outstanding' (Annual Report of the Commissioner of the SAP 1962: 3). By the end of the period under review here, only one-tenth of the SAP's married quarters were rented from private owners, and less than a quarter of the stations (Annual Report of the Commissioner of the SAP 1974: 4).

These organizational developments need to be set in context. After the Sharpeville massacre in 1960, internal Black politics became quiescent, relying on the external movements. The political protests of the 1950s were the zenith of Black opposition, and while this was effective in pressurizing the state to reformulate its urban policies in the second phase of apartheid (Posel 1991: 236–7), the greatest effect on the police occurred with the shift from internal to external protest in the 1960s. Because protest went underground and militarized, the police became engrossed with the external threat posed by guerrilla warfare. The process of decolonization elsewhere in Africa seemed to confirm the police in the necessity of this shift (on policing and decolonization see Anderson and Killingray 1992). The expansion in SAP manpower, resources, and equipment, and the diffusion of policing roles throughout South African society as various volunteer and reserve forces sprang up, reflected these broader events. But there were other consequences. The legal powers of the police were extended, training was given in riot control and counter-insurgency skills, police were deployed on border patrol, and the SAP's tendency towards militarization was enhanced by co-operation with the SADF and various internal changes to its rank structure and the reorganization of headquarters. Ordinary crime in the townships was left to flourish as resources and manpower focused more than usual on policing aspects of race relations. It is to these events, and their consequences for police work, that we now turn.

POLITICS, THE POLICE, AND COUNTER-INSURGENCY

The Pondoland massacre in June 1960 is always forgotten in the light of Sharpeville three months earlier. Admittedly half the number of people were killed (thirty as against sixty-nine), and it was in an isolated rural area rather than a township, and thus was not connected with the infamous pass laws, but the atrocity was if anything worse, since it was unprovoked. The police landed by aircraft in this barren part of Transkei (aircraft had been in use for a long time and helicopters since 1957), and opened up on the crowd at a peaceful meeting with sten guns, continuing to fire until nobody was left to shoot at. They then raided huts looking for instigators (on the massacre see Kiley 1960; for background on the Pondoland area see Beinart 1982). Had the protest been about a more prominent issue than administration in rural areas, Pondoland would rival Sharpeville as the nadir of police misconduct up to this juncture. As it is, the SAP is remembered at this time for Sharpeville.

On 16 March 1960 Robert Sobukwe, leader of the Pan-African Congress (PAC), wrote to the Commissioner of the SAP informing him of the PAC's intention to hold peaceful demonstrations throughout South Africa on 21 March in protest at the pass laws. He expressed concern about 'trigger-happy, African-hating' police, and assured Rademeyer that demonstrators would disperse if given clear orders and sufficient time to do so (the letter is reprinted in Karis and Carter 1977: 565–6). The PAC's call to protest went largely unheeded, save in a few of their strongholds such as Sharpeville and Langa, and the PAC had difficulty in controlling many of the unemployed and embittered youths who participated in the protest. Sharpeville police station had three White staff and thirty-five Black, and when a crowd of twenty thousand assembled on the morning of 21 March, massive reinforcements were sent in from elsewhere, only to be initially withdrawn to protect nearby White Vanderbijlpark; numbers of regular police were such that men were always spread thinly. Later on all leave was to be rescinded, including permissions for weddings, in order to prevent policemen from being massively outnumbered by large crowds. The police often used aircraft to dive-bomb at crowds and tear-gas in the hope that it would disperse them. Finding themselves outnumbered in Sharpeville, despite using aircraft to dive-bomb the crowd, the police opened fire on a hostile crowd (even critics of the police admit the hostility, see Gerhart 1978: 236–9, although the police were not themselves fired upon as Dippenaar claims, 1988: 278). Although no order was given for the police to open fire they killed 69 protesters and injured 180. On the same day, 28 were shot in Langa, leaving two dead. Official commissions of inquiry later absolved the police of blame, but the killings sparked off the sorts of unrest that Sobukwe's call had failed to ignite. Deaths occurred in Durban, Port Elizabeth, and Bloemfontein.

The police could not cope in terms of manpower or tactics; in his Annual Report for the year, the Commissioner records that the SAP 'constantly had their hands full to combat the situation' (p. 8). The government declared a state of emergency on 30 March, giving the SAP broad powers of arrest and detention. The government also used the SADF in concert with the SAP; the air force supplied planes and pilots to dive-bomb crowds, and the army cordoned off townships while the police rounded up people. Thousands of Africans were arrested and charged with minor infractions, and nearly two thousand political activists were detained. On 8 April the government announced the banning of the ANC and PAC, and any other organization attempting to further their aims, under the hastily enacted Unlawful

Organizations Act. This enabled further political activists to be detained, and imposed more severe penalties for various forms of political action. The following day an unsuccessful assassination attempt was made on Prime Minister Verwoerd's life; the second, in 1966, was successful, bringing the then political head of the police to power as Prime Minister. The assassination attempt added to the general sense of panic in the police, and among many Whites. But by then the powers were in place for the police to quell the unrest, and political protest was not to resurface on this scale again until 1976. The Commissioner's reference in the 1960 Annual Report to the SAP's 'firm action' to restore order underscores the extent of their brutality in quelling this and subsequent unrest, and his anodine remarks about 'firing on rioters' conceals the human tragedies caused. The SAP's methods for dealing with township protests in 1960, however, do not explain the long period of quiescence after Sharpeville. The banning of organized politics was critical, as were the difficulties experienced by the external movements, but the events of March and April 1960 set in train various changes to policing, the consequences of which also help to explain the state's ability to engineer a hiatus in Black politics.

It has already been emphasized how the manpower and expenditure of the SAP expanded markedly after 1960, and how policing roles were diffused throughout society by means of voluntary forces and other compatible agencies. Within the year the Police Amendment Act was passed establishing the Reserve Police. There was an expansion in police legal powers as well. The very broadly-defined offence of 'sabotage' was enacted with the 1962 General Law Amendment Act, allowing the police to charge people with this crime if they threatened or injured the public's health and safety; reference was even made to the disruption of the free flow of traffic as being an act of sabotage (see SAIRR 1978: 443–5). The 1963 General Law Amendment Act gave ninety-day detention powers to any commanding officer of a police station; the detainee could not be released in that period other than on the recommendation of the Minister of Justice. Allegations of mistreatment of detainees began almost immediately, and some detainees were found hanged, having supposedly committed suicide. In 1965 a new Official Secrets Act was passed, and there were various amendments to the Suppression of Communism Act and the Criminal Procedure Act, which curtailed the right of newspapers to report on police matters, and narrowed the public's recourse to the courts. The infamous Terrorism Act was passed in 1967 which increased the severity of the penalties for subversion and gave the police the powers to act, in the Prime Minister's words when introducing the legislation, 'as if the country were at war'. 'Terrorism' was defined in the Act in such an encompassing manner that it covered action intended to bring about any social or economic change (SAIRR 1978: 445–6). Finally, the Public Service Amendment Act of 1969 established the Bureau of State Security (BOSS) to co-ordinate military intelligence and the SAP's Special Branch. Various powers were accorded to BOSS, including the prosecution of anyone in possession of documents or information which related to the police and which was thought prejudicial to the interests of the country.

More than this, however, further legislation was passed which tightened the police's control over the population. Turk estimates, for example, that the proportion of legislation which dealt with legal controls over the population averaged 13.8 per cent for the period 1960–75 compared with 11.7 per cent for the 1949–59 period (1981: 139). Between 1970 and 1978, parliament passed thirty-five Acts dealing with the control of Africans, twenty with Coloureds, and seven with Asians. Nine dealt with Group Areas restrictions and locations. The substantive and procedural criminal law was the focus of twelve Acts; two Acts extended censorship. The Police Act was amended eight times, and the law governing prisons five times. Six Acts tightened control over the production and possession of arms and ammunition. Fourteen concerned liquor regulation. For this period Turk estimates that 16 per cent of legislation dealt with legal control over the population (1981: 140). And it was primarily through the police that this control operated, making them the main mediators of oppression.

The organization of the police was affected by the events of 1960. For example, the episode demonstrated that equipment and tactics for public-order policing were inadequate, and the same year the SAP began riot-control training for eighty-two men at the Police College, and thirty-nine from the SARHP. Riot drill was shortly to be made part of normal training for White recruits, and eventually Black, and the period of training was extended from six months to a year to accommodate this. Training was remilitarized, and within a few years the SAP was congratulating itself that its basic training for policemen was considered by military experts to be one of the toughest military-oriented training courses in the world (Dippenaar 1988: 372).

Training in the use of firearms was also given. Sixteen members were given training in the handling of the new Browning machine-gun in 1960, and another 109 did special firearms training in 1961. The police also started giving firearms training to other bodies. In 1961, for example, staff of DBAD were given training in the handling of revolvers, as were Iscor's private security guards, staff of Pretoria municipality, and sixteen members of government departments. By 1965 training in the use of firearms was even given to postmen. The Reserve Force was armed from 1963 onwards and given training in firearms by the SAP. As fear of *swart gevaar* extended in South Africa with various bomb incidents in the early 1960s, some committed by Whites, and the experience of violent wars of independence elsewhere in Africa, the police trained the staff of many private companies and banks in self-defence and firearms, as well as members of private gun clubs and self-protection groups.

To accompany the SAP's new riot-control training, new equipment was purchased, the Browning machine-guns being an example. In 1960 the SAP also purchased 322 water-cannon; it already possessed 383 troop-carriers and 80 Saracen armoured vehicles. A quicker and more mobile riot truck was introduced in 1962; 429 were in the SAP's possession by the end of the year. By 1966/7 the SAP's stock of vehicles included 129 riot lorries, 151 riot trucks, 417 riot landrovers, 80 Saracen armoured vehicles, two aeroplanes, and two helicopters (Annual Report of the Commissioner of the SAP 1966/7: 3). The planes did 667 flying hours during the year and the helicopters 3,076. However, the helicopters were used as much to check for infiltration by drug, stock, and diamond smugglers as guerrillas. By 1973 the number of riot landrovers had increased by 41 per cent from 1966/7, and riot lorries by 68.2 per cent. There was also an additional aircraft. In other words, the SAP's response at one level was to reinforce its weaponry, equipment, and skill in fire-power.

At another level, the SAP underwent significant reorganization, which became more apparent as time passed. In 1960 headquarters was centralized under the overall direction of an advisory board, comprising the Adjunct-General, the Detective-General, Quartermaster-General, Inspector-General, Director of the Security Branch, Director of Training, and the Chaplain-General, who advised the Commissioner on policy and its execution. In its structure and nomenclature the advisory board was military in style, and, having co-operated with the SADF in quelling the unrest, a decision was taken in 1961 to reinforce the SAP's militarization. The titles of the ranks were changed and new ones adopted, copied from the army, such as major, captain, warrant-officers, and lieutenant; in the past the SAP was entitled to use military ranks but only alongside constabulary ones. The board also held discussions with the SADF to strengthen operational links, and the boundaries of the police divisions were altered to coincide with those of the SADF in order better to effect joint command. The Defence Further Amendment Act of 1961 provided for the appointment of an interdepartmental committee to co-ordinate internal security work between the SADF and SAP; this Act also lengthened military service for White youths. (In the midst of this, the SAP reverted in 1962 to the blue uniform of the London bobby.) By 1973 Grundy reports that the SADF's 'Departmental Strategic Plan' required the SADF to assist the SAP at all times, both in counter-insurgency and preserving internal order (1983*a*: 137). In 1975 young national servicemen were transferred from the SADF to the SAP to offset the latter's manpower shortage, and from 1977, joint staff courses have been held for officers from the defence and police forces (see Brewer *et al.* 1988: 177–8).

Further reorganization occurred with the establishment of specialist units to deal with unrest-related incidents. The SAP's first riot police were formed in 1962, although they were initially called mobile police squads. Three were established in Witwatersrand, Northern Transvaal, and Durban. Each was given thirty-two vehicles, a mobile radio station, and five water-cannon (Annual Report of the Commissioner of the SAP 1962: 3). Over the years the riot squads expanded rapidly in manpower and equipment. The Commissioner's Annual Reports document the progress in equipment, although no mention is made any more of manpower. By 1966/7 the squads had radio fitted to their vehicles; in 1970 the riot squads had 97 radio-controlled vehicles. Within a further five years this had risen to 412 vehicles. This was perhaps not rapid progress in the context of the shift to motorization and radio technology in the police generally, as we shall see shortly, but the riot squads were generally underused in the period before 1976. Today, each police division has its special riot squad. Another specialist unit begun in the context of Sharpeville was the Firearms Unit, whose intention was to recover stolen firearms lest they get into Black hands, and to check for the smuggling of arms over the borders. In 1973 the unit was responsible for the confiscation of 702 firearms, 146 home-made weapons, and 433 rounds of ammunition (Annual Report of the Commissioner of the SAP 1973: 11).

The Special Branch was also reorganized in 1963, with the appointment of Hendrik van den Bergh as its commanding officer. By 1966 it had trebled in numbers and had as many high-ranking officers as the CID; van den Bergh received accelerated promotion to the rank of brigadier within eighteen months of his appointment (United Nations 1967). Early in 1964 the SB began training regular members of the SAP in aspects of security work; the Commissioner's Annual Report in 1965 mentioned 5,106 members being trained in internal security. And the SAP's regulations were changed in the 1960s to require policemen immediately to pass on any information to the SB. The mania with internal security led to the formation of a separate security agency in June 1963 known as Republican Intelligence (see Rees 1980). Senior staff were seconded from the SB. Its head was Mike Geldenhuys, and it was based in Johannesburg; he was later to become Commissioner of the SAP. Its focus was on the growing threat of guerrilla incursion from northern borders. One of the early members of the agency was Gordon Winter, a journalist who later wrote an exposé of the security forces (1981). He claims that most agents were journalists whose job was to report on liberal White activists and organizations (1981: 38–9). It was Republican Intelligence which was responsible for the swoop on the ANC in Rivonia, resulting in the imprisonment of Mandela (Winter 1981: 42), and all the other important security successes at this time.

In 1969 Republican Intelligence was transformed into a new security agency known as BOSS and given legal sanction by parliament, with van den Bergh moving to be its head. He took with him many men from the SB, who comprised BOSS's initial manpower. Lt.-Gen. Ventor became head of the SB. The role of BOSS was to co-ordinate the gathering of intelligence between the SB and military security, and it was given considerable legal power and financial resources to gather its own security information. Its activities were not subject to the authority of the Public Services Commission and its budget was not audited in the usual way, leading to allegations of secret accounts. Van den Bergh was to have been appointed Commissioner of the SAP, but moved instead to BOSS, which is indicative of where he saw the power lying. In terms of statutory powers, the Act which legalized BOSS made it an offence to possess documents or information on police, military, or security matters if they were thought to be prejudicial to the interests of the country, and made provision for the Minister of Justice to withhold evidence from presiding judges if the information involved state secrets. The English-language press claimed this was to enable the government to engage in damage limitation by avoiding embarrassing revelations in the press involving SB brutality. And the government was at the time under attack arising from the death in detention of James Lenkoe, found hanged in his cell, supposedly a suicide, but, as the inquest found, he also had electrode burns to his body.

But BOSS not only had strong legal powers, its financial position was strong. According to figures provided by Talbot (1980), the emergence of BOSS led to a 95.3 per cent drop in the budget for military intelligence between 1968/9 and 1969/70, while the expenditure on BOSS rose 208.5 per cent between 1969/70 and 1974/5, to total R12.5 millions. However, these figures must be treated with caution because of the secret accounts and the difficulty of knowing the precise sums granted for security policing. Rees claims that Republican Intelligence started with fifty men while BOSS had around a thousand at its height (1980), although these again must be treated as very rough estimates.

Relations between BOSS and the SB were never good, and became worse once van den Bergh's close friend, B. J. Vorster, stepped down as Prime Minister, in part because of a series of allegations about corruption in which BOSS, among others, was involved. These included allegations that BOSS had used its spying skills against other government departments and ministers; the earliest allegation of this sort appeared in 1971 when the deputy leader of the Herstigte Nasionale Party, a far-right Afrikaner group, claimed that his telephone had been tapped by BOSS. After an internal commission of inquiry in 1977 BOSS was renamed the Department of National Security, and later the Department of National Intelligence; van den Bergh was removed from his position in 1979 (Seegars 1989: 11). Once this happened, revelations about BOSS and van den Bergh began to appear in the press more frequently. For example, on 22 October 1979 Venter admitted in the *Sunday Times* that there had been clashes between BOSS and the SB over van den Bergh's enticement of the best members away from the SB, and the latter's difficult personality and negative attitude towards other security forces. When the new Prime Minister, P. W. Botha, had been Minister of Defence, he clashed several times with van den Bergh, threatening to resign on two occasions over van den Bergh's interference in military intelligence. He alleged that his phone had been tapped by BOSS. As soon as

Botha became Prime Minister he clipped van den Bergh's wings, and replaced him with a young professor from the University of the Orange Free State. Three shifts coincided with this. The new organization began to recruit from among university graduates in order to develop a more professional approach (Seegars 1989: 11), the emphasis moved towards intelligence-gathering rather than a more active policing role, and its focus was on external rather than domestic intelligence.

The transition in Black opposition towards the external movements and armed insurgency after the banning of the main political groups not only affected security policing, it encouraged the SAP to introduce counter-insurgency training and to form a special counter-insurgency unit, and required them to police the border and undertake dangerous border patrols. South Africa had occasional bomb attacks in the 1960s, but the armed wings of the ANC and PAC were effectively infiltrated by the SB and the armed struggle petered out after 1965 (see Barrell 1990: 1–30; S. Davies 1987: 12–20; Moorcraft 1990: 344–8). Between 1960 and 1974, there were 55 incidents of guerrilla attack inside the Republic, 89 per cent of which occurred in the first four years (Morris 1974: 282), although such statistics are notoriously unreliable (for another chronology of attacks see Moss 1979: pp. i–x). In what is the only study of the ANC's armed wing, Umkhonto we Sizwe, known to its members simply as MK, Barrell points out that by 1974 there was a virtual absence of an internal ANC underground network (1990: 29), and hardly any MK guerrillas had succeeded in making their way to South Africa since 1966 (p. 23). None the less, regular members of the SAP could apply for anti-terrorism training; by 1970 it was the most popular in-service course offered at the Police College, when 2,300 went through the course, which was more than did basic training that year. In 1973 500 African policemen took the course. But rather than dealing with the threat of attacks inside South Africa, the SAP's main thrust was in monitoring guerrilla infiltration from neighbouring states. Thus there was separate counter-insurgency training. In June 1968 the SAP started to train its own counter-insurgency units for duty on the Angolan border with Namibia, and 'loaned' men to the Rhodesian government. Training lasted four weeks and included familiarization with 'bush' terrain, and the use of special weaponry, such as mortars, anti-personnel mines, and hand-grenades. Skills in self-defence and survival in the bush were also part of the course.

Training was extended to African and Coloured policemen in 1972, when 294 did the course, and Indians in 1978. By this time, the number of deaths of policemen on border duty was beginning to rise. In the year in which the decision was taken to involve Black policemen in counter-insurgency, three White policemen died and twenty-two were injured. In the first year, four Black policemen died on border duty, and two Whites. The number of White fatalities had become problematic, forcing the Chaplaincy Unit to send chaplains to border areas monthly, and for morale-boosting publicity campaigns to be initiated (for example, White 1974), although this did not approach the scale of the 1980s (on which see Cock and Nathan 1989: pt. iv). But the decision to involve Black policemen in counter-insurgency was only in part motivated by the wish to reduce White fatalities. In his farewell speech to the first Black policemen sent on border duty, the Deputy Commissioner noted the manpower shortage in South Africa itself, which required, presumably, that Black policemen take their share of other duties. The men sang a Zulu version of Psalm 23 for the occasion, which may indicate that the majority were from this ethnic group. Gordon Winter, writing in *SARP* in 1974, gave perhaps the most important reason. In an article entitled 'South Africa's Answer to Terrorism: Blacks are now Killing Blacks', he wrote that the answer to guerrilla warfare was 'Black policemen who are prepared to turn apartheid on its head and kill fellow blacks who they recognize as terrorists, who are communist inspired and trained' (Winter 1974: 7). In short, committed, disciplined, and dedicated policemen to act as killers. He estimated that the number of Blacks in the counter-insurgency units was 500, and that Blacks in the regular police were fighting with one another to be sent on the training course for the units. In practice Black policemen are no more dedicated killers than Whites, but it facilitated image management by the police, and it is noticeable that once Black policemen participated in the bush war, Black faces began to appear more frequently in photographs and features in the SAP magazine (for example, *SARP* 1972). But this did not break down the apartheid barriers within the police. Rather than be integrated with their White colleagues in one unit, Blacks had to form their own unit, headed by a White officer, Major Smit, and had separate training.

Policing of the border pre-dated the establishment of the counter-insurgency units and began in earnest in 1964, when thirty-five border posts were established, providing ordinary policing duties, such as passport control and crime detection, as well as security work; in 1966 the security police assumed control of border posts on the Lesotho and Swaziland borders. However, as early as 1961, members of the SAP were deployed on the Angolan and Bechuanaland borders (Annual Report of the Commissioner of the SAP 1961: 7), and from 1967 the SAP were secretly assisting the police in Rhodesia in their war with guerrillas. Once this was admitted the following year, further units of South African policemen were deployed on border duty in Rhodesia, up to 300 at any one time. This went on until 1974. The first death of a South African policeman on border duty occurred in Rhodesia in 1968; in 1974 seven were killed in Rhodesia's guerrilla war, and fifteen elsewhere.

Above all, the externalization and militarization of Black opposition affected the mind-set of the police in South Africa. Significantly, this occurred before the shift in the state's own rhetoric towards 'total onslaught' and 'total war', from around 1977 (on the 'total onslaught' see Cock and Nathan 1989; Grundy 1983*a*, 1983*b*, 1988), which suggests that the police played an important role in this transition, although only the role of the SADF is acknowledged in the literature. The 'total onslaught' is particularly associated with the premiership of P. W. Botha and his Defence Minister, General Malan, and thus will be discussed in the next chapter, but briefly it describes the state's belief that the country was being besieged from outside by communist-inspired enemies, requiring a 'total war' in response. This involved the militarization of South African society, a growing role for the security and military chiefs in politics, and the increasing deployment of the SADF in a policing role inside South Africa. Interestingly, the mind-set of the SAP had already shifted in the direction of the 'total onslaught' by 1977 because of its involvement in riot control, border duty, and counter-insurgency. The Commissioner's Annual Reports had long made reference to communist agitators working amongst disaffected Blacks, but this was primarily in the context of public-order incidents, like industrial strikes and political demonstrations. But the obsession with internal security and the rhetoric of war only occurred towards the end of the 1960s, but this was well before the corresponding shift in the discourse of politicians and defence chiefs.

From the 1967/8 Annual Report, for example, the Commissioner began to devote part of his report to 'internal security', and to note the 'terrorist activity' inside South Africa. This accompanied all the organizational focus given to training in riot control and counter-insurgency. In terms of the police mind-set, the Commissioner commented upon the attack on the country by 'subversives'. 'The police have no assurance that the prosecutions instituted have put an end to the subversive campaigns. Consequently, active steps are being taken to restrict the activities of such organizations' (p. 3). The following year the Commissioner commented upon the 'threat of terrorism on our northern borders [which] will be the case for a very long time to come' (Annual Report of the Commissioner of the SAP 1968/9: 3), and the Commissioner appeared on Springbok Radio in September to advise listeners of the police response to 'the forces of anarchy', making particular reference to counter-insurgency work (Dippenaar 1988: 402). In 1970 the SAP put on file a copy of a book by a right-wing American alleging that Soviet- and Chinese-funded guerrillas were to launch an attack on South Africa that year (see Dippenaar 1988: 411–13), and in his 1971 Annual Report, the Commissioner wrote that proof now existed that 'subversive elements inside and outside the Republic will maintain and intensify their subversive activities . . . the threat against the Republic, from a security point of view, is intensifying' (p. 4). By 1973 the Commissioner was referring to the 'communist onslaught' of 'Soviet-funded and aided terrorists' (p. 10). A group of five alleged terrorists, fully armed, was arrested on board a boat at Port St Johns in 1973, leading the Commissioner to comment, 'with the arrest of the conspirators, the communist onslaught against South Africa was dealt yet another severe blow' (p. 10).

The onslaught did not just come in the form of guerrilla incursion, but also in communist infiltration of liberal White organizations. In his earlier 1971 Annual Report, the Commissioner noted that 'various organizations within the country are actively engaged in militant leftist subversion against the Republic' (p. 4). Thus, the White National Union of Students, long-time critics of apartheid, was described knowingly by the Commissioner in his 1973 Annual Report as 'so-called student leaders' (p. 10).

The management's demonology permeated the lower ranks as well. In a phrase redolent of the connection between bush warfare against guerrillas and containment of South Africa's own Black population, Constable Slabbert, who in 1970 single-handedly fought off guerrillas in Rhodesia, is quoted in the South African press afterwards as saying: 'what's so wonderful about it? War is only a state of emergency isn't it?' (quoted in Dippenaar 1988: 407). This mind-set was also reflected in the contents of the SAP's magazine, *SARP*. Thus, for example, Winter referred in its pages to 'terrorists who are communist inspired and trained' (1974: 7), and White's eulogy in *SARP* for 'our men on the border' was replete with the imagery of onslaught by communists (1974). So was the regular monthly column 'Chaplain's letter'; the Dutch Reform Church ministers in the SAP appropriated the values of the police rather than the New Testament. In justifying the SAP's deployment in Rhodesia in 1968, the Head Chaplain, Brigadier Cloete, remarked that if terrorists were not stopped at the Zambezi River, the police would have to stop them on South Africa's own border of the Limpopo River, such was the onslaught that would hit first Rhodesia, next South Africa. Another part of this mind-set was the ordinary policeman's fetish for guns. As an illustration of this fetish, Dippenaar reports that in 1964, for example, there were 107 accidents with guns, 82 cases of which involved recklessness, an example of which he cited was policemen's predilection for playing 'Russian Roulette' (1988: 358).

It is likely that the SAP's early use of the rhetoric of communist-terrorist onslaught influenced the state's later adoption of the discourse of 'total onslaught', but it certainly influenced the SAP management in its perception of policing priorities. The threat was an external and military one, emanating from northern borders. There was a danger that it could become internal as a result of the activities of 'agitators', which required considerable focus on the suppression of political activity inside South Africa and the tight control of the country's Black citizenry by means of administrative regulations. In comparison, the defeat of ordinary crime took a low place. Even though ordinary crime was rife, and there was little evidence of subversion inside South Africa itself after 1965, the decision to police beyond South Africa's borders in Angola and Rhodesia fed the SAP's mania with counter-insurgency, which negatively affected its policing of ordinary crime within the Republic. On the one hand, ordinary crime went relatively ignored, both in terms of police resources and effort. Conversely, when it was dealt with, the police tended to use paramilitary, colonial-style methods as if ordinary crime was an extension of guerrilla insurgency.

THE POLICING OF ORDINARY CRIME

From 1970 the Commissioner's Annual Reports became glossy, featuring photographs of policemen as part of a public relations presentation of the SAP. The image which was projected stressed the SAP's new role in counter-insurgency. Photographs mostly featured policemen in camouflage in the bush. This is one token of the SAP's shift towards the external threat and the relative neglect of ordinary crime (this emphasis is also reflected in the SAP's official history; see Dippenaar 1988: 353–419). Another token is the fact that only one in ten members of the SAP were involved in crime detection and investigation in 1968 (Dippenaar 1988: 374).

The crime statistics reflect this in two ways. First, the pursuit of ordinary crime was made subservient to the administrative offences which regulated the boundaries between the races, so that the ten most frequently committed offences each year primarily involved administrative offences rather than ordinary crime, although traffic offences were always number one. These included offences such as trespass, pass offences, possession of kaffir beer, curfew regulations, and offences under the Urban Areas Act. This explains why the prosecution rate each year was always lower for Whites than Blacks (Turk 1981: 141), although after 1968 the Commissioner ceased publishing race-specific tabulations. Secondly, the increase in these criminal offences fell well below those involving internal security. Between 1960 and 1973, there was an overall increase of 68.8 per cent in the number of offences committed for the top ten crimes of each year, compared to a 599.4 per cent increase in 'offences against the state' (worked from figures provided in the Commissioner's Annual Reports). Other statistical measures of this focus on internal security rather than ordinary crime are the rise in the SAP's expenditure on detainees, which increased by 131.1 per cent between 1961/2 and 1975/6 (worked from figures contained in the Auditor General's Annual Reports), and, as Table 5.6 illustrates, the low proportion of expenditure spent on 'detective work' throughout the 1960s, although this rose again in the 1970s. But throughout this period, the SAP spent in proportionate terms more than twice as much on 'arms, equipment, and ammunition' than 'detective work' (see Table 5.6).

The policing of ordinary crime in the Black townships was amongst the lowest priorities of all. The official inquiry into disturbances in Paarl in November 1963, under Justice Synman, provides a glimpse of what a police station was like in a township at this time. The Report described the station as a 'dilapidated old building with an unfenced back yard' (South Africa 1963: 22), with no accommodation for reinforcements, who had to be housed in a local hotel. There was no radio communication between the station and the district commander's office, and only one telephone in the station. Manpower shortage was critical. Stations were no better elsewhere in the district. In the entire Paarl district of 2,692 square miles there were forty men; one policeman for every 4,504 inhabitants or 0.22 policemen per thousand head of population. The expansion in police manpower and expenditure that was occurring at this time no doubt helped to alleviate this eventually, but resources were selectively targeted on White areas. In 1967, for example, the Indian township of Chatsworth, near Durban, had ninety policemen for a total population of 150,000 or 0.6 policemen per thousand head of population. By 1980 the number of policemen had risen only to 110, and failed to keep up with the rise in the township's population (Poodhun 1983: 186).

There were exceptions to this, pointed to as symbols of progress in police publicity literature. For example, Meadowlands Police Station was opened in 1959, and by 1967, *SARP* herald it as the most modern in the Republic. It was double-storey, with the top floor reserved for the CID, the SB, and administration. There were mess facilities, a bar, and various other buildings. The diameter of the station was 300 yards, making it very large. Its manpower numbered 215 uniformed men, all but nine of whom were African, and twenty-seven in the CID, all but four of whom were African, making the township heavily policed. Meadowlands was featured in order to give evidence of the SAP's commitment to the 'own areas' strategy, but development there was also affected by the fact that it was one of Johannesburg's African townships; the Rand's urban African population was the largest, and also the most tightly controlled. The area was also thought to be the centre of likely unrest. So focused was the police on the prospect of unrest in Johannesburg's African townships that the SAP established a Soweto District in 1973, of which Meadowlands was a part. The whole of the Transvaal area took the main share of SAP manpower. By 1975 37.5 per cent of manpower was based in this province, 15.1 per cent in Natal, 6.8 per cent in the Orange Free State, 23.1 per cent in the Cape, and 2.8 in Namibia. The remainder was unallocated to a district, but belonged to special squads, the training school, or headquarters. Meadowlands was also the township built to replace the long-standing shanty town known as Sophiatown, and thus the progress of its police station was made part of a broader public relations exercise for 'self-development' under apartheid.

The development of purpose-built townships under apartheid was also linked to crime prevention. DBAD's journal *Bantu* was surprisingly progressive in its criminological view when it wrote that 'squalor, slum conditions, and a restless society nurture crime and create criminals. Conversely, better living conditions, proper housing and a satisfied community tend to force the crime rate down' (*Bantu* 1964*a*: 279). Thus went the leading comment to the feature on Potchefstroom's new African township Ikageng. In 1954, it was claimed, no inhabitant of Klopperville felt safe: scarcely a week went by without its toll of stabbings and assaults. When residents were forcibly removed to Ikageng the same year, crime supposedly fell. The local police commander was quoted as saying that stabbings and assaults were almost unheard of in the township. 'The remedy for this crime-infected society', *Bantu* wrote, was 'the removal of the conditions which suckled the lawlessness, and to replace them by conditions for civilized living, adequate housing and recreational facilities' (p. 279), all provided in abundance in the new township. In short, apartheid's forced removals promoted crime prevention. The following year, however, the journal reverted to Afrikaner nationalist criminology in claiming that the *tsotsi* problem was caused by giving African youths too much education—or at least an education which did not equip Africans solely for manual labour. Thus, crime in Pretoria's townships was solved, it claimed, presumably because appropriately low educational standards were being inculcated (*Bantu* 1965: 166). Black crime, in other words, was used politically both to support the government's 'self-development' process and to oppose more radical reform.

In reality neither the development of new townships nor new purpose-built police stations could prevent the escalation in crime in the townships in the absence of jobs, a stable family life, rights to permanent settlement, and a legitimate civil police force. In Soweto, for example, there were 891 murders in 1966, 1,156 rapes, 7,747 aggravated assaults, 8,075 common assaults, and 33,489 thefts (SAIRR Annual Survey of Race Relations 1967: 73), this in an area where there were 1,051 regular policemen (p. 75), and, by the following year, another 443 African reserve police (SAIRR Annual Survey of Race Relations 1968: 52). The problem was that this high level of police surveillance was directed towards petty administrative offences and internal security. Defeating the high level of ordinary crime was not a priority. This concerned liberal Whites. The *Rand Daily Mail* ran a series of reports on ordinary crime in Soweto in February 1967, describing the gangs, racketeering, and vice. Gangs used knives to terrorize victims, leading the government to introduce the Dangerous Weapons Act in 1968, prohibiting the possession of knives in public places at set times. The Transvaal Regional Committee of the Black Sash also expressed concern about crime in the townships, urging the SAP to deploy more policemen on the beat. This criticism was linked to the SAP's focus on administrative offences rather than the high levels of ordinary crime. Writing in *Black Sash*, one of its members said: 'Logically it is the presence of policemen "on the beat" which deters criminals rather than this indiscriminate "picking up" of masses of technical offenders' (Katz 1967: 16).

The police did not, however, remain entirely distant from the plight of law-abiding township residents. In 1968 they started a special plain-clothes murder and robbery squad in Soweto, encouraged residents to join the reserve police, and senior officers made a series of public-relations visits to Soweto, to be photographed talking to local officers and members of the Urban Bantu Council, in an attempt to assuage fears; but crime soared. Nor was it just Soweto where crime rose. The United Party's MP for the area reported in parliament that in one weekend in Cape Town in 1973, there were 300 stabbings, eleven murders, and eight rapes (SAIRR Annual Survey of Race Relations 1973: 72). The SAP reassured the anxious that the majority of cases were solved. In 1970, for example, there was an average of eighty murders a month in Soweto, but the Chief of CID there, Colonel Gouws, said that seventy of these were solved (SAIRR Annual Survey of Race Relations 1971: 75). He added that during 1970, the police made 1,750 arrests in respect of the 2,425 robberies reported, and 460 arrests for the 640 cases of reported housebreaking (p. 75).

Indeed, the prosecution rate per thousand head of population in South Africa was high. In 1961, for example, it was 100, while in 1972 it had risen to 417. In the Netherlands for that year it was 25.4, Norway 44, Sweden 61, Belgium 63.2, France 70, and England and Wales 72.5 (SAIRR Annual Survey of Race Relations 1972: 86). A prosecution rate of this magnitude reflects the high level of crime in South Africa and the high number of cases the police solve, as well as the greater number of offences which South Africans could transgress against. And the fact that the prosecution rate for Whites stood at 86 per thousand head of population in 1972, compared to an overall figure of 417, illustrates how each factor selectively operated against Black South Africans: crime was higher in Black areas, the police prosecuted more Black people, and the law defined various administrative offences which only Blacks could commit.

The methods used by the police whenever they did give attention to ordinary crime are another relevant factor in explaining these figures. The police used a considerable degree of force in persuading Black people to confess to crimes. The clear-up rate of the South African police was high, but only because their standards of professional conduct were so low. Confessions were often obtained by brute force. Petty offenders were treated as if they were guerrillas. One measure of this brutality is the increase in the compensation payments made by the SAP to victims of their misconduct. In 1960/1, R65,877 was paid out to victims; in 1975/6 the figure was R510,219, representing an increase of 674.5 per cent.

Another method which drew in large numbers of Black offenders, and raised the level of prosecutions, was the strategy of mass arrests. Mass arrests began on the Rand on 7 December 1965, when 1,247 Africans were arrested in one swoop for offences ranging from the minor to the serious. The Divisional Commander for the area remarked the following day that he would not be satisfied until all armed robberies on the Rand had stopped (see Katz 1967: 15), although some offenders were later charged with transgressions of administrative regulations, such as vagrancy, trespass, tax offences, and influx-control infringements. In 1966 further mass arrests took place, ostensibly to deal with ordinary crime, but mostly ending up with prosecutions for administrative offences. The police swooped on Alexandra township in August 1966 and arrested people for minor offences, the most serious being possession of dangerous weapons and dagga (cannabis). A month before in Jeppe, 1,158 Africans were arrested and charged with minor technical offences.

Mass arrest is a very crude method for catching serious criminals, but is effective as a form of pass raid, and in the absence of finding serious criminals, people were charged with minor technical offences. In one raid where over a thousand Africans were arrested, only five housebreakers were caught (Carlson 1966: 12). The Commissioner said that the 'large scale clean up of the huge complex of Bantu villages on the south-western outskirts of Johannesburg [has] led to a marked decrease in serious crime. Most of the inhabitants of the Bantu townships were extremely thankful' (quoted in Katz 1967: 16). To emphasize this last point, the Divisional Commander for Johannesburg said that the SAP had been greeted with smiles by Africans in the townships. Since most of those arrested were charged with minor technical offences, it is unlikely that the residents welcomed the method; very few were not found to have contravened some administrative regulation. Hansard figures indicate that only about a fifth of people caught in mass arrests were released without charge (p. 16). So large numbers of policemen were deployed, with vehicles, dogs, and arms, in a massive round-up, which roped in thousands of otherwise law-abiding Africans, whose only crime was to offend against the battery of administrative regulations which controlled their lives in minute degree. It did little to deal effectively with ordinary crime, as Table 5.7 shows for 1974. Thus, the persistent high level of violent crime, and consequent disaffection from the police, contributed to the problems which led to the township uprisings in 1976.

TABLE 5.7 *Cases of serious crimes reported in 1974 in selected areas*

	Murder	Rape	Culpable homicide	Aggravated assault	Armed robbery
Soweto	854	1,282	92	7,682	—
Cape Peninsula'	425	1,024	435	8,614	3,440
Coloured townships in Johannesburg	97	329	41	988	329

Source: SAIRR Annual Survey of Race Relations 1974: 53–4.

Ordinary crime was not completely ignored; the SAP did try other methods on occasions. In some townships the police took to saturating the streets with policemen on pay-day in the hope of preventing theft of wages. In Johannesburg's Coloured townships in 1975, in a concerted attempt to stop the gangs of youths, the police agreed to withdraw certain charges for six months on condition that no further crimes were committed, and that the gangs were disbanded and received help to become social clubs instead (SAIRR Annual Survey of Race Relations 1975: 54).

Organizational reforms were also made in an attempt to deal with ordinary crime. As early as 1961, special units were formed on the Rand to combat car thefts, a murder and robbery squad was formed in Soweto in 1968, Soweto became a separate police division in 1973, and efforts were made to begin crime-prevention programmes in schools (see B. Visser 1973). The SAP also modernized its communication system and speeded up the process of motorization, although these developments were predicated by the security situation, as Dippenaar explains: 'The new communication system was vitally essential in view of the political development of the black population and associated upheaval among blacks' (1988: 305). In 1960 the SAP's fleet of vehicles was 3,055, 283 of which were fitted with two-way radios. Rapid response units with radios existed at this time only in Port Elizabeth, Durban, and on the East and West Rand; a unit in Pretoria was added in 1960. Although stimulated by the security situation, the development of radio communication was also linked to ordinary crime, as the Commissioner explained: 'This technology instils respect in the Bantu and the swift action on the part of the unit sometimes bewilders him' (Annual Report of the Commissioner of the SAP 1961: 4). By 1970 the vehicle fleet had expanded rapidly to 6,456 vehicles, 2,446 having two-way radios; some modernization was therefore taking place.

A crime that was given particular attention was the trafficking in and possession of dagga. In part this was an attempt to prevent the modern life-style of young Westerners from penetrating White South African youth, as well as a further means of control over the life of urban Africans, who used cannabis extensively, especially in migrant hostels. The SAP's aircraft were deployed in searches for drugs as much as for guerrillas, as were the tracker dogs. In 1974 the special South African Narcotics Bureau was formed to co-ordinate police effort. In 1969 the Commissioner's Annual Report noted the increase in offences under the Dagga Act, which totalled 27,578 for the year. Of the offenders, 85.9 per cent were male, and 4.9 per cent White. The vast majority were African (69.8 per cent), 84.9 per cent of whom were males. In short, it was a problem amongst migrant workers. The anti-drug campaigns the police started in White schools from 1971 indicate the SAP's fear that the practice would spread to White youths. Trafficking in dagga was also lucrative. In 1970 the police confiscated drugs to an estimated street value of R20.58 millions (Annual Report of the Commissioner of the SAP 1970: 7). White youths, however, tended to use more sophisticated drugs; dagga was an escape from the mindlessness of the hostels. In 1971 85 per cent of all prosecutions connected with hard drugs were of Whites (Annual Report of the Commissioner of the SAP 1971: 7), which is why this form of drug abuse was centred, according to police estimates, in the large conurbations of Cape Town, Durban, and Johannesburg. However, the total number of prosecutions for hard drugs that year was still only 248, minuscule compared to the prosecutions of migrant workers for use of softer drugs such as cannabis. Police effort, in other words, was on misuse of drugs by Blacks rather than Whites. Thus, in 1973 the SAP began Operation Reefer, which was the largest dagga-destroying operation in the history of the police; for nineteen days, the police uprooted and burnt cannabis plants in the Transkei.

CONCLUSION

The beginning of the 1960s marks the period of decolonization in Africa, where formerly colonial police forces were supposedly modernized and made more professional, although the resulting independence rarely saw them change into civil police forces (see Anderson and Killingray 1992). In South Africa, the 'self-development' for Blacks under the second phase of apartheid, which was the country's response to the same trend, was a chimera, and the SAP's role in policing race relations extended rather than diminished. However, the police thought themselves thoroughly professional now (a view less enthusiastically endorsed by van der Spuy 1989: 284). The Minister of Police explained in his New Year message to the SAP in 1969 that 'the arduous tasks of policing' in the Republic 'require more than just muscle power' (quoted in Dippenaar 1988: 404). The SAP's reputation for violence, brutality, and force gave the lie to the Minister's assessment. Equipment was modernized, reorganization undertaken, and expansion got under way but often under the stimulus of strengthening internal security; and by the end of the period under review in this chapter the minimum entry requirement to the SAP for Whites was still not Matriculation.

The police also thought themselves good at ordinary crime-fighting. Benjamin Bennett, a rank-and-file policeman, writing in *SARP*'s May issue in 1966, said: 'murderers, burglars, hold-up men, saboteurs, confidence tricksters and rapists are invariably arrested within days, even hours of their crime. No matter how cunningly they cover their tracks—and Bantu particularly can disappear quickly—they are relentlessly hunted down' (p. 93). But while the prosecution rate soared, as if to illustrate the SAP's efforts, so did the number of offences committed each year. Crime was endemic to South Africa's social conditions, and the police were helpless when crime was dealt with purely as a policing problem. In part this was because crime was not properly linked in the police mind-set to the social circumstances which fostered it, but the police also misdirected their efforts, under the influence of state policy, towards a largely non-existent guerrilla problem (at least it was non-existent in the Republic), and the minor technical offences which regulated the boundaries between the races.

The policing task, in other words, was still essentially a colonial one, and discharged by colonial policing methods. If the SAP was professional, it was so in counter-insurgency and its paramilitary role rather than in its benign role as a civil police force. Gone even was the ritual complaint by the Commissioner against the state's imposition of extraneous duties on the police. This is despite the fact that these duties increased by 238.4 per cent between 1966 and 1973, to total 2.4 million hours in 1973, the highest level that had pertained in the SAP's history. Whatever complaint was made about this was now done in private, for the following year, the number of hours decreased by 42.6 per cent, and a further 12.2 per cent in 1975. Yet in 1975 extraneous duties were still greater than they had ever been prior to 1970. In this sense also the state saw the police as its agent.

The period under review in this chapter began with the nadir of SAP's misconduct in the Sharpeville and Pondoland massacres, yet it was to sink even lower in the policing of township unrest in 1976, to which we turn in Chapter 6. The protests took everyone by surprise, given the long hiatus, but there were pointers in the style of policing between 1960 and 1975 to how the SAP reacted. The lessons of policing between 1960 and 1975 were: peaceful protest was seen by the police as part of the 'total onslaught'; force was used as a first resort; and skills in crowd control were underdeveloped in preference to proficiency in counter-insurgency and fire-power: in short, Soweto's schoolchildren were treated as if they were guerrillas.

6

Policing Reform and Reforming the Police: 1976–1992

INTRODUCTION

The uprisings in Soweto and elsewhere in 1976 marked the beginning of a substantial period of international economic pressure and political protest (on the effects of the uprisings on subsequent protest see Brewer 1986; Lodge and Nasson 1992), and showed once more the difficulties of an apartheid system without legitimacy and dependent upon coercive police power. The reform process that followed the crisis was at first hesitant, limited, and partial, but eventually culminated in President de Klerk's radical dismantling of apartheid. This chapter takes us from the events of Soweto in 1976 to de Klerk's reforms. The whole period, however, exposes the difficulties of the police in South Africa to transcend their origins as a colonial paramilitary force, whose primary function is the brutal containment of the subject population.

This assessment was valid at the beginning of the reform process in the late 1970s, when the South African state was caught in the cleft stick between the need of a reformist state to control the worst excesses of policing apartheid, and the historical tradition of policing in South Africa, where the police did not need to be circumspect in their treatment of Black Africans. This exemplified the tensions within the state at the start of the reform process, between some sections of its political arm, who were aware of the need to liberalize the police and of the domestic and international ramifications of police brutality, and some in the state's law-enforcement agencies, who in practice operated without constraint (as noted in Brewer *et al.* 1988: 176). And it is true at the end of the process now that de Klerk has finally abolished legalized racism, for the police are on the whole resisting their transformation into a civil police force. The old colonial police style and methods still hold sway despite the state's shedding of policies of internal colonialism and the interests served by radical police reform.

THE SOWETO UPRISING

The revolt that erupted in Soweto on the morning of 16 June 1976 had long roots in the period before: in the emergence of Black Consciousness in 1969, industrial unrest in 1973, the collapse of colonial regimes in Southern Africa from 1974 onwards, and the endless pressure in apartheid's townships and schools. And yet it took everyone by surprise, including the police (on the uprising see Brewer 1986: 65–105; Hirson 1979; Kane-Berman 1979). Discontentment among students over the decree that they be taught half their subjects in Afrikaans had been grumbling since February, but every time the police persuaded students either to return to school or disperse peacefully. The morning of 16 June was different for two reasons. The size of the protest had grown from a few hundred to ten thousand, and, being massively outnumbered, the police opened fire, leaving one African child dead and thousands smarting from tear-gas. Had the police not opened fire, the students might have dispersed after their meeting, but Hector Peterson's death transformed the situation. The children retaliated and the crowd swelled in number to thirty thousand in a few hours; incidents continued in Soweto for three days.

Dippenaar reports that the police were fully aware of the impending unrest, having 'kept a finger on the pulse of the community' (1988: 500), but the Cillie Commission into the disturbances (South Africa 1980) noted the police's lack of planning and foresight (p. 627). Soweto's riot squad had only 48 men, and on the day the entire SAP manpower on duty in the city was only 350 (p. 467). There was not even a loud hailer with which to address the crowd, and some of the tear-gas shells failed to explode because they were old stock and ineffective (p. 469). The chain of command broke down during the disturbance and policemen were left without instruction (p. 470). However, the report did support the principal claim that the police opened fire on protesters only after warning shots, and acted in self-defence. This is despite the evidence of a senior officer, reported in the *Rand Daily Mail* the following day, that no warning shots were fired. While the police claimed that the first death was of a child who had been taunting them, pathologists' evidence showed he was shot in the back. On 19 June the *Star* published an astonishing photograph of a fleeing person about to be shot in the back. However, the Cillie Commission reported that it simply 'cannot accept that the police used firearms when everything was still quiet and calm' (p. 433).

Put in historical perspective, this faith in the good sense of the police was entirely unfounded. But in the context of the evidence before it the Commission believed the police view of events because only fifteen Blacks under the age of 18 were among the 503 people who testified. Most witnesses were policemen. The attitudes of the police therefore bear consideration. Brigadier Visser, Divisional Commander in Soweto, spoke of the incident. 'Naturally,' he said, 'force had to be met with force' (quoted in Brewer 1986: 78): the children were an irrational and violent mob, and the community was scared either to oppose or stop them. The Deputy Commissioner of the SAP, Lt.-Gen. Venter, repeated the view that the children were an unruly mob. 'If we don't do anything the rioters will run amok burning, looting, killing, and injuring innocent people' (quoted in Brewer 1986: 79). Asked the following day why the police did not use less lethal ways of controlling the crowd, the Minister of Police, Jimmy Kruger, is reported in the *Rand Daily Mail* as saying that rubber bullets make the mob 'tame to the gun'. The implication was clear. The schoolchildren were a senseless, suggestible mob, uncontrollable, unpredictable, and irrational, and had to feel the cut of live ammunition.

As Olivier (1991*a*) shows with respect to all incidents of unrest in South Africa between 1970 and 1984, high levels of repression statistically increase the likelihood of further collective action rather than diminish it, and in 1976 the unrest spread throughout Soweto, and to other townships on the Rand and Cape. Workers became involved, and three successful stay-aways were organized. By November, nearly one million people in over two hundred communities had directly protested against apartheid in a way that they had not done since 1960. All of a sudden the police had to switch from the external guerrilla threat to an internal threat. But they continued to see the crowds of township residents much as they perceived guerrillas. The Cillie Commission reported that 575 people lost their lives in the following eight months of unrest, and 3,907 were injured. It attributed 78.4 per cent of the deaths and 61.1 per cent of the injuries to the police. In Uitenhage seven were left dead and thirty-three injured when police shot at protest marchers commemorating the first anniversary of the Soweto deaths. On the same day in Soweto nine were shot dead at barricades which they had erected to obstruct the police; unprovoked, the police fired tear-gas into Soweto's Regina Mundi church, where a memorial service was being held for the dead.

The police had no compunction in using a great deal of force to deal with internal protests. The damages paid for assaults by the police through civil courts or out-of-court sums rose markedly after the uprising in 1976—accepted claims exactly doubled between 1976 and 1978, and compensation paid increased by a factor of nearly four and a half (for figures see Brewer 1986: 119). The 1977 Indemnity Act specifically excluded the liability of the Minister of Police and any officer of the government for wrongs committed by the police, and the Police Act was revised in order to shorten the period of time in which proceedings against the police could be lodged. And with this protection, the number of assaults drastically increased: accepted claims increased by 112 per cent from 1978 to 1983, and compensation by 175.4 per cent. A series of *ad hoc* incidents at this time illustrate the SAP's resort to excessive violence when dealing with Blacks. They forced a 15-year-old African girl to have sex with them; assaulted a member of the public when he objected to them commandeering his car with a baby in the back seat just to transport them to the station; raped a 19-year-old African woman at gunpoint and said that they had become sexually excited after watching semi-naked women dancing; charged an African for blasphemy because he said 'Oh God' when they arrested him; beat up a nightclub owner when he refused them free drinks; set their dogs on suspects and refused them hospital treatment; instructed cell-mates to attack a prisoner 'like dogs' while they watched; shot an African because he had no pass; refused a mother the right to lay a wreath on her son's grave and fired tear-gas when she persisted; killed an 18-year-old schoolboy when he ran away from a road-block; shot and killed a taxi-driver for not parking his car properly; and were responsible for the death of two babies as a result of over-exposure to tear-gas (for documentation see Brewer 1986: 120–1).

The police showed no restraint in the use of violence even against colleagues. A police constable, on being asked to correct a fault in a parade, shot at his lieutenant; on breaking up a fight between two policemen, a third was shot dead by one of the fighters. Shoot first and ask questions later was the general police approach. Brigadier van der Westhuizen, from Natal, revealed this in a warning to Whites in the *Daily News* of 12 January 1980: 'never expect a robber to act like a normal person. Never argue with a robber. Shoot first and ask questions later.' In short, to threaten law and order meant the loss of one's right to life. Thus, between 1978 and 1983, the police killed, in the course of their duty, 1,005 Black adults and 102 juveniles, and seventeen White adults and two juveniles. Woundings totalled 2,505 Black adults and 341 juveniles, and sixty-four White adults and three juveniles (Brewer 1986: 122).

However, brute force and fire-power were not the only police responses to the new internal unrest. For the first time the police began to use vigilante groups as surrogates rather than simply sponsor and support them, as they had in the past. During the initial events in 1976, the police gave groups of mainly Zulu migrant workers authority to arm themselves without fear of prosecution in order to confront the students who were urging them to strike (SAIRR Annual Survey of Race Relations 1976: 97). At the Orange Free State Congress of the National Party later that year, the Minister of Police repeated his endorsement of the activities of vigilante groups, but indicated that they acted against 'criminals' rather than in any public order role, ensuring continuity with previous practice. (He also claimed that businessmen had the right to shoot anyone threatening their premises.) But even this subsequent qualification was too much for more reformist members of the government, and P. W. Botha, the Minister of Defence, said the following week that people should not take the law into their own hands: 'it is the state's duty to maintain law and order' (SAIRR Annual Survey of Race Relations 1976: 98). This commitment to a state monopoly of the use of force ensured that sanction of vigilante groups was unofficial.

It also ensured that the conservative *maghotla* never got the official recognition they requested. Seizing their chance during the unrest, ten members of the Soweto *maghotla* wrote to the Deputy Minister of Justice in September 1976 asking for official state recognition. The leader of Soweto's Urban Bantu Council, a member of the *maghotla*, as were many other councillors, urged that the *maghotla* be given further powers to make them more effective. Up to this point the *maghotla* had been active enough in dispensing rough justice. Four members of Meadowland's *maghotla* were found guilty in 1976 of culpable homicide, and a member of Soweto's *maghotla* of murder. However, the demand for official recognition was lost in the reform process that immediately followed the uprising. In October 1976 the Minister of Bantu Administration and Development announced the development of new Community Councils in the townships to replace the discredited Urban Bantu Councils. One feature of the reform of local government was the proposed development of community guards as a form of local policing, which would replace both the *maghotla* and the SAP in the townships, although the Municipal Law Enforcement Officers (MLEOs), as they were eventually called, did not appear until 1984; such was the pace of reform.

As part of the process of local government reform, the *maghotla* were to be severely curtailed. The Viljoen Commission of Inquiry into the Penal System, which tabled its report in January 1977, felt unable to recommend the recognition of the *maghotla*, and urged instead that they join the police reserve. There was even some thought at this time that the *maghotla* would be banned, but in May 1977 the Minister of Justice announced that they would be retained but their conduct would need to change: there was to be no more public thrashing of offenders, for example. In 1979 the Divisional Commander in Soweto warned the *maghotla* that it was the responsibility of the police to combat crime, and that members should join the reserve police.

Another method by which the police dealt with the uprising was detention and banning. The SAP immediately rounded up thousands of students and other activists, and treated them brutally in detention. Black Sash estimated that forty-four people died while in detention between March 1976 and July 1978. The police alleged that some students in detention had skipped the country, although no record was ever found of them again either side of the border, the implication being that they had died in custody and their bodies had been disposed of secretly. The death at this time of Steve Biko while in detention shows that this was not fanciful. At first the police denied that death was as a result of head injuries. When the cause was known much was made of Biko's alleged advocation of violence. The Minister of Police thus excused the assault as 'following automatically from an arrest with a stroppy person'. He was 'prepared to concede and accept that a policeman could lose his temper'; the violence was 'hardly serious enough to justify a charge before a police court' (quoted from Brewer 1986: 119).

In a five-minute inquest verdict, the magistrate accepted the police version and absolved them of any responsibility or criticism. This was despite the fact that Biko had been kept naked in his cell in leg-irons chained to a grille; that the doctor admitted that Biko should have been sent to hospital but the police initially refused; that when he was dispatched to hospital, he was transported in the back of an open van for 1,200 km., without medical supplies, supervision, or even notes, so that a Pretoria prison doctor treated a man dying of brain damage with vitamin injections and drip feed; and that the drip feed was later found empty. To inhibit public criticism, the government banned nineteen organizations in October 1977, including the two mostly widely read African newspapers. This gave the Port Elizabeth security police an effective public immunity, and the senior officer in charge of the interrogation was later promoted to the rank of deputy commissioner, although the Medical Association of South Africa eventually struck off the two doctors involved (on the medical ethics of the Biko case and other incidents see Berat 1989; Rayner 1990).

By 1978 the Commissioner noted in his Annual Report that the 'unrest situation is completely under control', the measures taken up to this point 'had the desired effect' (p. 1). This was Panglossian in its over-optimism given the unrest that was occurring continually, the re-emergence of the ANC inside South Africa after 1976, both as a political organization and guerrilla movement, and the fact that new bodies and newspapers almost immediately replaced those that had been banned. However, the Commissioner was probably reflecting confidence in a series of changes in police organization and manpower provoked by the uprisings, although Soweto's aftermath for the police was determined for the most part by the wider government response to the conflict, especially its reform initiatives.

THE AFTERMATH OF SOWETO

The events of 1976–7 showed in vivid relief the weaknesses of policing under apartheid that had been concealed or forgotten by the SAP's superordinance in the era of quiescence after 1960: the police were managerially incompetent and professionally undeveloped, under-staffed in terms of regular manpower, lacking in legitimacy, and crude and brutal in their strategy of relying on violence as a first resort, as well as outmodedly colonial in believing that Black demands could be met only with suppression and force.

In his Annual Report for 1976, the Commissioner noted how

the uprisings strained the resources of the SAP to breaking-point, requiring massive numbers to be withdrawn from ordinary police duties; all leave was cancelled for two consecutive years. The ratio of police per thousand head of population in 1976, at 1.13, was lower in South Africa than England and Wales (2.0), the USA (2.1), West Germany (2.7), and Israel (3.5), although the ratio underscores the South African state's policing resources by omitting members in compatible forces. The official figure was the same in 1976 as 1913, when the SAP was formed. 'It is apparent', the Commissioner wrote, 'that this state of affairs cannot be permitted to continue indefinitely, or, as during the past few years, to deteriorate. In order to remedy the matter, considerable expansion is imperative' (p. 1). The manpower situation was made worse by the high number of resignations following the Soweto disturbances, primarily by Black policemen in the urban townships who, presumably, had come under severe pressure to resign from a radicalized Black community. The Cillie Commission noted that only one policeman on duty in Orlando police station on the day of the uprising was still in the force at the time of the Commission's investigations (South Africa 1980: 475).

This is reflected in Table 6.1, which shows the declining proportion of Black policemen in the SAP for the three years following 1976 despite the increase in overall membership. Indeed, Black membership fell by 6.1 per cent between 1976 and 1979 compared to a 3.7 per cent increase for Whites. There was no similar effect after Sharpeville, where Black membership fell by only 0.8 per cent between 1960 and 1963, because it did not lead to the radicalization of the Black community and hence pressure on Black policemen to resign. It is also worth noting from Table 6.1 that the expansion desired by the Commissioner did not take place. Although the authorized complement increased markedly, actual manpower rose more slowly, and not fast enough to keep pace with the increase in population, so that the ratio of police per thousand head of population decreased. Large increases in actual manpower occurred only in 1982, with the beginning of township unrest, and 1986, when the kitskonstabels and special constables were recruited to deal with further township revolts (to be discussed later) and the SARHP was absorbed into the SAP.

Unfortunately 1976 marks the period from which the Commissioner reduced the level of information about the force in his annual reports, reflecting a new insularity, so no breakdown was given again of the social composition of the Black police (nor on many other things

TABLE 6.1 *Manpower trends 1976–1991*

Year	Authorized	Actual	% change*	% Black*	% under-staffed	Ratio per 1,000 population
1976	35,635	34,437	–	48.3	3.3	1.31
1977	–	35,019	1.6	46.2	–	1.29
1978	–	35,965	−0.1	44.6	–	1.26
1979	38,565	34,076	2.7	45.8	11.6	1.19
1980	–	34,214	0.4	46.8	–	1.19
1981	43,526	34,271	0.1	49.5	21.6	1.16
1982	44,004	42,527	24.0	47.9	3.3	1.41
1983	–	42,740	0.5	49.1	–	1.38
1984	45,561	44,696	4.5	48.0	1.8	1.41
1985	48,991	45,539	1.8	46.9	7.0	–
1986	55,234	48,921	7.4	45.9	11.4	–
1987	61,197	60,390	23.4	–	1.3	–
1988	64,851	60,878	0.8	–	6.1	–
1989	–	–	–	–	–	–
1990	–	–	–	–	–	–
1991	123,000	108,000	77.4	56.4	12.2	–

* Based on actual membership.

Source: Annual Reports of the Commissioner of the SAP.

as well), although in 1991 former Deputy Commissioner van Eyk revealed in a private communication to the author that the proportion of Black policemen had increased to 56.4 per cent of total manpower, and that 80.3 per cent were African, 13.9 per cent Coloured, and 5.8 per cent Asian, roughly the same proportion that has pertained since the inception of the SAP. To further help with manpower shortage, national servicemen could transfer from the SADF to the SAP: 360 did so in 1976, and 491 in 1977. By 1986 the number had reduced to 160. To avoid people using the SAP as a means to skip national service, the police initially only accepted transfers from the SADF, but in 1980 those who elected to do national service in the SAP rather than SADF were required to serve double the normal period of time.

Nor did the Commissioner's projected expansion occur with respect to police expenditure. As Table 6.2 illustrates, the percentage increases in expenditure were relatively small for the first two years following the uprisings, except for 1976 itself, reflecting perhaps the government's economic problems caused by the flight of capital out of South

TABLE 6.2 *Trends in SAP expenditure, 1975/6–1990/1*

Year	Total Rm.	% increase	% detective work	% equip-ment*	Ratio to SADF expenditure†	% of government expenditure
1975/6	170.1	–	1.0	2.4	550	2.3
1976/7	192.5	13.2	0.9	4.2	700	2.1
1977/8	204.0	5.9	–	4.1	830	2.3
1978/9	220.4	8.6	–	6.9	730	2.1
1979/80	245.2	11.2	–	7.5	680	2.0
1980/1	346.4	41.2	–	8.6	560	2.3
1981/2	418.5	20.7	–	–	580	–
1982/3	517.7	23.7	–	–	510	–
1983/4	564.2	9.1	–	–	540	2.4
1984/5	795.6	41.0	–	–	–	3.0
1985/6	954.7	19.9	–	–	–	2.9
1986/7	–	–	–	–	–	–
1987/8	1,530.0	60.2	–	–	430	–
1988/9	1,800.0	17.6	–	–	450	–
1989/90	2,456.4	41.4	–	–	–	–
1990/1	2,927.7	14.9	–	–	–	–

* Defined as 'arms, equipment and ammunition'.
† SAP expenditure = 100.

Source: Annual Reports of the Auditor General.

Africa after the disturbances. The increases rose massively in later years, however. Yet police expenditure has progressively fallen as a proportion of total government expenditure, and in 1984/5 only reached a level that pertained before 1970. It has never reached again the levels of the early 1960s, indicating how much more expensive reform is over repression, so that the coercive agencies of the state have to accept a declining share of the overall budget in periods of reform (which is a lesson for the new South Africa in the 1990s). However, the imbalance between police and defence expenditure has narrowed in this period in favour of the SAP, indicating the shift back from an external to an internal threat, but is still large in gross terms. Another noteworthy trend from Table 6.2 is the increasing proportion of police expenditure given to 'arms, equipment, and ammunition', which is the highest it has ever been, suggesting that the internal threat is still dealt with by force irrespective of the government's reform initiatives, although figures are only available for the early reform period.

But if the threat of widespread Black unrest in 1976 did not provoke the state significantly to strengthen police resources, as did the unrest from 1983 onwards, it stimulated the policeman-citizen tradition amongst Afrikaners, and led to an increase in reserve force membership. Between 1976 and 1978, the number of Whites active in the Reserve Police Force rose by 14.8 per cent, and that of Blacks by 5.7 per cent (showing how the events had a different bearing on Whites compared to Blacks), while active members in the Police Reserve increased by 38.2 per cent. Numbers in the Wachthuis also rose by 8.6 per cent in the same two-year period. Women were allowed into the reserve forces in 1982, the same year as Black women were allowed to join the regular SAP. In 1988 there were 406 women reservists, and a total of 20,058 members of the Police Reserve, although only 3,572 were active (Annual Report of the Commissioner of the SAP 1988: 7).

Another reserve force was also established in the aftermath of the 1976 uprisings. In 1980 the Minister of Police announced the intention to begin a force of schoolboy auxiliaries, composed of male volunteers over the age of 16 years. The following year the Junior Reserve was formally established, giving schoolboys basic training, including firearms training, although they were not allowed to carry arms on duty. Duty was restricted to school holidays; members had no powers of arrest. By the end of the first year, 375 boys had enlisted. Like all the reserve forces, the Junior Reserve was entirely voluntary; policing, as it were, on the cheap, with the state taking advantage of the policeman-citizen culture. This tradition also partly infused the growth of the private security industry after 1976 (on which see Grant 1989), and by 1979 the Commissioner was complaining about private security firms luring policemen away by higher salaries (Annual Report of the Commissioner of the SAP 1979: 1).

In addition to manpower shortage, managerial inefficiency was another lesson taught the police by the events of 1976. In the second half of 1976 senior managers extended and expanded the special division within headquarters known as the Inspectorate, to enable it to look at all staff matters, transport availability, methods of operation, codes of conduct, and make prescriptions to step up efficiency. It particularly looked at the deployment of staff between the SAP's various branches and divisions in order to make better use of existing manpower. There was also some internal reorganization of the riot squads. In the absence of significant internal unrest between 1960 and 1975, the police realized during 1976 that the organization of the riot police had been neglected (SAP 1986: 34). In 1976 each police division was given its own riot squad, making them more responsive to local circumstances, although a riot unit known as Unit 19 remains under the control of headquarters; even the police reserve formed its riot squad in July 1977. Riot police were also allowed to wear camouflage uniform from 1978, bringing something of bush warfare into the townships. They stopped this in Soweto in 1979 because it was provocative. But, working in the opposite direction, the police experimented with new riot-control technology after 1976: live ammunition was replaced with buck shot, sneeze machines (using a combination of tear-gas and ordinary sneeze powder), and water-cannon. Riot police were also given protective shields, safety helmets, gas masks, and rubber batons; before 1976 this was considered to display fear to the crowd, but after 1976 it was considered important in taming policemen's ready resort to live ammunition. The mine-resistant but highly mobile riot vehicle known as the casspir was also introduced in 1979. An airborne riot unit was formed in 1988, based on the helicopter riot squads in Argentina (van der Spuy 1988: 19).

In addition to trying to reduce fatalities, the police also began to take a low profile in some incidents of collective protest after 1976, although by no means all. One of the largest incidents, in terms of both numbers participating and geographical spread, was the April 1980 boycott by Coloured students (see Brewer 1986: 86–7). By the final day of the protest, there had been few incidents of baton-charging and tear-gas, and no shooting. It was not until the ninth day of the protest that the police made arrests, and then only under the Riotous Assemblies Act, not the more rigorous terrorist laws. Police even took to shepherding students while they marched and leaving them to make their speeches unhindered, although it was significant that the police reserved their most vigorous action for African children who participated in the protest. However, as we shall see below, all restraint had gone by 1983, when protest escalated to a plane that exceeded even the events of 1976.

Other managerial innovations introduced in the wake of the 1976 uprising included the computerization of records; up to 1977 the SAP was still using the antiquated card-index system to record data in its criminal bureau. Progress was also made on the computerization of the details of stolen property. In 1978 the SAP installed a computer for general use to flash information immediately on display screens throughout the Republic. After 1976 the force was also able to modernize to some extent by accelerating the academicization of policing, as Dippenaar describes it (1988: 558). In part this merely reflected advances in the educational standards of the Afrikaans-speaking community, but the management also renewed its commitment to raise the educational levels of the police. Training was made more academic, greater encouragement was given staff to enrol for degrees and diplomas in police science, as well as other subjects, and an ever-increasing number of new entrants joined with Matriculation qualifications. This increase in Matriculants is not explained solely by the number of English-speakers recruited to the police after 1976 to avoid national service in the SADF, although the proportion of English-speaking recruits rose from 7.9 per cent in 1975 to 16.6 per cent in 1977. On the whole it mirrored general educational advancement in South African society and a dramatic shift in preference by the SAP towards the employment of educated Africans. Thus, in 1973, only one quarter of new recruits had Matriculation; in 1976 it was nearly three-quarters. Eight out of ten new recruits had Matriculation in 1979. The new Commissioner appointed in 1983 had a postgraduate degree for a thesis on Trotskyism.

Above all, the uprisings in urban townships throughout 1976 and 1977 demonstrated vividly the residents' alienation from the apartheid system and the impossibility of a police force lacking in legitimacy to maintain control there by coercion alone. This was a lesson for the state as a whole rather than just its police force, and it persuaded the government to reform local government in the townships through the development of community councils, and in the process to introduce an African police force for operation there with, hopefully, more legitimacy.

The SAP continued with its 'own areas' policing strategy, and by 1978 there were sixty-nine police stations manned exclusively by Blacks, most of these being in African areas. But a new initiative seemed necessary after the uprisings. Within months of the initial demonstration in Soweto, the Minister of Bantu Administration and Development issued a statement in which he outlined plans to transfer increased powers to councillors who helped to administer the townships. Part of the plan was to encourage 'a well organized system of traditional disciplinary courts and community guards' (SAIRR Annual Survey of Race Relations 1976: 99). The conservative *maghotla* believed this to be official endorsement of their role as vigilantes, but this idea was quickly quashed. The 1977 Community Councils Act gave the new bodies the right to confer judicial powers on community guards, and the Chairman of Soweto's new Community Council announced immediately that the council would create the new force as an alternative to the 'barbarous' *maghotla*, and gave assurance that they would operate within the law, be subject to legal safeguard, and would not act against political dissidents. However, more radical members of the community rejected the idea as yet another apartheid surrogate, and Percy Qoboza, writing in the *Transvaal Post*, urged people to boycott them.

It was not until 1979 that regulations were drafted to enact the provisions of the 1977 Act. The regulations stated that persons found guilty of obstructing the guards would be fined R90 or ninety days in prison. Guards would be allowed to carry a knobkierie and other weapons at the discretion of the local police commander, but not to have firearms. Three ranks were defined; at all times they were to be subordinate to the SAP, and obliged to obey the lawful orders of the police. Before a council could appoint guards, it needed the permission of the local police and Bantu Administration Board. In the absence of permission, some political leaders established their own personal guards, such as David Thebehali's 'All Nation Guard', formed in Soweto in 1980, which marked the beginning of the descent into vigilantism later in the 1980s. Thebehali's guards were reported to be assaulting residents, and the head of Soweto's CID distanced them from the SAP, saying that they were not recognized as police reservists and had no official sanction. The police there also distanced themselves from the *maghotla*, refusing them permission to patrol Soweto's streets.

But the government left a vacuum in the townships in which vigilantes and the *maghotla* could flourish because it was not until 1984 that the first community councils were actually granted the right to form their own police forces. By October 1986, 1,259 MLEOs had graduated from the Lenz military base, where they were trained separately from the SAP. These numbers came nowhere near the expected 5,000 which the government proudly boasted would be in service in the first six months of 1985. The financing of the force was the responsibility of the local council, although the government gave a grant of R24.6 million in 1985 to help. Soweto Council (the largest African authority) had 270 officers in 1985 and spent R1.7 million on security, which only partially included policing (Brewer *et al.* 1988: 160–1). The *Weekly Mail* mentioned a figure of 900 MLEOs in Soweto by September 1986. Lekoa Council, in the Vaal Triangle, spent R2.7 million on security in 1988.

The powers granted by the central government insisted that commissioned officers within these township forces be drawn from those policemen from the SAP seconded to the White-appointed development boards; the whole of Soweto's force in 1986 consisted of policemen formerly attached to the West Rand Administration Board. The role of MLEOs was an auxiliary one to the SAP. They were charged with protecting the lives of African councillors and guarding municipal installations and government buildings, thus freeing the SAP to concentrate on policing the townships. But the force could also be called upon to assist the SAP in 'riotous conditions'. They also had the role of ensuring 'the implementation of council decisions', which could range from tracing outstanding library books and distributing council notices to pursuing residents for non-payment of township service charges. This suggested that the new force was seen as a type of community policing, as a senior officer remarked in 1986 at the first passing-out parade. But they were also active in suppressing township unrest in the mid-1980s. Thus, operationally, the MLEOs were in an ambiguous position, for they fell partly under the direction of local African politicians (although their powers of control come from central government) and partly the SAP; they were absorbed into the SAP in 1989.

A more rapid development to improve police–public relations with Black South Africans was the acceleration in the formation of homeland police after 1976 as more homelands became self-governing, itself part of the government's response to the uprising in order to deal with the vexed question of African political rights (on the growth of defence forces in the homelands after 1976 see C. Cooper 1989). Homeland governments place considerable prestige on having their own police force and all independent homelands have established their own police, as have some of the non-independent ones. There are several reasons for this. Bantustan leaders recognize the localized power a police force affords them, enabling them to deal effectively with homeland-based unrest, whether against themselves or the central government. Homeland forces, therefore, tend to be heavily involved in public-order policing. Homeland police forces also act as a buffer between the borders and the main industrial and population centres, giving them an important role in counter-insurgency and monitoring the infiltration of guerrillas. In 1978 110 policemen from the Transkei and Venda forces underwent training by the SAP in counter-insurgency. They thus perform critical functions for the SAP,

TABLE 6.3 *The Transkei Police*

Year	Expenditure Rm.	% change	Manpower	% change	% equipment	% crime*	% government expenditure
1977/8	4.62	–	1,356	–	5.9	0.7	1.9
1978/9	7.12	54.1	1,497	10.3	7.2	0.6	2.1
1979/80	5.61	−21.2	1,930	28.9	9.1	0.7	2.2
1980/1	9.29	65.5	2,061	6.7	2.2	0.4	2.8
1981/2	–	–	–	–	–	–	–
1982/3	–	–	–	–	–	–	–
1983/4	17.94	93.1	2,268	10.0	5.9	0.3	2.8
1984/5	20.02	11.5	2,240	−1.2	5.9	0.2	2.5
1985/6	26.38	31.7	2,239	0	1.5	0.2	2.0
1986/7	33.39	26.5	5,357	139.2	8.3	0.1	3.3

* 'detection and investigation of crime'.
Source: Estimates of the Expenditure of the Transkei Revenue Fund.

TABLE 6.4 *The Lebowa Police*

Year	Expenditure Rm.	% increase	Manpower	% increase	% equipment	% government expenditure
1978/9	0.69	–	–	–	–	0.9
1979/80	1.27	84.0	268	–	–	1.4
1980/1	2.63	107.0	476	77.6	1.5	2.3
1981/2	3.82	45.2	533	11.9	4.4	2.4
1982/3	5.31	39.0	632	18.5	2.6	2.6
1983/4	7.0	31.8	697	10.2	4.2	2.6
1984/5	8.92	27.4	763	9.4	3.5	2.6
1985/6	9.46	6.0	823	7.8	1.9	2.1
1986/7	17.52	85.2	–	–	7.5	3.1
1987/8	29.04	65.7	1,179	43.2	7.1	3.3
1988/9	46.26	59.2	1,376	16.7	5.8	4.2

Source: Lebowa Legislative Assembly, Estimates of Revenue and Expenditure.

and the SAP has not relinquished control over these nominally separate forces. Senior members of the SAP are seconded to the homeland forces in leadership positions, and all homeland policemen are trained by the SAP at the African police training centre in Hammanskraal.

In 1976 the Transkei was the first homeland to be granted independence, and thus the first to form its own police force. Statistics on the Transkei Police are provided in Table 6.3.

The Transkei government spent heavily on policing, giving generous annual increases in both police expenditure and manpower, although the proportion of its total expenditure devoted to policing was roughly the same as the national figure for the SAP. Table 6.4 provides comparative figures for Lebowa, another independent homeland which has had its own police force since 1981. The commitment to policing is even greater in the latter case, where annual increases in expenditure exceed those of Transkei despite being a smaller force, which is reflected in the greater proportion of state expenditure spent on policing by the government in Lebowa. However, per capita expenditure per head of police was still lower in both than in the SAP. Reflecting the public-order and counter-insurgency roles of the homeland police, it is interesting to note the low (and declining) proportion of police expenditure on 'the detection and investigation of crime' in the Transkei, and the high proportion in both on 'arms, equipment, and ammunition'. The focus was also upon the internal threat; up to 1986–7, the Transkei government, which has its own defence force, spent more on policing than on the military. The Transkei also has a separate traffic police.

Between 1978–9 and 1982–3, the Bophuthatswana government increased its expenditure on policing by a factor of four, to total R1.24 million. Venda formed a 'National Force' upon independence, which merged policing, military duties, and control of the prison service. It was headed by Lt.-Col. Mulautzi, a former member of the SAP. Within the year it had formed its own counter-insurgency unit, and its budget rose by 88 per cent. In a show of strength by ANC guerrillas, insurgents attacked a police station in the capital of Venda, Sibasa, in the first year, killing two policemen. The role of homeland police in political policing is perhaps best exemplified by the Ciskei Police. In 1977 the Ciskei government formed its own Intelligence Service as a branch of BOSS, and with independence it formed the Central Ciskei Intelligence Service, with thirty men. Overall the Ciskei Police numbered 392 men in April 1980, with a further 400 in the Ciskei Defence Force. Major-General Sebe, brother of the then Chief Minister and a former member of BOSS, was the first chief of police. The Ciskei Police became notorious for their brutality in suppressing rural unrest, but all such forces have a tendency toward brutal treatment, as well as bureaucratic inefficiency and financial irregularity.

In 1984/5 the accounts of the Transkei government show that R100,000 was paid out in compensation to members of the public for their treatment at the hands of the police. The same sum was paid the following year. Between 1983 and 1985, the KwaZulu Police paid R38,500 in compensation. Two of the incidents involved R2,500 for attempted rape and theft of the victim's Bible, and R3,500 for assault on a prisoner who was dropped in a drain of human faeces and urine. Policemen involved in the incidents were dismissed from the force, but the Chief of the KwaZulu Police, Colonel Mathe, described the numbers dismissed as 'just a drop in the ocean'. In 1983 a child was given R25,000 after being shot in the neck during disturbances at school. Corruption was as common as brutality. The Report of the Sessional Committee on Public Accounts complained that the book-keeping of the Bophuthatswana Police was inadequate and irregular. The KwaZulu Legislative Assembly's Sessional Committee on the Accounts of the KwaZulu government complained about the activities of the Chief of the KwaZulu Police in 1983, alleging irregularities in stocktaking in the quartermaster's stores for the previous three years. He was dismissed the following year, and the new chief, Brigadier Laas, made an undertaking to stamp out irregularities within the force. He noted that eleven constables from the KwaZulu Police had been implicated in theft of property from prisoners and police stations, including station typewriters.

The KwaZulu Police acts as an exemplar of police forces in non-independent Bantustans. In the independent homelands, the Bantustan government pays for all policing out of its grant from the central government, but in non-independent homelands the central government continues to pay for the work of the SAP in the Bantustan, and the homeland authority for its own police force (if it has one) from its grant from the central government. In 1974/5, the central government spent R5.85 million on policing in KwaZulu, more than it spent on any other service save the Bantu Trust, but it was not until 1980 that Buthelezi set up KwaZulu's own police force. In 1983/4, the KwaZulu government spent R5.4 million on policing, representing 1 per cent of its total expenditure, but the South African government spent a further R20.62 million. In the same year, the central government gave R0.28 million from its funds to 'community development' in KwaZulu, thus spending nearly seventy-five times more on policing (Brewer 1988: 261).

Along with budgetary complications, police forces in non-independent homelands also have to work out jurisdiction with the SAP. To begin with, the KwaZulu Police was responsible for the rural areas and the

SAP for the urban townships near to Durban (Maré and Hamilton 1987: 215). In mid-1986, at the height of the township uprisings, Buthelezi pressed for the government to hand over responsibility for all police stations in KwaZulu, which it granted in 1987. Along with this came the power to issue firearm certificates, effectively allowing the KwaZulu government to arm Inkatha vigilantes, as will be discussed further below.

Within two years the KwaZulu Police formed a Reaction Unit of thirty-six men, who were fully trained in all aspects of counter-insurgency and riot control, with training provided by the SAP. The Annual Report of the Commissioner of the SAP for 1984 indicates that forty-one policemen from the KwaZulu Police underwent training in counter-insurgency that year, with another thirty-three from the police in Transkei, and thirty-eight from Ciskei. In its first year, the Reaction Unit of the KwaZulu Police overspent by R333,250, 94 per cent over budget. Other policemen in the KwaZulu Police were often untrained. Since the SAP concentrated on training its own police, places were not always available for policemen from the separate homeland forces. In 1983 the KwaZulu Legislative Assembly Sessional Committee on the Accounts of the KwaZulu government indicated that KwaZulu had a 'considerable number of untrained policemen', and that eventually it was intended to set up a training college for the KwaZulu Police. The lack of training reinforced the tendency towards corruption and brutality in the KwaZulu Police, and was worrisome given that members were issued with firearms. Eventually, Brigadier Laas introduced in-service training for KwaZulu policemen, although their interpenetration with Inkatha has led to little improvement in policing skills in the homeland.

The acceleration in independence for homelands after 1976 offers an illustration of how the SAP was affected by the government's reform process. Another example is its effects on apartheid in the SAP's organization and structure. In 1976 Black officers were allowed to wear the same uniform as White officers, and Black constables were given this dispensation in 1980; from then all members of the SAP wore blue. Blacks were allowed to join the SAP's Staff Association in 1979, and in 1981 Black officers were granted authority over lower-ranking White policemen. The first Black major was appointed in 1978 and the first lieutenant-colonel in 1980. Discrimination in pay, and housing and pension rights was eventually abolished in 1984, although racial bias in the command structure ensures the perpetuation

TABLE 6.5 *Command structure of the SAP by race, 1983*

Race	Rank				
	Major	Captain	Lieutenant	Warrant-officer	Sergeant
African	11	25	28	1,138	2,626
Coloured	1	8	13	246	505
Asian	2	4	14	247	330
White	470	741	1,085	5,337	4,685

Source: Brewer *et al.* 1988: 167.

of inequality in overall economic rewards within the SAP, as shown in Table 6.5. However, training is still racially segregated, and no Black chaplains have yet been appointed.

In shedding its own apartheid, the SAP acted as it did in the early period of Prime Minister Botha's reforms as a whole: slowly, begrudgingly, and hesitantly. Overall it used the velvet-gloved fist, a combination of repression and reform. The government and the SAP became concerned at the public image of the police after the negative publicity caused world-wide by the shootings in 1976–7 and Steve Biko's death, and began to present the SAP as a civil police force, underemphasizing its colonial style and methods. The new Commissioner in 1978, General Geldenhuys, although formerly connected with BOSS and long-time head of the SAP's special branch, announced, on taking office, that the fundamental concepts of his tenure would be 'discipline and courtesy'. To emphasize that the force had a service role in society, the SAP magazine changed its name in 1979 to *Servamus*, from the new motto for the force, *servamus et servimus* (we protect and we serve). The magazine also began to publish more material in English, to broaden its appeal among the public, although after a letter of complaint about this to the editor from the head of the women's police, Doveen Botha, an editorial explained that the magazine would revert to exclusive use of Afrikaans. The SAP also produced its own publicity film called *Intruder*, shown at commercial cinemas, which stressed the ordinary policing role of the force. In 1979 the SAP formed its first public relations branch, with the stated intention of ensuring that more 'objective' information was released to the public about the police.

In effect this was an attempt to control public information about the SAP, and needs to be understood in conjunction with new legislative limits placed on press comment on police activities, and the Minister's warning in 1980 that criticism of the SAP by any of its members would be regarded as an act of disloyalty to the force and a disciplinary offence. Under no circumstances were members to discuss complaints with the press (a similar restriction applies to members of the Royal Ulster Constabulary in Northern Ireland). It was also part of this process to limit the information made available about the force in the Commissioner's annual reports. Behind this attempt to control public information about the SAP lay the view that the poor image of the police was the result of exaggerated reporting by the press rather than misconduct by the police themselves. In the midst of the 1976 unrest, the Commissioner and the Chairman of the Press Union of South Africa negotiated an agreement to ensure more favourable reporting of the police. But in his 1978 Annual Report, the Commissioner still complained of untruths and half-truths about the police in the press (p. 1), although this was attributed primarily to the English-language press (Dippenaar 1988: 511–12). The Police Act was thus amended in 1979 to make it illegal to print any 'untrue matter' about the police, with the onus of proof being on the defendant to show grounds for believing its veracity: guilty until proved innocent.

The image-making extended to the introduction of community policing initiatives. The SAP formed a 'help-u' patrol car, known as the jolly patrol, painted yellow with rotating lights and a siren on the top. It patrolled the streets and could be stopped by any member of the public to give assistance, although they functioned only in Cape Town, Johannesburg, and Durban, thus engaging in image-making amongst Whites only. Trainee policemen were also released from college on Saturday mornings to undertake foot-patrol duty in shopping areas as an attempt to reduce the estrangement between the police and the White public. Crime-prevention schemes were also introduced to reinforce the image that the SAP was concerned with ordinary crime. In 1981 the SAP began public involvement in crime detection through a television programme. By 1982 every police division had a full-time crime-prevention officer, and one and a half million crime-prevention leaflets had been distributed to members of the public. However, ostensibly under the guise of 'crime prevention', the police and the army would also cordon off African townships and undertake massive searches for political opponents.

The crime statistics bear out the impression that in the immediate wake of the 1976 uprisings, the SAP devoted more effort to public-order and unrest-related offences than to ordinary crime. The statistics provided in the Annual Reports of the Commissioner of the SAP distinguish between 'offences', being the more serious cases, and 'law infringements', for minor and petty crimes. Between 1975 and 1977, the number of 'offences' dealt with by the police increased by 6.4 per cent and 'law infringements' fell by 25.9 per cent. With 1976 as the base year of 100, public-order offences rose to 562.3 in 1977, and offences against the 'security of the state and good order' rose to 133.9, whereas ordinary crimes fell in 1977, such that drunkenness was 89.7, common assault 82.2, and rape 97.1. Even the administrative regulations which controlled the boundaries between the races were relatively underscored with the emphasis on more serious offences, so that contravention of curfew regulations fell to 64.4, pass law infringements 81.2, possession of kaffir beer 84.2, and offences under the Urban Areas Act to 72. By 1979, however, with the public-order situation more under control, the police began to focus once again on the administrative regulations which monitored race relations. Thus, with 1976 as the base year of 100, curfew regulations had risen to 91.9, pass law infringements to 110.4, possession of kaffir beer to 110, and offences under the Urban Areas Act to 116.2.

Therefore, whilst the SAP was busily constructing a public image as a civil police force, dedicated to service to the community and crime detection and prevention, their efforts, as reflected in the crime statistics, seemed to be directed more to the containment of political opposition. Another good measure of this is the resources of the forensic investigators. In the course of his investigation into the 1992 Boipatong massacre, Waddington discovered that there were only ten forensic specialists in the Vaal Triangle, an area encompassing eighteen police districts (1992: 40). Their normal daily work-load consisted of between thirty and forty cases, plus the demands of frequent court cases, which resulted in only the most superficial investigation by scene-of-crime officers. But to reinforce the public image of a force devoted to investigating ordinary crime, the Commissioner complained about the extraneous duties imposed on the SAP by the state, urging that the force be allowed to concentrate on 'normal' police duties. This complaint came after a long period of silence on the issue, and in 1977 there was a drop in the number of man-hours given to these duties, but only by 3.1 per cent, to total over one and a half million hours (Annual Report of the Commissioner of the SAP 1977: 5). Yet while the SAP kept its role in policing Black opposition, the image as a civil police force always stood to be undercut by the deleterious consequences arising from the latest atrocity, which required that the police continually massage their tattered image. The death in detention of Neil Aggett in February 1982 serves as a good example (on which see Foster and Luyt 1986).

After Biko's death, the new Commissioner issued rules regarding the treatment of detainees. These included instructions about medical treatment, nutritional requirements, and sleeping and exercise facilities. Three years later, in March 1982, the Detainees' Parents Support Committee approached fifty foreign medical associations to ask for support for a campaign to force the government to allow independent doctors to examine political detainees. In April the Committee sent a memorandum to the Minister of Law and Order alleging that detainees were being tortured. It presented statements from seventy detainees and ex-detainees claiming that systematic and widespread torture was being used by the police. The claims included 20 cases of sleep deprivation, 22 cases of electric shock, 11 cases of mid-air suspension, 25 cases of suffocation, 28 cases of enforced standing for long periods, 54 cases of physical attack, 14 cases of attacks on the genitals, and 25 cases of being kept naked for long periods. All this was revealed at the time of the inquest into Aggett's death. Aggett had alleged assault and torture during interrogation, and on three occasions magistrates were denied access to see him because the police were 'too busy'. It appeared that Dr Aggett underwent a sixty-hour interrogation session, and witnesses reported that the police abused and beat him, and used electric shock on his testicles. The interrogators claimed that they were not aware of the rights of detainees nor that prisoners were not to be subject to 'intensive interrogation'. Their claim was that Aggett hung himself in remorse at implicating two friends. The magistrate believed this version of events.

There was widespread condemnation at the verdict, and the 1982 Rabie Commission into security legislation recommended that magistrates and doctors should have regular access to detainees. Within five months another detainee died in police custody. The liberal Afrikaans-language press criticized the actions of the security police and pointed to the disastrous effects such incidents had on the image of the police, government, and South Africa abroad. This prompted the Minister to announce a new code of conduct for the humane treatment of detainees, similar to that adopted by the British government in Northern Ireland. Responsibility for guarding detainees was moved from the SB to uniformed officers, and the code clearly stated that non-compliance would result in both criminal and disciplinary charges. The code is laudable in its sentiments: 'a detainee shall at all times be treated in a humane manner with proper regard of the rules of decency and shall not in any way be assaulted or otherwise ill-treated or subjected to any form of torture or degrading treatment.' It became a disciplinary offence for interrogators to torture or mistreat detainees.

But, typical of the SAP's velvet-fist approach to police reform, the system of control and monitoring remained weak. Regular visits were to be made by state medical and judicial officials, and no procedure was specified by which detainees could make complaints. Visits from detainees' personal doctor were forbidden. Investigations of mistreatment were not to be independent but carried out by an officer from another branch. The chief advance in this code was that it prevented police officers pleading ignorance of the rules governing interrogation. The main caveat was that the code's force was suspended and officers given indemnity from prosecution when a state of emergency was promulgated. During 1984, 530 people were detained under the terms of the security legislation, and in February 1985 the Minister announced that 1,611 visits had been made to detainees during 1984 by inspectors and 1,833 by magistrates. Only forty-nine complaints of ill-treatment were received. However, during the state of emergency in 1985, the number of detainees rose to over 7,000 and the legal indemnity granted the police led to widespread allegations of mistreatment of detainees.

Thus, the problem was not the absence of rules governing police conduct, but the opportunity afforded officers to disregard them, enabling repression at the hands of the police to continue alongside any reform of police conduct. Further police powers were granted to strengthen the repressive role. Section 49(2) of the 1977 Criminal Procedures Act allowed the SAP (and others, including mines police and private security guards) to use such force 'as may in the circumstances be necessary' to overcome or stop a fleeing person. The killing of a person who could not be arrested or stopped in flight by other means was deemed to be justifiable homicide. In 1984 98 people were killed in terms of this provision. In 1978 the Commissioner stated that he was prepared to call for further change in legislation in order for the SAP to take better counter-measures against public disorder in urban areas (Annual Report of the Commissioner of the SAP 1978:

1), and the SAP was granted further powers in the 1979 Amendment to the Police Act. The Amendment gave policemen and women the right to conduct searches without warrant and seize materials at any point within ten kilometres of the Republic's borders, and gave the State President the power to place the police 'under the orders and directions as the State President may for that purpose appoint'. Grundy took this to mean the SADF and cites it as evidence of the further militarization of the SAP (1983a: 140–1). The 1982 Internal Security Act gave officers in the SAP of the rank of lieutenant-colonel or above the power to order preventive detention, detention of witnesses, and for interrogation. Under the 1977 Criminal Procedures Act the SAP had the power of short-term detention, being able to arrest and detain 'in specific situations of unrest', without good cause being shown, for a period of forty-eight hours.

But strengthening police powers was only part of the SAP's velvet-fist approach under Botha's premiership. The SAP became dominated by the security police. Both Commissioners appointed in 1978 and 1983 were linked with BOSS and former heads of the SB, and the senior officer involved in the Biko death was promoted to head the SB. As we saw in the last chapter, Botha also successfully restored the predominance of the SB over BOSS in security matters. All this was a gesture of support by the government for the activities of the security police, and was considered necessary because of the guerrilla insurgency that began to take place after 1976, feeding the mania about security.

In August 1979 the police issued statistics on the quantities of arms seized during the previous year, which included 61 assault rifles, 21 sub-machine-guns, 3 machine-guns, 14 hand-carbines, 29 machine pistols, 32 automatic pistols, two rocket-propelled grenade-launchers, 304 grenades, 31,805 bullets, 235 kg. of explosives, and numerous associated detonators, primers, cord, and safety fuses. The police success in this respect did not prevent armed attacks by the ANC (on this see Barrell 1990: 30–52; Brewer 1986: 130–8). Insurgents attacked their first police station inside South Africa in 1977, and three more followed in 1979 and 1980. In one instance, the insurgents were assisted by a former policeman who, under instruction from the ANC, had infiltrated the SAP (S. Davies 1987: 140). A chronology of guerrilla activity, compiled in 1981, records 112 attacks between October 1976 and May 1981 (quoted in Brewer 1986: 134), and statistics compiled by the Centre for Intergroup Studies at the

University of Cape Town showed that between 1977 and September 1983, the ANC had undertaken 210 instances of political violence, killed 52 people, and injured 286 (quoted in Brewer 1986: 134). Some of these incidents were high-profile explosions and bomb attacks on oil depots, banks, shopping centres, and offices, reflecting an intensification of the ANC's confidence, planning, and daring. Barrell notes a further escalation, in that in 1983 the ANC took the decision that the avoidance of civilian casualties should no longer be allowed to constrain guerrilla activities (1990: 60); and in that year car bombs exploded in the city centres of Port Elizabeth, Pretoria, and Durban. In that year the SAP formed special guard units to protect dignatories and key sites from guerrilla attack. In 1988 the ANC mounted its largest number of actions to date, with 281 being reported (Barrell 1990: 66), although security force success in capturing guerrillas fell from the previous year.

As S. Davies explains in his analysis of the ANC (1987: 139, 175), the police had great difficulty in identifying ANC insurgents and the new, mostly young, activists. Their informer network broke down as the ANC assassinated those suspected of infiltrating the organization and informers feared reprisals from the ANC. The police came increasingly to rely on information obtained from detainees under interrogation (p. 84). This explains the state's reliance on the SB, the ambivalence of the security police to the rights of detainees, and the complicity of the state in endorsing the SB's breach of them: reform of police practice was not to obstruct the SAP's colonial-like task of maintaining White minority rule.

POLICING UNDER BOTHA'S REFORMS

The concepts through which reform was understood in the Botha era were 'total onslaught' and 'total strategy' (the writing on this is legion; for examples see: Frankel 1981, 1984; Grundy 1983*b*; Hansson 1990; Swilling and Philips 1989). The communist-inspired onslaught against the country, shown in nation-wide political unrest, guerrilla insurgency, and industrial strikes, necessitated a national strategy of counter-revolution. There were two features to this: repression and reform. The reforms comprised carefully constructed changes to policies on the homelands, urbanization, trades unions and labour, regional development, and, above all, the constitution. It became popular in the literature to describe the reform component as a strategy 'winning hearts and minds' along the lines of American counter-insurgency theory (Hansson 1990; Spence 1988; Swilling and Philips 1989). However, the state made it absolutely clear that reform could proceed, and accelerate, only once law and order was restored (Hansson 1990: 30). Thus from the state's point of view, the security forces were critical. On the one hand they were the bulwark protecting South Africa from the onslaught, and their success in repressing these evil forces, often by crude and brutal violence, facilitated and widened the process of reform. However, from a more objective stance, the security forces essentially provided a bulwark for the maintenance of White minority rule, since the Botha reforms were solely intended to co-opt sections of the Black population and accommodate them to their subjugation. As Selfe aptly puts it, Botha's reforms were a judicious mix of security action and socio-economic uplift, raising the costs of challenging the state whilst simultaneously enhancing the benefits of co-operating with it (1989: 155).

The consequence of the importance of the security forces to the state was that they were drawn increasingly into a direct political role inside the state apparatus, something unknown before in such an obvious manner. There was no change in police–state relations, but the police's functional importance to the state's agenda now saw them, and other security forces, being accorded a direct political role. This degree of penetration of civil administration by the security forces needs to be distinguished from previous periods when politics was militarized because of the centralization of government under P. W. Botha, giving police and military personnel direct access to enormous power (Moorcraft 1990: 409), although others argue that there is a continuity with the Boer tradition of politician generals (Seegars 1986). This access was accorded by means of the state security council (SSC) and the system of joint management committees (JMCs) (on which see, for example, Boraine 1989; Hansson 1990; Seegars 1991; Selfe 1989; Spence 1988). Decision-making in this structure was centralized around a managerial committee system which co-opted, among others, top military and security personnel, including the SAP. At the centre was the SSC. It was supposed to oversee security matters and to this end the heads of the SADF, SAP, National Intelligence Service, Prisons Service, and 'other military and police personnel' sat on the committee. A variety of government ministers were co-opted, illustrating the ministries which were felt to touch security matters. These included the ministers of Law and Order, Defence, Foreign Affairs, Justice, Constitutional Development and Planning, and Co-operation and Development, the latter two dealing with urban Black affairs. The SSC was serviced by a secretariat, which was also dominated by military and police personnel. In March 1986 there were thirteen interdepartmental working committees to assist the SSC, consisting mostly of politicians, civil servants, and representatives of the military and security forces.

The SSC became one of the major decision-making forums within the Botha government, with some commentators claiming it to be more important than the cabinet. It increasingly involved itself in a wide spectrum of issues beyond security, including foreign policy, economic matters, and constitutional change (Grundy 1983*b*: 14). The inter-departmental committees gave advice to the SSC on such questions as security force manpower, cultural matters, civil defence, transport, national supplies and resources, telecommunications, community services, the economy, and political affairs. Allegations were made that the SSC involved itself in specific political issues, ranging from particular industrial disputes to land redistribution between KwaZulu and Swaziland. The states of emergency were said to have been imposed on the recommendation of the committee against the advice of some leading members of the cabinet. Therefore, inasmuch as the SSC had a decision-making role and the SAP had membership of the committee, the SAP had a direct input into decision-making. In this context it is significant that upon retiring as Commissioner of the SAP in 1987, General Coetzee was given a post in the Department of Foreign Affairs, to oversee difficulties in relations between Transkei and Ciskei.

Another component of the 'security establishment', as Grundy called it (1983*b*, 1988), was the system of JMCs to co-ordinate security at local and regional levels. They also assumed a political role, giving the local representatives of the military and police who sat on them an input into community politics (on the Mamelodi JMC see Boraine 1989). These committees worked under the overall direction of the SSC, which also funded them. By March 1986 the SSC had established twelve JMCs covering the large conurbations, another sixty working in smaller towns, and a further number operating at the level of local authorities. The names of 348 of these were listed in the South African press in October 1986. They had no executive power, but were primarily deployed to ensure the co-ordination of government security at local and regional levels, and to act as an early warning system to identify areas of unrest. They reported on these matters to the secretariat of the SSC. Membership comprised local representatives of the military and SAP, as well as civil servants and members of the business community. Each JMC had its own chairperson, which in every case happened to be a member of the SAP or SADF, but little else was publicly revealed, so that it is difficult to identify membership or assess the relative weighting of the police and army on the committee.

They were especially involved in overseeing the co-operation of the SADF and police in instances of joint action. In the post-1983 unrest, the SADF became heavily involved in policing the townships. The 1957 Defence Act was even amended to enshrine the SADF's role in civil unrest, giving it conventional policing duties of promoting internal security, maintaining law and order, and preventing crime. The SADF had the same powers under the state of emergency as the civil police, including indemnity. To accomplish these duties, army personnel were given 'between three and four days training' in patrolling townships, covering riot-control techniques, road-blocks, vehicle and foot patrol, 'immediate action drill', and searches. Co-operation between the SADF and SAP was departmentally institutionalized in 1985 when the Deputy Minister of Defence also became the deputy in the ministry of Law and Order, subsequently going on to become Minister. Although the army and police maintained their separate command structures while on joint operations, security policy itself was co-ordinated by the JMCs. But some JMCs took political decisions regarding local unrest, such as the decision by the Cape Town JMC to initiate a strategy to counter the influence of a residents' association in the Atlantis township. In August 1986 the press in South Africa published a document which showed that the JMC in Johannesburg had decided to break the service charge boycott in the townships of the Vaal Triangle. Their plans included the formation of local 'collective action groups', composed of police and government officials, which would enforce the collection of rents and the eviction of non-paying tenants. It was also seeking employers who would be prepared to deduct service charges directly from the wages of employees, an idea subsequently withdrawn by the government and then reintroduced. The JMC also took the decision to institute a system of weekend camps in an attempt to win 'the hearts and minds' of the young and to recruit them to persuade their parents to abandon the boycott. Documents were leaked to the press which also showed that some local JMCs had instructed Black township authorities not to negotiate an end to the boycott with 'radical organizations'. As a result of actions like this the SAP, through its membership of the JMCs, had an input into political decision-making at the community level.

Under old-style apartheid, policing was coercive and repressive. The SAP undermined Black political resistance to White minority rule, and strictly policed boundaries between the races, ensuring that Blacks were kept in their proper social, political, and economic place. The state's reliance on the police to effect this internal colonialism was complete, making the SAP the medium through which apartheid was experienced. Under Botha's reforms, however, policing became wrapped up with the state's attempt to accommodate as well as suppress Black demands (on the SAP's role in Botha's reformist politics see Brewer 1988: 264–74; also see Shearing 1986). The state's reliance on the police was as total as before, but now in order to achieve limited reforms as well as to maintain repression. The police became passive actors in implementing or upholding the government's accommodative measures, as when protecting African local government and Black parliamentary candidates, or enforcing some of the deracialization policies, such as tearing down notices unlawfully imposing segregated facilities and policing multiracial facilities and events. The police were also more proactive in the reform process in that they were used by the state as a means to achieve accommodation through such measures as police reform of the treatment of detainees, the development of more legitimate forces in the urban areas and homelands, and the abolition of apartheid in the organization and structure of the force.

The policing of apartheid under Botha thus involved the SAP supporting the state's limited reforms and repressing more radical activities and movements, with its own reform being used as an exemplar of reform within apartheid generally. Botha extended the Black-on-Black policing strategy, co-opted Black officers into senior positions, deracialized the SAP, and instituted some controls on police conduct. But police reform was inhibited by the limitations of Botha's reform process generally. Botha's reform of apartheid did not extend to dismantling White control of politics, and where this was threatened by popular unrest, repression by the police was intense, widespread, and violent. The necessity in the reform period for the police to be seen as accountable and under political control, and thus to have themselves been changed by the reform process, was less important in the final analysis than the maintenance of White political domination. This is illustrated by the policing of township unrest from 1984, when Black protest escalated dramatically under dissatisfaction with Botha's cautious and limited approach to political reform. Old-style policing was without abandon, and it was the sustained barbarity and brutality of it which led in part to the fall of Botha and the prospect of more genuine police reform.

RENEWED TOWNSHIP UPRISINGS AND THE STATES
OF EMERGENCY

By 1983 Black politics had strengthened significantly from 1976 by becoming organizationally sophisticated, integrated with the guerrilla campaign and industrial protests by the unions, and willing and able to take to the streets in massive collective action. Botha's reforms themselves afforded political space to organizations like the United Democratic Front (UDF) and the Black trade unions to agitate and protest, as well as providing much to protest against, such as the new constitution which excluded Africans, the service charge increases imposed on residents as part of the upgrading of the townships, the lack of legitimacy of the new community councils, and independence for more homelands. The escalation in protest was matched with an upward spiral in police brutality.

During 1984, for example, collective protests against rent and service charge increases spread. In August, rioting broke out in Tumahole, near Parys. Police used whips and tear-gas to halt the disturbances. Protests in Sharpeville led to fourteen deaths. The introduction of the new constitution and service charge increases in the townships was an explosive mix. On 4 September, the day the State President was elected under the new constitution, twenty-nine deaths occurred and 300 injuries. In October, the police and army undertook a joint manœuvre to seal off the townships of Sharpeville, Sebokeng, and Boipatong, detaining 350 people. The liberal press thought the intervention of the military in a civil incident unprecedented, but their memories were short. In the first thirty years of the Union, the army was called out four times to support the police. In the more recent past, they had been used in 1960 and 1976 (see Prior 1989: 199).

Other critics of the police, who alleged in 1984 that the police were responsible for atrocities, were threatened with legal action under the Police Act for revealing publicly information about the police (see Southern African Catholic Bishops' Conference 1984 for some of the allegations). Charges against two churchmen, Allan Boesak and Archbishop Hurley, were eventually dropped.

To illustrate just how little police tactics had developed under Botha's reforms, the march in Sharpeville to commemorate the twenty-fifth anniversary of the 1960 shootings was fired upon without warning by the police, leaving forty people dead. It was significant, President Reagan said when discussing the deaths at a press conference, that Black policemen had been involved and had done the firing; so at least some things had changed, but the end result was the same. In one year between September 1984 and October 1985, police killed 514 people and imprisoned 4,806 (Brewer *et al.* 1988: 180). Funerals of the dead became politicized and highly-charged events, often resulting in more deaths. One funeral in Uitenhage in March 1985 ended in nineteen deaths as a result of police action, although the Kannemeyer Report into the deaths exonerated the police, making only mildly critical remarks about their manner towards the mourners. In these ways the police demonstrated that they had learned very little from 1976, for collective protest was only intensified by vigorous police action.

The government responded by imposing a state of emergency. The regulations promulgated a number of new offences punishable by a prison sentence of up to ten years. They included such innocuous acts as: verbally threatening harm to another person; preparing, printing, publishing, or possessing a threatening document; hindering officers in the course of their duty; destroying or defacing any notice of the emergency regulations; disclosing the name or identity of anybody arrested under the regulations before their name had been officially confirmed; causing fear, panic, and alarm or weakening public confidence; and advising people to stay away from work or to dislocate industry. While in detention people were forbidden to sing and whistle, make unnecessary noise, cause unnecessary trouble, or be a nuisance. Anybody committing these offences could be placed in solitary confinement, deprived of meals, and given six strokes if they were under 14 years of age.

What is more, in the state of emergency the police were given further repressive powers. Under the regulations any police officer, soldier, or prison officer of any rank could arrest and detain without warrant. In the first state of emergency during 1985 such detentions were restricted to fourteen days, unless extended further by the Minister of Law and Order, but this was lengthened to 180 days in the second state of emergency. Police officers could use force 'resulting in death' if people refused to heed instructions given in 'a loud voice'. The Commissioner of the SAP had the power to ban gatherings, close premises, control traffic, essential services, and the dissemination and reporting of information, to seal off areas, and remove people from particular places, and impose curfews. Were this not enough, the regulations allowed the Commissioner command over 'any other matter which, in the Commissioner's opinion, affects the safety of members of the public or the maintenance of law and order'. These orders gave the police powers to control every facet of resistance and organizational activity, even down to the issuing of statements and the placing of newspaper advertisements. All gatherings came within the terms of the regulations, irrespective of their nature, venue, or purpose. During the second state of emergency, when the courts agreed that divisional police commissioners had unlawfully given themselves the same powers, the government redrew and backdated the regulations to extend the definition of 'Commissioner of the SAP' to include divisional commissioners, even those deployed in independent homelands (for a study of the operation of emergency powers see Ellmann 1992).

The state of emergency also suspended the few controls on police conduct provided by the Internal Security Act and the 1960 Children's Act, which protects the rights of children under 16 years of age. This latter suspension was important because 22 per cent of the 18,966 people detained for 'unrest offences' in 1985 were under 16 years of age (72 per cent were under 21 years of age and hence were juveniles in terms of the 1959 Prisons Act). There was widespread mistreatment and torture of minors. The public could initiate a complaints procedure against the security forces, but an increasing number of security personnel patrolled the townships without identification tags. In response to a parliamentary question, the Minister of Law and Order estimated this to be 20 per cent of all security force personnel in March 1986. But after a lengthy departmental inquiry he claimed it to be simply the result of the failure of suppliers to provide enough identification tags. This was after a judge had described those who patrolled in this way as inept, ham-fisted, and threatening. Moreover, the state of emergency gave all members of the police force, security force, and prison service indemnity from civil and criminal prosecutions, so long as they 'acted in good faith'. They were deemed to be acting so when under the 'orders, direction, command and instructions' of superior officers. The SAP had a reputation for violence and brutality even without indemnity. For example, between 1976 and 1985 the SAP alone killed or wounded 9,771 people in the course of their duty and paid compensation of R8.25m. for assault, wrongful arrest, and injury (Brewer 1986: 119, 122). But along with indemnity came an increase in the number of deaths and injuries: 32 per cent of the deaths and woundings in this nine-year period occurred in 1985, when the first state of emergency operated for part of the year. The first month of the 1985 state of emergency saw a death-toll double that of the month before, most of the increase in which was the result of action by the security forces; the SAIRR estimated that 50 per cent of the 879 deaths due to unrest in 1985 were the responsibility of the security forces. However, figures vary. Hansson, for example, argues that the police killed 763 people in 1985 alone (1989: 119). By 1987 the rate of fatal shootings by the SAP was double that of police in the United States (for other comparative figures on deaths by police action see Foster and Luyt 1986: 304), and the average age of victims was only 22 years; 23 per cent were under 18 years of age and thus legally children (Hansson 1989: 125). In an

TABLE 6.6 *Percentage of wastage due to dismissals, 1976–1988*

Year	White	Black
1976	1.0	20.3
1977	–	–
1978	1.4	10.8
1979	1.4	23.2
1980	–	–
1981	–	–
1982	–	–
1983	2.2	16.7
1984	2.4	17.8
1985	3.4	23.3
1986	1.5	15.6
1987	8.9	
1988	6.2	

Source: Annual Reports of the Commissioner of the SAP.

excellent account of the law governing police rights to use force in this way, Nicolas Haysom refers to the SAP as having, in effect, a licence to kill (1987). Yet despite this misconduct, the proportion of wastage due to dismissals fell, save for 1985 itself, as shown in Table 6.6.

There was a second feature to the states of emergency besides the increase in police powers and brutality: namely, an expansion in the state's policing capacity. The army was given a policing role, and Black forces grew considerably. In 1985, for example, 35,372 troops were being deployed in 96 African townships, rising to 40,000 in 1986 (Prior 1989: 199). By 1987 they had largely succeeded in their efforts in quelling unrest and began to play a less prominent role (see Nathan 1989: 67; also Sandler 1989). In part this was because the expansion in the police force in 1986 allowed the police to reassume position in the front line of attack, regaining some of the initiative from the SADF. However, the primary responsibility in the African townships was given over to Black forces. The SAP's 'own areas' strategy was proceeding very slowly. By the end of 1984, only seventy-three stations were controlled by Blacks, less than one in ten. This was in great part because the SAP could change its attitudes about the negative qualities of Black policemen slower than the state needed. Hence, separate forces were created. In this respect the MLEOs became important in public order policing rather than any community service role. Known colloquially as 'greenflies', 'greenbeans', and 'blackjacks' because of their green and khaki uniforms, there were 9,000 deployed in December 1987 according to the *Weekly Mail*. They were armed with shotguns and side arms and trained for three months. In October 1989 they were incorporated into the SAP, although retaining a separate uniform.

Recruitment to the force was not a problem despite the pejorative publicity (unlike that of the SAP which was affected by political circumstances in the urban areas) because the authorities tended to recruit MLEOs from the rural areas, where police action was less overt, job prospects more bleak, and conservative political attitudes more prevalent (Prior 1989: 195; cf. Frankel 1980: 490–1, who says that this emphasis on rural recruitment is true of the SAP as well). The Development Boards which helped to run townships, sponsored advertisements in newspapers seeking recruits, asking for people between the ages of 18 and 35 years, with Standard 6 education, and who were physically fit. Some members later talked to the press during a strike and indicated their motivations to join. Sanuse Mathanda came from the Transkei to Soweto in search of work. After several weeks he joined the municipal police; as an inducement, the job came with residence rights, and a good salary, as well as medical insurance and other insurance policies. Quoted in the *New Nation* on 6 November 1986 he said: 'I can't resign from this job as my family back home would starve.' Another from Venda said that 'hunger and unemployment compelled me to join'.

Within weeks, MLEOs developed a reputation in the press for being 'trigger happy', as the *City Press* commented on 28 September 1986. Some of the incidents are barbaric in the extreme. The *Sunday Tribune* carried a report on 22 June 1986 that MLEOs in Lekoa had tortured two schoolboys, sprinkled their hands and feet with petrol, and set them alight. Twenty-six people were shot dead in Soweto on 26 August 1986 by MLEOs for resisting eviction. In Katlehong on 9 April 1987, a member shot and injured a 13-year-old boy after becoming annoyed at the boy cheering too loudly at an athletics match; civil damages of R25,000 were paid. A young African girl was sexually assaulted in Ibhang, having to perform obscene acts with her boyfriend and have objects forced into her vagina. In Gompo, the MLEOs had thirty-three charges of violence laid against them by 4 August 1987, one of which included assaulting a 7-year-old boy. Part of the problem was that MLEOs were not under the direct supervision of trained policemen from the SAP; indeed, one member of Soweto's municipal force said that the attraction of the job was being able to work without White supervision (quoted in *New Nation*, 6 Nov. 1986). Where there was supervision, young, inexperienced Afrikaners tended to be employed by the council for the purpose or transferred from the SAP. In the sexual assault case in Ibhang, it transpired that the sergeant was a young Afrikaner of 21 years; another was only 20, with Standard 8 education and no previous police training, who had immediately been given the rank of sergeant.

The brutality of MLEOs made them subject to considerable hostility from township residents, and many were murdered, burned out of their homes, and their families attacked. In the first four months of 1986, ten policemen were killed, the homes of fifty-one burned, and there were fifty-three arson attacks on the cars of policemen (Dippenaar 1988: 779). The authorities took to housing them in barracks at police stations behind high fences and barbed wire. As one member in Tembisa remarked: 'I don't like the job because people hate and despise us. They regard us as their enemies. In fact we live as outcasts. I spend much of my time at the barracks behind the high wall—looking through it as guys of my age stroll with their ladies, freely and without fear' (*New Nation*, 6 Nov. 1986). Many thus complained of having being misled into joining, and not having been informed by the authorities as to what the job entailed. There was also disappointment that other promises were not met. As one member from Dobsonville in Soweto said, the authorities 'failed to give us the gold and glittering life promised during recruitment. It is a year since I was employed and I have heard promise and promise of more money which they haven't kept' (ibid.).

It was such dissatisfaction that led some members to go on strike in 1986, the first police strike in South Africa since 1918. Members in Kasigo went on strike for higher wages in November 1986, 115 were detained under emergency regulations for striking in Katlehong, and in December 1987 municipal police mutinied in Lekoa, attempting to kill their White commanding officer, resulting in a shoot-out with the local riot police. Critics understandably described the police as in crisis (Cato 1989). Ironically, many members of this repressive force took the opportunity to exploit the strategic space allowed by Botha's reforms to join the South African Black Municipal and Allied Workers Union, and became involved in the union's campaign for higher wages and better conditions for all municipal workers. The union secretary said that MLEOs had been recruited from the ranks of the starving and were being controlled by their stomachs: a mix which led them to engage in industrial action when left hungry. Some councils conceded their demands, others dismissed the strikers.

An additional complaint was that most councils paid the municipal police less than the state paid the 'special constables' recruited in 1986 as a further separate Black police force. Known as kitskonstabels (instant constables) because they received three weeks of training at most, this force proved more ruthless than MLEOs (for studies of kitskonstabels see D. Fine 1989; D. Fine and Hansson 1990; Institute of Criminology 1990). *Servamus* described the force as a new idea, but it built upon the civic guard tradition; the only difference being that it was exclusively African. Africans had volunteered before for various reserve police forces and vigilante groups, and the kitskonstabels extended this. Most recruits were rural Africans, employed in other parts of the state bureaucracy, or members of township vigilante groups, and were thus primarily conservative, although Heribert Adams, in a personal communication to the author, claimed that some came from the ranks of the radical youths known as the 'comrades'. Dippenaar writes that entry requirements were strict (1988: 788), although the authorities were desperate enough to take as many as they could; often by deceit and subterfuge. The authorities undertook recruitment tours in the homelands and roamed the streets of the townships with loud hailers urging youths to enlist. Large sums were offered, often falsely representing pay, which led to a similar disillusionment as experienced by the MLEOs, and a strike. Some later said they had been duped into joining, being given the impression that they were to engage in 'security work' for private companies rather than riot policing (see *Grassroots*, Oct. 1986). According to the *Cape Times* on 3 February 1987, some were misled into signing ten-year contracts which prevented them from resigning. By June 1987 2,250 kitskonstabels had been trained. At the time of their incorporation into the SAP in 1989, 5,167 had undergone training.

The popular explanation for the emergence of the kitskonstabels is that it facilitated Black-on-Black policing (see D. Fine 1989: 45), thus undercutting some of the bad publicity caused by White policemen killing Black youths, and perpetuating the old apartheid idea of divide and rule. In fact manpower shortage in the SAP was also a factor. Another factor in the emergence of kitskonstabels was the SAP's realization that it had lost the battle in the townships and that a more legitimate force was needed. Indeed, the initial image was that kitskonstabels were to provide community policing in the townships; an extension of the 'own areas' policing strategy. On 22 September 1986, the day after the announcement for the new force, the Minister of Law and Order said they would be deployed on foot to walk the beat in the townships to act as a link between the police and public in order to stimulate trust. If this were so, the SAP was handing over the most difficult of policing jobs in South Africa to the least trained and professional force; and it quickly showed. In fact, they were under the operational command of the SAP's riot squads, and the head was General Wandrag, commanding officer of the SAP's counter-insurgency unit. At the first passing-out parade of trained kitskonstabels, held in front of Wandrag, members paraded and baton-charged through smoke. The Minister was still referring to them in parliament as 'bobbies on the beat' in 1088, after two years of sustained brutality against township residents. However, the powers given to kitskonstabels far exceeded those needed by community policemen, and these powers made it clear that members were always intended to perform public-order policing.

Kitskonstabels were employed by the SAP rather than community councils, and thus appointed under the Police Act, having the same functions as the SAP: the preservation of internal security; the maintenance of law and order; and the investigation and prevention of crime. In terms of the state of emergency, kitskonstabels were defined as members of the security forces, and thus given the sweeping powers (and indemnity) of the security forces (see D. Fine 1989: 50–1), unlike MLEOs. Given the low educational standard of those recruited and general lack of literacy, training was not academic. Training covered riot control, weapons training, and aspects of crime prevention (D. Fine 1989: 55). Subsequent misconduct showed kitskonstabels to handle weapons dangerously, on and off-duty. One shot and killed his wife in a personal dispute; another flashed his gun when refused a free ride by a driver; one went berserk outside a New Brighton police station, firing at fellow kitskonstabels, the SADF, and MLEOs, eventually shooting two policemen before turning the gun on himself; two kitskonstabels killed five fellow guests at a drinking party in Katlehong; and several were shot by other kitskonstabels in fights. However, the brutality vented on each other was nothing to that vented on township residents.

The first shooting of members of the public occurred within a month of kitskonstabels being deployed on the streets. On 19 September 1987 the *Cape Times* reported that kitskonstabels had been implicated in twelve murders, and ninety-five other crimes; 607 had been disciplined in the Transvaal and twenty-five in the Cape for negligent duty and overstepping their authority. The supervision by members of the SAP that was supposed to operate broke down; circumstances made it impossible to operate. As a warrant-officer from Pretoria explained in court after two kitskonstabels were accused of assaulting residents in Hofmeyr, members were deployed in distant African townships and he could not be expected to watch over them twenty-four hours a day (*Sunday Tribune*, 15 Nov. 1987). As for the community they were supposed to win the trust of, they were subject to ostracism and rejection. Kitskonstabels were murdered, bombed out of their homes, and horrifically killed by means of the necklace (a burning tyre around the neck). A survey by D. Fine and Hansson shows almost universal contempt for them (1990). Wives often pleaded in the press for their husbands to resign or they would divorce (a tactic imposed on them by the township radicals in order to earn their own immunity); many kitskonstabels responded in the press by saying that they were forced to join by hunger—the dilemma of all native police in colonial societies.

Another way in which the state expanded its policing capacity to cope with the unrest was to employ vigilante groups as surrogates, who had even less hesitation in using brutal tactics to suppress political opposition. The role of the vigilantes has been well documented (Brewer 1988; Haysom 1980, 1989*b*, 1990; Plasket 1989), and while they appeared to critics to be a new feature in police strategy, as indeed they were to the extent of their involvement in policing, vigilante groups were not entirely novel. Communities themselves formed vigilante groups in the 1950s to counteract township gangs, and they were also associated with rival political organizations at this time and used to attack one another. The SAP's main connection was with the conservative vigilantes in the *maghotla*, although this was sometimes uneasy as a result of the latter's extreme methods. More recently, the police used Zulu migrant workers to attack students in 1976. But current groups, such as 'The A-Team', 'Phakathis', and 'AmaAfrica Poqo', sometimes wearing white armbands to distinguish colleagues in the mêlée, have become more prominent as the level of political violence for which some of them are responsible has escalated, and more closely connected with the security forces.

The popular portrayal in the academic literature is that vigilantes are used by the state in order to allow itself to be presented as the neutral arbiter in Black-on-Black violence and to de-escalate its own direct aggression (see, for example, Haysom 1990: 64). However, the emergency regulations made it extremely difficult to assess the upsurge of vigilante violence. None the less, Haysom points out that in 1988, twice as many persons died as a result of vigilante and counter-vigilante violence in the Pietermaritzburg area than in Beirut during the same period, and that township residents were more likely to die in vigilante violence than as a result of confrontations with the police (1990: 63). The emergency regulations also made it difficult to perceive the relationship between vigilantes and the police. But as far as it is possible to tell, there are six types of vigilante: those created by communities as alternative sources of law and order because they reject or fail to get sufficient protection from the police; Asian and Coloured vigilantes who protect their communities from attacks by Africans; those established by the African local community councils to act as their personal forces; those connected with homeland governments; groups dominated by conservative political organizations, such as Inkatha and the Afrikaner Weerstandsbeweging (AWB); and, finally, those directly sponsored by the security forces. Not all types engage in violence or work with the police, however the police seem to play four roles.

First, many policemen and women from the township and homeland forces are active members of vigilante groups. Indeed, vigilante groups were one of the main recruitment sources for the municipal and special forces established in 1984 and 1986. Thus, the UDF described the kitskonstabels as 'glorified vigilantes with shotguns and ammunition' (*New Nation*, 19 Feb. 1987), and kitskonstabels and MLEOs are suspected of heavy involvement in the vigilante groups established by the local councils. One group in Tumahole, which was responsible for whipping people found on the streets after the 9 p.m. curfew and for beating children who were late for school, was reputed to have at its core a Black policewoman and her family and friends. Vigilantes who attacked and killed three UDF supporters in Port Elizabeth described themselves as police and wore the blue overall of kitskonstabels. This also happened in Thembekile. Former Leandra vigilante boss, J. Maboy Zanda, joined the kitskonstabels, and it was later alleged that he harassed members of the democratic movement (*South*, 18 June 1987). A former vigilante godfather in Nyanga, Prince Gobingca, also joined the kitskonstabels; four thousand residents of Crossroads marched to the divisional headquarters of the SAP in April 1987 to complain about his activities as a policeman.

Secondly, some police forces have supported vigilante groups in their attacks on opponents of the state. In May 1986 conservative vigilantes known as 'the fathers' launched an attack on the satellite settlements that comprised Crossroads to drive out radical Black youths who opposed the move to Khayelitsha. It was widely alleged that the police had assisted the vigilantes, although this was denied by the authorities. Another group calling itself 'Witdoeke' is alleged to have aided the police and army in removing the squatters once resistance had been overcome. In December 1986 members of the radical Congress of South African Trades Unions were set upon by vigilante groups associated with Inkatha and by members of the KwaZulu Police, leaving thirty-nine people dead in a week of violence. Vigilantes connected with Inkatha have been seen being transported to townships in police casspirs, and while it is an offence for policemen and women to belong to 'extremist organizations', examples of which mentioned by the Minister of Law and Order included the AWB and

UDF, this did not apply to Inkatha membership. Inkatha membership is a prerequisite for membership of the KwaZulu Police, strengthening the link between Inkatha and the SAP (on which see Maré and Hamilton 1987: 213; a survey of attitudes in the Pietermaritzburg area shows that people overwhelmingly believe that the SAP is biased in favour of Inkatha; see Centre for Criminal Justice 1991).

The third role of the police is, in conjunction with other security forces, directly to sponsor and establish vigilante groups to work on their behalf, particularly to attack the neighbourhood and street committees lawfully established by radical resistance organizations as an alternative local government. Some of the vigilante groups set up grass-roots political structures to rival those they attacked, and the International Defence and Aid Fund alleged that some kitskonstabels took a leading role on these more conservative committees. Finally, the police fail to protect the victims of conservative vigilantes or pursue with sufficient vigour their criminal activities. This under-policing of vigilantism takes many forms. The police fail to intervene to protect victims, even when witnessing an attack, and their investigation of attacks is dilatory—statements are often not taken from victims, and the hostels where the suspected perpetrators are living are not searched. This only fuels counter-violence, as victims retaliate as a result of feeling unprotected by the law. Thus, there is considerable under-policing of Inkatha violence. In an interview with the author in 1992, a recently retired Zulu policeman in the SAP indicated that he had often been told by senior officers not to investigate crimes for which Inkatha members were thought to be responsible. The Trust Feeds case also illustrates how the police in Natal selectively favoured Inkatha over their political rivals affiliated to the UDF.

There are two caveats which need to be mentioned at this point. First, the expansion in Black police personnel opens up the opportunity for infiltration of the police by the ANC. In the American South, Alex shows that Black policemen and women were hired who shared the values of segregation and discrimination (1969: p. xvii), and while this is true in South Africa's case as well, many joined the police out of hunger and desperation for work. This gives some of them a more conditional loyalty to the police than their actions in suppressing unrest suggests. The strikes by kitskonstabels and MLEOs are illustrations of this, but the conditional loyalty extends even to some Black policemen and women in the more professionally trained SAP: the actions of Lt. Rockman are a case in point. In 1989 he refused to lead members of his riot squad in action in Mitchell's Plain, Cape Town, because he said that the riot police were out of control and acting too brutally. With other dissident Black members of the SAP, he later formed the Police and Prisons Civil Rights Union, which organized protest marches through Cape Town against police brutality. The ANC seized the strategic space and distributed pamphlets in 1989 urging Black policemen to disaffect, but this never occurred on any large scale, although figures for resignations are no longer published by the Commissioner. A few policemen and women, however, have been identified as ANC members and supporters. Two former Black security policemen went on trial in November 1986 charged with furthering the aims of the ANC, having been recruited as members in 1980. One of the insurgents involved in the attack on the Moroka police station in May 1979 was a former policeman. According to the issue of *Southscan* on 2 February 1990, former members of SAP death squads have defected to the ANC.

The second caveat is that some policemen have played a constructive role in trying to defuse the violence between Inkatha and the UDF and negotiate a truce. The role of senior officers in Pietermaritzburg is worth highlighting. This area witnessed some of the worst internecine violence between Inkatha and the pro-ANC UDF, and several officers negotiated a truce. Captain Ray Harrald, for example, who describes himself as a committed Christian, persuaded the two factions in Shongweni Valley to put away their arms and attend reconciliation meetings. The pact celebrated its first anniversary on 13 August 1990, and the *Natal Mercury* was moved to write that there had been a year of unprecedented peace. Another policeman involved in similar efforts elsewhere in the Pietermaritzburg area was Major TerreBlanche, commander of Pietermaritzburg's riot police. However, he was murdered by a right-wing Afrikaner terrorist group in March 1990. A representative of the UDF in the area described him as 'well respected', and the spokesman for the Mpumalanga Peace Committee said: 'he was well-liked and respected. People saw him as a man of his word' (*Natal Mercury*, 15 Mar. 1990). Such impartiality was, unfortunately, rare, and clearly put policemen at risk from those conservative groups who wished to perpetuate the violence. Generally, the SAP favoured conservative political groups, and worked through them.

The use of surrogates to attack opponents of the state during township unrest in the 1980s was a considerable extension of previous police involvement with vigilantism. The police have rightly been condemned both for their exploitation of internecine conflict between Blacks in order to defend the state, and their partisanship in support of conservative groups. It was a tactic seen before perhaps in the support given by some sections of the Royal Irish Constabulary to Protestant paramilitary gangs in the Irish war of independence between 1919 and 1922, and in the links today between a few members of the Royal Ulster Constabulary and Protestant paramilitary organizations, but never on such a manifest scale as found in South Africa. Nothing of its like existed in other forces who policed situations of decolonization (no mention is made of it, for example, in the volume by Anderson and Killingray 1992). But the SAP was to surpass itself once more in the death squads that operated as a tactic to neutralize the unrest. In the long history of policing in South Africa, the SAP finally reached its nadir when members became involved directly in assassinations of political opponents of the state (on death squads see Laurence 1990; Steytler 1990).

Evidence for the existence of death squads comes from the disclosure of former members and court cases, but as Steytler makes clear, it is also suggested by the lamentable failure of the SAP to arrest anyone for the sixty assassinations that occurred between 1978 and 1989 (1990: 108). In only one case were killers brought to trial, and this involved six members of the Ciskei Police, convicted after a tip-off from someone else within the force (Laurence 1990: 2). The revelations by ex-members of assassination squads offer firmer evidence, however. A former African security policeman, Butana Nofemela, signed an affidavit just before his execution for murder claiming to be a member of a squad (see Laurence 1990: 4–11; Steytler 1990: 109). One of the victims was Victor Mxenge, a prominent opponent of apartheid; there were seven other victims. In *Vrye Weekblad*, Captain Coetzee, head of one of the squads, confirmed Nofomela's allegations, and identified further members of death squads. He wrote: 'My men and I had to murder political and security opponents of the police and the government. I myself am guilty of, or at least an accomplice to, several murders' (quoted in Laurence 1990: 11). He implicated several top policemen, including a former Commissioner, Johann Coetzee, former heads of the security police, as well as the SAP's forensic expert. Apparently, they tended to use defectors from the ANC, known as 'Askaris', as gunmen, although serving policemen were also responsible for murders; many Askaris went into the security police themselves (some of the murders are recounted in Laurence 1990: 15–23).

Other revelations were made. The SB had a special unit known as C-1, commanded by Brigadier Schoon, whose purpose was to engage in counter-insurgency through widespread use of the Askaris (Steytler 1990: 117), and 'dirty tricks'. Two colonels from the SB admitted in the *Johannesburg Star* in 1986 to running dirty-tricks campaigns, whereupon the Minister of Law and Order reported the paper to the Media Council. But the Council ruled in favour of the newspaper when the Colonels repeated their admission that they had distributed misleading pamphlets and tape recordings about Allan Boesak. The SADF also had a Civil Co-operation Bureau that was allegedly responsible for political assassinations (Laurence 1990: 25). The SAP's response was to deny the allegations, prosecute those policemen whose involvement was incontrovertible, and claim that their actions were never sanctioned by senior officers or the government. Subsequently, blame was diverted to right-wing Afrikaner paramilitary organizations, some of whose members have tangential connections with the police. Justice Harms's Commission of Inquiry into the allegations exonerated the police, although it made critical remarks about the SADF's Civil Co-operation Bureau, which was almost immediately disbanded. An international delegation to South Africa by Amnesty International in November 1991 was more sanguine, and supported allegations of hit-squads within the police, as did the International Commission of Jurists.

As innovative as the SAP clearly was in its tactics, it failed to suppress political protest against the state, while knowledge of the tactics added to the government's political problems and intensified opposition to it; the police contributed greatly to the government's crisis. It was a while before elements in the government realized this, and initially the SAP was not thought to need major reform. The SAP's image was presented positively by the Botha government, and their activities in the unrest excused by several factors. In excellent accounts of state discourse between 1985 and 1988, Posel (1989, 1990) argues that it sought to explain why township residents resorted to violence, and to justify the activities of the security forces. In terms of the former, unrest was presented as random, mindless, and mob-like Black-on-Black violence. Thus, the SADF and SAP were neutral arbiters providing order and control, upholding the values of civilized behaviour both in society as a whole and in their own conduct. To allege anything more was, according to the Minister of Law and Order in a statement issued from Pretoria on 4 August 1988, 'vicious propaganda, a carefully orchestrated campaign of wilful lies and distortions . . . deliberate false perceptions' (on government responses to criticism of the police see Weitzer 1991: 262–4).

This wove neatly in with the SAP's own discourse (on which see Rauch 1991; van der Spuy 1988). It was from this time that the SAP began to articulate a religious discourse, stressing a mandate from God, and that, in the Commissioner's words, the SAP in the townships was 'serving the King of Law and Order—Jesus Christ' (Annual Report of the Commissioner of the SAP 1985: 31). The Chaplaincy Unit was no longer presented just as a mechanism to ensure social integration for new members, but as providing moral guidance in difficult police work; the activities of the SAP in the townships were being guided by God—an idea which resonated with Afrikaner versions of Calvinism.

Another theme in SAP discourse was that of professionalism. They acted impartially, expediently, and with integrity. The 1988 White Paper on the organizations and functions of the SAP (South Africa 1988) stressed that the force kept abreast of latest technology, had developed its own research unit to avail of the latest work in universities and research institutes, and applied scientific principles to policing (p. 49). Dippenaar makes much of changes to police training in 1985 to make it more academic (1988: 758–60). Thus, when under attack in the townships, the SAP acted with professionalism, and 'astonishing calm and self-control' (Dippenaar 1988: 782). As part of this discourse on professionalism, the SAP also stressed its benign policing role. Thus in the midst of suffering and slaughter in the townships caused by the police, the SAP began a large public relations exercise to find its neatest station, opened up a museum to the public, set up a new Social Service Unit and ran training courses for homeland police in 'social services', ran large celebrations to commemorate various anniversaries in SAP history, reintroduced foot patrols in city centres, as well as bicycle patrols in Johannesburg, and began to use the rhetoric of 'community policing'. In this last respect, the 1988 White Paper on the SAP emphasized the obligation to provide service to the community, mentioning such things as searching for children's lost pets, giving advice on various problems, and providing assistance in times of need (South Africa 1988: 6). The new Minister of Law and Order, Adriaan Vlok, a noted liberal who replaced the more hardline Minister le Grange in 1986, sought to present the human face of the SAP, urging members in his first speech as Minister to perform their duties with a smile. Later he said that friendliness, reasonableness, and service should not be seen by policemen as weakness, and that the SAP should live up to its motto— we protect, we serve. The new Commissioner appointed in 1987, General de Witt, also stressed the importance of the SAP winning the trust of the public.

The response to police misconduct in the township unrest of the 1980s was thus exactly the same as following 1976: the civil policing model was drawn on to recast the SAP's image in a more favourable hue. The themes of religion, community service, and professionalism that structure the SAP's public image are exemplified in the SAP Creed, which was devised during the worst excesses of police misconduct in the townships.

In humble submission to Almighty God, who controls the destinies of nations and the history of peoples, who gathered our forebears together from many countries and gave them this their own, who has guided them from generation to generation, who has wondrously delivered them from the dangers that beset them, we, as members of the South African Police, declare that whereas we are conscious of our responsibility towards God and man, are convinced of the necessity to stand united to safeguard the integrity and freedom of our country, to secure the maintenance of law and order, to further the contentment and spiritual and material welfare of all in our midst. We are prepared to assume our task and . . . foster sound international relations based on Christian and religious principles to realize the ideal of peaceful co-existence, and in the fulfilment of our task pledge our sincere devotion to the Republic even if we shall be asked to bring the highest sacrifice, for at thy will to live or perish Oh South Africa, dear land.

THE POLITICIZATION OF POLICING

The high profile of the police in suppressing opposition to the government after 1984 had the effect of politicizing policing. There were three dimensions to this: the emergence of policing as a political issue, competition between political parties to represent the police, and the increasing openness with which some policemen and women expressed support for the Afrikaner right wing.

Even in Black politics policing issues were rarely given prominence because they were subsumed within a broader attack on apartheid, although criticism of the police was a constant feature of Black politics, but they featured on the agenda of White politics even less. However, the splits within Afrikanerdom in the early 1980s over Botha's reform (on which see, for example, Schrire 1992), propelled policing issues on to the White political agenda, in a way that was reminiscent of the conflicts over policing between Smuts and Malan forty years before. The particular concerns that featured most in the political debate were issues about police conduct and the question of police reform. In a review of élite conflicts over policing in the 1980s, Weitzer (1991) identifies three positions. The liberal position criticized the partisanship of the police, as well as their methods and lack of concern for civil liberties, and although it recognized the need for law and order, it argued that this should be coupled with peace and progress. Thus, in this view, the SAP was in need of extensive reform. The conservative critique, proffered by the Conservative Party and Herstigte Nasionale Party, supported the police and their methods, believing the police to have been undermined by unwarranted criticism. It also attacked the government for shackling the police by means of ill-judged mechanisms of control, in the belief that law and order could be restored only by tough policing. Reform was not necessary; indeed, measures of police reform introduced by Botha should be rescinded.

The early position of the National Party likewise defended the police against criticism, claiming that their methods were measured, proportionate, and professional. But this public defence tended to be matched with private concerns over police atrocities. Reformist members of the cabinet found police misconduct increasingly embarrassing politically. Botha was reported as believing in 1984 that the police were out of control, and that two-thirds of policemen and women rejected his reforms (Spence 1988: 252). Even the Minister of Law and Order at the time, Louis le Grange, was believed to be opposed to reform but could not be removed, despite serious illness, because of support for him among the conservative sections of the National Party (ibid.). It was for this reason that Adriaan Vlok, a supporter of Botha's reforms, was moved in as le Grange's deputy while retaining his position as Deputy Minister of Defence. Vlok was eventually made Minister of Law and Order, although it is reported that he had little influence among the police (ibid.). However, with Vlok the idea of police reform was promoted privately, and many of his public defences of the police were double-edged, by having a tinge of exhortation for the police to improve. In this respect, the rhetoric of the civil policing model, which was used by the government to counteract criticism of the police, became partly a statement of the goals the police should themselves aim for. Thus, in the volume celebrating the seventy-fifth anniversary of the SAP in 1988, Vlok wrote: 'While I wish to thank the SAP for their seventy-five years of devoted service, and while I praise every individual member for his or her contribution, I also wish to encourage every member of the force to meet the future with the same courage and daring which they have displayed in the past' (Dippenaar 1988: p. v). The later position of the National Party, therefore, saw a widening of the divisions between the National and Conservative Parties over the question of police reform, and the National Party distanced itself from right-wing critics. Demands for police reform were publicly voiced, placing police reform on the political agenda again, as it had been in 1948.

The Conservative Party tends to feel that police conduct is justifiable given the threat to law and order which Black unrest poses. It defends the police against criticism from wherever it emanates, even endorsing the mistreatment of minors on the claim that no police force should tolerate being humiliated and goaded by children. Casper Uys told the White parliament in March 1985 that South Africa owed a debt of gratitude to the police, who were simultaneously being pilloried in the eyes of the world and undermined by the reforms introduced by the government. In by-elections in October 1985, a National Party poster ran 'Don't shoot. Think', emphasizing the party's commitment to control police excesses; the Herstigte Nasionale Party reversed it to 'Shoot. Don't think', while the leader of the Conservative Party argued that the security forces should be 'unleashed', portraying government security policy as the cause of continued unrest. Thus, government supporters frequently attacked the Conservative Party on the grounds that they were blind to the necessity of police reform, as they were to reform generally. There were two other telling complaints. The Conservative Party was accused of trying to politicize the police, and attempting to hijack support for themselves from within the police. The mode of political representation for the police was traditionally through the National Party, but the intensified political debate on policing created a situation where, for the first time, the political loyalty of the police to the National Party was threatened.

There is now a strong suspicion that many members of the police support the Conservative Party and even the more right-wing AWB. Helen Suzman has made this allegation in parliament and the Conservative Party believes it to be the case, although the Minister of Law and Order has issued strong denials. However, Adam (1987: 42) argues that right-wing sentiments are widespread within the police, and P. W. Botha reportedly believed that nearly two-thirds of White members of the SAP supported the Conservative Party against his reform policy (Spence 1988: 252). The evidence for this is circumstantial but does build to be convincing. First, lower echelons of the SAP tend to come from that part of the Afrikaner social structure most threatened by the reforms implemented by the National Party and from which the Conservative Party draws its electoral support (on which see Bekker and Grobbelaar 1987). A former Black policeman in the SAP indicated in an interview with the author that pro-AWB policemen would taunt Black colleagues and often give the AWB's Nazi-like salute. This affinity with the Afrikaner right wing also explains why some former policemen came out of retirement to stand as candidates for the Conservative Party in the 1987 general election. Secondly, if the experience of Northern Ireland is applicable, the contradictory position the police have been left in as a result of government reforms might create a sense of alienation among some ordinary members of the SAP as they feel they can no longer call upon the same unthinking loyalty from the state as before or act with the same lack of restraint. If this alienation exists, it is likely to increase police support for more right-wing parties, such as the Conservative Party, who urge stronger support for, and greater understanding of, the problems of the SAP.

Finally, there are incidents which show that the police failed to act against right-wing extremists or did so only after considerable delay. However, some have contended that under- or over-policing of political groups does not reflect malevolent intent but sheer incompetence (for example, Waddington 1992). This is sometimes the case, as with the investigation of the Boipatong massacre which Waddington studied as part of the Goldstone Commission, although even here there was partisanship shown by the police in their respective conduct towards the hostel dwellers and victims (see Waddington 1992: 36), and police tapes were tampered with which could have proved that policemen assisted the attackers. But as a general principle, selective policing evinces much malevolent intent and partisanship. Adam and Moodley argue, for example, that the potential reservoir for the Latin American-style death squads that operate in the SAP is found in the AWB link with local police (1986: 61). But there is firmer evidence of collusion. In April 1985, for example, around one thousand members of the AWB marched on Pretoria central police station to deliver 'a message of gratitude' to the police for their efforts in maintaining law and order. The march was illegal and could have led to prosecutions under the Internal Security Act, but the police failed to take any action, yet similar occurrences were dealt with severely when involving Blacks. A meeting in May 1986 which would have been addressed by Pik Botha was broken up by AWB members. Amidst wild chanting and considerable fighting the AWB took over the meeting, whereupon its leader, Eugene TerreBlanche, delivered a speech attacking the government's reform policies. The local police refused to protect the meeting and a special squad from outside had to be brought in, using tear-gas to clear the hall. Nor did the police prevent the AWB from holding an illegal gathering in a nearby rugby stadium to continue the speeches attacking the government. The pro-government Afrikaans-language newspaper *Rapport* was shocked at the conduct of the police, asking the police authorities 'to ensure that the actions of its men do not in the least create the impression of partiality', and a cabinet colleague of Pik Botha publicly criticized the local police division. In February 1988 police allowed an illegal march by the AWB and permitted them to present a petition to the State President in Pretoria, whereas two days later the police arrested and detained a group of clergy, armed only with Bibles, when they were on an illegal march in Cape Town to present a petition.

This demonstrates the difficulties that the more technocratically-minded and impartial senior officers have in enforcing their authority on relatively autonomous local junior commanders (Adam 1987: 42). A former lieutenant-colonel in the SB explained the problem thus: 'decisions are left to the local units and only the minimum of information passed up the system. The police only feed up the line problems they can't cope with' (quoted in the *Independent*, 24 June 1992). Thus, after riot police opened fire on a crowd in Boipatong in June 1992 that had harassed de Klerk after his ill-fated visit to the scene of the massacre, an officer was heard to shout at the men asking who had given permission for them to shoot. The SAP's lack of professional contingency planning and mobilization plans for dealing with major public-order incidents (discussed by Waddington 1992:

27–30) thus hands control of very fluid situations to junior officers who have to make *ad hoc* decisions, and they sometimes do so in line with their more conservative political beliefs. Moorcraft claims that most right-wing support within the SAP is in the middle and lower ranks (1990: 410): precisely the people who determine practice on the ground rather than operational policy.

But this local autonomy cuts both ways, and it is symptomatic of the political divisions within the SAP that some attempts by AWB members to break up National Party meetings or marches met with a vigorous police response and court appearances, although magistrates sometimes treated their offences quite leniently. Charges of terrorism against TerreBlanche were rejected by a magistrate in 1983 and reduced to possession of firearms, which included four AK-47 automatic rifles and more than four thousand rounds of ammunition. Mr Justice van Dyk described him and his two accomplices, all ex-policemen, as 'civilized and decent people'. 'The fact that they were in possession of these articles was an unfortunate occurrence of events. The community would certainly not expect me to send them to jail' (*Rand Daily Mail*, 5 Nov. 1983). This was the same judge who imprisoned Barbara Hogan for ten years merely for membership of the ANC. However, in 1983 two AWB members were given fifteen-year sentences for terrorism, although they were freed in 1987 along with political prisoners from the ANC and PAC, including Govan Mbeki, thus softening the release among Afrikaner right-wingers.

Shortly after one of the incidents of police partisanship towards the AWB, the Deputy Minister for Law and Order confirmed in parliament that members of police forces and reservists could belong to any political organization as long as it was not radical, specifically identifying that this precluded membership of the AWB (and the UDF), although many AWB members serve in auxiliary commando units and therefore liaise with the police. In February 1988 the government banned seventeen organizations associated with the UDF and the White Liberation Movement, one of whose members, an ex-policeman, massacred seven Black people and injured fifteen after opening fire on innocent Black shoppers in Pretoria (for details of the incident see Marks and Andersson 1990: 59). However, the AWB was not banned, despite making continual warnings since its formation in 1973 that it would take to arms to defend the Afrikaner *volk* (on the AWB see Adam 1987; B. du Toit 1991). The AWB is the leading paramilitary group on the Afrikaner right wing (Posel shows how the

AWB has occasionally had favourable television coverage in South Africa, 1989: 271, 1990: 164), although there are several minor organizations. The AWB is not on good terms with them all; TerreBlanche was on the death list of one of them, as was de Klerk (Steytler 1990: 122). The AWB is the best organized. It has vigilante groups, called *Die Boere Brandwag* (Boer Sentry), as well as a para-military section known as *aquila* (eagles). There are separate sections for women and a youth movement. B. du Toit quotes a former assistant leader (who was also a former policeman) as saying that although the AWB claims 150,000 active supporters, 15,000 are registered members (1991: 645).

The AWB thus prompts comparisons with OB in the 1940s. Both were large organizations, appealed to militant Afrikaners, drew on Nazi symbolism, claimed big support within the police, and posed a serious challenge to law and order, which led constitutional nationalists eventually to distance themselves from both. The Conservative Party has an ambivalent attitude towards the AWB and has failed to endorse it fully. The parliamentary right wing today has as little strategic space in which to give support to extra-parliamentary right-wing groups as it did during the Second World War. Stanley Uys rightly points out that the AWB is puny compared to OB (1988: 211), but its main influence comes from its connections with the police. These associations are not insignificant, although not as strong as between the SAP and OB during the war. The main leaders of the AWB are ex-policemen, including TerreBlanche, who was once B. J. Vorster's bodyguard. Its intelligence officer and co-leader of one of its paramilitary wings is a former lieutenant-colonel in the security police who was involved in the interrogation of Dr Aggett. His duties in the AWB apparently include the training of children, from the age of 10, in the use of firearms (Foster and Luyt 1986: 300–1). In March 1988 seven police reservists in Northern Transvaal were forced to resign because of their support for the AWB. One of the expelled members claimed afterwards that at least 40 per cent of reservists in the Northern Transvaal were members (quoted in van der Spuy 1988: 20). Lt.-Col. Horak, who had been working for or in the SB between 1957 and 1990 before fleeing to Britain in 1990 with the help of the ANC, revealed in the *Independent* on 24 June 1992 that the recruits in the SAP to whom he lectured at training college were mostly AWB supporters. He is quoted as saying: 'the police are totally AWB, especially the young ones.' It is not surprising therefore that some policemen allow their sympathies for the AWB to affect their work; nor that the changed political partisanship of the police should persuade the new de Klerk government to begin a process of police reform.

THE DE KLERK ERA

Frederik de Klerk assumed the state presidency in September 1989, and although his government comprised almost the same personnel as the cabinet of his predecessor, the style and policies of the new government were entirely different. Heribert Adam (1990: 68) noted that de Klerk was not a securocrat, with a power base in the military and security apparatus, but a lawyer with a preference for constitutional government. Immediately the rhetoric on policing changed. In 1990 the Minister of Law and Order acknowledged the need to change 'the face of the force' (cited in Weitzer 1991: 265). His deputy remarked that there was a need to 'remove the old attitude, the aggressive attitude' among the police (ibid.). Within three months of de Klerk's appointment, the Commissioner of the SAP remarked that the police function in modern South Africa would have to be carried out with 'particular understanding, insight, and even pity. Sensitivity can be achieved only by ensuring that all police personnel are trained in the minimizing of conflict' (*Financial Mail*, 26 Jan. 1990). A former deputy commissioner, in a private communication with the author, said in 1991 that the SAP would develop trust and a partnership with the community, and remove all stumbling-blocks that inhibited this. But the clearest statement of the new policing principles came with de Klerk's speech at the opening of parliament in February 1991. Outlining a 'manifesto for the new South Africa', special attention was given to policing. All people would be equal before the law and enjoy equal rights. The protection of, and respect for life, liberty, and property would be amongst the first principles of the SAP. Violence and intimidation would end, and the police would no longer be subject to political expediency.

The rhetoric of the civil police tradition, however, has been used by South African governments since the 1930s, while the reality of policing remained very much colonial in style and methods. But, to his credit, de Klerk did set about trying to change the SAP from above.

Commissions of inquiry were announced to investigate police conduct in public violence and the allegation of police death squads. This was sweetened by an immediate pay increase for the police of 79 per cent in de Klerk's first budget, a real shift in expenditure from defence towards the police, and a commitment to increase manpower by ten thousand in the first year. More civilians were to be employed to free members from administrative work. Reforms were also immediate. The kitskonstabels and MLEOs were incorporated into the SAP in 1989 as a mechanism of control. In November 1989, two months after de Klerk took office as State President, the new government announced that Botha's complex system of security committees would be abolished. It was significant that the statement to this effect was made during a speech at the SAP's training college: more civilian authority would be established in security matters, and the political influence of the military and police would be curtailed, even though this was opposed by military and police chiefs (Moorcraft 1990: 400; on the changes see Hansson 1990: 56–7; Seegars 1991: 265–6). De Klerk was also against the 'winning hearts and minds strategy' of Botha that was linked to the SSC, because it was not an end in itself and transformed the majority of the population into an enemy (Hansson 1990: 55–6). However, the new government did not abandon the co-ordination of security policy in the regions, but handed it over to civilians and reduced the power of the SSC, whose position was taken by a committee of the cabinet with de Klerk as its head. An ex-policeman revealed, however, that the local police commanders still retained considerable influence by controlling the amount of information given to the civil authorities (quoted in the *Independent*, 24 June 1992).

The new State President quickly overruled the objections of his senior security advisers and permitted mass protests and marches; reduced the initial period of national service by a half; cut the defence budget in real terms, while raising that of the SAP; released political prisoners; and abandoned the destabilization policies in neighbouring countries in favour of diplomacy (Baynham 1990: 429). The SAP was demilitarized in one sense because men were removed from border duty in 1990, but in a broader sense de Klerk announced that the policing emphasis would shift from a focus on political activity towards ordinary crime. The police would no longer play 'a control function connected to a specific political policy' but would instead concentrate on the prevention of crime. In a speech to senior officers in January

1990, de Klerk said: 'matters that have in the past been dealt with by strong-arm tactics will in the future be dealt with differently' (*Sunday Times*, 28 Jan. 1990).

Several associated changes occurred. De Klerk's insistence that the SAP shift towards ordinary crime has been accompanied by a proposal to decentralize the force and devolve 'elements of policing' to elected local authorities, which counters the very essence of the centralized colonial policing model. Vlok announced in 1991 that there would be increased patrols on foot, and temporary offices would be opened where crimes could be reported quickly. Specialist police units dealing with ordinary crime were established or strengthened, such as the Child Protection Unit and the Tourist Support Unit. Training methods were to be reviewed, and the SB was merged with the CID, coming under the latter's direction. 'Mechanisms of communication' were established in 1990 with representatives of the ANC, PAC, and Inkatha in order to form a united front to combat crime under the code-name 'Operation Sentry': an initiative for the community to police itself, and for the broadening of political input to the SAP. What is more, this was accompanied by an attempt to depoliticize the SAP.

In January 1990 the new State President spoke to an audience of the top five hundred officers in the SAP, and after admitting that the SAP had been involved in politics in the past, he urged upon them the need to remove the SAP from the political battle front. He said, 'we want to take the police out of it. We will not use you any longer as instruments to attain political goals' (*Sunday Times*, 28 Jan. 1990). Three months later the Minister of Law and Order announced that police personnel, in the regular and reserve forces, would no longer be allowed to hold membership of any political party, or any movement or organization with political objectives. The Conservative Party and AWB correctly interpreted this as an attack on policemen and women with right-wing sympathies. The Conservative Party's Chief Whip commented wryly that partisanship was not prohibited when the majority of police supported the National Party, although to spare the dilemma of policemen and women the Conservative Party suspended their membership (Weitzer 1991: 265).

However, the proposed shift in emphasis away from 'high' to 'low' policing (Brodeur 1983), from political activity against the state to ordinary crime, was not only implemented as a strategy to avoid police partisanship in favour of the Afrikaner right wing, but a reflection of deep concern over the astronomical rise in crime. In his 'manifesto for the new South Africa', de Klerk linked the high crime rate to reform, arguing that crime had the potential to abet serious delays and undermine the progress already made. It has been recognized by liberal criminologists since the 1930s that apartheid generates crime, but the massive operations against township unrest between 1983 and 1990 left little time for 'normal' policing, and the violence provided manifold cover for criminals. Indeed, Scharf claims that the police actually sponsored the township *tsotsis* in the 1980s in order to impede the work of political organizations in the townships and as a source of information about political activists (1990: 255). Thus, ordinary crime flourished. According to figures provided in the Commissioner's Annual Reports, between 1981/2 and 1988 there was an overall increase in 'offences' of 22.2 per cent, and 'law infringements' of 17.4 per cent, which is over twice the rate of population growth.

The relative balance between the two sorts of crime shows the SAP's emphasis on the more serious offences. This is perhaps best illustrated by comparing figures for 1984 and 1986, when township unrest was at its height. In this period 'offences' rose by 7 per cent, while 'law infringements' fell by 34.4 per cent. Either less minor offences were being committed, or the police focused more on the serious ones. Certainly more serious crimes were being committed. In 1989, for example, there was a murder in South Africa every forty-five minutes; it was one every hour in 1986. Table 6.7 shows the number of serious offences reported between 1981–2 and 1988, most of which exceeded the increase in the overall crime rate in the same period; crime was not only increasing, serious crime was escalating faster. Another crime trend is noteworthy. In the 1988 Annual Report, the Commissioner provided a racial breakdown for certain crimes, which showed that only 4.4 per cent of rape victims were White, and only 2.9 per cent of murder victims (the race of the perpetrator was not given however), whereas 48.6 per cent of burglaries were of White residential properties compared to 24.1 per cent of Black residential properties. Thus, crimes of violence against the person tend to be on Blacks, while crimes of property reflect the patterns of wealth in society and are thus against Whites (on this point generally see Marks and Andersson 1990: 33–4, 56–7). With crime high, people's opinion of the SAP was low. In a survey of 364 Black respondents in the Pietermaritzburg area in 1991, 38.8 per cent said that the SAP was doing a good job in dealing with non-political crime, 6.3 per cent believed them courteous and friendly, and 29.1 per cent helpful and

TABLE 6.7 *Number (in thousands) of cases reported of selected crimes, 1981/2–1988*

Crime	1981/2	1982/3	1983/4	1984/5	1985/6	1987	1988	% rise
Murder	8.0	8.5	9.4	8.9	9.6	9.8	10.6	31.5
Robbery	38.6	38.2	37.7	39.3	45.9	46.2	45.8	18.6
Rape	15.5	15.3	15.7	16.0	14.9	18.1	19.3	24.6
Burglary	139.2	148.7	153.4	166.8	197.4	194.2	182.7	31.2
Assault	119.8	121.7	125.1	123.1	110.3	120.7	125.5	4.7
Car theft	44.4	44.7	44.3	48.5	59.4	59.9	57.8	30.0

Source: Annual Reports of the Commissioner of the SAP.

approachable; low enough, but higher than might be expected given their reputation in dealing with political crime, although the positive views held by respondents with affiliations to Inkatha distort the overall figures considerably (see Centre for Criminal Justice 1991: 21–2).

The high crime rate therefore constituted a significant spur to police reform besides any political considerations. However, as P. W. Botha discovered in his earlier and less far-reaching attempts to change the apartheid bureaucracy, reform from above can be stymied by resistance from below, and low-ranking policemen and women have been slow to implement these changes or act in their spirit, and senior officers unwilling or unable to assert them. At least eighteen people died in police custody under suspicious circumstances in 1990, and in only one case did the government order a judicial inquiry (Amnesty International 1991*a*: 2). During 1991, the police continued to use their powers of detention without trial against political activists. On 21 June 1991 new security legislation was passed which repealed some of the draconian powers conferred on the police by the 1982 Internal Security Act, but three were retained: an amendment allowing for fourteen-day preventive detention, the detention of state witnesses, and Section 29, which permitted the police to detain a person indefinitely, incommunicado, and in solitary confinement for purposes of interrogation (Amnesty International 1991*b*: 2). Detention without charge or trial was strengthened further in legislation in June 1992, and in July 1992, the State Pathologist, Dr Gluckman, a supporter of de Klerk's government, revealed that deaths in detention were occurring at the rate of one a week. He had on file two hundred cases of suspicious death, nine out of ten of which he said were the responsibility of the police. The government's first reaction was to order an investigation into the cases, but the Minister of Law and Order subsequently denied police responsibility, explaining that deaths in custody occur because of natural causes and suicide, a reaction reminiscent of the then Minister's initial comments on Steve Biko's death fifteen years before.

The SAP's conduct in political violence also seemed to have changed little. In January 1990 de Klerk issued the following instruction to senior policemen: 'when people gather politically to voice their views in an orderly fashion you will be asked to keep law and order. But you will not be required to prevent people from gathering to gain support for their views' (*Sunday Times*, 28 Jan. 1990). There have been instances since then where the police negotiated with marchers in order to avoid violence, but there are also counter-instances. In Sebokeng on 26 March 1990, for example, five people were shot dead and 161 injured when the police opened fire on a peaceful demonstration organized by the UDF. A further seven were killed and 127 wounded on the same day. De Klerk ordered a judicial commission of inquiry under Justice Goldstone, and the judge strongly criticized the undisciplined conduct of the police. The majority of people were shot in the back and no warning was given of the SAP's intention to open fire with live ammunition. The judge recommended that the Attorney-General investigate the possibility of bringing criminal charges against thirty-one of the policemen, although no charges had been laid by the end of 1991. In October 1990 the police fired upon a group of people protesting about rent increases and killed one. The Minister of Law and Order admitted in parliament that 197 people had been shot dead by the security forces in the first eleven months of 1990, while the United Nations's Human Rights Commission put the figure at 265 by the end of September. Two million Rands was paid out by the police in out-of-court settlement of compensation claims between January and August 1990, and 1,870 policemen were found guilty of criminal acts during the year. In January 1992 the police fired upon demonstrators in Ennerdale, most of whom were shot in the back. Five people were shot dead in disturbances in Boipatong in June 1992 after de Klerk visited the scene of earlier killings.

The warnings against political partisanship have also not diminished the scale of discriminatory policing. Serious communal violence occurred in Welkom during May 1990 between Black and White miners, in which AWB vigilantes were allowed to roam freely by the local police. In May the following year, AWB members and local farmers surrounded and then attacked an African settlement in

Goedgevonden in protest against it being handed back to Africans. They were unmolested by the local police, who seemed unaware of the 250 men on horseback harassing the local community over an extended number of hours. However, when the AWB attacked de Klerk's political rally in Ventersdorp in August 1991, the police reacted vigorously, leaving three AWB members dead. But partisanship in Black politics had been overcome even less. Hit-squads continued to be used, and the police aided Inkatha in attacking ANC supporters.

The de Klerk government was seriously affected by the revelations of the commissions of inquiry it set up to investigate security force conduct, and the admissions of former members now coming clean after defecting to the ANC. The Harms Commission reported that members of the SADF's Civil Co-operation Bureau, working in conjunction with some members of the police, had 'tried and sentenced people without due legal process'. De Klerk asked that the Black community let bygones be bygones, although the Minister of Defence resigned and the Bureau was abolished. However, while the Harms Commission largely exonerated the SAP from participation in death squads, former members of such units made embarrassing admissions, and confirmed police involvement (as did two international delegations). In July 1991 a former member of Five Reconnaissance Regiment, an élite squad of security personnel, revealed that the unit had carried out attacks on residents in Alexandra township and in Pietermaritzburg during 1991, and been responsible for the massacre of twenty-six train commuters on 13 September 1990. A man claiming to be a member of a hit-squad told the *Natal Mercury* in February 1991 that the unit had been involved in the murder of Chief Maphumulo, a prominent anti-Inkatha activist, on the 25th of the month. It was later revealed in the Supreme Court that Maphumulo's supporters had earlier come under attack from armed Inkatha members with the active support of the police (see Amnesty International 1991*b*: 6–7). In December 1992, twenty-nine senior staff from the Defence Force were asked to resign because of their involvement in illegal activities.

The police have worked with, or for, Inkatha on several occasions since de Klerk came to power. On 12 May 1991 at least twenty-seven people were killed when an estimated thousand *impis* from Inkatha launched an attack on the Swanieville squatter camp near Kagiso. The police did not prevent the attack nor detain the *impis* despite the area coming under emergency regulations and a curfew, and the fact that the Inkatha supporters trekked ten kilometres from their hostel to the scene of the attack without being spotted or detained. The police even escorted them back to their hostel (Amnesty International 1991*b*: 7). Some residents claimed in sworn statements that policemen participated in the attack. On 14 August 1991 the police actually transported one thousand Inkatha supporters in armoured vehicles to the scene of an attack on ANC members in Thokoza and did not intervene in the fighting. Another incident in December was recorded on video tape by the ANC; the tape clearly showed police ferrying armed Inkatha supporters in armoured vehicles. On 17 June 1992 the police did nothing to prevent or seriously investigate the attack on Boipatong squatter camp by Inkatha supporters from a nearby hostel, which left forty-two people dead, one of them a young baby in its mother's arms, sliced by a panga. A former Black policeman admitted in an interview with the author that the police in Boipatong had been deliberately incompetent, had lied to the Goldstone Commission, and, indeed, did escort perpetrators back to their hostels in casspirs with goods stolen from the victims. The international furore over the case eventually persuaded the police to assign 'over two hundred' investigators to the case, but this was some days later. They did not act on at least two warnings that the attack was planned, and they arrived on the scene six hours after the event. Two days later residents had still not had statements taken by the police; several survivors said the attackers were led by White men with blackened faces (*Sunday Times*, 21 June 1992). Five men from a local hostel were later arrested; the SAP selected as its spokesperson on the incident the policeman who had earlier been involved in reconciling the warring factions in the Pietermaritzburg area. On 20 July an international inquiry by Peter Waddington and two British police officers for the Goldstone Commission condemned the SAP's lack of professionalism in investigating the incident, although found no evidence of direct collusion (Waddington 1992). A few days prior to the report, the police arrested seventy-six Zulu from the hostel on thirty-six counts of murder.

However, it would be wrong to present the violence as one way; the SAP's superficial investigation of the Boipatong massacre was not made more thorough by the ANC's instruction to residents to boycott the investigation and avoid co-operation with the police. ANC supporters have been responsible for many attacks on Inkatha; twenty-three members were massacred by ANC supporters in April 1992.

The level of violence for which each is responsible is high. The British Defence and Aid Fund for Southern Africa estimated in July 1992 that eight thousand people had lost their lives in political violence since February 1990. Indeed, between the signing of the Peace Accord in September 1991 and June 1992, 2,400 people were killed in township violence between Inkatha and the ANC. Many of these lie at the hands of the ANC, and on the first day of the ANC's general strike on 3 August 1992, leaders in the organization called upon supporters to desist from violence. What distinguishes Inkatha's violence is that it is sponsored by elements of the state.

Few people doubt that there is collusion between Inkatha and the SAP, and other security personnel, although this is denied by the government, despite its admission that it funded Inkatha in 1989 and 1990. The government attributes collusion to a few renegade members of the police and SADF who engage in free-lance attacks on the ANC and its supporters, but critics claim that it goes higher. The issue is just how far up knowledge of this collusion goes: to senior officers in the SAP, the securocrats in the intelligence network, or to de Klerk himself, as the ANC believes. Certain sections of the state do not want to see a strong ANC develop: some because they want to undermine negotiations between the ANC and the government, others because they want to negotiate with a weak ANC. The attacks serve this purpose in three ways: by increasing the pressure on Mandela from younger radicals either to withdraw from the talks or permit counter-violence, both of which serve the propaganda interests of the government; by undermining the faith supporters have in the ANC's capacity to deliver protection or peace generally; and by preventing it from organizing in the townships politically. A former Black policeman argued in an interview with the author that there is a conspiracy to destabilize the ANC and alleged that this went up as high as the Commissioner. He claimed that Black police had even been used to attack Inkatha supporters in an attempt to provoke them to retaliate against the ANC.

If de Klerk does not directly dictate this policy or tacitly endorse it, he must show his opposition by reining in the culprits. So far he has been unwilling or unable to do this. Weitzer suggests he is unwilling (1991: 266), since de Klerk has shied away from advocating extensive structural and ideological reform of the police. For example, the government does not countenance the abandonment of the SAP's security role, which means that it does not favour the dismantling of the SB, nor radical demilitarization and disarming of the SAP. It does not see the need to appoint new senior officers unconnected with the past, nor purge the force of its most aggressive and sectarian members. Finally, Weitzer shows that the government does not support the introduction of public accountability for the SAP, quoting a spokesman from the Department of Law and Order as saying it would be 'a sad day in any country when you have to have a body to police the police' (ibid.). Thus, it seems justified to conclude that either the political will is lacking for serious police reform or the government feels unable to force change upon the police. This brings us to the heart of the relationship between policing and the state, which is addressed in the next chapter.

CONCLUSION

As it passes its eightieth year, the SAP is in the worst crisis of its history. Having been neglected from the very beginning in favour of a focus on policing race relations, ordinary crime is at a higher level than ever before, yet the SAP also seems incapable of keeping political order. Having always been very effective in policing race relations, the SAP now confronts a government which finds its past partisanship an embarrassment and which criticizes its success in bolstering the state's previous policy of internal colonialism. The force is reeling under evidence of collusion with groups on the Afrikaner and African right wing, as well as allegations of police death squads, the murder of suspects in custody, and patent general incompetence.

In reaching, in this way, a nadir in the SAP's reputation, the conduct of policemen and women may come to haunt them in the future as a change in government turns their past victims into pursuers. As a possible portent, ANC radicals recently killed a policeman in Sharpeville: he was dismembered and mutilated, his limbs and head displayed on lamp posts and road signs. What remained of his torso was then necklaced, with the burning tyre dragged around the township behind a van. Defections to the ANC, in anticipation of retribution like this, have led to embarrassing revelations of just how contemptuously the police treated Black South Africans in the past. Not surprisingly, morale in the SAP is reported to be low (Baynham 1990: 415). Work-loads are crippling, the work hazardous, and the future uncertain. How the force reacts to this situation in the forthcoming period of transitional government will have a large bearing on the prospects of peace and stability in the new South Africa.

Conclusion

The SAP was formed on 1 April 1913 and, in the context of the following eight decades, this was an inauspicious date; and it proved to be eight decades of bad luck for the majority of the population—an April Fool's day that lasted a life span. This study has addressed the conduct of the SAP down the years which has made it appear thus. In one sense the study disappoints because this emphasis neither focuses on, nor provides firm evidence to prove, the allegations which currently dominate people's interest in the SAP. Rather, the study places the misconduct in a broader historical context, enabling us to see why such things occur. Contemporary policing has been approached via a consideration of its past because the SAP never transcended its origins as a colonial force. Thus, the allegations which direct immediate attention on the police in South Africa, such as incompetence in investigating ordinary crime, collusion with the Afrikaner and Black right wing, political partisanship, and police involvement in death squads and political assassinations, among others, refer to conduct which befits the essentially colonial style of policing in modern South Africa. The first section of this Conclusion will review the main features of the colonial-style policing in South Africa, before consideration is given to its consequences for police–state relations and the prospects of future police reform.

THE HISTORY AND DEVELOPMENT OF POLICING IN SOUTH AFRICA

The SAP never transcended its origins as a colonial police force. While colonial forces elsewhere modernized during the nineteenth and twentieth centuries, the SAP was always structured by the colonial-like role it continued to discharge. The SAP's primary task has been to police race relations, and thus to contain and control Black South Africans by keeping them in their political, economic, social, and moral place as a subject population. The structure, style, and methods it used for this throughout the twentieth century remained characteristic of the nineteenth: it was centralized and under political control, acted as the servant of the state in suppressing part of the populace, performed several non-police duties on behalf of government, and its methods relied on brute force as the first resort. In this regard, the conduct and characteristics of the SAP are not unique; they were once quite common among colonial forces elsewhere. The oddity is that this colonial style should survive into the last decade of the twentieth century, which is also the only thing strange about South Africa's policies of internal colonialism.

This is not to argue that the SAP has been completely locked in the nineteenth century, but modernization was achieved only within the constraints of its colonial-like role. The modernization of equipment and training, for example, was conditioned by the need to control the Black population by force and to monitor the boundaries between the races. Thus, the emphasis on militarism within the force, the development of universal riot-control training, and the deployment of efficient armoured vehicles, for example, was necessary given the police role in subjugating the majority of the population. Professional contingency and mobilization plans of sorts exist within the SAP for dealing with large crowds and public order incidents, but these are very underdeveloped (as revealed by Waddington 1992: 27–30), primarily because of the SAP's willingness and capacity to rely on the colonial strategy of maximum force as a first resort. Even the extensive use of Blacks in the police in South Africa, seemingly an enigma, is a reflection of its colonial context. It is consistent with the absence of other stable and well-paid forms of employment for the colonized population in a very racially structured economy, and the colonial policy of getting the colonized to share in the administration of their oppression.

In this last respect, the existence of a large Black police personnel illustrates the democratization of the machinery of policing under South Africa's internal colonialism, although not its decision-making structures, since Blacks are invariably in the lower echelons of the police; in this regard they are like Afrikaner policemen before the

Second World War. This long tradition of Black policemen in South Africa ensures there is continuity between the kitskonstabels and MLEOs in the townships of the 1980s, the 'own areas' strategy of the 1950s, and the development of homeland forces from the 1960s: they are intended to mask the colonial nature of police work by facilitating Black-on-Black policing.

The success of the state's policy of internal colonialism explains other anomalies about the police in South Africa. Despite the popular image, South Africa was never a police state in the sense of having a large, well-resourced and equipped police force. The SAP has suffered almost continually from being understaffed, under-funded, and under-equipped. It usually took a catastrophe for the state to respond to the Commissioner's persistent demand for more resources, although this redirection of funds quickly dissipated and never made up for past neglect. The smallness of the SAP is explained in part because the state could never attract sufficient numbers of Whites to the police because of the greater opportunities provided elsewhere in the economy for this privileged group, and the unwillingness to appoint Blacks outside their own areas. But in most part, it reflected the fact that a large police force was unnecessary in South Africa because of the volunteer tradition of citizen-policemen which survived from its colonial past, allowing the SAP to have its regular manpower supplemented by numerous reserve forces, the degree of social control embedded in every institution of South Africa's structures of internal colonialism, and the political and technological capacity of the police to resort to maximum force as a first resort.

The public accountability of the SAP needs to be understood in this context (on this topic see Brewer 1992). In South Africa controversial police interventions were not largely *ad hoc* responses to particular traumatic events, but reflected structural relations between the social groups, so that the police deliberately reproduced traditional social cleavages rather than attempted (even if unsuccessfully) to mediate them impartially. Thus, police accountability needs to be located in terms of dominant–subordinate group relations and the intervention of the police to guarantee the position of Whites, and Afrikaners especially. Therefore, it is not the case that the SAP have been impervious to external control, but police accountability extended only to the dominant communal group, and they were rarely held to account for the way they maintained and reinforced boundaries between the races: indeed, this was their main task. Historically, the mechanisms of accountability have been weak in South Africa, mostly comprising after-the-fact explanations of police misconduct by means of official commissions of inquiry into specific incidents, or legal judgements on cases brought to court. The commissions of inquiry rarely found fault with the SAP and certainly never challenged their right to regulate and control the Black population. Most acts of misconduct never came before the courts, and guilty policemen were often not dismissed from the force when they were prosecuted.

Colonial policing is avowedly political, and policing in twentieth-century South Africa has therefore always been a political activity; it is inseparable from the state's policies of internal colonialism. However, there are two dimensions to political partisanship. Not only have the police served the state by implementing and enforcing these policies, police work was defined in such a way that was consistent with them. The political partisanship of policing in South Africa was something recognized from the beginning by the Black population, since the police were the key institution which implemented policies of internal colonialism and thus mediated their oppression. It was the police which enforced the administrative regulations which controlled their movements, limited their rights and opportunities, monitored and controlled their contact with Whites, and allowed state penetration of their ordinary daily lives. So although control was also embedded in the pass office, labour bureau, factory, and building site, policing was easily seen as a political activity by Blacks because the police enforced and symbolized a system of internal colonialism which accorded them second-class citizenship. In this sense South Africa has always been a police state because the police have from the beginning been experienced by the subject population as the main mediation of social control (for a discussion of the concept of social control see Mayer 1983; Stedman-Jones 1983).

But policing in South Africa is also politically partisan for the way in which police work is defined under policies of internal colonialism. This results in police work almost exclusively being conceptualized as the control and containment of the Black population, and thus the policing of race relations rather than ordinary crime. This extends the ways in which policing is perceived by Black South Africans. Ordinary crime in Black areas is high because of the very inequalities the police help to enforce, and the SAP's near complete focus on policing race relations to the neglect of ordinary crime placed the majority of law-abiding Blacks in a situation where they were caught between the twin evils of the gangsters and the police. The police did not protect them from the *tsotsis*, but only harassed and intimidated them for different reasons. The desire of law-abiding Blacks for law and order in the townships provided the SAP, at one time, with the opportunity to meet the needs of Black South Africans for crime prevention and detection, and thus to act towards them as a civil police service. But this went unsatisfied with the focus on policing race relations, and thus the containment and control of Blacks. The SAP was therefore also perceived by township residents as incompetent and ineffective when it came to dealing with ordinary crime.

Black South Africans withdrew all legitimacy from the SAP, as they did from the whole process of policing under White minority rule, irrespective of the skin colour of the person who discharged it. This shows the enormity of the pull factors Black policemen are under before deciding to join. But there is never a shortage of applicants; the racially structured employment opportunities left for Blacks makes many join out of hunger and desperation. The lack of legitimacy accorded to the police by Blacks resulted in various initiatives from Black communities to police themselves. The perceived incompetence and inefficiency of the SAP in dealing with ordinary crime also resulted in the state searching for more effective Black forces to police the townships. However, the illegitimacy of the whole process of policing affected the perception of all police forces, and, what is more, by their conduct Black policemen quickly demonstrated that their real purpose was to enhance the policing of race relations rather than deal with ordinary crime.

The entire thrust of this study has therefore been that the development of policing in South Africa needs to be placed in the context of broader state policies towards the Black population. These policies have constrained the SAP's modernization into a civil police force, allowed the perpetuation of brute force as a first resort well after it was abandoned in police forces with similar colonial origins, determined that police work be defined primarily as the policing of race relations, encouraged the growth of various forces drawn entirely from the subject population, and made policing a manifestly political activity. Critical junctures in the development of policing in South Africa therefore follow the evolution of state policies of internal colonialism.

In this respect, the election victory of Afrikaner nationalists in 1948 on a policy of apartheid is not the significant benchmark that it is usually presented as being since internal colonialism was state policy before 1948, albeit in slightly different form. Significant junctures in the development of policing also occurred much later, such as the emergence of the second phase of apartheid around 1960, which brought with it the 'own areas' policing strategy and homeland forces, and the reform era from the late 1970s, which culminated in de Klerk's attempt to reformulate radically the police role.

With this broader historical perspective it is possible to see what sort of transition was marked by 1948. The police had already established that their primary duty was the control and containment of Blacks. Their reputation for violence also pre-dated 1948, and from the very beginning the SAP had the centralized structure, militarism, and extraneous duties characteristic of colonial forces. Police reform, however, was taken off the political agenda by Afrikaner nationalists. Development towards the civil police model was possible on several occasions before 1948, when police reform was made a political issue by liberal critics of the SAP. There was also tension within the SAP at this time with some senior officers demanding reform along the lines of a civil police force. But always the state withdrew from reform because of its continued need for the colonial-like role played by the SAP. And at most, liberal critics of the police called for the police to perform the colonial task with the style and methods of a civil police force. However, while this demand was still being made in 1950 by a government commission of inquiry on the police, 1948 does signify a juncture of sorts. As state policies of internal colonialism evolved into apartheid, police powers were expanded, political, legal, and organizational constraints on police conduct were withdrawn, and police methods became more brutal. This brutality presented no political problem for the new government, save with the exception of Sharpeville, since police reform was not on the political agenda until developments in Black politics placed it there again in the late 1970s, whereupon police methods became an immense political embarrassment to reformist politicians.

This is a useful reminder that developments in policing were also affected by circumstances within the opposition movement. As the political challenge intensified during the 1950s, for example, police misconduct and lawlessness also increased, and the later emergence of armed struggle affected police training and methods, and ideological mind-set. But until the late 1970s, developments in Black opposition invariably reinforced the colonial-like character of the SAP rather than mounting up pressure for police reform. Thus, it was not until the end of the period of police omnipresence, a time marked by the Sharpeville and Soweto massacres between 1960 and 1976, that Black protest re-emerged, whereupon the rhetoric of the civil police tradition was drawn on by the police and government spokespeople when they were under attack for the colonial-like brutality and political partisanship of the police. This rhetoric became part of P. W. Botha's more general reform policy, and the government's rhetoric added pressure to Black demands for police reform by pointing to the contradiction between state discourse about policing and police practice. This pressure has risen significantly now that the contradiction has become wider because of de Klerk's more radical discourse on police reform and yet his continued inability to control the SAP's worst excesses.

POLICING AND THE STATE

It is clear from this review that policing in twentieth-century South Africa exemplifies a close relationship between policing and the state. This was determined by the colonial nature of the police style and the South African state's use of the police. Colonial policing is by character closely allied to the interests and structure of the colonial state: the police are centralized under the control of the state, they serve the state rather than the law, and perform several non-police duties for government. The relationship deepened in South Africa's case because of the state's reliance on the police to effect its policies of internal colonialism against often bitter internal opposition and an international environment where decolonization was the norm. The South African state used the police to implant an alien rule on a subject population that resisted it, requiring the police to intervene in social conflict in a politically partisan fashion. For all these reasons, the South African case offers a good opportunity to comment on the general issue of police–state relations.

It is now a commonplace in the literature on police studies to claim that policing is political and closely tied to the nature and project of the state (for a selection see: Bayley 1982; Brogden 1987a, 1987b; Brewer *et al.* 1988; Brodeur 1983; Enloe 1980; Hillyard and Percy-Smith 1988; Mosse 1975; Reiner 1985, 1989; Turk 1982). This trend reflects growing disillusionment with the liberal model of policing, which was once the only prism through which the police were understood. The model was an empirical and normative one. It was axiomatic that British police forces were of the liberal type—indeed, the model was extrapolated from what police practice in Britain was thought to be like empirically; and other police forces were normatively judged according to their proximity to British practice. Reiner calls this the 'consensus stage' of police research (1989), and these early authors on the police looked contemptuously on policing practice on the European continent (discussed by Tobias 1972), for example, and valorized the British bobby, seeing the avuncular figure as a metaphor for British social and political values.

Four features about British policing were stressed, which describe the liberal model. The first refers to various organizational practices characteristic of British policing, such as decentralization, an absence of militarism and arms, and a police membership which fairly represents the social composition of society as a whole. The liberal model also saw police–public relations in a distinct way. The police obtained their mandate from the public and could only operate on the basis of public consensus and legitimacy. This fed into conceptualizations of the police role, which emphasized crime detection and prevention as well as a service role in the community. Finally, the model proffered the idea that policing was apolitical. Two things were meant by this: as an institution, the police were independent of political parties and governments; and individual members divorced their political views from their conduct as policemen and women. At the organizational and individual levels, therefore, political neutrality was both principle and practice, so that the police impartially upheld the law rather than partisanly advanced political causes.

Changes in the nature of contemporary policing in Britain led to a reassessment of the liberal model (for a general review of these processes see: Fielding 1991; Reiner 1985: 48–84). Critics of the British police detected various tendencies towards centralization (see Brewer *et al.* 1988: 23; R. Fine and Miller 1988), the emergence of paramilitary-style policing methods (Jefferson 1990), and a deterioration in police relations with the public, in large part because of their ineffectiveness in stemming the rise of crime (Kinsey *et al.* 1986), notorious public order incidents which damaged the police image (Brewer *et al.* 1988: 25–7), or racial bias in dealing with ethnic minorities in the inner cities (Cashmore and McLaughlin 1991*b*).

Once the model was under threat in this way, critics looked back and disputed that there had ever been a 'golden age' in Britain when policing conformed to the model. Others also pointed to the colonial origins of the British police (Brogden 1987*a*, 1987*b*), arguing that tendencies of the colonial model survived throughout, including the habit of 'policing by strangers', as Brogden shows with respect to Liverpool between the wars (1991), and the excessive use of force in policing industrial disputes (Geary 1985).

It also became popular to identify a relationship between politics and the police (R. Fine and Miller 1988; Grimshaw and Jefferson 1987: 282–97; Reiner 1985, 1989). In part this reflected changes in British society which made it less homogeneous and more divisive, increasing intervention by the police in social conflict (on which see Fielding 1991), and on changes that were said to be occurring in the British state under Thatcher governments, to which changes in policing were allied. Thus, the militarism, centralization, and bias of the police were linked to the authoritarianism and centralization of the British state under Thatcher, and its legitimacy crisis, which expressed itself in various public order challenges to the government, and inner-city disturbances, in all of which the police intervened aggressively on behalf of the state (for a selection of this literature see: Bridges 1983; R. Fine and Miller 1988; Hain 1980; Hall *et al.* 1978; Scraton 1985; Uglow 1988). This is what Reiner calls the 'conflict stage' of police research (1989), and within the paradigm it is widely recognized that the police are an institution within the domain of state influence, operate to consolidate and maintain state authority, take a share of the state's fiscal pie, and have an impact upon people's views of the state.

However, it is necessary to unpack what is meant precisely by the claim that there is a relationship between policing and politics. One or more of six claims are implied by the relationship, and each claim comes in a weak and strong form:

1. The first concerns political beliefs. In its weak version the claim is that policemen and women are political animals and hold political beliefs and opinions. In its strong form, this becomes the argument that members of the police allow their conduct to be influenced by their beliefs. In the South African case we can see evidence for the stronger version of the claim, in that many ordinary policemen and women have shown support for the Afrikaner political right wing, especially in the way right-wing violence is under-policed and organizations like OB and AWB leniently treated. Afrikaner racial

beliefs have clearly influenced the way Afrikaner policemen and women have treated Blacks, and go some way to explain the gratuitous violence, sexual abuse, and inhuman and degrading treatment accorded them. What is also important here is the organizational culture of the SAP, which provided little disciplinary constraint on the open expression of members' political and racial beliefs in their practice.

2. A second claim concerns the politicization of policing as an issue. In its weak form the claim is that policing has become an issue of dispute in party politics, and thus part of political debate and intrigue. In its strong version, the claim is that the police 'side' with one party rather than another, and thus directly engage in party political disputes. South Africa provides an example of the strong form. Members of the police have at various times supported Afrikaner nationalism rather than Smuts, the Conservative rather than National Party, and Inkatha rather than the UDF or ANC; it is this partisanship which helps to dispute the claim that selective policing reflects incompetence rather than malevolence. Partisanship is shown in open political support, but more often in selective enforcement of the law, and the under- or over-policing of the activities of respective political groupings.

3. The third claim relates to police resources. In its weak form the claim is that the police are part of the state's fiscal pie, and the resources devoted to it reflect the political and other priorities of the state. In its strong version, this becomes the claim that the police manipulate the state's priorities in order to obtain a disproportionate share of resources. In South Africa's case, it is clear that the state increased the SAP's resources under such exigencies as the aftermath of war and public-order incidents, and in line with guerrilla insurgency and other developments in Black politics. But the SAP was also able on occasions to manipulate the state's perceptions of circumstances in order to effect an increase in financial and manpower resources. It did this by warnings of low morale in the police over pay (for a similar example from the Royal Irish Constabulary in 1914 see Brewer 1989) or poor working conditions, such as the lack of accommodation; exploiting members' dissatisfactions by warnings of high resignations, or even strikes, as occurred in 1918; by threats of widespread guerrilla insurgency, political opposition, or communist incursion, which predicated the SAP's early recognition of the so-called 'total on-slaught'; and by using crime figures to warn of an unbridled escalation

of lawlessness and anarchy, especially appealing to White fears of *swart gevaar*.

4. The fourth claim concerns the police relationship to state policies. In its weak version the argument is that the police implement state policies by the enforcement of laws which enact them. The strong form of this claim is that the police are partisan in the bias shown against legitimate opposition to these policies. The SAP always claimed that they exemplified the former: that they merely implemented the law rather than determined the policies thus enacted by it. But the force, aggression, and brutality used by them against the state's opponents engaged in lawful and peaceful opposition, belied claims to impartiality and reflected their contempt for any opposition to state policies. But this was not just evinced in gratuitous violence towards the state's opponents, it was reflected also in the SAP's circumvention, and sometimes complete disregard, of the legal protections which opponents were accorded when engaging in lawful and peaceful opposition, and the use of openly illegal means to suppress this opposition, such as death squads and vigilantes, and the murder and torture of detainees. Again, this is evidence for political malevolence within the police rather than simple incompetence.

5. Another claim concerns the permeation of state values and ideology within the police. In its weak form, the argument is that the police are affected by the values and ideology of the state. In its strong version, the claim is that the police support these values and ideology and reinforce them by denying legitimate opposition to them, or the expression of alternative values and ideologies. The best example of the stronger version of the claim in South Africa is the SAP's criminalization of peaceful political activity against the state by alleging it to be furthering the aims of communism or to come within the very encompassing legal definitions of terrorism and sabotage. The South African state itself denied opponents the opportunity to express alternative values and ideologies through its tough security legislation, but the police often used the legislation as a catch-all by which to criminalize quite innocuous forms of protest, such as carol-singing, the wearing of certain T-shirts, funeral marches, and newspaper copy, which were alleged at one time or another to be furthering the aims of communism.

6. The final claim posits, in its weak form, that the conduct of the police affects people's perceptions of the state, and thus influences politics indirectly. The strong version of this claims that the police

manipulate these perceptions by trying both deliberately to manufacture a positive image of the state by careful presentation of its conduct, and to avoid negative images arising from the deleterious consequences of police misconduct. In South Africa's case, evidence for the stronger version comes in the form of the public-relations exercises engaged in by the SAP after highly publicized police atrocities which threatened the state, the adoption of the rhetoric of the civil policing tradition to massage the SAP's image on these occasions, and various publicity enterprises to stress its benign policing role after the paramilitary role was revealed to dominate. The SAP's 'helping hand' poster campaign is but one example of the latter amongst the White population; the occasional drive to defeat ordinary crime in the townships is another relating to Black South Africans.

Different conclusions about the relationship between politics and the police emerge from the weak and strong versions of these claims. While clearly denying the arguments of the liberal model that policing is apolitical and independent of the state, the weak versions cast the relationship as one-way, in which the police manifestly come within the domain of the state's influence and will always be affected by it, but are passive and reactive to that influence. In this form, the relationship describes a truism, since there is hardly an institution which cannot in some way claim to be influenced by the political process and state power; and like all truisms, the relationship tells us the obvious. It advances our understanding of policing only by making apparent what was not obvious to advocates of the liberal model. In the stronger versions, the relationship between politics and the police is two-way, in which the police are proactive in politics and partisanly advance the policies and ideologies of the state.

Clearly, the SAP, and all other compatible forces in South Africa, illustrate the strong case; they have been very proactive in politics by furthering the state's policies of internal colonialism, by supporting the values and ideology which underlay the state, and in suppressing opposition thereto beyond the limits which the law laid down as permissible for the police. They have been politically partisan in the way policing has been defined, carried out, and in the ends to be realized by it. The SAP are more than incompetent: they are, in short, politically biased. However, precisely because it is such a good exemplar of the strong version of police–state relations, the South African case is also useful in providing a cautionary footnote to discussions of this form of the relationship.

Even in societies like South Africa where the police are so pro-actively political and partisan, it is over-simplistic to argue that the police are a tool of the state, automatically reproducing state policy and interests. Robinson (1975: 287) has argued similarly with respect to the local connection between American mayors and the city police, which has long been portrayed as politically corrupt. The history and development of policing in South Africa suggests two closely associated caveats which weaken the strong version of the police–state relationship. First, the state often has internal contradictions and policy disputes within it, which are reflected in political conflicts within the police and contradictory political interventions by them. This does not affect the link between politics and the police, but weakens the police–state bond because the political support and interventions can be on behalf of subordinate factions within the state, or for political causes and groupings outside the state. Secondly, even in situations where police–state relations are close, this relationship can be weakened by the police trying to assert their independence from the state, although this is always limited if the state has a readiness and capacity to impose its influence on the police.

These qualifications amount to what can be called, borrowing a term from Althusser, the relative autonomy of policing from the state. The South African case illustrates this well. The history of the SAP over the last eight decades shows that they had a capacity for independent action within the overall constraints imposed by the state. This relative autonomy had organizational and political expressions. With respect to organizational manifestations, the South African state's continual need for colonial policing, because of its policies of internal colonial-ism, was in conflict with the occasional pressure emerging from within the police management to professionalize, as many former colonial police services had done. At certain periods, especially before 1948, the tension between the civil and colonial models erupted in conflict within the police, and therefore between sections of the police and the state. The state's need to retain features of the colonial police style was also in conflict with the requirements of modern urban dwellers for a civil police force focused on combating crime and on service to the community. There has always been a constituency inside South Africa (more or less powerful on occasions) complaining about outdated police methods and tactics and misdirected efforts, to which the police were required occasionally to respond by improving their crime prevention and detection capabilities, and service role. Thus, relative autonomy showed itself in the police management's demand for organizational independence within the structure of the state, leaving the management free to determine key organizational concerns and priorities, and free from the burden of performing non-police duties for government departments. The perennial complaint of Commissioners about extraneous duties is the best illustration of the demand for organizational autonomy.

But this organizational autonomy was, in the final analysis, relative. The demand was made by a centralized force under the effective institutional control of the state, so that Commissioners could do little but complain. Moreover, the complaint was uttered only occasionally by the police management, who were fully aware of their subservience to the state, and the demand for civil policing duties was always treated by the state as secondary to the need to police race relations and thus to control and regulate the Black population. Thus, when the Commissioner said after the Second World War, for example, that strident steps would be taken to lessen the burden of extraneous duties, they actually increased; as they have done progressively throughout most of the SAP's history.

Relative autonomy was also manifested in political opposition by the police to particular state policies. This interacts with the existence of internal contradictions within the South African state, so that the police, or sections thereof, have sometimes supported subordinate factions within the governing class, as many Afrikaner nationalist policemen did, for example, during the fusion and United Party governments prior to the Second World War, when they opposed Smuts's entry into the war. A contemporary example is provided by the support of some members of the police for the old-style apartheid policies of certain factions of the state, such as the Conservative Party, against de Klerk's policies of reform. This autonomy can also amount to a political challenge to the state as a whole, so that some sections of the police intervene to give active support to the policies of extra-constitutional groups outside the state. Good examples of this are provided by the opposition of some policemen and women to the ethnic and racial policies pursued by the South African state at various times, such as police involvement in the 1914 Afrikaner rebellion against General Botha's Union government and in the 1940–1 Afrikaner rebellion by the OB against Smuts, support today for the AWB, and, in the opposite direction, support for the ANC among some members of the police before it was unbanned. Autonomy of this sort amounts to a complete challenge to the political interests of the state. This political autonomy is also evident in police protest against the economic policies of the state, such as police strikes over low pay and poor working conditions, which occurred in 1918 and during 1985–6.

But again this political autonomy is relative. Discontent was restricted to minor or junior sections of the police, the state was always able successfully to manage or sidestep the protest, and the loyalty of most members was retained. The majority of members continued to support the policies of the state or its dominant faction. Sometimes police discontent over the state's policies was simply crushed by superior force, as happened in the 1914 and 1940–1 Afrikaner rebellions. The state resorted to prosecution in some cases where policemen were revealed to be members of illegal organizations, like the OB and formerly the ANC, or other disciplinary measures. On other occasions the state simply bought police loyalty by the temporary redirection of resources for pay increases, improvements in accommodation, or extra manpower. But as a demonstration of how relative is the SAP's autonomy, its ability to manipulate a lion's share of the state's resources was always conditional on the state's other priorities, which is why it has persistently remained understaffed and under-resourced.

It is symptomatic of how loyal the majority of police officers are to the racial and class interests of the state's former policies of internal colonialism that perhaps their greatest assertion of political autonomy is occurring in the contemporary period, when de Klerk is abandoning that project in favour of radical reform. The opposition to political reform among many policemen and women today is constrained in its expressions because it reflects relative rather than complete autonomy from the state, which is why it mostly shows itself in dissimulation, the use of surrogates, free-lance activities, and localized examples of under- or over-policing. None the less, many members of the SAP are using their capacity for limited independent action to defend those sections of the state and extra-constitutional groups who support the colonial status quo ante: old-style apartheid. This is ironic because the colonial nature of policing in South Africa has made the police so closely associated with the state that the relative autonomy shown at this juncture is difficult for de Klerk to accept. But police opposition to political reform today can only be understood in the context of a set of police–state relations where the SAP possess relative autonomy.

It is also in this context that one must locate the problem of future police reform.

POLICING THE NEW SOUTH AFRICA

It is appropriate to close a book that has focused on policing in South Africa's past with some comments on policing in the future. This is not pandering to the topical because any review of the SAP's history and development reveals policing in the old South Africa to be very relevant to policing in the future. The policing errors and failures disclosed by the past predicate the proposals for policing the new South Africa by showing the nature of the task and what needs to be avoided.

Changes are necessary to the current role, style, organization, and structure of the police, and various proposals can be devised to effect this. But the task goes further, for proposals are needed which restrict the relative autonomy of the SAP so that these other changes can be more easily implemented. The arguments here suggest that it is necessary for the state to assert complete control over the police, at least in the short term, rather than abandon the future to the mythology of the liberal model. Unless this is done and, ironically, the SAP placed more firmly under the political control of a liberal and reformist state, the general reform process will be stymied by police actions intended to subvert or obstruct it. In this respect, the liberal model of policing is the wrong one for de Klerk to invoke when discussing police reform. In an analytical sense it is wrong because the model is a chimera. It is erroneous in a practical sense because what South Africa needs in the short term is more not less political control of the police, so long as it is control by a reformist state, and more not less political intervention by the police, so long as it is intervention to sponsor reform rather than reaction.

In one sense, this is more important than internal changes to police organization and structure, for the suggestion of this study is that President de Klerk is a prisoner of the SAP's relative autonomy. It is popular amongst radical critics to portray him as working to some grand design in which the police are being cleverly used by the government deliberately to slow down the reform process, scupper the ANC by advancing Inkatha, and frighten most electors into voting for the steady hand of the National Party and its eventual coalition allies by exaggerating the power and influence of the Afrikaner right wing. This view fits most people's experience of past National Party leaders as being mischievous and downright dishonest when it came to promises of reform, and the image of the SAP throughout its history as being fully in the domain of the state's control.

However, it cannot be denied that de Klerk has done more than any previous leader to dismantle the legal pillars of apartheid, and has gone furthest in reforming the police. But once it is accepted that the SAP is not completely derivative of the state in how it acts, and that police–state relations have not always conformed to the image of complete subservience, current resistance to state policies can be seen as reflecting the SAP's relative autonomy rather than Machiavellian manipulation by the government. In this view, de Klerk does not lack the political will to control the police; he is a prisoner of their relative autonomy and is unable to rein them in completely. Any consideration of policing the new South Africa therefore must begin with proposals for establishing state control over the police. This is what many programmatic statements for police reform omit, preferring instead to see the police as autonomous and able to be reformed solely by internal changes to the police (for example Weitzer 1990*a*, 1990*b*). However, police reform in South Africa should not be conceived of narrowly.

It is important to put police reform in a broader context. This is so for two reasons. First, reform of the Royal Ulster Constabulary in Northern Ireland since 1969 illustrates the obstacles to police reform when it occurs within a political vacuum (on police reform in Northern Ireland see Brewer 1991: 275–8; Weitzer 1985). Police reform must be part of a wider process of social change which addresses the political and economic problems which the police would otherwise have to deal with. The Northern Ireland case shows that unless the structural inequalities and problems of the society are addressed, no amount of police reform will alter the nature of police–public relations. In this sense, it is possible to be relatively optimistic about police reform in South Africa because it appears to be part of a process of broader reform.

This broader approach to police reform is necessary for a second reason. Police reform should be placed in the context of police–state relations, so that it addresses more than the organizational structure and role of the police. Police reform is not being approached in its proper context if it is divorced from the state. However, a case for state control of the police can only be made if the state is committed to police reform as part of a wider process of genuine reform, a commitment which can be gauged by its efforts to impose both the necessary change and control on the police.

Assuming that the state after transition is genuinely reformist, the following proposals seem appropriate as means by which it can assert control over the police:

1. There should be one single national force under direct and centralized control of the (presumably) multiracial government. All reserve and volunteer forces, homeland forces, and other compatible policing agencies should be absorbed into the SAP or disbanded, so that policing functions are brought within one agency, which can be more easily controlled politically.

2. Political control should be exercised by a committee of political representatives and nominated lay people, responsible to the elected government, along the lines of the Northern Ireland Police Authority.

3. There should be a purge of senior officers within the police, and the state should retain only those officers who are committed to broader reform and prepared to implement police reform. A new police oath should be devised which requires expression of partisanship towards the political values of the new democratic South Africa, and this loyalty should be a major criterion for appointment to senior office.

4. A new and stricter disciplinary ethos needs to be introduced by senior officers, to ensure that ordinary policemen and women are placed under close organizational control. This disciplinary ethos should be supported by strict sanctions and facilitated by close supervision. Supervision should be provided by senior officers and lay inspectors nominated by the new government; lay inspectors should have the right to intervene in police practice, and would report directly to the committee responsible for policing.

5. Mechanisms of legal and public accountability should be introduced, which strictly limit the legal powers of the police, institute legal control over the police, and provide for public input into police practice and policy. This can be done by such means as liaison committees, upon which police and elected political representatives sit, independent lay visitors to police stations, and independent complaint procedures (these proposals for accountability are expanded in Brewer 1992).

6. There should be a purge of the rank and file, so that the police

retain only those with good disciplinary records in the past and those committed to the political values of the new democratic South Africa. Support for the process of change, in society and within the police, should be made a criterion of appointment via an expression of loyalty in the form of a new police oath.

Clearly, these proposals increase the political partisanship of the new police and strengthen the bond with the new state, but it would now be partisanship in favour of democratic political ideologies, and loyalty to the policies of reform and the values which underlie them. It is feasible to contend that the political impartiality espoused by advocates of liberal models of reform would simply provide cover for policemen and women to continue their covert loyalties to the colonial status quo ante.

Several changes are also necessary internal to the organization and role of the police. These are addressed in the following proposals:

1. The police should refocus all their efforts towards ordinary crime. Their role in policing race relations would by definition already be abolished with the election of a new government, but their responsibility for internal security should be granted to a separate body unconnected with the police, along the lines of the current Internal Stability Unit, set up in 1991. The nomenclature of this new force should emphasize its distance from policing, by using such a name as the 'national guard', as in the United States, to avoid the police being associated with riot control and 'political' policing. The training, equipment, and crowd-control tactics of this force should be made the subject of extensive review, as already proposed by the group of international experts collected together by Justice Goldstone (see Heymann 1992), and it should come under the forms of state control mentioned above.

2. There should be an enormous expansion in the manpower of the police in order to combat the increase in ordinary crime by placing many more policemen and women on the streets, thus building on the wish within townships for legitimate law-and-order policing.

3. The police will need to be re-educated and retrained to make them capable of dealing with ordinary crime (proposals for this are expanded in Brewer forthcoming). Re-education would need to correct the SAP's past demonology and mind-set by means of such things as race-awareness training, a stress on the philosophy of community policing, and on the service role of the police.

Training should place emphasis on crime detection and prevention, and community policing.

4. Community policing initiatives should be introduced to strengthen the police–public relationship and overcome negative images of the police. Local liaison committees should operate to give local communities an input into police operational policy as a form of problem-solving policing for the neighbourhood.

5. The police should be demilitarized and disarmed.

6. Members of the police would be required to use minimum force. Excessive force and gratuitous violence should be made grounds for immediate prosecution and dismissal.

7. The command structure of the police should be democratized, so that there is rapid expansion in the number of senior Black officers to make the command structure more representative of South African society.

8. The deployment of police manpower and resources should make no reference to race, and 'own areas' strategies should be abolished, so that police work can provide policemen and women with opportunities to establish real relationships with members of other communities, thus undercutting negative stereotypes and demonology.

9. The police should develop professional contingency and mobilization plans for dealing with incidents, based on the examples of other forces more experienced in minimum policing methods, which take decision-making out of the hands of junior officers and the rank and file. Mechanisms should be introduced to hold officers to account for the decisions taken on the ground.

It is important to end by noting that police reform is a two-way process. As these proposals suggest, the police are required to make a considerable number of changes in order to procure peace and stability in the new South Africa, but people in the country can also do a great deal in order to facilitate the police in making these changes. First, it is necessary for former policemen and women to be assured that they will not be subject to reprisals and intimidation under the new government, and that bygones are truly bygones, thus reducing their fear and anxiety about the future. The new South Africa needs to forget its past and build on new foundations rather than have these shaken continually by fighting over past battles: policing in Northern Ireland cannot be normalized because the past is such a burden on the future. Secondly, there needs to be an end to township violence. The police cannot switch attention to ordinary crime while political violence remains unchecked: Northern Ireland again offers a case in point. Thus, political leaders have a responsibility to control their supporters and persuade them to peace. The policies of the new government will do much to alleviate the causes of violence, but the police paramilitary role cannot be abandoned while political groups refuse to take their responsibility to desist from violence. The 1990 Peace Accord between the government, ANC, and Inkatha promised to deliver this but has palpably failed. This is a measure of the enormity of the task of police reform in South Africa: we can but hope for South Africa's sake that they pull it off.

BIBLIOGRAPHY

PRIMARY SOURCES

General

Annual Estimates of the Expenditure of Transkei Revenue Fund.
Annual Estimates of the Expenditure to be Defrayed from the Revenue Account, South African Railways and Harbours Service.
Annual Estimates of Revenue and Expenditure, Lebowa Legislative Assembly.
Annual Reports of the Commandant of the Natal Mounted Police.
Annual Reports of the Commissioner of the SAP.
Annual Reports of the General Manager of Railways and Harbours.
Annual Reports of the Native Affairs Commission.
Annual Reports of the Proceedings of the Native Representative Council.
Annual Reports of the Sessional Committee on Public Accounts, Bophuthatswana Legislative Assembly.
Annual Reports of the Sessional Committee on the Accounts of the KwaZulu Government, KwaZulu Legislative Assembly.
Annual Reports of the South African Institute of Race Relations.
Annual Reports of the South African Transport Service Board.
Annual Survey of Race Relations, South African Institute of Race Relations.
Bantu, journal of the Department of Bantu Administration and Development.
Black Sash, journal of the Black Sash.
Race Relations, journal of the South African Institute of Race Relations.
South African Police magazines, *Nongqai*, *SARP*, *Justitia*, and *Servamus*.
South African Public Service Lists.
South African Railways and Harbours Service, Estimates of the Expenditure to be Defrayed from the Revenue Account, 1956.

Archive Material

Rhodes House Library, Oxford University

MSS Afr. r. 92. Sir Robert Hall, Unofficial Diary of a Visit to South Africa in 1944 to Assess the African Question.
MSS Afr. r. 102. Lt. J. E. Thomas, Tanganyika Diary.
MSS Afr. s. 8, ff. 71–4. Mr Justice Saul Solomon, Typed Copy of a Letter to Sir Herbert Baker Concerning the Political Situation in South Africa in 1939.

MSS Afr. s. 1250. Sir Herbert Stanley, Correspondence 1910–41.

MSS Afr. s. 1277. Richard Gethin, Impressions with the 1st South African Division and East African Military Corps, Jan.–Apr. 1941.

MSS Afr. s. 1638. Lt. Arthur Weatherhead, Diaries of the South African Constabulary 1904–7.

MSS Afr. s. 2015. Col. Rowland Daniel, Letters to his Mother from Bechuanaland 1896–1914.

MSS Brit. Emp. s. 308. Lt.-Col. H. W. Bamford, Police Service in Natal and Malta, 1920 and 1921.

South African Police Archive, Pretoria

Conf/6/5/10, Cost of Police Needed Under Draft Regulations Framed Under the Police Bill, 1911.

Conf/6/5/10/A, Regarding Revised Police Regulations, 1911–12.

Conf/6/7/10, Absorption of Railway Police in the South African Police Force, 1925.

Conf/6/8/10, Criminal Investigation Department for the Union, Reorganization by Deputy Commissioner, 1912.

Conf/6/8/10/A, Reorganization of Criminal Investigation Department, 1906–11.

Conf/6/268/14, Vryheid: Suspect, 1914.

Conf/6/281/15/A, Report by Detective Cuffs, Criminal Investigation Department Regarding Meeting of Railwaymen, 1915.

Conf/6/288/15, Alleged Plot to Assassinate Generals Botha and Smuts, 1914–15.

Conf/6/301/15, Anti-Government and Anti-British Rioting in Johannesburg, 1915.

Conf/6/610/18, Local Allowance: Alleged Unrest, 1918–19.

Conf/6/610/18/1, Alleged Unrest Between Railway Employees, 1918.

Conf/6/610/18/2, Alleged Industrial Unrest—Cape Peninsula, 1918.

Conf/6/611/18, Regarding Contemplated Reduction of Establishment of SAP, 1918.

Conf/6/641/18, Political Meetings, Police Reports Regarding, 1918.

Conf/6/657/18/1–13, Proposed Amalgamation Police and South African Mounted Riflemen, 1919–25.

Conf/6/658/18, Regarding Native National Congress: Meetings of, 1918–19.

Conf/6/658/18/1, Regarding Native National Congress: Reports Regarding Meetings of, 1920.

Conf/6/658/18/2, Native National Congress, Rex Versus ShThema and Others, 1920.

Conf/6/726/19/1–5, South West Protectorate, Commissioner's Report on Police Requirements, 1919.

Conf/6/731/19, Nationalist Party, Police Arrangements for Meetings of, 1919–20.

Conf/6/758/20, Holding-up of Banks at Doornfontein and Jeepes, 1920.

Conf/6/760/20, Durban Borough Police, Regarding Union Government Taking Control of, 1920.

Conf/6/766/20/1, Overseas Recruiting to the SAP, 1920–8.

Conf/6/967/23, Marcus Garvey, 1923–30.

Conf/8/233/A, Estimates 1909–10 Native Affairs—Number of Police to be Perployed, 1909.

Conf/8/385, re Illicit Liquor Traffic in Basutoland, 1910.

Conf/8/397, re December 1909 Enrolments for Transvaal Police, 1910.

Conf/8/414, Point of Complaint Raised by District Commandant Ermelo, 1910.

Conf/8/415, Confidential Circular Letter to all Officers—Administration of Punishment to Members of Transvaal Police, 1910.

Conf/8/423, re Alleged Contravention of Diamond Trade Ordinance, 1910.

Conf/8/431, re Proposed Conference at Bloemfontein of all Commissioners of Police in South Africa, 1910.

Conf/8/433, Police Telephone Requirements, 1910.

Conf/8/438, Application for Extra Native Court at Nauwpoort Lydenberg District, 1910.

Conf/8/446, Complaint by District Commandant Ermelo re Class of Men Transferred to that District, 1910.

Conf/8/447, Complaint by District Commandant re Conduct of Mr C. Rothman Concerning the Police at Klerksdorp, 1910.

Conf/8/504, Postal and Telegraph Duties Performed by Members of Transvaal Police, 1910.

Conf/8/507, Clerical Staff, 1910.

Conf/8/513, Enquiry re Thomas re Maintenance of Children, 1910.

Conf/8/520, Anonymous Letter Received from East Rand, 1910.

Conf/8/522, Complaint by Native Women at Amsterdam, 1910.

Conf/8/533/A, A. Burcharth, Detective CID: Allegation Against the Deputy Commissioner CID, 1911.

Conf/8/534, re Illicit Liquor Traffic East Rand, 1910.

Conf/8/540, Depot Instructors, Educational Qualifications of, 1910.

Conf/8/550, Regarding Policing of Johannesburg, 1911.

Conf/8/551, Regarding Policing in Johannesburg, 1911.

Conf/8/553, Establishment of the Police Area Benoni-Springs, 1911.

Conf/8/556, Regarding Schilpadfontein Post Pretoria District, 1911.

Conf/8/564, Enquiry Regarding Alexander Storeman, Wife and Children Destitute in Edinburgh, 1911.

Conf/8/566, Regarding Native Outrages on Rand, Question of Increase of Police, 1911–12.

Conf/8/571, Regarding Native Police Attached to Native Affairs Department, 1911.

Conf/8/572, Regarding Sale of Tobacco Pouches to Natives on Rand Containing Indecent Picture, 1911.

Conf/8/579, Regarding Whippet Racing, 1911.

Conf/8/580, Regarding Cutting from the *Transvaal Critic* of 24 Feb. 1911 Referring to a Police Official, 1911.

Conf/8/581, Regarding Cutting from *Sunday Times* of 5 Mar. 1911 and *Transvaal Chronicle* of 6 Mar. 1911, 1911.

Conf/8/591, Regarding Police and Coloured People, Cuttings from *Transvaal Leader* 3 Mar. 1911, *Volkstem* 21 Feb. 1911, 1911.

Conf/8/771, Anonymous Letter re Police Germiston, Also Cutting from *Transvaal Critic* 4 Oct. 1912, 1912.

Conf/8/772, Anonymous Letter re Benoni, 1912.

Conf/8/787, re Suspected Trouble with Natives, Communication from Mr J. Lundman, 1912.

Conf/8/796, Complaint from Johannesburg Police re Treatment of Dutch-Speaking Members, 1912.

Conf/8/838, Circular, Efficiency of Police and Suggestions for Increasing Same, 1913.

Conf/8/848, re Police Boksburg District—Cutting from *Leader* of 26 Sept. 1913, 1913.

SAP/1/62/27, Murder of Member of SAP and Members of the Public by one Swart, 1927.

SAP/1/93/27, Members of the South African Police, 1915.

SAP/1/161/26, School Attendance, Police Assistance, 1926–34.

SAP/1/185/13, Points Discussed Between Commissioner and Acting Secretary as to Measures to be Adopted Throughout Union for Protection of Life and Property in Event of Disorder, n.d.

SAP/1/185/13/1–52, Miners' Strike 1913, 1913.

SAP/1/895/14/3, Application to Proceed on Active Service in Europe by Members of SAP, 1915.

SAP/2/14/21/1, Review of Various Police Forces, South Africa Prior to Reorganization, 1911–13.

SAP/2/14/21/2, Actual Strength of all Forces Incorporated in the SAP, 1914–15.

SAP/20/10/24, Training Baton Drill, 1915–34.

Official Government Reports and Documents

Cape of Good Hope (1882), *Report by Bernard V. Shaw on Police and Gaol Establishments* (Cape Town: Government Printer).

Department of Justice (1936), *Correspondence Which has Passed Between the Rt.*

Hon. Minister of Justice and the Durban City Council Relevant to the Question of Adequately Dealing with Crime Committed within the Limits of the Borough of Durban (Cape Town: Government Printer).

South Africa (1963), *Report of the Commission Appointed to Inquire into the Events on 20–22 March 1962 at Paarl* (Pretoria: Government Printer).

—— (1980), *Report of the Commission of Inquiry into the Riots at Soweto and Elsewhere from 16 June 1976 to 28 February 1977* (Pretoria: Government Printer).

—— (1988), *White Paper on the Organization and Functions of the SAP* (Pretoria: Government Printer).

Union of South Africa (1914*a*), *Report of the Native Grievance Inquiry 1913–14* (Cape Town: Government Printer).

—— (1914*b*), *Report of the Commissioner, Hon. Mr Justice Gregorowski, into the Deaths of Senator General de la Rey and Dr S. Grace* (Cape Town: Government Printer).

—— (1917), *Report of the Committee on Retrenchment in Public Expenditure* (Cape Town: Government Printer).

—— (1918*a*), *Report of the Select Committee on the Police Strike and Recruiting, 1918* (Cape Town: Government Printer).

—— (1918*b*), *Report of the Public Service Commission of Inquiry* (Cape Town: Government Printer).

—— (1922), *Report of the Martial Law Inquiry Judicial Commission* (Cape Town: Government Printer).

—— (1923), *Report of the Commission into the Rebellion of the Bondelzwarts* (Cape Town: Government Printer).

—— (1926), *Report of the Commission of Inquiry Appointed by His Excellency the Governor General into the Organization of the SAP* (Cape Town: Government Printer).

—— (1937*a*), (The Lansdown Commission) *Report of the Police Commission of Inquiry into the SAP and SARHP* (Cape Town: Government Printer).

—— (1937*b*), *Report of the Commission into Riots and Disturbances at Vereeniging on 18 and 19 September 1937* (Cape Town: Government Printer).

—— (1944), *Report of the Public Services Commission of Inquiry* (Cape Town: Government Printer).

—— (1946), *Third Report of the Public Services Commission of Inquiry* (Cape Town: Government Printer).

—— (1947), *Report of the Commission of Inquiry into the Disturbances at the Moroka Emergency Camp* (Cape Town: Government Printer).

—— (1948), *Report of the Public Services Commission of Inquiry* (Cape Town: Government Printer).

—— (1950*a*), *Report of the Commission of Inquiry into Allegations Against Members of the SAP* (Pretoria: Government Printer).

—— (1950*b*), *Report of the Commission of Inquiry into Acts of Violence Committed by Natives at Krugersdorp, Newlands, Randfontein, and Newclare* (Pretoria: Government Printer).

SECONDARY SOURCES

Acta Juridica (1989) (ed.), *Policing and the Law* (Cape Town: Juta).
Adam, H. (1987), 'The Ultra-Right in South Africa', *Optima*, 35: 36–43.
—— (1990), 'Prisoners of Presidents: South Africa and Eastern Europe', in J. Olivier (ed.), *Eastern Europe and South Africa* (Pretoria: Human Sciences Research Council), 63–76.
—— and Giliomee, H. (1979), *The Rise and Crisis of Afrikaner Power* (Cape Town: David Philip).
—— and Moodley, K. (1986), *South Africa Without Apartheid* (Berkeley, Calif.: University of California Press).
Adebisi, B. (1976), 'Alliance for Oppression', *Co-Existence*, 13: 190–208.
Alderson, J. (1979), *Policing Freedom* (Plymouth: MacDonald and Evans).
Alex, N. (1969), *Black in Blue* (New York: Appleton, Century and Croft).
Amnesty International (1991a), Statement by Amnesty International to the 47th Session of the United Nations' Commission on Human Rights.
—— (1991b), Statement by Amnesty International to the United Nations' *Ad Hoc* Working Group of Experts on South Africa.
Anderson, D. (1991), 'Policing, Prosecution, and the Law in Colonial Kenya', in Anderson and Killingray (1991a), 183–201.
Anderson, D., and Killingray, D. (1991a) (eds.), *Policing the Empire* (Manchester: Manchester University Press).
—— (1991b), 'Consent, Coercion, and Colonial Control', in Anderson and Killingray (1991a), 1–17.
—— (1992) (eds.), *Policing and Decolonization* (Manchester: Manchester University Press).
Ashforth, A. (1990), *The Politics of Official Discourse in Twentieth-Century South Africa* (Oxford: Clarendon Press).
Attwell, J. (1926), *The Fighting Police of South Africa* (Pietermaritzburg: Natal Witness).
Atz, J. (1988), 'The British Colonial Police Service', Ph.D. thesis (Temple University).
Bantu (1959), 'Meadowlands', *Bantu*, 2: 9.
—— (1960), 'Editorial', *Bantu*, 7/8: 473.
—— (1961), 'Editorial', *Bantu*, 8/6: 277–8.
—— (1962), 'Keepers of the Peace', *Bantu*, 9/9: 526–7.
—— (1964a), 'Ikageng Township: Crime Hardly Ever Heard of', *Bantu*, 11/9: 279–81.
—— (1964b), 'Prisoners' Friend Keeps Thousands out of Gaol', *Bantu*, 11/10: 469–71.
—— (1964c), 'Sound Relations Between Police and Bantu', *Bantu*, 11/10: 356–7.
—— (1965), 'Tsotsi Problem Almost Solved in Pretoria', *Bantu*, 12/4: 164–6.

Bantu Educational Journal (1963), 'My Future Career: Occupations in the Disciplinary Services', *Bantu Education Journal*, 9: 236–43.

Barrell, H. (1990), *MK: The ANC's Armed Struggle* (London: Penguin).

Bayley, D. (1982), 'A World Perspective on the Role of the Police in Social Control', in R. Donelan (ed.), *The Maintenance of Order in Society* (Ottawa: Canadian Police College), 87–96.

—— and Mendelsohn, H. (1969) (eds.), *Minorities and the Police* (New York: Free Press).

Baynham, S. (1990), 'Security Strategies for a Future South Africa', *Journal of Modern African Studies*, 28: 401–30.

Beinart, W. (1982), *The Political Economy of Pondoland* (Cambridge: Cambridge University Press).

—— (1987), 'Worker Consciousness, Ethnic Pluralism, and Nationalism: the Experiences of a South African Migrant 1930–60', in S. Marks and S. Trapido (eds.), *The Politics of Race, Class, and Nationalism in Twentieth-Century South Africa* (London: Longman), 105–23.

—— and Bundy, C. (1987), *Hidden Struggles in Rural South Africa* (Johannesburg: Ravan Press).

Bekker, S., and Grobbelaar, J. (1987), 'The White Right-Wing Movement in South Africa: Before and After the May 1987 Election', in D. van Vuuren, L. Schlemmer, H. Marais, and J. Latakgona (eds.), *South African Election 1987* (Cape Town: Owen Burgess), 65–80.

Bennett, B. (1959), *Genius for the Defence* (Cape Town: Timmins).

Berat, L. (1989), 'Doctors, Detainees, and Torture: Medical Ethics Versus the Law in South Africa', unpublished seminar paper given to the Southern African Research Programme (Yale University).

Black, D. and Reiss, A. (1967) (eds.), *Studies in Crime and Law Enforcement in Major Metropolitan Areas* (Washington, DC: Government Printer).

Black Sash (1956), 'Are Nats Nazis?', *Black Sash*, July, 1–2.

—— (1959*a*), 'Passes and the Police', *Black Sash*, June/July, 10–11.

—— (1959*b*), 'Sash and Police in Verbal Battle', *Black Sash*, Dec., 16–17.

Bloom, H. (1957), 'The SAP', *Africa South*, 2/1: 7–17.

Bonner, P. (1988), 'Family, Crime, and Political Consciousness on the East Rand', *Journal of Southern African Studies*, 14: 293–340.

Boraine, A. (1989), 'The Militarization of Urban Controls: The Security Management System in Mamelodi 1986–88', in Cock and Nathan (1989), 159–73.

Bowden, T. (1975), 'Policing Palestine 1920–36', in G. Mosse (ed.), *Police Forces in History* (London: Sage), 115–30.

—— (1978), *Beyond the Limits of the Law* (London: Penguin).

Brewer, J. (1984), *Mosley's Men* (Aldershot: Gower).

—— (1986), *After Soweto: An Unfinished Journey* (Oxford: Clarendon Press).

Brewer, J.(1988), 'The Police in South African Politics', in S. Johnson (ed.), *South Africa: No Turning Back* (London: Macmillan), 258–82.

—— (1989), 'Max Weber and the Royal Irish Constabulary: A Note on Class and Status', *British Journal of Sociology*, 40: 82–96.

—— (1990), *The Royal Irish Constabulary: An Oral History* (Belfast: Institute of Irish Studies).

—— (1991), *Inside the RUC: Routine Policing in a Divided Society* (Oxford: Clarendon Press).

—— (1992), 'Police Deviance and Accountability in Divided Societies: A Comparative Framework', paper for the conference on Policing the New South Africa, University of Natal, Durban, Sept. 1992.

—— (forthcoming), 'Re-educating the South African Police: Comparative Lessons', in T. Mathews, P. Heyman, and M. Mathews (eds.), *Policing the Conflict in South Africa* (Gainsville, Flo.: University Press of Florida).

—— Guelke, A., Hume, I., Moxon-Brown, E., and Wilford, R. (1988), *Police, Public Order, and the State* (London: Macmillan).

Bridges, L. (1983), 'Policing the Urban Wasteland', *Race and Class*, 25: 31–47.

Brodeur, J. (1983), 'High Policing and Low Policing: Remarks about the Policing of Political Activities', *Social Problems*, 30: 507–20.

Brogden, M. (1987*a*), 'An Act to Colonize the Internal Lands of the Island', *International Journal of the Sociology of Law*, 15: 179–208.

—— (1987*b*), 'The Emergence of the Police—the Colonial Dimension', *British Journal of Criminology*, 27: 4–14.

—— (1989), 'The Origins of the SAP', in *Acta Juridica* (1989), 1–19.

—— (1991), *On The Mersey Beat* (Oxford: Clarendon Press).

—— Jefferson, T., and Walklate, S. (1988), *Introducing Policework* (London: Unwin Hyman).

Buitendag, F. (1951), 'The Emergence of the Urban African', *Race Relations*, 13: 73–7.

Bulpin, T. (1955), *Storm over the Transvaal* (Cape Town: Timmins).

Bunting, B. (1964), *The Rise of the South African Reich* (London: Penguin).

Butler, J., Rotberg, R., and Adams, J. (1977), *The Black Homelands of South Africa* (Berkeley, Calif.: University of California Press).

Cain, M. (1979), 'Trends in the Sociology of Policework', *International Journal of the Sociology of Law*, 7: 143–67.

Carlson, J. (1966), 'Mass Arrests and Crime', *Black Sash*, Feb./Apr., 12–13.

Carr, W. (1953), 'Administration of Non-Whites: The Organizational Framework of the Johannesburg City Council', *Journal of Racial Affairs*, 4: 6.

Cashmore, E., and McLaughlin, E. (1991*a*), 'Out of Order?', in Cashmore and McLaughlin (1991*b*), 1–11.

—— (1991*b*) (eds.), *Out of Order: Policing Black People* (London: Routledge).

Cato (1989), 'Apartheid's Armed Forces in Crisis', *The African Communist*, 116: 20–32.

Centre for Criminal Justice (1991), *Policing in the Greater Pietermaritzburg Area: A Perception Study* (Pietermaritzburg: Centre for Criminal Justice).

Chimutengwende, C. (1978), *South Africa: The Press and the Politics of Liberation* (London: Barbican Books).

Cock, J. (1989), 'Introduction', in Cock and Nathan (1989), 1–15.

—— and Nathan, L. (1989) (eds.), *War and Society* (Cape Town: David Philip).

Cohen, S. (1977), 'South Africa: Police State', *Nation*, 224: 143–6.

—— and Scull, A. (1983) (eds.), *Social Control and the State* (Oxford: Martin Robertson).

Cooper, C. (1989), 'The Militarization of the Bantustans', in Cock and Nathan (1989), 174–87.

Cooper, F. (1972), *The Police Brigade* (Cape Town: Constantia Publishers).

—— (1972–3), 'A Short History of the SAP', *SARP*, 7/8–9/6.

Courtney, R. (1939), *Palestine Police* (London: Herbert Jenkins).

Cox, E. (1977), *Police and Crime in India* (London: Stanley Park).

Critchley, T. (1978), *A History of Police in England and Wales* (London: Constable).

Dandy, M. (1989), 'When the Force Frolics', in *Acta Juridica* (1989), 20–43.

Davenport, R. (1968), 'African Townsmen?: South African Natives (Urban Areas) Legislation Through the Year', *African Affairs*, 271: 95–109.

Davenport, T. (1963), 'The South African Rebellion of 1914', *Economic History Review*, 77: 62–85.

Davies, D., and Slabbert, M. (1985) (eds.), *Crime and Power in South Africa* (Cape Town: David Philip).

Davies, R. (1979), *Capital, State, and White Labour in South Africa 1900–60* (Brighton: Harvester).

Davies, S. (1987), *Apartheid's Rebels* (New Haven, Conn.: Yale University Press).

De Klerk, W. (1975), *The Puritans in Africa* (London: Penguin).

Dep, M. (1979), *A History of the Ceylon Police* (London: Stanley Parker).

Department of Information (1917), *South Africa Yearbook 1917* (Cape Town: Government Printer).

—— (1948), *South Africa Yearbook 1948* (Cape Town: Government Printer).

—— (1990), *South Africa Yearbook 1989–90* (Pretoria: Government Printer).

Dippenaar, M. (1988), *The History of the SAP 1913–88* (Silverton: Promedia).

Douthit, W. (1975), 'Police Professionalism and the War Against Crime in the United States', in G. Mosse (ed.), *Police Forces in History* (London: Sage), 317–33.

Dubow, S. (1987), 'Race, Civilization, and Culture', in S. Marks and S. Trapido (eds.), *The Politics of Race, Class, and Nationalism in Twentieth-Century South Africa* (London: Longman), 78–93.

Duigan, P., and Jackson, R. (1986), *Politics and Government in African States* (Stanford, Calif.: Hoover Institute).

Dunbar Moodie, T. (1975), *The Rise of Afrikanerdom* (Berkeley, Calif.: University of California Press).

—— (1988), 'Migrancy and Male Sexuality on the South African Goldmines', *Journal of Southern African Studies*, 14: 228–56.

Duncan, P. (1964), *South Africa's Rule of Violence* (London: Methuen).

Du Toit, B. (1991), 'The Far-Right in Current South African Politics', *Journal of Modern African Studies*, 29: 627–67.

Du Toit, M. (1976), *South Africa's Trade Unions* (New York: McGraw-Hill).

Elks, K. (1986), 'Crime, Community and Police in Cape Town 1825–50', MA thesis (University of Cape Town).

Ellmann, E. (1992), *In a Time of Trouble: Law and Liberty in South Africa's State of Emergency* (Oxford: Clarendon Press).

Enloe, C. (1980), *Police, Military, and Ethnicity* (London: Transaction Books).

Erikson, S. (1973), 'An American Looks at South Africa: Hybrid of Democracy and a Police State', *Journal of Thought*, 8: 106–16.

Feit, E. (1967), *African Opposition in South Africa* (Stanford, Calif.: Hoover Institute).

Fielding, N. (1991), *The Police and Social Conflict* (London: Athlone Press).

Fine, D. (1989), 'Kitskonstabels: A Case Study of Black on Black Policing', in *Acta Juridica* (1989), 44–85.

—— and Hansson, D. (1990), 'Community Responses to Police Abuse of Power', in Hansson and van Zyl Smit (1990), 209–31.

Fine, R. (1990), *Beyond Apartheid: Labour and Liberation in South Africa* (London: Pluto).

—— and Miller, R. (1988) (eds.), *Policing the Miners' Strike* (London: Lawrence and Wishart).

Finnane, M. (1991), 'The Varieties of Policing: Colonial Queensland 1860–1900', in Anderson and Killingray (1991*a*), 33–51.

First, R. (1958), 'Bethal Case Book', *Africa South*, 2–3: 20–1.

Foran, W. (1962), *The Kenyan Police* (London: Robert Hale).

Foster, D., and Luyt, C. (1986), 'The Blueman's Burden: Policing the Police in South Africa', *South African Journal of Human Rights*, 2: 297–311.

Frankel, P. (1980), 'South Africa: The Politics of Police Control', *Comparative Politics*, 12: 481–99.

—— (1981), 'Race and Counter-Revolution in South Africa's Total Strategy', *Journal of Commonwealth and Comparative Politics*, 18: 272–92.

—— (1984), *Pretoria's Praetorians* (Cambridge: Cambridge University Press).

Frederikse, J. (1986), *South Africa: A Different Kind of War* (London: James Currey).

—— (1990), *The Unbreakable Thread* (London: Zed Press).

Gann, L., and Duigan, P. (1981), *Why South Africa Will Survive* (Cape Town: Tafelberg).

Garson, N. (1962), 'The Boer Rebellion of 1914', *History Today*, 12: 132–9.

Geary, R. (1985), *Policing Industrial Disputes 1893 to 1985* (London: Methuen).

Gellately, R. (1990), *The Gestapo and German Society* (Oxford: Clarendon Press).

Gerhart, G. (1978), *Black Power in South Africa* (Berkeley, Calif.: University of California Press).

Godley, R. (1935), *Khaki and Blue* (London: Dickson and Thompson).

Goffery, A. (1940), 'The Liquor Problem in Urban Areas', *Race Relations*, 7: 88–94.

Grant, E. (1989), 'Private Policing', in *Acta Juridica* (1989), 92–117.

Griffiths, D. (1971), *To Guard My People* (London: Benn).

Grimshaw, R., and Jefferson, T. (1987), *Interpreting Policework* (London: Allen and Unwin).

Grotpeter, J. (1980), 'Changing South Africa', *Current History*, 78: 119–23.

Grundlingh, A. (1991), 'Protectors and Friends of the People: The South African Constabulary in the Transvaal and Orange River Colony 1900–8', in Anderson and Killingray (1991*a*), 168–82.

Grundy, K. (1983*a*), *Soldiers Without Politics* (Berkeley, Calif.: University of California Press).

—— (1983*b*), 'South Africa's Domestic Strategy', *Current History*, 82: 110–14.

—— (1988), *The Militarization of South African Politics* (London: Tauris).

Gupta, A. (1979), *Crime and Police in India* (New Delhi: Concept Publishing).

Guy, J. (1987), 'TheMa-Rashea', in B. Bozzoli (ed.), *Class, Community, and Conflict* (Johannesburg: Ravan Press), 198–212.

Hain, P. (1980) (ed.), *Policing the Police*, vol. ii (London: John Calder).

Hall, S., Crichter, C., Jefferson, T., Clark, J., and Roberts, B. (1978), *Policing the Crisis* (London: Macmillan).

Hancock, W. (1968), *Smuts: The Field of Force* (Cambridge: Cambridge University Press).

Hansson, D. (1989), 'Trigger Happy: An Evaluation of Fatal Shootings in the Greater Cape Town Area from 1984 to 1986', in *Acta Juridica* (1989), 118–38.

—— (1990), 'Changes in Counter Revolution: State Strategy in the Decade 1979 to 1989', in Hansson and van Zyl Smit (1990), 28–62.

—— and van Zyl Smit, D. (1990) (eds.), *Towards Justice?* (Cape Town: Oxford University Press).

Hare, A. (1985), *Social Interaction as Drama* (Beverly Hills, Calif.: Sage).

Hattersley, A. (1960), *The First South African Detective* (Cape Town: Timmins).

Hawkins, H., and Thomas, R. (1991), 'White Policing of Black Populations: A History of Race and Social Control in America', in Cashmore and McLaughlin (1991*b*), 184–98.

Hawkins, R. (1991), 'The "Irish Model" and the Empire', in Anderson and Killingray (1991*a*), 18–32.

Hayman, R. (1941), 'Kaffir Beer and the Law', *Race Relations*, 8: 55–7.

Haysom, N. (1980), *Mabangalala: The Rise of Right-Wing Vigilantism in South Africa* (University of Witwatersrand: Centre for Applied Legal Studies).
—— (1987), 'Licence to Kill', *South African Journal of Human Rights*, 3: 3–27.
—— (1989a), 'Policing the Police', in *Acta Juridica* (1989), 139–64.
—— (1989b), 'Vigilantism and the Militarization of South Africa', in Cock and Nathan (1989), 188–201.
—— (1990), 'Vigilantism and the Policing of African Townships', in Hansson and van Zyl Smit (1990), 63–84.
Hellmann, E. (1940), *Problems of Urban Bantu Youth* (Johannesburg: SAIRR).
—— (1943), 'Non-Europeans in the Army', *Race Relations*, 10: 45–52.
Heymann, P. (1992), Testimony of Multinational Panel Regarding Lawful Control of Demonstrations in the Republic of South Africa, Before the Commission of Inquiry Regarding the Prevention of Public Violence and Intimidation Under The Hon. Mr Justice Goldstone, 9 July.
Hickman, A. (1960), *Men Who Made Rhodesia* (Salisbury: British South Africa Company).
Hill, R. (1986), *Policing the Colonial Frontier* (Wellington: Government Printer).
—— (1991), 'The Policing of Colonial New Zealand', in Anderson and Killingray (1991a), 52–70.
Hillyard, P., and Percy-Smith, J. (1988), *The Coercive State* (London: Collins).
Hirson, B. (1979), *Year of Fire, Year of Ash* (London: Zed Press).
HMSO (1900), *Correspondence Relating to the Defence of Natal*, Cd. 44.
Holt, H. (1913), *The Mounted Police of Natal* (London: John Murray).
Hook, M. (1906), *With Sword and Statute* (London: Greaves and Pass).
Institute of Criminology (1990), *Kitskonstabels in Crisis* (Institute of Criminology, University of Cape Town).
Jefferson, T. (1990), *The Case Against Paramilitary Policing* (Milton Keynes: Open University Press).
Jeffries, C. (1952), *The Colonial Police* (London: Max Parrish).
Johnson, D. (1991), 'From Military to Tribal Police', in Anderson and Killingray (1991a), 151–67.
Johnson, H. (1991), 'Patterns of Policing in the Post-Emancipation British Caribbean', in Anderson and Killingray (1991a), 71–91.
Kane-Berman, J. (1979), *South Africa: A Method in the Madness* (London: Pluto Press).
Karis, T., and Carter, G. (1972–7), *From Protest to Challenge* (Stanford, Calif.: Hoover Institute).
Katz, E. (1967), 'Mass Arrests', *Black Sash*, Nov., 15–16.
Kiley, D. (1960), 'The Pondoland Massacre', *Africa South*, 5/1: 14–19.
Killingray, D. (1991), 'Guarding the Extending Frontier', in Anderson and Killingray (1991a), 106–25.
King, J. (1988), 'The United Kingdom Police Strike of 1918–19', *Police Studies*, 11: 128–38.

Kinsey, R., Lea, J., and Young, J. (1986), *Losing the Fight Against Crime* (Oxford: Blackwell).

Koch, E. (1978), 'The Development of the Police Force on the Witwatersrand 1886–1906', *Africa Perception*, 8: 65–82.

Lacey, M. (1989), '*Platskiet–Politiek*: The Role of the Union Defence Force 1910–24', in Cock and Nathan (1989), 28–39.

La Hausse, P. (1990), '"The Cows of Nangoloza": Youth Crime and Amalaita Gangs in Durban 1900–36', *Journal of Southern African Studies*, 16: 79–111.

Lambert, J. (1970), *Crime, Police, and Race Relations* (Oxford: Oxford University Press).

Laurence, P. (1990), *Death Squads* (London: Penguin).

Lewin, J. (n.d.), *Africans and the Police* (Johannesburg: SAIRR, Pim Pamphlet Series).

Lewis, J. (1984), *Industrialization and Trade Union Organization in South Africa 1924–55* (Cambridge: Cambridge University Press).

Lipton, M. (1985), *Capitalism and Apartheid* (Aldershot: Gower).

Lodge, T. (1983), *Black Politics in South Africa Since 1945* (London: Longman).

—— and Nasson, B. (1992), *All Here and Now: Black Politics in South Africa in the 1980s* (London: Hurst).

Lorch, A. (1922), *A Story of the Cape Mounted Riflemen* (Pretoria: Proctor).

Luckhardt, K., and Wall, B. (1980), *Organize or Starve* (London: Lawrence and Wishart).

Maré, G., and Hamilton, G. (1987), *An Appetite for Power: Buthelezi's Inkatha and South Africa* (Johannesburg: Ravan Press).

Marks, S., and Andersson, N. (1990), 'The Epidemiology and Culture of Violence', in N. Chabani Manganyi and A. du Toit (eds.), *Political Violence and the Struggle in South Africa* (London: Macmillan), 29–69.

—— and Trapido, S. (1988), 'South Africa Since 1976: An Historical Perspective', in S. Johnson (ed.), *South Africa: No Turning Back* (London: Macmillan), 1–51.

Martin, H., and Orpen, N. (1979), *South Africa at War* (Cape Town: Purnell).

Mathews, A. (1971), 'Security Legislation and Social Change in the Republic of South Africa', in H. Adam (ed.), *South Africa: Sociological Perspectives* (Oxford: Oxford University Press), 228–48.

Mayer, J. (1983), 'Notes Towards a Working Definition of Social Control in Historical Analysis', in Cohen and Scull (1983), 44–61.

Mayet, H. (1976), 'The Role and Image of the SAP in Society from the Point of View of the Coloured People in Johannesburg', MA thesis (University of South Africa).

Meintjers, J. (1966), *De La Rey: Lion of the West* (Johannesburg: Keartland).

Michelman, C. (1975), *The Black Sash in South Africa* (Oxford: Oxford University Press).

Moorcraft, P. (1990), *African Nemesis* (London: Brassey's).

Morris, M. (1974), *Armed Conflict in Southern Africa* (Cape Town: Spence).

Morrison, W. (1985), *Showing the Flag* (Vancouver: University of British Columbia Press).

Moss, G. (1979), *Political Trials in South Africa* (University of Witwatersrand, Development Studies Group).

Mosse, G. (1975), 'Introduction', in G. Mosse (ed.), *Police Forces in History* (London: Sage), 1–7.

Mphahlele, E. (1956), 'The Evanton Riots', *Africa South*, 1/2: 57–62.

Nasson, B. (1991), 'Bobbies to Boers: Police, People, and Social Control in Cape Town', in Anderson and Killingray (1991*a*), 236–54.

Nathan, L. (1989), 'Troops in the Townships 1984–7', in Cock and Nathan (1989), 67–78.

Ndibongo, M. (1991), 'South Africa: The Care of Black Police/Black Community', M.Sc. thesis (Michigan State University).

Ngakane, W. (1957), 'Passes and Africans', *Black Sash*, Nov., 5–6.

Nokwe, D. (1959), 'The SAP: Laws and Powers', *Africa South*, 2/2: 16–18.

Nongqai (1922), 'The Police of the Past', *Nongqai*, Mar., 141–2.

Odenkunle, F. (1979), 'The Nigerian Police', *International Journal of the Sociology of Law*, 7: 89–99.

Olivier, J. (1991*a*), 'State Responses to Collective Action in South Africa 1970–84', *South African Journal of Sociology*, 22: 41–56.

—— (1991*b*), 'Dynamic Methods for Dynamic Progress: The Case of Civil Unrest in South Africa', mimeo, Human Sciences Research Council, Pretoria.

Omar, D. (1990), 'An Overview of State Lawlessness in South Africa', in Hansson and van Zyl Smit (1990), 17–27.

O'Meara, D. (1975), 'The 1946 African Mine Workers' Strike in the Political Economy of South Africa', *Journal of Commonwealth and Comparative Politics*, 19: 146–73.

—— (1983), *Volkskapitalisme* (Cambridge: Cambridge University Press).

Orpen, C. (1980), 'Effects of Job Involvement on the Work–Leisure Relationship: A Correlational Study Among Bank Clerks and Police Officers', *Psychological Reports*, 50: 355–64.

Philips, M. (1989), 'The Nuts and Bolts of Military Power', in Cock and Nathan (1989), 16–27.

Pinnock, D. (1985), 'Breaking the Web: Gangs and Family Situation in Cape Town', in Davies and Slabbert (1985), 87–102.

—— (1987), 'Stone Boys and the Making of a Cape Flats Mafia', in B. Bozzoli (ed.), *Class, Community, and Conflict* (Johannesburg: Ravan Press), 143–65.

Plasket, C. (1989), 'Sub-Contracting the Dirty Work', in *Acta Juridica* (1989), 165–88.

Poodhun, E. (1983), 'The Role of Indian Policemen in the SAP', D.Phil. thesis (University of Durban-Westville).

Portia (1956), 'Who May Come Into My Home?', *Black Sash*, Apr., 7.

Posel, D. (1989), 'A "Battlefield of Perception": State Discourse on Political Violence', in Cock and Nathan (1989), 262–74.

—— (1990), 'Symbolizing Violence: State and Media Discourse in Television Coverage of Township Protest, 1985–7', in N. Chabani Manganyi and A. du Toit (eds.), *Political Violence and the Struggle in South Africa* (London: Macmillan), 154–71.

—— (1991), *The Making of Apartheid 1948–61* (Oxford: Clarendon Press).

Prior, A. (1989), 'The SAP and the Counter Revolution of 1985–7', in *Acta Juridica* (1989), 189–205.

Rankin, D. (1957), 'Our Traditional Way of Life in South Africa', *Black Sash*, Mar., 5–6.

Rauch, J. (1991), 'The Challenge of Policing in the New South Africa', paper for the annual conference of the American Society of Criminology, San Francisco, 20–2 November.

Rayner, M. (1990), 'From Biko to Wendy Orr: The Problem of Medical Accountability in Contexts of Political Violence and Torture', in N. Chabani Manganyi and A. du Toit (eds.), *Political Violence and the Struggle in South Africa* (London: Macmillan), 172–204.

Rees, M. (1980), 'The BOSS-DONS Story', *Rand Daily Mail*, 1–5 Feb.

Reiner, R. (1985), *The Politics of the Police* (Brighton: Harvester).

—— (1989), 'The Politics of Police Research', in M. Weatheritt (ed.), *Police Research: Some Future Prospects* (Aldershot: Avebury), 3–20.

Rheinnallt-Jones, J. (1936), 'Race Relations in 1935: A South African Survey', *Race Relations*, 3: 1–7.

—— (1938), 'Race Relations in 1937: A South African Survey', *Race Relations*, 5: 14–19.

Rich, P. (1984), *White Power and the Liberal Conscience* (Manchester: Manchester University Press).

—— (1989), 'Doctrines of "Change" in South Africa', in J. Brewer (ed.), *Can South Africa Survive?* (London: Macmillan), 281–311.

Robb, P. (1991), 'The Ordering of Rural India', in Anderson and Killingray (1991*a*), 126–50.

Robinson, C. (1975), 'The Mayor and the Police', in G. Mosse (ed.), *Police Forces in History* (London: Sage), 277–316.

Rock, P. (1983), 'Law, Order, and Power in Late Seventeenth-Century and Early Eighteenth-Century England', in Cohen and Scull (1983), 78–97.

Roux, E. (1964), *Time Longer Than Rope* (Madison, Wisc.: University of Wisconsin Press).

Ruchelman, L. (1974), *Police Politics* (Cambridge, Mass.: Ballinger).

Sachs, A. (1975), 'Instruments of Domination in South Africa', in L. Thompson and J. Butler (eds.), *Change in Contemporary South Africa* (Berkeley, Calif.: University of California Press), 123–46.

SAIRR (1978), *Laws Affecting Race Relations in South Africa* (Johannesburg, SAIRR).

Sandler, D. (1989), 'The Psychological Experiences of White Conscripts in the Black Townships', in Cock and Nathan (1989), 79–89.

SAP (1948), *Yearbook of the SAP* (Pretoria: Government Printer).

—— (1986), 'Historical Developments and Activities of the SAP', *Annual Report of the Commissioner of the SAP* (Pretoria: Government Printer), 32–43.

SARP (1972), 'Our Non-White Counter Insurgents', *SARP*, 8/7: 34.

Scharf, W. (1989), 'Community Policing in South Africa', in *Acta Juridica* (1989), 206–33.

—— (1990), 'The Resurgence of Urban Street Gangs and Community Responses in Cape Town During the Late Eighties', in Hansson and van Zyl Smit (1990), 232–64.

Schrire, R. (1992), *Adapt or Die: The End of White Politics in South Africa* (London: Hurst).

Scraton, P. (1985), *The State of the Police* (London: Pluto Press).

Searle, E. (1928), *With a Policeman in South Africa* (London: Abbey Press).

Seegars, A. (1986), 'The Military in South Africa: A Comparison and Critique', *South Africa International*, 16: 184–98.

—— (1989), 'The Rise of an Authoritarian Mode of Policing in South Africa', paper to the Friedrich Naumann conference on divided societies, Bonn, September.

—— (1991), 'South Africa's National Security Management System 1972–90', *Journal of Modern African Studies*, 29: 253–73.

Selfe, J. (1989), 'South Africa's National Management System', in Cock and Nathan (1989), 149–58.

Servamus (1980), 'Lt. Col. Sibramonia Pillai', *Servamus*, Dec.: 20.

—— (1984), 'The ANC in Perspective', *Servamus*, July: 10–13.

Shearing, C. (1986), 'Policing South Africa: Reflections on Botha's Reforms', *Canadian Journal of Sociology*, 11: 293–307.

Simkins, C. (1983), *Four Essays on the Past, Present, and Possible Future Distribution of the Black Population in South Africa* (Cape Town: David Philip).

Simons, H. (1939), 'Disabilities of the Native in the Union of South Africa', *Race Relations*, 6: 59–67.

—— (1956), 'Passes and Police', *Africa South*, 1/1: 53–8.

Skinner, L. (1975), *Police on the Pastoral Frontier* (St Lucia: Queensland University Press).

Smuts, J. (1952), *Jan Christian Smuts* (London: Cassell).

Southall, R. (1982), *South Africa's Transkei* (London: Heinemann).

Southern African Bishops' Conference (1984), *Report on Police Conduct During Township Protests* (Durban: Southern African Bishops' Conference).

Spence, J. (1988), 'The Military in South African Politics', in S. Johnson (ed.), *South Africa: No Turning Back* (London: Macmillan), 240–57.

Spink, K. (1991), *Black Sash* (London: Methuen).

Stadler, A. (1979), 'Birds in the Cornfields: Squatter Movements in Johannesburg 1944–7', in B. Bozzoli (ed.), *Labour, Townships, and Protests* (Johannesburg: Ravan Press), 54–68.

Stedman-Jones, G. (1983), 'Class Expression Versus Social Control', in Cohen and Scull (1983), 234–56.

Steedman, C. (1984), *Policing the Victorian Community* (London: Routledge).

Steytler, N. (1990), 'Policing Political Opponents: Death Squads and Cop Culture', in Hansson and van Zyl Smit (1990), 106–34.

Strijdom, H., and Scarink, W. (1979), 'Victims of Serious Crime in Soweto', *Humanitas*, 5: 39–45.

Stultz, N. (1974), *Afrikaner Politics in South Africa 1934–48* (Berkeley, Calif.: University of California Press).

Sturgis, J. (1991), 'Whiskey Detectives in Town', in Anderson and Killingray (1991*a*), 202–18.

Swilling, M., and Philips, M. (1989), 'State Power in the 1980s: From "Total Strategy" to "Counter-Revolutionary Warfare"', in Cock and Nathan (1989), 134–48.

Talbot, S. (1980), 'The CIA and BOSS', in E. Ray (ed.), *Dirty Work: The CIA in Africa* (London: Zed Press), 266–75.

Tamuno, T. (1970), *The Police in Modern Nigeria 1861–1965* (Ibidan: Ibidan University Press).

Tobias, J. (1972), 'Police and Public in the United Kingdom', *Journal of Contemporary History*, 7: 201–20.

Trew, T. (1978), 'Theory at Work', *UEA Papers in Linguistics*, 6: 39–60.

Turk, A. (1977), 'The Problem of Legal Order in the United States and South Africa', *Sociological Focus*, 10: 31–41.

—— (1981), 'The Meaning of Criminality in South Africa', *International Journal of the Sociology of Law*, 9: 123–55.

—— (1982), 'Policing in Political Context', in R. Donelan (ed.), *The Maintenance of Order in Society* (Ottawa: Canadian Police College), 176–89.

United Nations (1967), *Military and Police Forces in the Republic of South Africa* (New York: United Nations).

Uglow, S. (1988), *Policing Liberal Society* (Oxford: Oxford University Press).

Uys, S. (1988), 'The Afrikaner Establishment', in S. Johnson (ed.), *South Africa: No Turning Back* (London: Macmillan), 206–39.

Van der Poel, J. (1973), *Selections from the Smuts Papers* (Cambridge: Cambridge University Press).

Van der Spuy, E. (1988), 'Policing the Eighties: *Servamus et Servimus?*', paper for the Association of Sociologists in Southern Africa, University of Durban-Westville.

—— (1989), 'Literature on the Police in South Africa: A Historical Perspective', in *Acta Juridica* (1989), 262–91.

Van der Spuy, E. (1990), 'Political Discourse and the History of the SAP', in Hansson and van Zyl Smit (1990), 85–105.

Van Heerden, J. (1959), 'The Structure and Function of the Department of Bantu Administration and Development', *Bantu*, 1/10: 50–2.

Van Heerden, T. (1986), *Introduction to Police Science* (Pretoria: University of South Africa).

Van Onselen, L. (1960), *A Rhapsody in Blue* (Cape Town: Timmins).

Van Zyl Slabbert, F. (1975), 'Afrikaner Nationalism, White Politics, and Political Change', in L. Thompson and J. Butler (eds.), *Change in Contemporary South Africa* (Berkeley, Calif.: University of California Press), 234–56.

Van Zyl Smit, D. (1990), 'Introduction: Contextualizing Criminology in Contemporary South Africa', in Hansson and van Zyl Smit (1990), 1–16.

Venables, L. (1951*a*), 'Juvenile Delinquency', *Journal of Racial Affairs*, 2/1: 12–24.

—— (1951*b*), 'Crime in Johannesburg', *Journal of Racial Affairs*, 2/2: 1–13.

Visser, B. (1973), 'The Police Approach to Crime Prevention', *SARP*, 9/11: 8–9.

Visser, G. (1976), *OB: Traitors or Patriots?* (Cape Town: Macmillan).

Waddington, P. (1992), Report of the Inquiry into the Police Response to, and Investigation of, Events in Boipatong on 17 June 1992, Submitted to the Commission of Inquiry Regarding the Prevention of Public Violence and Intimidation Under The Hon. Mr Justice Goldstone, 20 July.

Walsh, D. (1988), 'The RUC—A Law unto Themselves?', in M. Tomlinson, T. Varley, and C. McCullough (eds.), *Whose Law and Order?* (Dublin: Sociological Association of Ireland), 92–108.

Walshe, P. (1971), *The Rise of African Nationalism in South Africa* (Berkeley, Calif.: University of California Press).

Waters, G. (1979), 'South Africa's Urban Transformation', paper for the Association of Sociologists in Southern Africa, Lesotho.

Webb, H. (1916), *The Causes of the Rebellion* (Pretoria: Northern Printing Press).

Weitzer, R. (1985), 'Policing a Divided Society', *Social Problems*, 33: 41–55.

—— (1990*a*), 'Policing a New South Africa', *The Christian Science Monitor*, 4 Apr.: 18.

—— (1990*b*), 'Police in Need of New Ethos', *IDASA Bulletin*, Sept.–Oct.: 7–8.

—— (1991), 'Elite Conflict Over Policing in South Africa 1980–90', *Policing and Society*, 1: 257–68.

White, B. (1974), 'With our Men on the Border', *SARP*, 11/2: 7–9.

Williams, O. (1959), 'The Sinister Spy and Other Stories', *Black Sash*, Mar.: 6.

Willis, J. (1991), 'Thieves, Drunkards, and Vagrants', in Anderson and Killingray (1991*a*), 219–35.

Wilson, E. (1884), *Reminiscences of a Frontier Armed and Mounted Police Officer in South Africa* (Dublin: James Duffy).

Wilson, M., and Thompson, L. (1969) (eds.), *The Oxford History of South Africa* (Oxford: Clarendon Press).

Winter, G. (1974), 'South Africa's Answer to Terrorism: Blacks Killing Blacks', *SARP*, 10/8: 7.

—— (1981), *Inside BOSS* (London: Penguin).

Wintersmith, R. (1974), *The Police and the Black Community* (Cambridge, Mass.: Lexington).

Wollheim, O. (1950), 'The Cape Skolly', *Race Relations*, 17: 48–53.

Wolpe, H. (1988), *Race, Class, and the Apartheid State* (London: James Currey).

Yudelman, D. (1983), *The Emergence of Modern South Africa* (Westport, Conn.: Greenwood).

INDEX

Adam, Heribert 2, 304, 317, 321
African National Congress 98, 166, 214,
    247, 252, 254, 309, 310, 311, 319,
    320, 329, 330, 341, 345, 346, 347,
    352
  and MK 254, 293, 311–12
  see also Native National Congress
Afrikaanse Kultuurvereniging van die
    Suid-Afrikaanse Polisie 211, 240
Afrikaner Party 168
Afrikaner rebellion:
  (1914) 63–6, 345
  (1940–2) 156–63, 345
Afrikaner Weerstandsbeweging 308, 317,
    318, 319–21, 326, 327, 345
Aggett, Neil 290, 320
Alexandra 179, 327
Althusser, L. 13, 344
Anderson, D. 5, 6
Anglo-Boer wars 27, 28, 45, 63, 64, 68,
    94, 102
Angola 258
apartheid 1, 2, 16, 70, 105, 146, 168,
    172, 183–4, 191, 195, 204, 206, 209,
    211, 220, 221, 222, 226, 234, 235,
    237, 268, 269, 270, 274, 281, 297,
    315, 335, 345, 346
  and policing 168–9, 183–4, 195–6,
    207, 225, 234, 274, 297, 336–7
Australia 6, 9, 59, 142

Baden-Powell, Maj.-Gen. 28
Bamford Lt.-Col. 27
Bantu 226, 227, 228, 261
Bantu Education Journal 227
Belfast 26
Biko, Steve 273–4, 290
Black Consciousness 269
Black Sash 262
Bloemfontein 55, 85, 161, 247
Boipatong massacre 289, 298, 317, 318,
    328–9
Bondelzwarts massacre 100–1, 105
Boputhatswana 224, 284, 285
Botha, Duveen 241, 287
Botha, General 55, 57, 63, 64, 66, 97, 345

Botha, Pik 318
Botha, P. W. 253, 256, 272, 287, 293,
    294, 297, 298, 299, 315, 317, 322,
    325, 338
Bowden, T. 7
Brink, Commissioner 184, 185, 211
Britain 6, 8, 9, 10, 14, 15, 17, 18, 20, 21,
    22, 23, 24, 26, 27, 29, 32, 33, 40, 45,
    47, 48, 51, 64, 73, 90, 106, 115, 118,
    148, 174, 211, 243, 262, 275, 339–40
British Empire 5, 7, 58, 63, 69, 160
Brogden, M. 3, 6, 7, 51, 340
Bulhoek massacre 100, 105
Bureau of State Security 249, 252–3,
    284, 287, 292
Burn-Beggs, Commissioner 30, 32, 35
Buthelezi, Chief 285
  see also Inkatha

Canada 6, 9, 59, 142
Cape 14, 15, 16, 17, 19, 21, 24, 26, 29, 30,
    31, 33, 39, 40, 45, 59, 88, 101, 113,
    118, 128, 144, 184, 196, 227, 260, 270
Cape Mounted Police 16
Cape Mounted Riflemen 17, 19, 22, 39
Cape Times 216, 217, 220, 305, 306
Cape Town 26, 81, 84, 86, 113, 127,
    133, 139, 154, 157, 172, 176, 179,
    219, 262, 265, 283, 296, 318
Cato Manor 225
Ceylon 7
Chatsworth 232, 260
Cillie Commission 269, 270, 275
Ciskei 224, 284, 286, 295
Ciskei Police 284, 311
citizen-policeman tradition 16, 17–18,
    26, 59, 278, 334
City Press 303
colonial policing model 5–10, 12
Columbo 7
community policing 313–14, 350–1
Conservative Party 315, 316, 317, 320,
    323, 341, 345
Cooper, F. 82, 151, 152
crime 15, 16, 20, 23, 24, 26, 49–53, 89,
    90–3, 128–30, 131–6, 196–8, 200–2,

crime (*cont.*):
212–14, 221, 226–7, 258–61, 288–9, 323–5, 335–6, 350, 351
fear of crime 23, 25, 30, 40, 50, 51, 139
liquor raids 53–4, 135–6, 140, 179, 205
youth gangs 132–4, 196, 200–1, 203, 261–2, 264
Criminal Investigation Department 50, 75, 85–90, 112, 114, 126–7, 211, 212, 245, 252, 262, 287, 323
in pre-Union police 25, 30, 33
criminological theories 16, 100, 131–2, 175, 200, 212, 262

Daily News 228, 272
Dartnell, Maj.-Gen. Sir 17, 18, 19, 26, 27
Davies, S. 293
de Klerk, F. W. 1, 3, 5, 74, 318, 320, 321, 322, 323, 324, 325, 326, 327, 329, 338, 345, 347, 348
de la Rey, Senator 57, 64
Department of Bantu Administration and Development 224, 225, 226, 227, 231, 234, 243, 261
de Villiers, Commissioner 112, 113, 114, 115, 116, 126, 127, 143, 144, 150, 152, 166, 182
de Wet, General 64
Dippenaar, M. 115, 155, 157, 175, 187, 258, 265, 280, 305, 313
Dominion Party 108
Dublin 8, 26
Dunbar-Moodie, T. 132
Durban 25, 27, 41, 69, 75, 78, 81, 111, 112, 133, 157, 161, 162, 172, 176, 205, 215, 216, 225, 228, 232, 247, 251, 260, 265, 286, 288, 292
Durban Borough Police 25, 41, 42, 76, 78, 111, 112

Fagan Commission 181, 192
Financial Mail 3, 321
Fine, D. 306
Fine, R. 165, 166
Foster gang 65, 90
Fourie, Jopie 65, 66
Frontier and Armed Mounted Police 17, 25
Fusion government 107–8, 110, 181, 345

Garvey, Marcus 93
Geldenhuys, Commissioner 252, 287

Giliomee, H. 2
Gluckman, Dr 325
Goldstone Commission 317, 326, 328
Grundy, K. 251, 292

Hall, Sir Robert 163, 165
Hansson, D. 301, 306
Harms Commission 312, 327
Hartigan, Lt.-Col. 69
Hattersley, A. 19
Henry, Sir Edward 25
Hertzog, General 45, 48, 63, 95, 96, 97, 98, 105, 106, 107, 108, 109, 110, 142, 149, 155, 156, 162
Hickman, A. 7
Hirson, B. 215
Holland 15, 84
Holt, H. 19
Human Sciences Research Council 236

Independent 320
India 10, 25, 37
influx control 23, 107, 108–9, 137–41, 164–5, 180–1, 199, 213, 225–7
Inkatha 286, 308, 309, 310, 327, 329, 341, 347, 352
Isandhlwana 17
Israel 243, 245, 275
Israelites 100

Jeffries, C. 9
Johannesburg 40, 41, 46, 52, 54, 57, 66, 72, 78, 81, 85, 96, 97, 98, 103, 127, 148, 152, 153, 157, 159, 161, 172, 176, 178, 200, 203, 204, 213, 216, 221, 230, 260, 263, 264, 265, 288, 296
Johannesburg Star 312
Joint Management Committees 294, 295, 296, 297
see also State Security Council
Justicia 227, 228

Kannemeyer Report 299
Kenya 6, 33, 142
Killingray, D. 5, 6
King, John 21
kitskonstabels 303, 305, 306, 308, 309, 322, 334
Kliptown 178
Koffiefontein 162, 186, 219
Kruger, Jimmy 270
KwaZulu 224, 225, 284, 286, 295, 308, 309

KwaZulu Police 285–6, 308, 309

Lacey, M. 64
Lansdown Commission 113, 116, 117,
    121–2, 124, 134, 140, 141–7, 153,
    154, 177
Lebowa 224, 283, 284
Lebowa Police 283, 284
le Grange, L. 314, 315
Leibbrandt, S. 159, 160, 185
Lesotho 256
liberal model of policing 1, 9, 146,
    339–40
Lipton, M. 223
Liverpool 51, 73
London 15, 17, 18, 20, 21, 23, 24, 90,
    101, 143, 149, 154, 215, 217, 251
London Metropolitan Police 17, 21, 24,
    25, 90, 101, 114, 143, 154, 175, 217
London Standard 18

maghotla 133, 202, 234, 242, 272, 273,
    280, 281, 307
Malan, Dr 108, 110, 111, 156, 162, 315
Mandela, Nelson 166, 252, 329
    see also African National Congress
Mavrogordato, Mr 50
Meadowlands 209, 260, 310
miners' strike (1946) 177–8
Moorcraft, P. 319
Moroka 178, 179, 193, 207, 310
Municipal Law Enforcement
    Officers 302, 303, 304, 305, 306,
    309, 322, 334

Nairobi 89, 148
Namibia/South West Africa 57, 63, 64,
    66, 67, 69, 78, 79, 142, 147–8, 254,
    260
Natal 14, 16, 17, 18, 19, 21, 26, 27, 29,
    30, 32, 34, 39, 40, 45, 59, 76, 78, 79,
    88, 115, 118, 128, 196, 260
Natal Legislative Assembly 19, 26
Natal Mercury 310, 327
Natal Mounted Police 16, 17, 18, 19, 22, 26
Natal Police 11, 21, 25, 27, 30, 32, 34,
    39, 79
National Council for Women 81, 119
National Party 4, 63, 66, 95, 96, 107,
    108, 147, 184, 186, 188, 189, 204,
    222, 315, 316, 317, 341, 348
Native Affairs Commission 170, 175,
    176, 179, 192

Native National Congress 98
Native Representative Council 136, 163,
    164, 206
Nazism 2, 111, 147, 148, 157, 159, 220
Newclare 179, 204, 205
New Statesman 215
New Zealand 6, 9, 59, 142
Nigeria 6
Nongqai 11, 20, 27–8
Northern Ireland 10, 177, 243, 288, 290,
    311, 348, 349, 351, 352

O'Meara, D. 108
Orange Free State 14, 28, 30, 39, 40, 58,
    63, 65, 88, 118, 128, 166, 184, 196,
    260, 272
Orlando 180, 193, 201, 204, 233, 275
Ossewbrandwag 110, 150, 151, 155–63,
    186, 320, 345, 346

Palestine 6
Palmer, Commissioner 58, 152, 157,
    166, 169, 170, 179, 183, 184, 185
Pan African Congress 246, 247, 254, 319
Pietermaritzburg 24, 25, 39, 41, 69, 75,
    85, 324, 327
Pietermaritzburg Borough Police 25, 41,
    42, 76, 78, 111
Pinnock, D. 76, 128
police–state relations 12–13, 33, 37, 45,
    156, 294, 338–47
Pondoland massacre 246, 267
Port Elizabeth 81, 100, 176, 247, 274,
    293, 308
Posel, D. 140, 181, 182, 213, 226
Pretoria 18, 40, 43, 84, 85, 86, 133, 159,
    174, 176, 274, 293, 306, 313, 318,
    319

Qoboza, Percy 287

Rabie Commission 290
Rademeyer, Commissioner 114, 153,
    211, 214, 223, 247
Rand Daily Mail 51, 216, 220, 227, 261,
    269
Rand strike:
    (1914) 57
    (1922) 93–6, 105, 106
Rankin, D. 221
rapid response policing 174, 202
Reiner, Robert 339, 340
reserve police 59, 149, 241–3, 278

Rheinnallt-Jones, J. 131, 134, 137, 138
Rhodesia/Zimbabwe 6, 7, 254, 257, 258
Rich, P. 107
Rock, P. 23
Rorke's Drift 16
Royal Irish Constabulary 5, 6, 8, 16, 22, 142, 143, 146, 311, 341
Royal Ulster Constabulary 177, 288, 311, 348

SARP 227, 228, 237, 238, 240, 255, 260, 266
Scharf, W. 324
Searle, E. 19
Seegars, A. 114
Selfe, J. 294
separate development 223–5, 231
Servamus 227, 287, 304
Sharpeville 298, 330
Sharpeville massacre 223, 231, 235, 241, 245, 246–7, 251, 267, 299, 338
Shaw, G. V. 21, 22, 24, 26, 30
Sisulu, Walter 166
Smuts, General 48, 55, 63, 66, 93, 95, 96, 97, 105, 107, 108, 110, 111, 122, 148, 149, 150, 151, 153, 155, 156, 158, 160, 162, 163, 164, 168, 172, 175, 180, 181, 183, 185, 188, 203, 315, 341, 345
Sobukwe, Robert 246, 247
see also Pan African Congress
South African Communist Party 166, 203, 214
South African Constabulary 28, 42
South African Criminal Bureau 87–90
South African Defence Force 38, 243, 246, 247, 251, 276, 280, 292, 294, 296, 306, 312, 329
South African Institute of Race Relations 131, 133, 137, 139, 140, 180, 200, 201, 202
South African Mounted Riflemen 4, 5, 14, 28, 38, 39, 40, 41, 42, 43, 48, 54, 55, 59, 67, 68, 74, 75, 77, 78, 87, 111, 231
South African Party 96, 107
see also Smuts, General
South African Police:
    accountability of 218–19, 220, 248, 330, 334–5, 349
    Afrikaner–British relations within 45–7, 48, 69, 73, 153–5, 159
    Black police in 62, 70, 83, 119, 120–3,
        169–70, 176, 182–3, 189–90, 191–2, 192–4, 208–9, 227–8, 231–3, 236–7, 238, 255, 275, 287, 333
    as colonial force 5, 12, 94, 101–4, 146, 180, 332–8, 343, 344
    counter-insurgency 254–8, 292–3, 294–6, 341
    and crime 40, 48–51, 90, 128–35, 195–8, 200–2, 212–13, 226, 259–60, 261, 262, 264–5, 266, 289, 323, 324–5, 335–6
    death squads 311–12, 322, 327
    discipline and misconduct 43, 47–8, 82–3, 100, 114–16, 136–8, 143, 179, 194–5, 215–20, 230, 246–8, 263, 269–72, 279, 290, 301, 326, 327, 337, 342
    employment of English-speakers 118–19, 154, 190, 240, 280
    employment of women 81, 177, 241
    expenditure on 43, 59–61, 67, 76, 117, 124–7, 186, 188, 210, 239–40, 244–5, 276–7, 341
    in First World War 58–60, 63, 66
    as liberal force 11, 40, 101–4, 145, 180, 229, 287, 288, 312–13, 314, 343, 347
    links with Afrikaner extremists 159–62, 185–6, 316–21, 326, 340–1, 345
    links with Black vigilantes 234–5, 272–3, 280–1, 307–9, 310–11
    links with Inkatha 327–8
    literature on 3–4
    manpower levels 42, 44, 61, 68–9, 81, 117–18, 120–1, 169, 170–2, 188–9, 190, 207–8, 238–9, 275, 276
    modernization 74, 82, 84, 177, 279–80, 313, 333, 344
    motorization in 127, 172–3, 187, 210
    organizational structure 40–1, 67, 78, 101, 103, 249, 250–1, 264, 278
    origins of 14, 31–8, 332
    and pass laws 107, 164–5, 178, 198–9, 204–5, 213, 225–7, 263, 289
    police state 2, 335
    policing Afrikaner unrest 63–6, 94–7, 149–63, 185, 345
    policing Black politics 93, 98, 99, 100, 105, 139, 165–6, 178, 203–5, 214–15, 245, 246–8, 254, 269–70, 273–4, 298–9, 300, 301, 322, 326, 327, 337–8, 342

policing industrial strikes 54–5, 57, 93–6, 99, 100, 177–8
policing race relations 48, 51–4, 75, 97–8, 130, 135, 139, 163, 165–6, 182, 289, 297
reform of 1–2, 13, 136, 140–7, 167, 220–1, 268, 321, 323, 325, 329, 330–1, 337, 346, 147–52
relations with kitskonstables 306
relations with SAMR 39, 43, 75, 76, 77, 78
relative autonomy of 13, 145, 211, 344–7
riot police 250, 251, 278–9, 305, 309–10, 350
in Second World War 147–67
on strike 71–3
training 43, 80–1, 102–3, 112, 118, 145, 175–7, 190, 240–1, 250, 254–5, 280, 286
treatment of detainees 273–4, 290–1
see also Criminal Investigation Department; reserve police; Special Branch
South African Railways and Harbour Police 79, 112, 113, 114, 116, 124, 147, 159, 169, 209, 238–9, 249, 275
South African Wachthuis 243, 278
South West African Constabulary 78, 148
Soweto 234, 235, 242, 260, 261, 262, 264, 270, 271, 272, 273, 279, 280, 281, 282, 303, 304
Soweto uprising 2, 267, 268–74, 307, 338
Special Branch 85, 131, 174–5, 214, 223, 249, 250, 252, 253, 292, 312, 323
squatting 178–81
see also influx control
Stanley, Sir Herbert 63, 106
state of emergency 299–302
State Security Council 294, 295, 296, 322
Sunday Times 253
Sunday Tribune 303

TerreBlanche, E. 318, 319, 320
see also Afrikaner Weerstandsbeweging
Te Water Commission 56, 74, 80–1, 87, 91, 92, 103, 113, 115, 182
Tomlinson Commission 223
trades union movement 165–6
Transkei 176, 224, 231, 232, 233, 235,

237, 246, 266, 282, 283, 284, 286, 295, 308
Transkei Police 232–3, 283, 284
Transvaal 14, 16, 18, 25, 28, 29, 30, 31, 32, 34, 35, 39, 40, 44, 45, 63, 65, 78, 86, 88, 117, 118, 128, 140, 144, 150, 154, 157, 161, 171, 196, 260, 289
Transvaal Leader 40, 47
Transvaal Post 281
Transvaal Republic Police 15, 211
Transvaal Town Police 25, 28, 32, 35, 37, 42
Truter, Commissioner 30, 32, 36, 39, 40, 41, 43, 44, 45, 46, 48, 59, 62, 67, 68, 69, 70, 71, 72, 75, 76, 77, 78, 79, 80, 81, 85, 91, 100, 101, 102, 103, 111, 143, 182, 189
tsotsis 132, 133, 200, 212, 242
see also crime: youth gangs
Turk, A. 249

Uitenhage 299
Umtata 176
United Democratic Front 298, 308, 309, 310, 319, 326, 341
United Party 108, 110, 163, 172, 180, 181, 189, 191, 345
see also Fusion government; Smuts, General
United States of America 10, 15, 275, 350
Urban Bantu Councils 234, 262, 272, 273

van den Bergh, H. 186, 252, 253, 254
see also Bureau of State Security
van der Spuy, E. 3, 150, 151, 240
van der Walt, J. 160
van Heerden, J. 212
van Heerden, T. 3
van Onselen, L. 44, 81, 84, 160, 188
van Rensberg, Dr 155, 158
see also Ossewbrandwag
van Riebeeck, Jan 15
van Zyl Smit, D. 131
Venables, L. 200, 201, 202
Venda 224, 282, 283, 284
Vereeniging 134, 135, 136, 140, 179
Verwoerd, Dr 248
vigilantes 202, 214, 234, 242, 272, 281, 304, 307–9, 311, 320
Visser, G. 150, 159
Vlok, A. 313, 314, 315, 316

Volkstem 46, 47
Vorster, B. J. 186, 219, 230, 237, 253, 320
Vrye Weekblad 311
Vryheid 163

Waddington, P. 289, 317, 328
Weekly Mail 281, 302

Weitzer, R. 329, 330
Wilson, E. 19
Windhoek 66, 89, 148
Winter, G. 252, 255

Zulu rebellion (1905) 22, 27
Zululand Mounted Police 16, 22